Expert Office 365

Notes from the Field

Nikolas Charlebois-Laprade, Evgueni Zabourdaev,
Daniel Brunet, Bruce Wilson, Mike Farran, Kip Ng,
Andrew Stobart, Roger Cormier, Colin Hughes-Jones,
Rhoderick Milne and Shawn Cathcart

Apress®

Expert Office 365: Notes from the Field

Nikolas Charlebois-Laprade
Gatineau, Québec, Canada

Evgueni Zabourdaev
Ottawa, Ontario, Canada

Daniel Brunet
Laval, Québec, Canada

Bruce Wilson
Winnipeg, Manitoba, Canada

Mike Farran
Strathmore, Alberta, Canada

Kip Ng
Mississauga, Ontario, Canada

Andrew Stobart
Winnipeg, Manitoba, Canada

Roger Cormier
Mississauga, Ontario, Canada

Colin Hughes-Jones
Mississauga, Ontario, Canada

Rhoderick Milne
Mississauga, Ontario, Canada

Shawn Cathcart
Edmonton, Alberta, Canada

ISBN-13 (pbk): 978-1-4842-2990-3
DOI 10.1007/978-1-4842-2991-0

ISBN-13 (electronic): 978-1-4842-2991-0

Library of Congress Control Number: 2017954393

Cover image designed by Freepik

Managing Director: Welmoed Spahr
Editorial Director: Todd Green
Acquisitions Editor: Gwenan Spearing
Development Editor: Laura Berendson
Coordinating Editor: Nancy Chen
Copy Editor: Michael G. Laraque
Artist: SPi Global

Distributed to the book trade worldwide by Springer Science+Business Media New York, 233 Spring Street, 6th Floor, New York, NY 10013. Phone 1-800-SPRINGER, fax (201) 348-4505, e-mail orders-ny@springer-sbm.com, or visit www.springeronline.com. Apress Media, LLC is a California LLC and the sole member (owner) is Springer Science+Business Media Finance Inc (SSBM Finance Inc). SSBM Finance Inc is a Delaware corporation.

For information on translations, please e-mail rights@apress.com, or visit www.apress.com/rights-permissions.

Apress titles may be purchased in bulk for academic, corporate, or promotional use. eBook versions and licenses are also available for most titles. For more information, reference our Print and eBook Bulk Sales web page at www.apress.com/bulk-sales.

Any source code or other supplementary material referenced by the authors in this book is available to readers on GitHub via the book's product page, located at www.apress.com/9781484229903. For more detailed information, please visit www.apress.com/source-code.

Printed on acid-free paper

To the Make-A-Wish Foundation: May this book help put some smiles on the faces of kids in need.

—Nik

Contents at a Glance

Contents

A Word from the Editor

As part of the Business Productivity group inside Microsoft, I have had the chance to collaborate with some of the smartest people the planet has to offer. During my first year in my role as a Premier Field Engineer within Microsoft Canada, I've been able to observe several of my colleagues help others solve problems in areas of expertise they simply mastered. This book is a realization of a crazy idea I had to capture that deep knowledge that these talented people possess. Whether we want it or not, even if it feels like today's IT world is forcing us to become more generalists than specialists, we all possess this area of knowledge we prefer or excel at. The current book captures these niches of knowledge my colleagues in Microsoft Canada possess into what is one of the most complete sources of knowledge on Office 365 there is out there. May it be a motivation for you to step out of your comfort zone and learn things in an area you don't feel comfortable in.

The simple fact that the authors' revenues from this book are entirely going to the Make-A-Wish Foundation for kids in America should be a great indication of the passion the authors have for the technology. I want to thank each and every one of them for the hard work they put in making this project a reality. Evgueni, Shawn, Rhoderick, Roger, Colin, Daniel, Mike, Andrew, Bruce, and Kip, thank you for responding to the call and stepping up to the plate. A special thank you also to James Parkes, Neil Hodgkinson, and Bob Fox for helping out with the technology review for this book. Last but none the least, thank you to all of you the readers for taking the opportunity to invest time in improving your skill set and to open your horizons to the wonderful opportunities offered by Office 365.

—Nik

About the Contributors

Nikolas Charlebois-Laprade Nik is a software engineer with a background in management. He is always trying to think outside the box, and he's a fervent early adopter of anything worth a try. Nik has the rare ability of being able to see the bigger picture, identify gaps, and envision creative solutions to bridge those gaps. This ex-PowerShell MVP joined the ranks of Microsoft Premier Field Engineers in 2015. Based in Gatineau, Quebec, he focuses on the latest development technologies and on PowerShell Automation.

Evgueni Zabourdaev With a background as a system engineer, analyst, infrastructure architect, and consultant spanning 20 years, **Evgueni Zabourdaev** has long been passionate about topics surrounding information architecture, enterprise content and information management, document collaboration, taxonomy development, search, and other traditional subject matter that extends and improves knowledge management across organizations.

A proud French Montrealer, **Daniel Brunet** has a career that is highly focused on content management. After ten years at a law firm managing many flavors of enterprise content management, he found love, with all its challenges, when SharePoint 2007 was introduced. It was only natural to join Microsoft and work with this product for the following ten years. Today, Daniel is still at home coaching customers on content-management strategies, of which a big part is, of course, recovery. Known by the nickname Dano at Microsoft, when he is not with customers, Daniel can be found on his boat or motorcycle, on which he can stop thinking about governance.

Bruce Wilson Since early 2000, **Bruce Wilson** has been supporting customers with troubleshooting various technical issues. After joining Microsoft in 2007, he supported each of the mail filtering cloud offerings provided by the company. Over the years, Bruce has developed multiple techniques to identify where breakdowns and failures occur during mail flow. He trusts that you will find this book helpful as you use the cloud services offered by Microsoft.

Mike Farran His true passion is in produce; however, he's been sidetracked in the IT industry for more than 20 years. He likes to say his focus is on learning and helping others to learn and improve their skills and knowledge. This pursuit of knowledge has lead him to a Help Desk for an Oil & Gas company, various consulting companies, programming, managing a data center, and then finding his second love, SharePoint, in 2006. Microsoft boosted his ego six years ago by hiring him as a Premier Field Engineer, whereby his thirst for knowledge never goes unquenched.

Kip Ng Kip has more than 20 years of working experience in IT consulting, IT delivery, and IT technical leadership. Kip has strong global exposure. He can speak four languages and has worked with hundreds of organizations worldwide. He currently manages and runs the Business Productivity delivery team at Microsoft Canada, focusing on driving digital transformation and leading the cloud strategy and delivery.

Andrew Stobart Andrew is currently a Support Escalation Engineer for Exchange Online and lives with his family in Winnipeg, Manitoba, Canada. He is a dedicated and passionate professional with more than 20 years of experience in IT consulting, support, and operations. He has expertise and an in-depth technical skill set in Windows client and server, Active Directory, Microsoft SQL, Exchange, Office 365, MySQL, IIS, SCCM, SCOM, Hyper-V, Visual Studio (C#), PowerShell, and many others. He is recognized for his strong client relationships and exceptional communication abilities with diverse audiences. Andrew has been with Microsoft since 2011.

Roger Cormier Roger has worked with SharePoint since March of 2004 and has been learning about SharePoint since that day. He enjoys working with people and leveraging technology to deliver business solutions. Aside from IT, Roger enjoys playing guitar and strength training.

Colin Hughes-Jones Colin started providing support for SharePoint as a contractor at Microsoft in December 2005. He joined Microsoft in Texas as a Support Escalation Engineer in June 2007. In November 2007, he moved back to Canada and assumed the role of Premier Field Engineer. He recently celebrated his ten-year anniversary working at Microsoft.

Rhoderick Milne Rhoderick is currently a Senior Premier Field Engineer with Microsoft, based out of Mississauga, Ontario, Canada. With more than 15 years of IT experience, he specializes in cloud, messaging, and virtualization. Prior to moving to Canada, Rhoderick worked in the UK's largest financial institutions and has a proven track record in consulting and training. Rhoderick is a charter Microsoft Certified Solutions Master (MCSM) in Exchange 2013, Microsoft Certified Master (MCM) in Exchange 2007 and 2010, in addition to holding regular Microsoft Certified Systems Engineer + Internet (MCSE+I) and Microsoft Certified IT Professional (MCITP) credentials.

Shawn Cathcart His 20-years career has seen him excel at the architecture, implementation, and operational management of Microsoft technologies. While he has covered a wide array of the Microsoft product stack, his primary focus is on universal communication and messaging. That mix of operational management and project implementation experience gives Shawn a very honest and practical approach to the utilization of Microsoft technologies. Shawn has been a Microsoft Premier Field Engineer since 2014. Prior to that, he worked as a consultant for a Microsoft Gold Partner for ten years. He lives in Edmonton, Alberta, Canada, with his wife, Stacey, and son, Nolan.

Acknowledgments

To all my mentors in life, for helping me shape the professional that I am today.

—Nik Charlebois-Laprade

To Mom, Dad, Natalia, Steven, and Mark, at whose time expense my chapter was written

—Evgueni Zabourdaev

To my daughter, Mariska, who dealt so well with all my traveling, and to Roger Cormier, who believed in me nine years ago. Thank you both. You are a big part of my success at Microsoft.

—Daniel Brunet

I would like to thank my family and coworkers who supported me through this time.

—Bruce Wilson

To all in my life thus far who have helped me learn and grow and to Nik Charlebois-Laprade for his gentle yet firm progress update requests.

—Mike Farran

First and foremost, I would like to thank God. You gave me the opportunities to meet and work with all the highly talented experts who have authored this book. A special thanks to Nik, who has been so patient, professional, and dedicated to this book project. It has been a joy for me to work with all of you!

—Kip Ng

Dedicated to my incredible family, for their amazing love and support of me.

—Andrew Stobart

I would like to thank my wife and children for supporting me while I was working on this project. I would also like to thank each of the authors and reviewers who have contributed to this book, though there are too many of them to name individually. I also have to thank Neil Hodgkinson. His constant community contribution and his willingness to propagate his knowledge have profoundly affected my work.

—Roger Cormier

I would like to thank Roger Cormier for introducing me to SharePoint back in 2005, Jon Waite for igniting my passion for the Search functionality of SharePoint, and Neil Hodgkinson and Manas Biswas for authoring so much great content on the hybrid Search functionality of SharePoint on-premises and SharePoint Online.

—Colin Hughes-Jones

Thanks to all the outstanding people who have helped me grow over the years, both personally and professionally. Thank you to my wife for insisting I do the Exchange MCM and to my Parents who demonstrated what is possible with passion and hard work. To Charles and Andy who took the opportunity to hire someone for racking servers at the top of a 42U rack, you provided unsurpassed opportunities. I tried adding a reference to Turkish oil wrestling to the book, but it was denied... To my managers and colleagues at Microsoft - you all rock!

—*Rhoderick Milne*

Secial thanks are due to my wife Stacey, whom both encourages me to think outside the box and to get outside my comfort zone. And who supports me through the ensuing chaos whenever I step out on a new limb. And to my son Nolan, whose kind heart, gentle smile and infectious laughter remind me every day that joy in life is found in the simple things.

—*Shawn Cathcart*

CHAPTER 1

Records Management in SharePoint Online

BY EVGUENI ZABOURDAEV

A record, in a nutshell, is a piece of content (with its associated metadata) that serves as evidence of an activity and, therefore, requires special treatment, such as distinct security and storage considerations, dedicated routing rules, and retention for a certain period.

Records management is generally considered to be part of a broader Information Lifecycle Management (ILM) discipline. While ILM covers formal creation, management, storage, and disposition of all information across its life cycle, not all content has to become records (Figure 1-1).

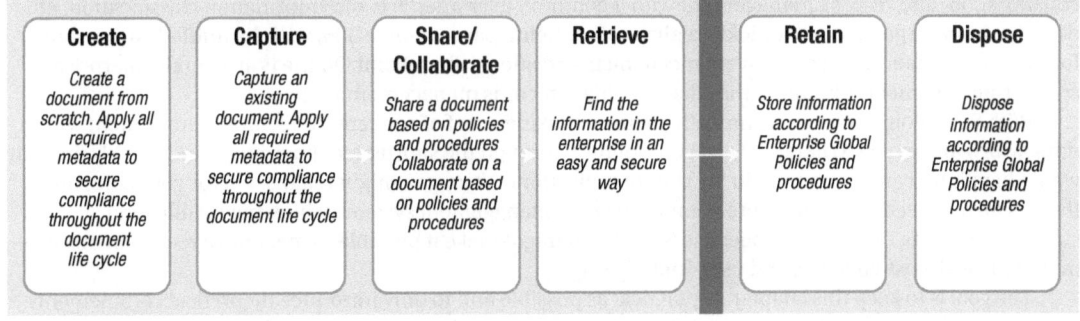

Figure 1-1. *Content life cycle*

Records management is only concerned with certain types of information, and its processes are typically applied on a selective basis to manage security, declaration, routing, retention, and disposition for specialized use cases, such as legal, finance, human resources, etc. (Figure 1-2).

© Nikolas Charlebois-Laprade et al. 2017
N. Charlebois-Laprade et al., *Expert Office 365*, DOI 10.1007/978-1-4842-2991-0_1

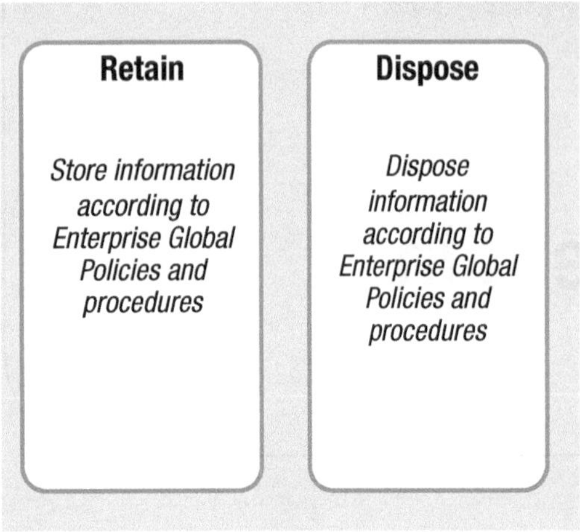

Retain	Dispose
Store information according to Enterprise Global Policies and procedures	Dispose information according to Enterprise Global Policies and procedures

Figure 1-2. Records-management phases

Enterprises have been embracing SharePoint as a records management platform since SharePoint 2007. While many companies are evolving their IT environments into the cloud with Office 365 and hybrid deployments, records management itself has been transforming. Some organizations still have (or choose) to play by the "paper era" rules and continue to deal with increasingly complex requirements for their records management systems (RMSs). Others, however, strive for a more agile and streamlined world of electronic records and are willing to simplify their requirements for records management. For the latter, SharePoint offers a great opportunity to create a highly usable solution that covers document management, collaboration, and records management with a common user interface and information classification, all of which helps organizations quickly realize value. Being part of Office 365, with its unified Governance, Risk and Compliance, and eDiscovery mechanisms positions, SharePoint Online is an overall enterprise content-management solution, rather than a solitary records management tool.

With SharePoint, you can technically set up a working proof of concept for records management within days, which allows you to iteratively test the solution through the shorter feedback loops and quickly find out what SharePoint can and cannot do for your organization. Often, you might realize that for your company, there is no real need to pursue more complex records management systems with strict certification standards, such as DoD 5015.2,[1] because SharePoint might make it possible to meet most requirements in a more practical, cost-effective, and user-friendly way.

The goal is to keep this chapter as practical as possible and to only introduce theoretical complements on an as-needed basis. Instead of merely listing all the relevant features and their descriptions in an academic manner, I will go through the process of building an end-to-end sample records management solution. Also, while records might include both physical and digital content, I will be focusing on electronic information. The concepts covered in this chapter are demonstrated using SharePoint Online (Office 365); however, most of the information discussed should also be valid for SharePoint 2016 and even SharePoint 2013 on-premises. Finally, for all the demonstrations in this chapter, only the Classic user interface (UI) is being used. However, the gap between Classic and Modern sites is rapidly getting narrower, so we may soon be able to use the Modern UI without any limitations.

---

[1]Department of Defense, Executive Service Directorate, "DoD Directives Division," www.dtic.mil/whs/directives/corres/pdf/501502p.pdf.

Sample Scenario

To make it practical, I will organize this chapter around a sample scenario that is close to a situation you might come across in the real world. Of course, it will be a simplified scenario. However, I will go through all the necessary steps required to design and build a fully functional records management system.

Let's start. Imagine, we have a customer who would like to try SharePoint for their records management needs. As a pilot, they chose two types of documents for the initial test. Here is the pilot content, along with some initial requirements for each document type.

- Manuals

    - No change or relocation is allowed after the final review.

    - Records should still be accessible among active documents until destroyed.

    - Delete all previous version history two years after declared as a record.

    - Final review state is triggered by end users manually.

- Company Guidelines

    - Only records managers should have access to records.

    - No artifacts should be left behind among active documents, once declared as a record.

    - Delete all previous version history at the time of record declaration.

    - Documents are active until finally approved.

Equipped with these requirements, we are ready to start planning our new system design.

Records Management System Design

Before we dive into the architecture activities, let's define some general rules about the overall approach. The three guiding principles we will be following to design our records management system are the following:

- The interest of the company comes first. After all, it is the company compliancy requirements that drive the whole RMS project.

- Ease of use for end users is optimized. The solution should be as transparent to the end users as possible. The easier it is to deal with, the higher the chances it actually will be used. How many greatly (over-) engineered solutions were stalled by end users, by their finding more convenient workarounds or plainly sabotaging the new system altogether? We definitely want a different fate for our solution.

- Only SharePoint Online standard functionality is used. "Out of the box" is a mantra we hear more and more often, and rightfully so.

Essentially, to design a records management system, we would have to answer the following four questions:

1. Who? Who the main stakeholders are and why they should care

2. What? What information should become records and what the retention and disposition policies are

3. How? How active content should become records

4. Where? Where records should be stored

Let's proceed with the system-design activities, by tackling those questions one by one.

Who?

Creating requirements for a records management solution is particularly difficult, because they originate from the overall business needs and there are many stakeholders, so multiple aspects have to be looked at thoroughly. Therefore, records managements should not be undertaken as merely an IT project. Let's make it clear: implementation with SharePoint is just the final step of the journey.

By defining the roles and understanding the needs of the different stakeholders, we also indirectly answer the "Why" question—Why should they care? Why are we doing it at all? As mentioned before, this kind of projects is always driven by the needs of the organization (Figure 1-3).

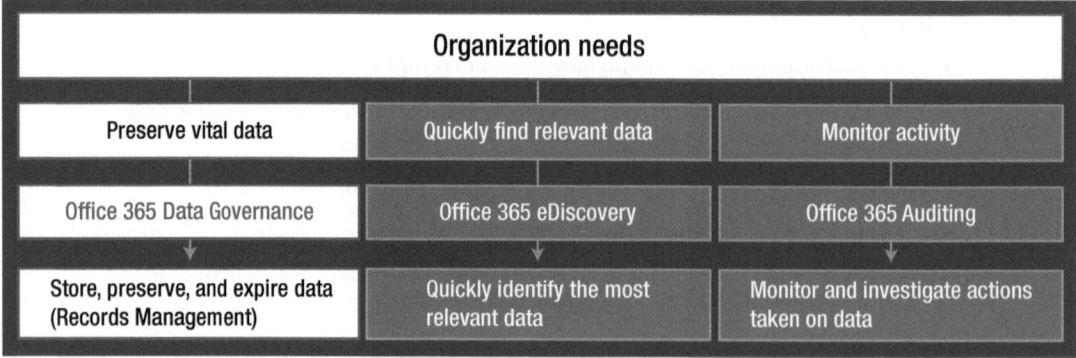

Figure 1-3. Organizational data compliance needs

Preserving vital data is covered by the broader Office 365 Data Governance capabilities, under which falls the SharePoint Online records-management functionality. You would require the following organizational roles around the table, to have a discussion (or, most likely, a series of discussions) about the RMS design:

- Records managers and compliance officers to categorize the records in the organization and to oversee the overall records management process

- IT personnel to implement the systems that efficiently support records management

- Content managers to find where organizational information is kept and to make sure that their teams follow records-management practices

- General users who work with content daily, to get honest feedback on the system's usability

Now, when all the right people are engaged, we can have the remaining three questions answered as accurately as possible.

What?

We will first have to find out what information should become records and what the retention and disposition policies are. That is, how long each record type should be retained and how records should be disposed.

Records and content managers will survey document usage in the organization to determine which documents and other items should become records. This content-analysis exercise, along with the compliance requirements documentation, usually results in the Holy Grail of the records management—the File Plan, also known as a Retention Schedule. What information does it usually capture?

- Types of items for records

- Retention periods for records

- Who is responsible for managing the various kinds of records

For each record type, the File Plan determines

- When this type of content is no longer active

- How long it should be retained after that

- How it should ultimately be disposed of

File Plan is typically owned by records managers and in our sample scenario looks like this (Figure 1-4).

Sample File Plan						
Prepared by:		Katie J		Date:		02-Jan-17
Kind of Record	Category	Description	Media	Retention Period	Disposition	Contact
105 - Reference	100 - General	Materials produced by the Company and third parties that are kept for reference purposes.	Electronic Document	5 years	Destroy	Garth F
740 - Compliance	700 - Legal	Content related to the Company's global and business unit compliance management programs. Include compliance policy, program, procedures, and guidelines.	Electronic Document	10 years	Destroy	Sara D
750 - Contract	700 - Legal	Content related to contracts between the Company and third parties for provision of services and goods.	Electronic Document	15 years	Destroy	Sara D

Figure 1-4. Sample file plan

We are also told that from the records-management perspective, Manuals fall under the Reference type, and Company Guidelines are considered the Compliance kind of record. Records managers then additionally asked for a "soft delete" functionality in case of Manuals. They would like to have a "back door" and be able to un-delete any purged records of this kind within a short period of time following the disposition. On the contrary, for all Legal records (including the guidelines), they want permanent destruction without any recovery option. Let's update the requirements based on the "What?" information from the File Plan.

Refined Requirements

- Manuals (Record Type: 105—Reference)
    - Retain for five years as a record, then move to Recycle Bin.
    - No change or relocation is allowed after the final review.
    - Records should still be accessible among active documents until destroyed.
    - Delete all previous version history two years after declared as a record.
    - Final review state is triggered by end users manually.
- Company Guidelines (Record Type: 740—Compliance)
    - Retain for ten years as a record, then destroy permanently.
    - Only records managers should have access to records.
    - No artifacts should be left behind among active documents, once declared as a record.
    - Delete all previous version history at the time of record declaration.
    - Documents are active until finally approved.

How?

We now have a good idea about what type of records we are dealing with as well as their retention and disposition needs. But how should we convert active documents into records? In SharePoint, we can use the following techniques for records declaration:

- Records can be declared manually by end users.
- Records can be declared automatically
    - via Information Management (IM) Policies
    - or by creating a workflow that sends a document to a Records Center

Let's have a closer look at those methods.

Manual Declaration

This technique can be a good fit for low-volume content that should be converted on an ad-hoc basis triggered by the end users' decision.

Information Management Policy

An information management (IM) policy specifies actions to take on documents at certain points in time. Policy actions occur automatically, so users do not have to manually start them. Two available policy actions relate specifically to managing records and are therefore of particular interest to us:

- Transferring a document to another location
- Declaring a document to be a record

If a connection to a Records Center site exists, you can create a policy that sends documents to it. The policy also specifies whether to copy the document to the Records Center site, move it, or move it and leave a link in the document library.

I'll be discussing in-place records management later, but if it is enabled for the site, you can create a policy that declares a document to be a record.

Also, it is important to know that each information management policy can have multiple stages. For example, you could create a policy that deletes all the earlier versions of a document one year after the document creation date and then transfer the document to a Records Center five years after the document was last modified.

For a centralized approach, it is a good idea to add an information policy to a content type. It makes it easy to associate policy features with multiple lists or libraries. You can choose to add an existing information management policy to a content type or create a unique policy specific to an individual content type.

In addition to associating a policy with content types, you can define a location-based retention policy that applies only to a specific list, library, or folder. Note that each subfolder inherits the retention policy of its parent, unless you choose to break inheritance and define a new retention policy at the child level. If you create a retention policy this way, however, you cannot reuse this policy on other lists, libraries, folders, or sites.

If you want to apply a single retention policy to all types of content in a single location, you will most likely want to use location-based retention. In most other cases, including our sample scenario, you will want to make sure that a retention policy is specified for content types.

Workflows

When creating a workflow, you can add an action to send an item to a repository. By using this action, you can create workflows that send documents to a Records Center site. You can also include other actions in the workflow. For example, you could create a workflow that sends an e-mail message requesting approval to a document's author and then send the document to a Records Center site. You could even combine policies and workflows, by creating a retention policy that runs the new workflow one year after a document is created.

Please note that even though the workflow option is what you would most likely end up with in the real-world implementation, in this chapter we will be using IM policy just to keep our focus on the records management features.

Site Retention

In our scenario, we will not be dealing with site retentions; however, it is worth mentioning this additional type of policy, which is now available in SharePoint and defines a retention policy for the whole site.

Refined Requirements

When looking at the requirements, it seems like manual declaration would be a good conversion method for Manuals. Also, because this content type is subject to the less strict rules, we were asked to allow records to be "undeclared" by the content owners.

For Company Guidelines, on the other hand, we would have to define an information management policy that declares records based on the Final Approval Date metadata. Alternatively, a workflow can be created that would take care of the approval process, eventually converting a document to a record.

Now, after answering the "How?" question, let's further update the requirements, as follows:

- Manuals (Record Type: 105—Reference)

    - Retain for five years as a record, then move to Recycle Bin.

    - No change or relocation is allowed after the final review.

- Records should still be accessible among active documents, until destroyed.

- Delete all previous version history two years after declared as a record.

- Declare as records manually by end users.

- Company Guidelines (Record Type: 740—Compliance)

    - Retain for ten years as a record, then destroy permanently.

    - Only records managers should have access to records.

    - No artifacts should be left behind among active documents, once declared as a record.

    - Delete all previous version history at the time of record declaration.

    - Declare as a record automatically, using information management policy triggered by Final Approval Date.

Where?

Phew! We have crossed three questions off our design list. There is now the last "Where?" question remaining unanswered before we can get to the most exciting part of the project: implementation.

Location-wise, SharePoint provides two strategies for managing records:

> In-place records management allows you to archive content directly in your site. That is, the site can contain both active documents and records. SharePoint blocks in-place records, as a result of which they can no longer be manually altered, removed, or relocated. You can even specify different retention policies for active documents and records.

■ **Note**   One limitation is that you cannot use in-place records management with document sets.

> Records Center site collection(s) can serve as a content vault. The last version of the source "active" library (whether this is a major or minor version) becomes the first version in the target "record" library.

The fundamental attribute of in-place records is that the records stay in the same location and exist alongside active documents. All previous versions remain visible and accessible. From the end user perspective, in-place records largely act as active documents, still have the same permissions, and don't disappear anywhere, therefore fully preserving the context. On the other hand, downsides for this management approach are an increased difficulty of records discovery and a weaker security model. Also, by combining active content and records in the same library, we cause its size to grow more rapidly.

For a Records Center, structure and security are on its strong side. All records are distinct and easily accessible by records managers in a centralized and secured manner. Stricter rules are applied, and the records cannot be altered or deleted for the duration of the retention period. The drop-off library and its routing rules enforce structure. On the flip side of the advantages coin, there is a reduced visibility for the end users: documents are removed from the original libraries and context.

Refined Requirements

While reading the preceding characteristics of each method, you had probably already made a mental note of the approach that is most appropriate for each content type we deal with. The requirements here are pretty straightforward and don't leave much room for guesswork. You've got it: In-place for Manuals and Record Center for Guidelines.

Here is how our complete design requirements now look:

- Manuals (Record Type: 105—Reference)

  - Retain for five years as a record, then move to Recycle Bin.

  - No change or relocation is allowed after the final review.

  - Records should still be accessible among active documents, until destroyed.

  - Delete all previous version history two years after declared as a record.

  - Declare as records in-place manually by end users.

- Company Guidelines (Record Type: 740—Compliance)

  - Retain for ten years as a record, then destroy permanently.

  - Send to Records Center and restrict access only to records managers.

  - No artifacts should be left behind among active documents, once declared as a record.

  - Delete all previous version history at the time of record declaration.

  - Declare as a record automatically, using information management policy triggered by Final Approval Date.

Other Things to Keep in Mind

At each point, you should thoroughly document your records management guidelines, plans, and any defined metrics. If your enterprise becomes engaged in any records-related litigation, you might be obliged to present this type of documentation. Make sure you also have the auditing, monitoring, and reporting covered.

Records Management System Implementation

Enough of the paperwork! Now that we have our design components finalized, let's get to our SharePoint Online tenant and begin the implementation.

Solution Elements

We will be working with a few SharePoint components, among which the following major ones:

- Content Type Hub (sometimes also referred to as Content Type Publishing Hub), to centrally manage Enterprise Content Types

- Document Collaboration site, which is just a classic team site with the following document libraries:

  - "Manuals" library (with in-place records management enabled)

  - "Legal" library

- Records Center site

Of course, there are other components involved, such as the Taxonomy Term Store for Managed Metadata, but they are not directly specific to the RMS solution we are implementing and, therefore, will be considered generic SharePoint elements in the context of this chapter.

Be aware that the implementation process is not linear and will require us to frequently switch between different sites, so bear with the progression and stay focused. You will see that, logically, all the steps are nicely aligned and, at the end, should make total sense to you and your customers.

Create Records Center

We will start our implementation activities with the Document Center site collection creation (Figure 1-5).

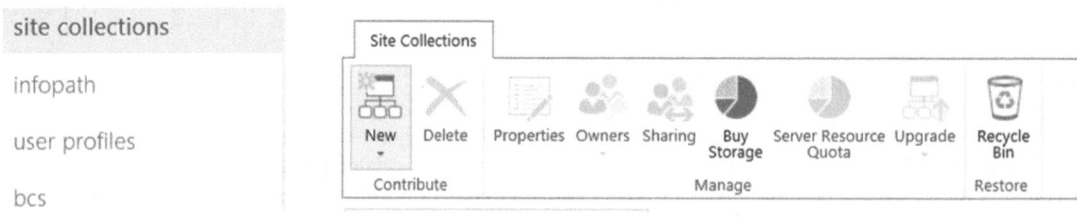

Figure 1-5. *Create New Site Collection*

In SharePoint admin center, create a new site collection.

▪ **Note** If you want to quickly navigate to the SharePoint admin center, use its URL, which should be similar to `https://contoso-admin.sharepoint.com`.

Select a Records Center template under the Enterprise tab (Figure 1-6).

Select a template:

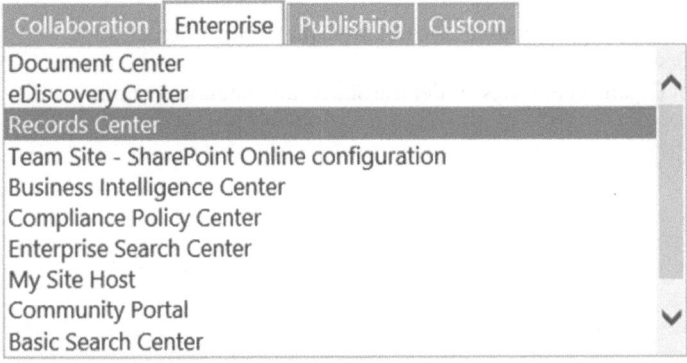

This template creates a site designed for records management. Records managers can configure the routing table to direct incoming files to specific locations. The site also lets you manage whether records can be deleted or modified after they are added to the repository.

Figure 1-6. *New site collection template selection dialog*

After some time, your brand-new site collection will be created.

Right out of the box, this new site is optimized for high-volume document submission and equipped with many useful enterprise records management features (Figure 1-7).

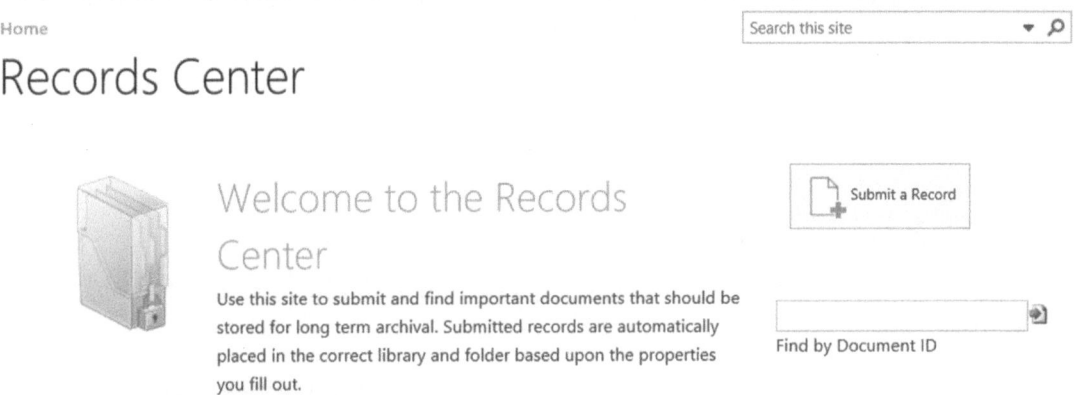

Figure 1-7. *Records Center home page*

In the spirit of focusing only on the practical aspects of the implementation, I will not be providing a detailed theoretical description of all the Records Center site collection capabilities (or, for that matter, one of any other standard SharePoint components we are about to create). There is more than enough general information about all of those, which is readily available on TechNet.com and via your favorite search engine.

Configure "Send To" Location

We must now make SharePoint aware of our newly created site. Do not leave the Records Center yet; we must get some information about it first.

Go to Site Settings and click Content Organizer Settings, under the Site Administration section (Figure 1-8).

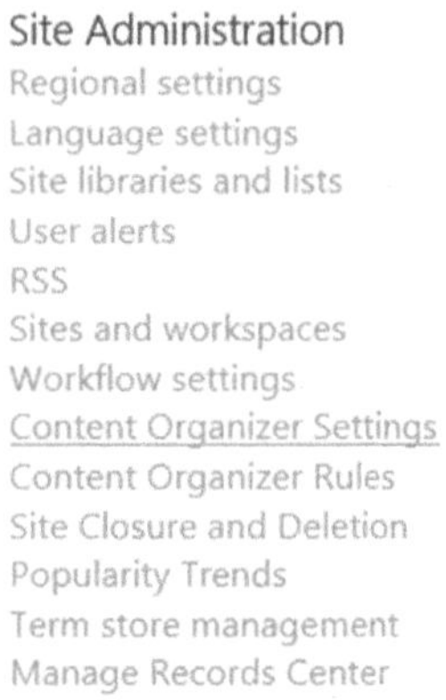

Site Administration
Regional settings
Language settings
Site libraries and lists
User alerts
RSS
Sites and workspaces
Workflow settings
Content Organizer Settings
Content Organizer Rules
Site Closure and Deletion
Popularity Trends
Term store management
Manage Records Center

Figure 1-8. *Content Organizer Settings link*

On the settings page displayed, scroll all the way down and copy the Submission Points URL (Figure 1-9).

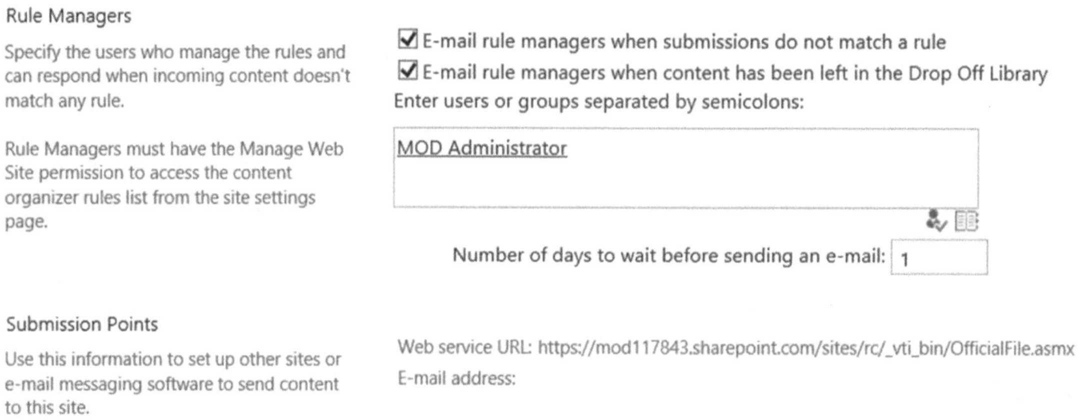

Rule Managers

Specify the users who manage the rules and can respond when incoming content doesn't match any rule.

☑ E-mail rule managers when submissions do not match a rule
☑ E-mail rule managers when content has been left in the Drop Off Library
Enter users or groups separated by semicolons:

Rule Managers must have the Manage Web Site permission to access the content organizer rules list from the site settings page.

MOD Administrator

Number of days to wait before sending an e-mail: 1

Submission Points

Use this information to set up other sites or e-mail messaging software to send content to this site.

Web service URL: https://mod117843.sharepoint.com/sites/rc/_vti_bin/OfficialFile.asmx
E-mail address:

Figure 1-9. *"Send to" URL*

The URL will look similar to this: `https://contoso.sharepoint.com/sites/rc/_vti_bin/OfficialFile.asmx`.

Now, let's get back to the SharePoint admin center (remember—a lot of switching!). This time let's click the records management link in the left-hand navigation panel (Figure 1-10).

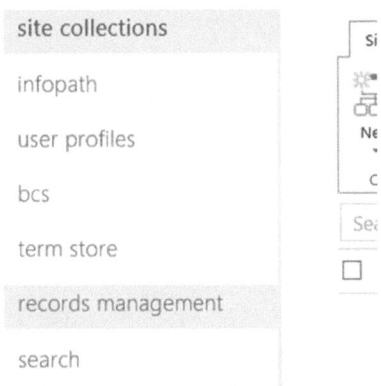

Figure 1-10. *Records management settings*

Here, you will configure a new "Send To" connection. Just give it a name ("Records Center," on the following screenshot) and paste the "Send To" URL you have obtained in Step 2. The end result will look similar to Figure 1-11.

Send To Connections

Send To Connections allow content to be submitted to sites with a configured Content Organizer. Send To connections will appear as locations that content can be submitted to when configuring Information Management Policy. Optionally you can make Send To Connections available for users to manually submit content.

Send To Connections

| New Connection |
| Records Center |

Connection Settings

Each connection requires a display name and a URL to a content organizer. Optionally, this connection can be made available as a Send To option on the item's drop-down menu and on the Ribbon.

Display name:

| Records Center |

Send To URL:

| https://mod117843.sharepoint.com/sites/rc/_vt | (Click here to test)

Example: "http://site url/_vti_bin/officialfile.asmx"

☑ Allow manual submission from the Send To menu

Send To action:

| Move ▾ |

Explanation (to be shown on links and recorded in the audit log):

| Sends to Records Center |

| Update Connection | | Remove Connection |

Figure 1-11. *"Send To" configuration*

Just to verify that the connection is successfully configured, you may want to check out the Send To drop-down in the document ribbon menu of a site collection of your choice, within the document library ribbon's Files tab. You should see your connection available there (Figure 1-12).

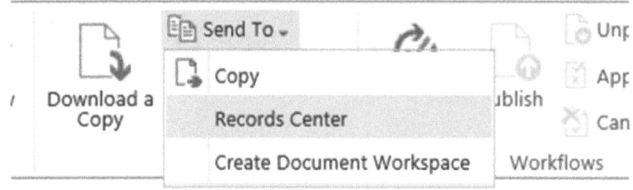

Figure 1-12. *"Send To" drop-down*

It can take a while before the connection is propagated to all the sites. The timer job will eventually pick it up, so be patient.

Create Content Types

Now we proceed to the creation of what I call "pillars of document management"—the mighty content types. In SharePoint, you can control content types at different levels, but we will be doing it in a centralized "enterprise" manner. Our approach will allow maximum control over the metadata and policies to the records managers, while hiding most of the complexity from the content owners and end users.

I would like to point out a very important piece of information: Enterprise Content Type Hub is, in fact, pre-created for you in SharePoint Online. However, if you try to find it under the list of existing site collections in SharePoint Online admin center, you will be disappointed; it is not there. To get to this hidden site collection, you will have to specify its URL directly. Just add "contenttyphub" after the "sites" managed path of your SharePoint Online URL. For the Contoso tenant, the URL will look like this: `https://contoso.sharepoint.com/sites/contenttypehub`.

You will then see a standard site collection based on the Team Site template. The only difference from a regular out-of-the-box team site will be an activated "Content Type Syndication Hub" site-collection feature.

In my case, I just removed all the clutter from the home page, changed the color theme, and updated the site icon, so it can be easier to differentiate visually (Figure 1-13).

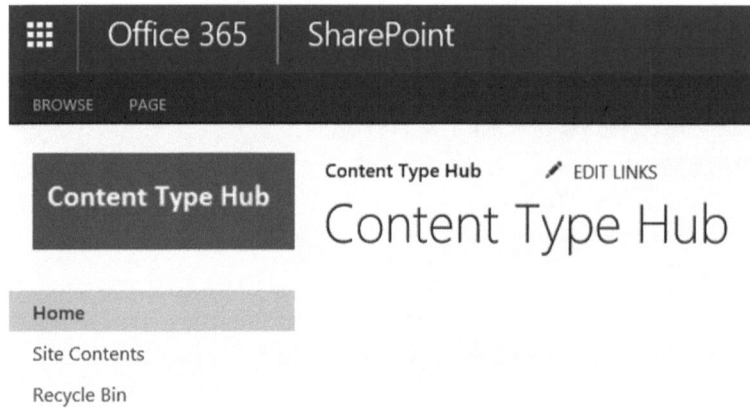

Figure 1-13. *Enterprise Content Type Hub home page*

Go to Sites Settings and click the Site Content Types link under the Web Designer Galleries section (Figure 1-14).

Web Designer Galleries
Site columns
Site content types
Web parts
List templates
Master pages
Themes
Solutions
Composed looks

Figure 1-14. *Link to Site content types settings*

Using the standard Content Type controls, create the hierarchy of content types for both General and Legal kinds of records (Figure 1-15).

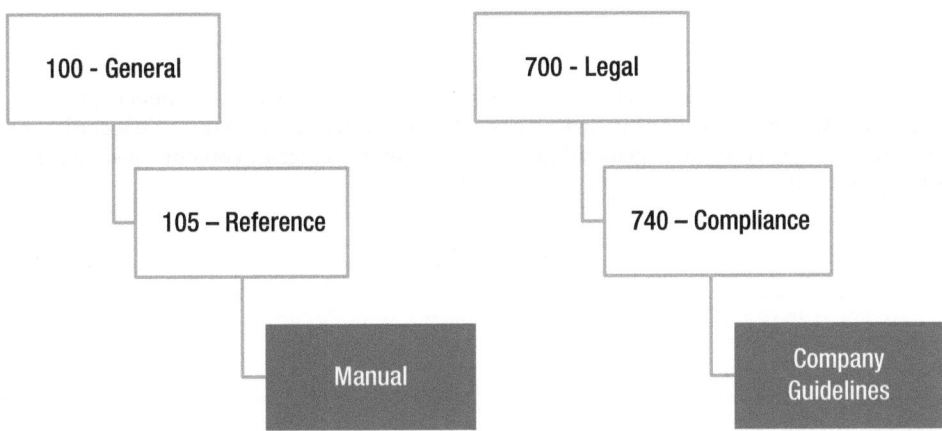

Figure 1-15. *Content types hierarchy*

This is mostly a document management exercise, so you can plan your hierarchy differently and add as much metadata as needed at any level. This approach is a great way to control the enterprise metadata and be in compliance across your entire SharePoint environment. Just make sure you create your Managed Metadata using the centralized Taxonomy Term Store.

In our sample implementation, we will keep the metadata to a minimum, to avoid unnecessary cluttering.

Starting with "100—General" and build your way down to the "105—Reference" (Figure 1-16).

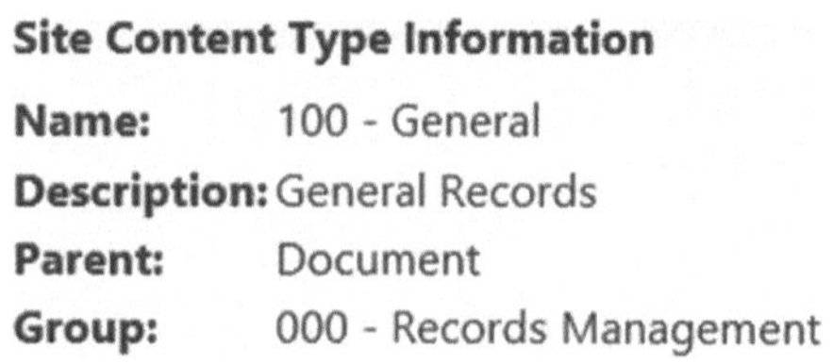

Site Content Type Information

Name: 100 - General
Description: General Records
Parent: Document
Group: 000 - Records Management

Figure 1-16. *General content yype*

You can see the inheritance relationship in the following screenshot (Figure 1-17**).**

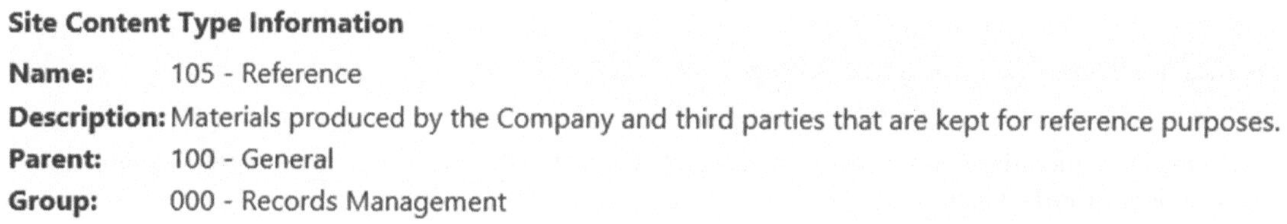

Site Content Type Information

Name: 105 - Reference
Description: Materials produced by the Company and third parties that are kept for reference purposes.
Parent: 100 - General
Group: 000 - Records Management

Figure 1-17. *Reference content type*

Last, you create the Manual content type. In the example following, I chose to place it under a new group, called "Enterprise Content Types," just to make it easier to differentiate between the pure records management content types ("Records Management" group) and the end-user facing content types we are going to publish (Figure 1-18).

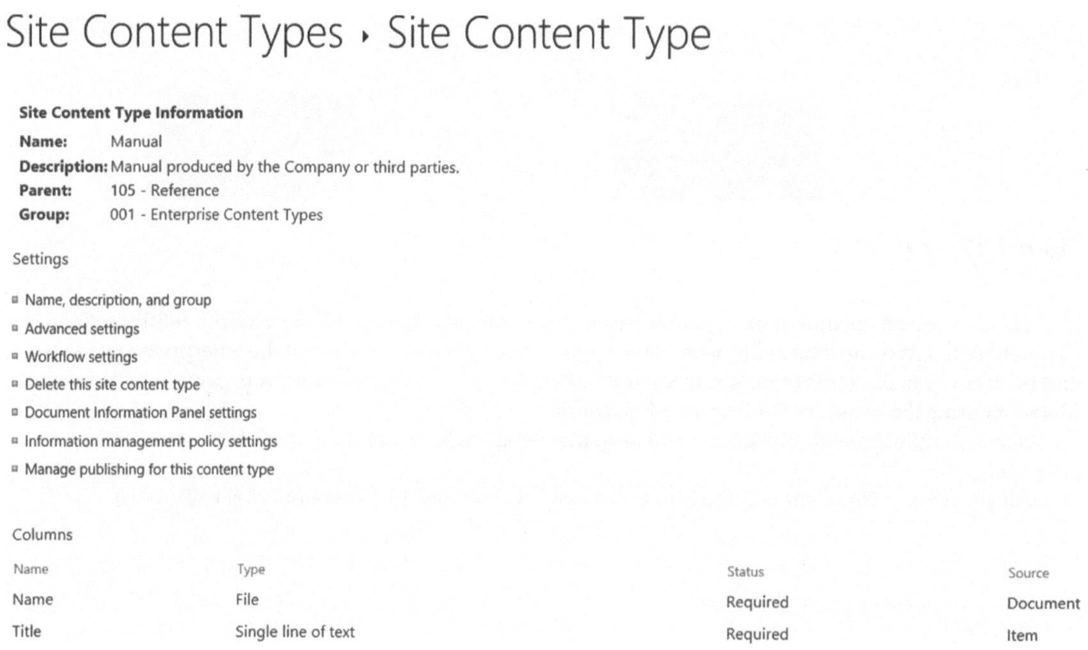

Site Content Types ‣ Site Content Type

Site Content Type Information

Name: Manual
Description: Manual produced by the Company or third parties.
Parent: 105 - Reference
Group: 001 - Enterprise Content Types

Settings

▫ Name, description, and group
▫ Advanced settings
▫ Workflow settings
▫ Delete this site content type
▫ Document Information Panel settings
▫ Information management policy settings
▫ Manage publishing for this content type

Columns

Name	Type	Status	Source
Name	File	Required	Document
Title	Single line of text	Required	Item

Figure 1-18. *Manual content type*

16

We will then go through the same motions for our Legal content type hierarchy, resulting in the Company Guidelines content type. The only difference for this content type is that we have added one custom column to it: "Final Approval Date" (Figure 1-19).

Site Content Type Information

Name: Company Guidelines

Description: Guidelines related to the Company's global and business unit compliance management programs.

Parent: 740 - Compliance

Group: 001 - Enterprise Content Types

Settings

▫ Name, description, and group

▫ Advanced settings

▫ Workflow settings

▫ Delete this site content type

▫ Document Information Panel settings

▫ Information management policy settings

▫ Manage publishing for this content type

Columns

Name	Type	Status	Source
Name	File	Required	Document
Title	Single line of text	Optional	Item
Final Approval Date	Date and Time	Optional	740 - Compliance

Figure 1-19. Company guidelines content type metadata

After you are done, the final content type structure should look like what you see in Figure 1-20.

Site Settings ‣ Site Content Types ⓘ

Create

Site Content Type	Parent
000 - Records Management	
100 - General	Document
105 - Reference	100 - General
700 - Legal	Document
740 - Compliance	700 - Legal
001 - Enterprise Content Types	
Company Guidelines	740 - Compliance
Manual	105 - Reference

Figure 1-20. *All our custom content types*

Create Information Management Policies

The next step will be to create and apply the appropriate information management policies. We will define them according to our design requirements. Also, we have decided to create content type-based policies to ensure centralized control. But then we are faced with a choice of to which level of the content type hierarchy the policies should be applied. Keep in mind that we can only assign a policy to a certain single point in this structure. The top level would be too generic, because we will have more kinds of records beyond Reference under the General category. The File Plan, in fact, defines retention and disposition policies at the record-kind level, which, in our case, is represented by "Reference" and "Compliance" in their respective categories. Therefore, we will assign the policies at that level (Figure 1-21).

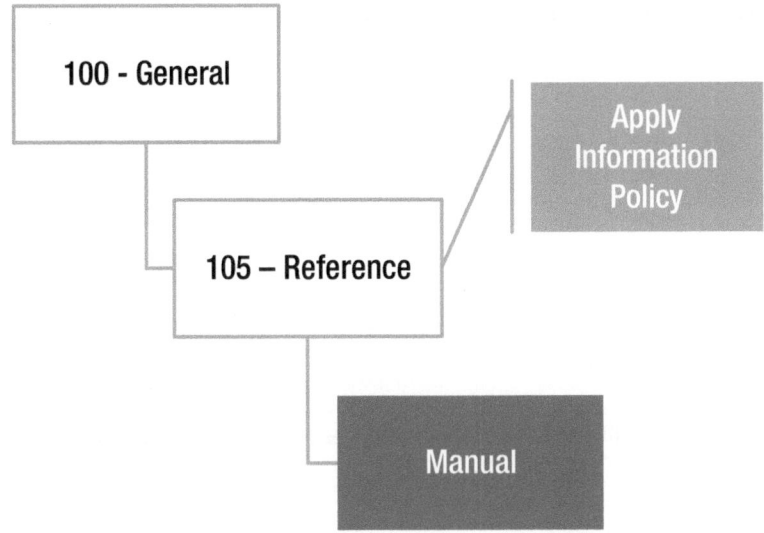

Figure 1-21. *Information management policy assignment*

We are still within the Content Type Hub site, and we should stay in its context, because all the policy configurations will be performed here. Remember: The first- and second-level content types are staying within the Content Type Hub and will not be published. Only records managers will be able to access the Enterprise Hub, to update the policies and other content type properties. For content owners and end users, the inherited policies will just "magically" work at the level of the published content types—Manual and Company Guidelsines.

To create a policy for a particular content type, just click the content type name (under Site Settings ➤ Site Content Types) and then, on the Site Content Type page, in the Settings section, click Information management policy settings. There, you can define a policy by updating the Edit Policy page.

To specify a retention period for documents that are subject to this policy, click Enable Retention, then specify the retention period and the actions that you want to occur (Figure 1-22).

Site Content Types ▸ Edit Policy

Name and Administrative Description

The name and administrative description are shown to list managers when configuring policies on a list or content type.

Name:

> 105 - Reference

Administrative Description:

> General Reference records.

Policy Statement

The policy statement is displayed to end users when they open items subject to this policy. The policy statement can explain which policies apply to the content or indicate any special handling or information that users need to be aware of.

Policy Statement:

> General Reference records are destroyed after 5 years.

Retention

Schedule how content is managed and disposed by

☑ Enable Retention

Figure 1-22. *Policy update form*

For the Reference content type, specify two retention stages, as shown in Figure 1-23.

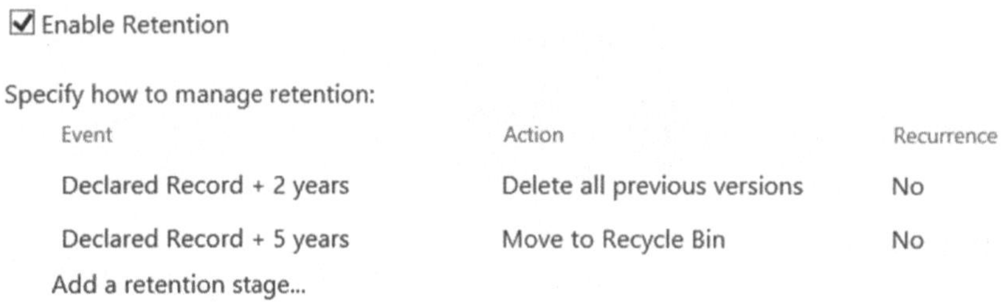

☑ Enable Retention

Specify how to manage retention:

Event	Action	Recurrence
Declared Record + 2 years	Delete all previous versions	No
Declared Record + 5 years	Move to Recycle Bin	No
Add a retention stage...		

Figure 1-23. *Retentiovn stages for Reference records*

For the Compliance content types, there will also be two retention stages to satisfy the requirements (Figure 1-24).

☑ Enable Retention

Specify how to manage retention:

Event	Action	Recurrence
Final Approval Date + 0 days	Send to the Records Center location	No
Declared Record + 10 years	Permanently Delete	No
Add a retention stage...		

Figure 1-24. *Retention stages for Compliance records*

The "Final Approval Date + 0 days" stage is somewhat artificial and is used here only for demonstration purposes. As mentioned previously, you will likely rely on a workflow to send documents to the Records Center in a real-world scenario. However, it is perfectly fine to use this stage when you are explaining to your customers how the policies work. In particular, there is one somewhat obscure point we are trying to convey by doing that.

Let's take a look at the second stage of the policy assigned to the Reference content type. To set a stage based on a date property, in the Event section, we click "This stage is based off a date property on the item" and then select the action and the increment of time after this action (number of days, months, or years) when we want it to be triggered (Figure 1-25).

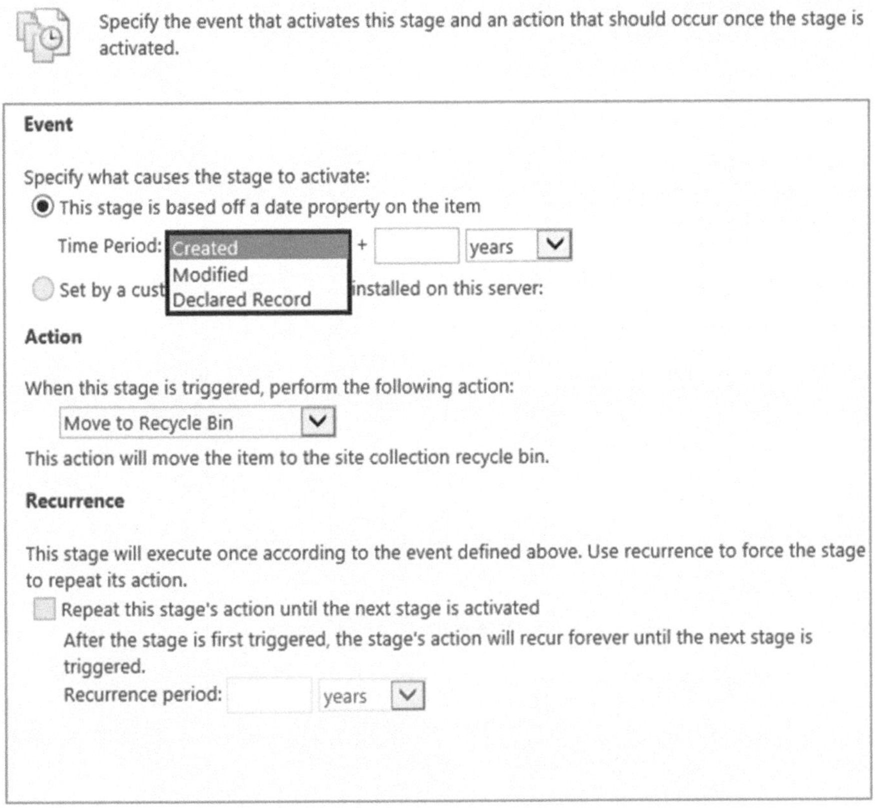

 Specify the event that activates this stage and an action that should occur once the stage is activated.

Event

Specify what causes the stage to activate:

◉ This stage is based off a date property on the item

Time Period: | Created | + | | years | ⌄ |
| Modified |
| Declared Record |

◯ Set by a cust... | | installed on this server: |

Action

When this stage is triggered, perform the following action:

| Move to Recycle Bin | ⌄ |

This action will move the item to the site collection recycle bin.

Recurrence

This stage will execute once according to the event defined above. Use recurrence to force the stage to repeat its action.

☐ Repeat this stage's action until the next stage is activated

After the stage is first triggered, the stage's action will recur forever until the next stage is triggered.

Recurrence period: | | years | ⌄ |

Figure 1-25. *Stage editing for Reference records*

Note that the only date properties available in the drop-down list are Created, Modified, and Declared Record. In some articles and blog posts, those three options are described as the only ones possible.

That, in fact, is not quite true. Any date-based property can be used here. And we can easily demonstrate it when creating a policy for the Compliance content type. Do you remember the custom column "Final Approval Date" of the Date and Time type that we created for this content type? When editing the first stage for its policy, low and behold, we now have the fourth option available (Figure 1-26).

Specify the event that activates this stage and an action that should occur once the stage is activated.

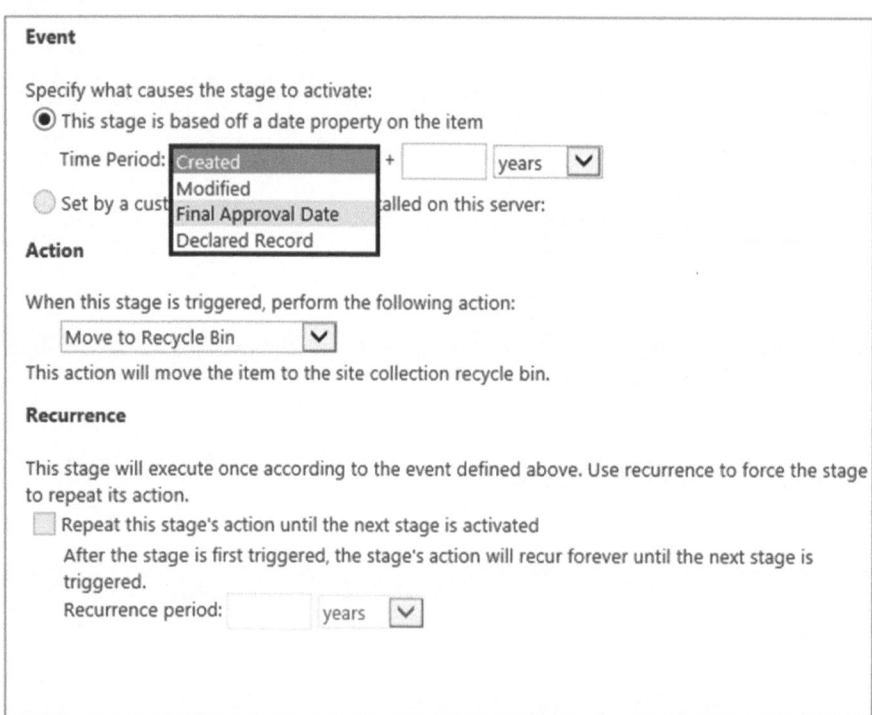

Figure 1-26. *Stage editing for Compliance records*

At this point, you should have two information management policies (each with two stages) created for the Reference and Compliance content types. Any content types created that are based on those two would automatically inherit, among other properties, their information management policies. And that is exactly what we want to achieve for the Manual and Company Guidelines content types.

■ **Note**   The "Set by a custom retention formula installed on this server" radio button is not available in SharePoint Online.

Publish Content Types

All the information management policies are now created, and it is time to publish our content types. As designed, we will only be publishing the business user-facing content types Manual and Company Guidelines (Figure 1-27).

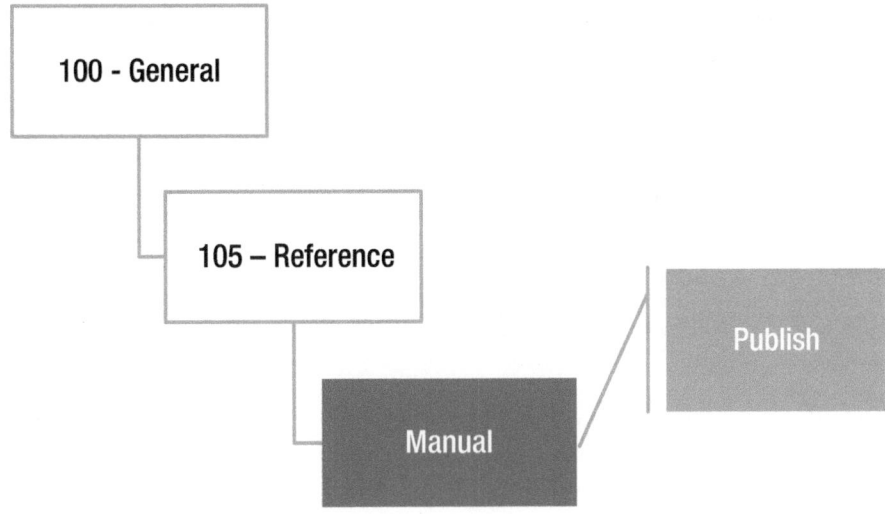

Figure 1-27. *Published content type*

Go to Site Content Types, choose "105—Reference," and click "Manage publishing for this content type." As you can see following, the "105—Reference" content type is not being published, even though we applied the Information Policy to it (Figure 1-28).

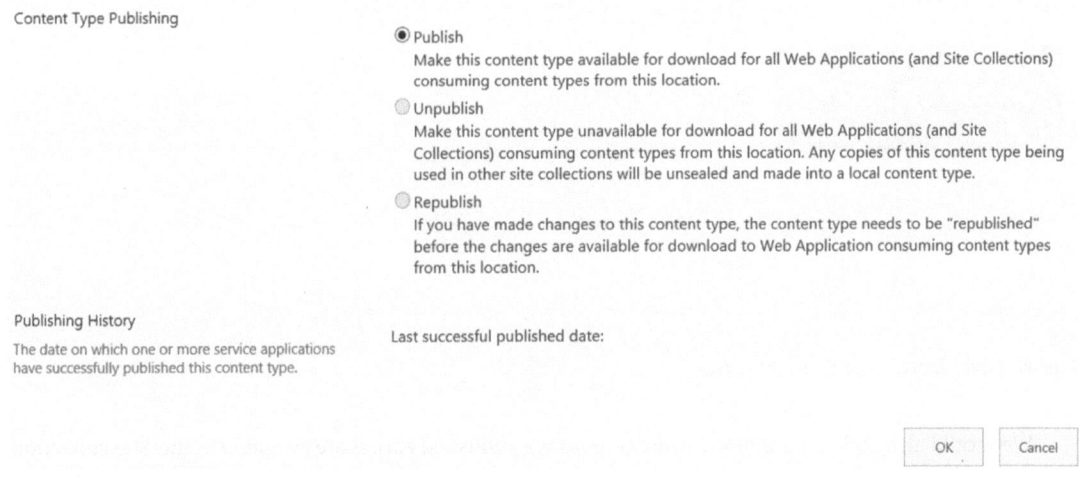

Figure 1-28. *Higher-level content type is not published*

Only the "Manual" content type (that is, that below "105—Reference" in the hierarchy) is getting published. After you publish it, the publishing settings for this content type will look as shown in Figure 1-29.

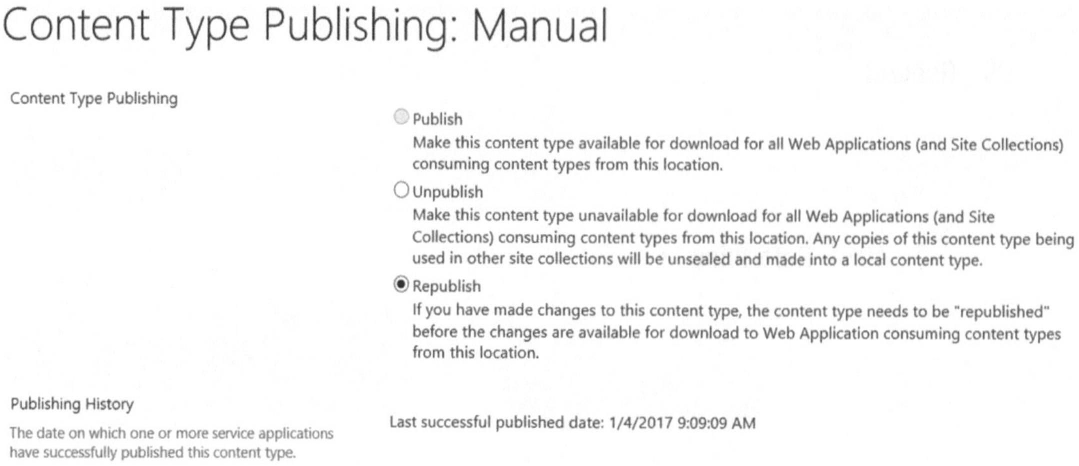

Content Type Publishing: Manual

Content Type Publishing

○ Publish
   Make this content type available for download for all Web Applications (and Site Collections)
   consuming content types from this location.

○ Unpublish
   Make this content type unavailable for download for all Web Applications (and Site
   Collections) consuming content types from this location. Any copies of this content type being
   used in other site collections will be unsealed and made into a local content type.

◉ Republish
   If you have made changes to this content type, the content type needs to be "republished"
   before the changes are available for download to Web Application consuming content types
   from this location.

Publishing History
The date on which one or more service applications
have successfully published this content type.

Last successful published date: 1/4/2017 9:09:09 AM

***Figure 1-29.** Manual content type is published*

The same goes for the "Company Guidelines" content type. It would be the only one published in the Legal content types hierarchy.

We now have all the content types ready to set up document libraries.

Create and Configure Collaboration Libraries

Let's now switch to the site collection whose documents the business user will be working with on a daily basis. Create two new document libraries here: "Legal" and "Manuals" (Figure 1-30).

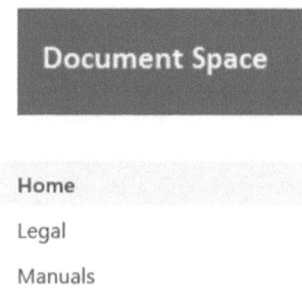

Home

Legal

Manuals

***Figure 1-30.** Document Space libraries*

We should also make sure that the content types we published earlier are available in this site collection (Figure 1-31).

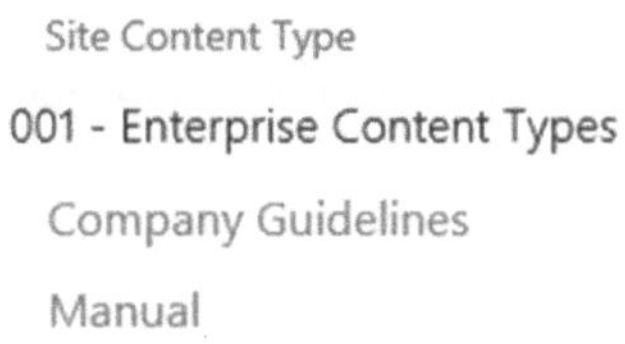

Site Content Type
001 - Enterprise Content Types
Company Guidelines
Manual

***Figure 1-31.** Available content types*

Again, it can take a while before the published content types are propagated to all the sites, so be patient.

Now, let's configure the Legal library to accept only a single content type, "Company Guidelines." Add it as the default custom content type and delete the out-of-the-box "Document" one (Figure 1-32).

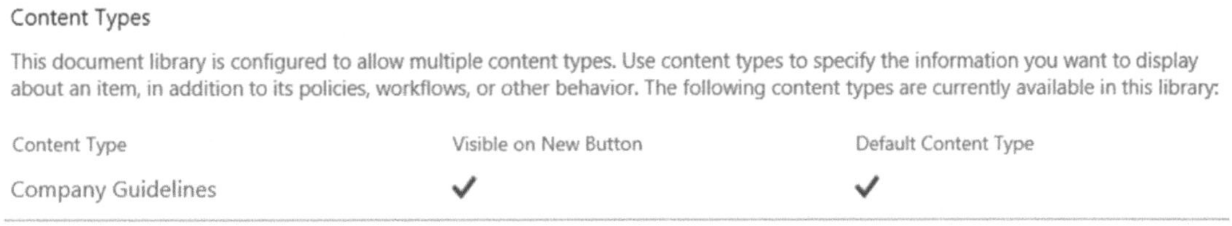

Content Types
This document library is configured to allow multiple content types. Use content types to specify the information you want to display about an item, in addition to its policies, workflows, or other behavior. The following content types are currently available in this library:
Content Type
Visible on New Button
Default Content Type
Company Guidelines
✓
✓

***Figure 1-32.** Company Guidelines content type in Legal library*

For the Manuals library, we will only allow Manual content type (Figure 1-33).

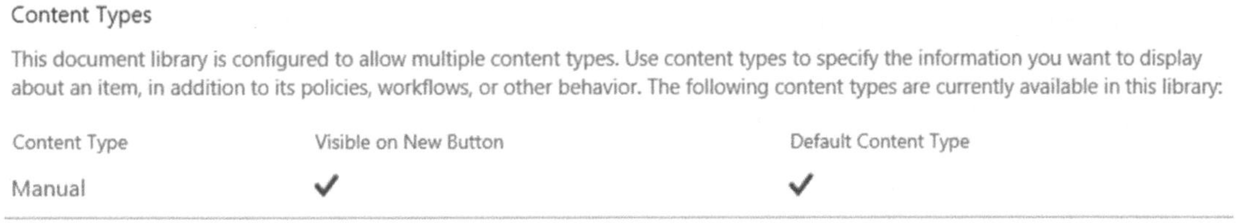

Content Types
This document library is configured to allow multiple content types. Use content types to specify the information you want to display about an item, in addition to its policies, workflows, or other behavior. The following content types are currently available in this library:
Content Type
Visible on New Button
Default Content Type
Manual
✓
✓

***Figure 1-33.** Manual content type in Manuals library*

Now the business users can start working with the documents.

Configure In-Place Records Management

As you remember, we decided to configure in-place records management for the Manuals library. Let's first activate the respective site collection feature (Figure 1-34).

In Place Records Management
Enable the definition and declaration of records in place.
Deactivate
Active

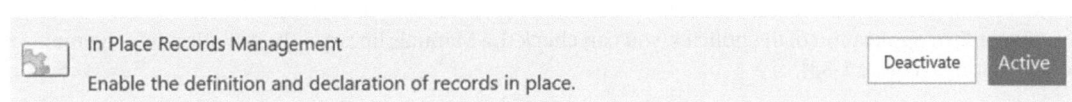

***Figure 1-34.** Activate In Place Records Management feature*

We will then disable location-based policies for the site collection, by deactivating the Library and Folder Based Retention feature. This enables content owners to ensure that the content type policies are not overridden by the list administrator's location-based policies (Figure 1-35).

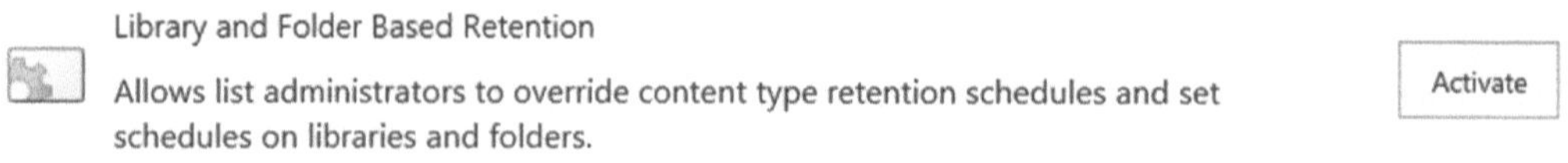

Library and Folder Based Retention

Allows list administrators to override content type retention schedules and set schedules on libraries and folders.

Activate

Figure 1-35. *Activate Library and Folder Based Retention feature*

We don't want our in-place records to be modified or deleted, so let's block Edit and Delete for records, via Site Collection's "Records Declaration Settings" (Figure 1-36).

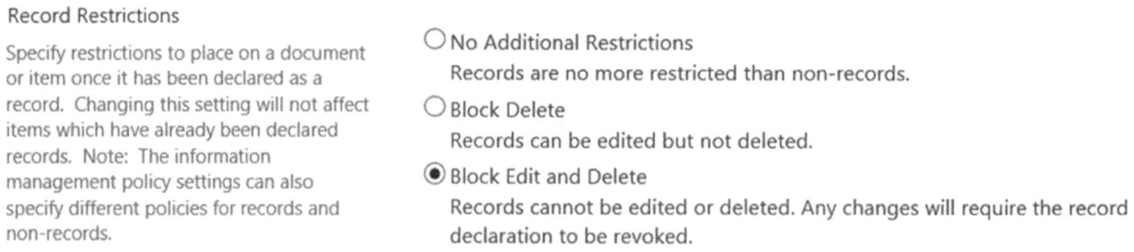

Record Restrictions

Specify restrictions to place on a document or item once it has been declared as a record. Changing this setting will not affect items which have already been declared records. Note: The information management policy settings can also specify different policies for records and non-records.

○ No Additional Restrictions
  Records are no more restricted than non-records.

○ Block Delete
  Records can be edited but not deleted.

◉ Block Edit and Delete
  Records cannot be edited or deleted. Any changes will require the record declaration to be revoked.

Figure 1-36. *Record Restrictions configuration*

Finally, let's enable in-place records management for the Manuals library, via the library's Library Record Declaration Settings (Figure 1-37).

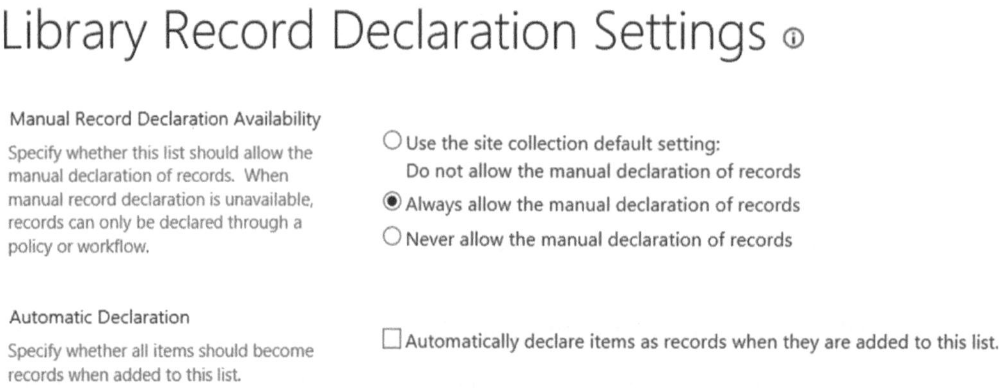

Library Record Declaration Settings ⓘ

Manual Record Declaration Availability

Specify whether this list should allow the manual declaration of records. When manual record declaration is unavailable, records can only be declared through a policy or workflow.

○ Use the site collection default setting:
  Do not allow the manual declaration of records
◉ Always allow the manual declaration of records
○ Never allow the manual declaration of records

Automatic Declaration

Specify whether all items should become records when added to this list.

☐ Automatically declare items as records when they are added to this list.

Figure 1-37. *Library Record Declaration Settings*

To confirm application of the policies, you can check the Manuals library's "Information management policy" settings (Figure 1-38).

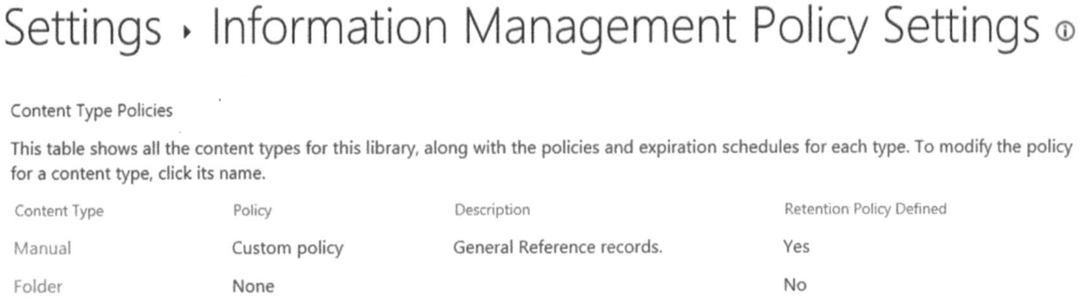

Settings ▸ Information Management Policy Settings ⓘ

Content Type Policies

This table shows all the content types for this library, along with the policies and expiration schedules for each type. To modify the policy for a content type, click its name.

Content Type	Policy	Description	Retention Policy Defined
Manual	Custom policy	General Reference records.	Yes
Folder	None		No

Figure 1-38. *Information Management Policy Settings of library*

Because we are controlling the policy at the higher level in our content type hierarchy, site collection administrators won't be able to modify it (Figure 1-39).

Information Management Policy Settings: Manual

Specify the Policy

Specify the information management policy for this content type. If you would like to use one of this site's predefined policies then select "Use a site policy". Alternatively, you can directly create or edit the policy settings.

You cannot change policy settings for this content type because it inherited the settings from its parent content type or a site level content type. To change these policy settings, change the settings for the parent of this content type.

○ None
◉ Define a policy...
○ Use a site collection policy:
[⌄]

Figure 1-39. *Information Management Policy Settings cannot change*

You can now upload a test document to Manuals library and check its compliance details. To access a document's compliance details, click "..." beside the document in the library, then click "..." again in the info panel, select "Advanced," and. Finally, click "Compliance Details" (Figure 1-40).

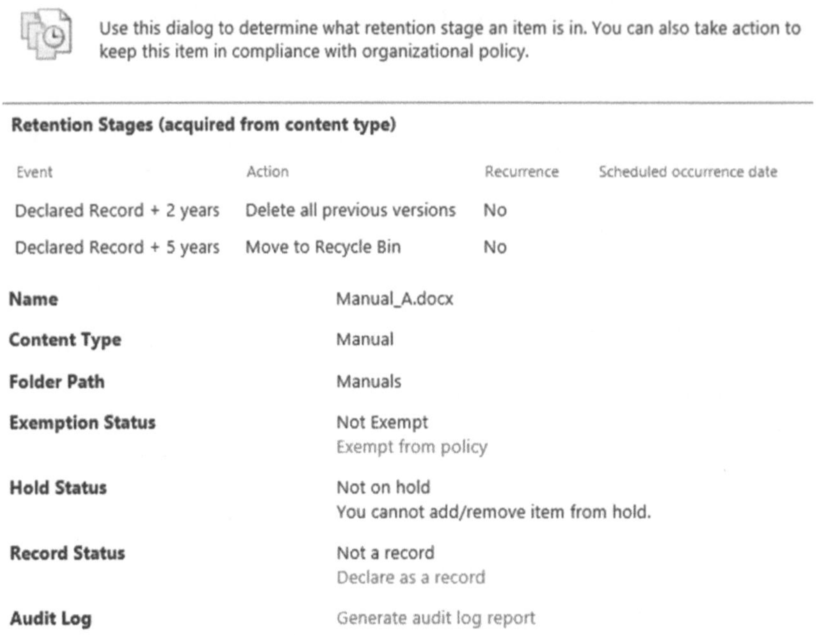

Use this dialog to determine what retention stage an item is in. You can also take action to keep this item in compliance with organizational policy.
Retention Stages (acquired from content type)
Event
Action
Recurrence
Scheduled occurrence date
Declared Record + 2 years
Delete all previous versions
No
Declared Record + 5 years
Move to Recycle Bin
No
Name
Manual_A.docx
Content Type
Manual
Folder Path
Manuals
Exemption Status
Not Exempt
Exempt from policy
Hold Status
Not on hold
You cannot add/remove item from hold.
Record Status
Not a record
Declare as a record
Audit Log
Generate audit log report

Figure 1-40. *Compliance details for non-record*

It's time to declare a document as a record in-place, via the ribbon menu (Figure 1-41).

View Properties
Edit Properties
Declare Record
Version History
Shared With
Delete Document
Manage

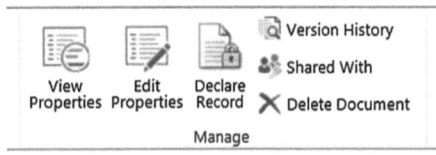

Figure 1-41. *Declare in-place record*

The lock icon will identify the in-place records (Figure 1-42).

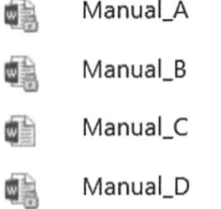

Manual_A
Manual_B
Manual_C
Manual_D

Figure 1-42. *In-place records*

You can check the document's compliance details again, to confirm that it's now a record (Figure 1-43).

 Use this dialog to determine what retention stage an item is in. You can also take action to keep this item in compliance with organizational policy.

Retention Stages (acquired from content type)

Event	Action	Recurrence	Scheduled occurrence date
Declared Record + 2 years	Delete all previous versions	No	1/18/2019
Declared Record + 5 years	Move to Recycle Bin	No	

Name	Manual_A.docx
Content Type	Manual
Folder Path	Manuals
Exemption Status	Not Exempt Exempt from policy
Hold Status	Not on hold You cannot add/remove item from hold.
Record Status	Declared record on 1/18/2017 Undeclare record
Audit Log	Generate audit log report

Figure 1-43. Compliance details for record

Go back to the ribbon menu, to ensure that no deletion or modification has been allowed (Figure 1-44).

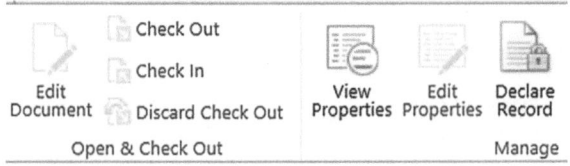

Figure 1-44. Record modification is disabled

Looks like we have just fulfilled all the requirements for Manuals. Hooray!

Configure Content Organizer Rules in Records Center

Now it's time to tackle all the remaining legal requirements for Company Guidelines documents. We must switch to the Records Center.

There, create a "Legal" records library.

We then add the Company Guidelines content type to the library's content types. Good thing we created all our content types centrally, so they are now readily available in all site collections throughout the entire SharePoint Online tenant!

The next step will be to create a new Content Organizer Rule, based on the content type we have just added (Figure 1-45).

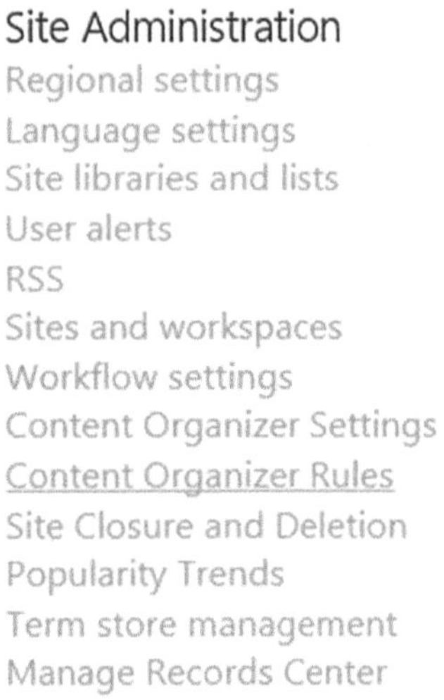

Site Administration
Regional settings
Language settings
Site libraries and lists
User alerts
RSS
Sites and workspaces
Workflow settings
Content Organizer Settings
Content Organizer Rules
Site Closure and Deletion
Popularity Trends
Term store management
Manage Records Center

Figure 1-45. *Content Organizer Rules settings link*

You should end up with something similar to what is shown in Figure 1-46 and Figure 1-47.

Content Organizer Rules ⓘ

⊕ new item

Group by Content Type   All Items   Group by Target Library   •••

✓	Title	Priority	Target Path

▲ **Submission Content Type : Company Guidelines** (1)

Company Guidelines (Legal)	••• 5	/sites/rc/Legal

Figure 1-46. *Content Organizer rule for Company Guidelines—overview*

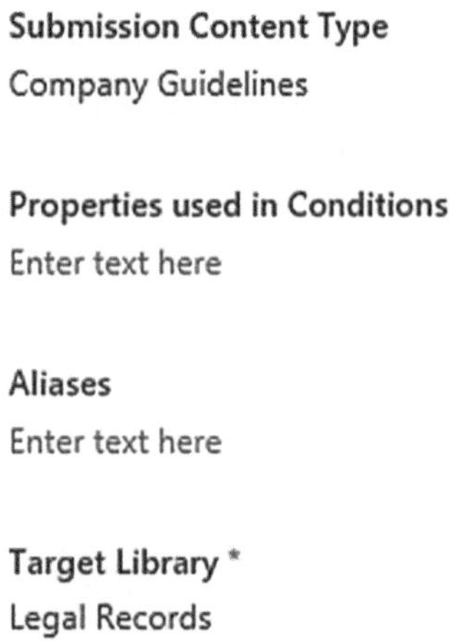

Submission Content Type

Company Guidelines

Properties used in Conditions

Enter text here

Aliases

Enter text here

Target Library *

Legal Records

Figure 1-47. *Content Organizer rule for Company Guidelines content type*

Now, get back to the Document Space site collection, navigate to the Legal library, select a document, go to the ribbon's Files tab, and test the new Routing Rule, by sending a document manually to the Records Center (Figure 1-48).

Figure 1-48. *Sending to Records Center*

When looking at the Records Center, you should see the document automatically routed and placed into the appropirate Legal records library.

■ **Note**   The Drop Off library, which is automatically created when activating the Content Organizer feature, serves as the default location to which documents are routed if they do not meet predetermined criteria.

Solution Overview

Congratulations! We now have a fully functional records management environment that is based exclusively on the out-of-the-box functionality of SharePoint Online. You can use it for quick pilots and demonstrations within your company or with customers.

Challenges

If it is all that simple, why do we hear again and again about failed RMS implementations? The challenges companies face when working on records management are not exclusive to SharePoint.

Here are some of them:

- Issues
    - Missing structure(s)
    - Missing business support
    - Poor process support
    - Treated as infrastructure
    - Low user focus/poor UX
    - Missing taxonomy
    - Missing metadata
    - Missing standards alignment
- Result in
    - Low capture ratio of business-critical information
    - Low perceived value for users and business
    - Duplications
    - Inability to find existing information
    - Information overflow
    - Information silos
    - Compliance risk

Those items should be addressed in order to achieve any success with records management projects.

What's Next for Office 365 Data Governance

There is more and more excitement building around the Advanced Data Governance in Office 365. It was recently announced and promises a lot of great things, such as true retention and classification across Office 365, event triggers, manual review and disposition, reporting, and improved client experience.

You should definitely keep an eye on those upcoming functionalities, because they can dramatically affect the records management landscape in Office 365, and in SharePoint Online in particular.

Summary

In this chapter, we have demonstrated how with SharePoint Online you can setup a working proof of concept for Records Management within days, which should allow to iteratively test the solution through the shorter feedback loops and quickly find out what SharePoint can (or cannot) do for your organization.

CHAPTER 2

■ ■ ■

Skype for Business Online

BY SHAWN CATHCART

The last few years have been a very exciting time for the universal communications (UC) space. Not only have the feature sets continued to expand, but the ubiquity of the end-user experience across many different platforms and types of end points has driven a much richer collaborative environment within Skype for Business. Around feature parity, it has also seen the gap close between the traditional on-premises product and what is offered in the cloud with Skype for Business Online. This chapter will explore that feature parity, as well as practical guidance around deployment of hybrid configurations, which allow the richest experience for customers moving from on-premises to the cloud.

Overview

The proliferation of cloud services has been transformational to the technology industry. It has challenged the way we think about the normal life cycle of IT services. From design, implementation, operational consumption, and maintenance through feature expansion, updates and upgrades, and implementation refresh of the service. What typically existed as a two-to-three-year life cycle for an IT service is now tracked in terms of months. There is a constant onslaught of feature set updates and improvements that are equally as huge benefit to end users as they are a challenge to IT service administrators.

The traditional focus on the underlying infrastructure supporting an IT service is now being transitioned to a focus on staying abreast of feature set updates, the integration of those features into other applications, and user consumption of the service as a whole. That being said, many of the hybrid configurations that are the cornerstone of most companies' cloud journey are a challenging mix of on-premises configuration, network connectivity, and migration planning. They also require a strong understanding of the cloud service features for users migrated to the cloud. The feature parity and coexistence state between on-premises users and cloud users is yet another layer of complexity.

I'm a strong advocate of cloud services—and not merely because of who I work for and what I do for a living. The cloud offers companies the opportunity to focus on the feature sets of an IT service that translate to operational efficiency and collaboration, without the additional effort of maintaining the underlying infrastructure for that service. But I'm also a very pragmatic and practical person. I have no desire to sugar coat the challenges in deploying the hybrid configurations that are common for most companies. My goal is to provide guidance in this chapter that is direct and technically applicable to the widest audience possible. My overviews are here to serve the purpose of clarifying what components of the Skype for Business service we are dealing with. While that seems an obvious statement, I've found that many customers get confused with the wide breadth of different modalities or components that make up the Skype for Business service. This confusion only increases when they attempt to understand how those components factor into a hybrid configuration. Figure 2-1 helps to summarize those components and will be key to drilling deeper into the specifics of hybrid configuration.

© Nikolas Charlebois-Laprade et al. 2017
N. Charlebois-Laprade et al., *Expert Office 365*, DOI 10.1007/978-1-4842-2991-0_2

Microsoft SaaS hybrid scenario architecture

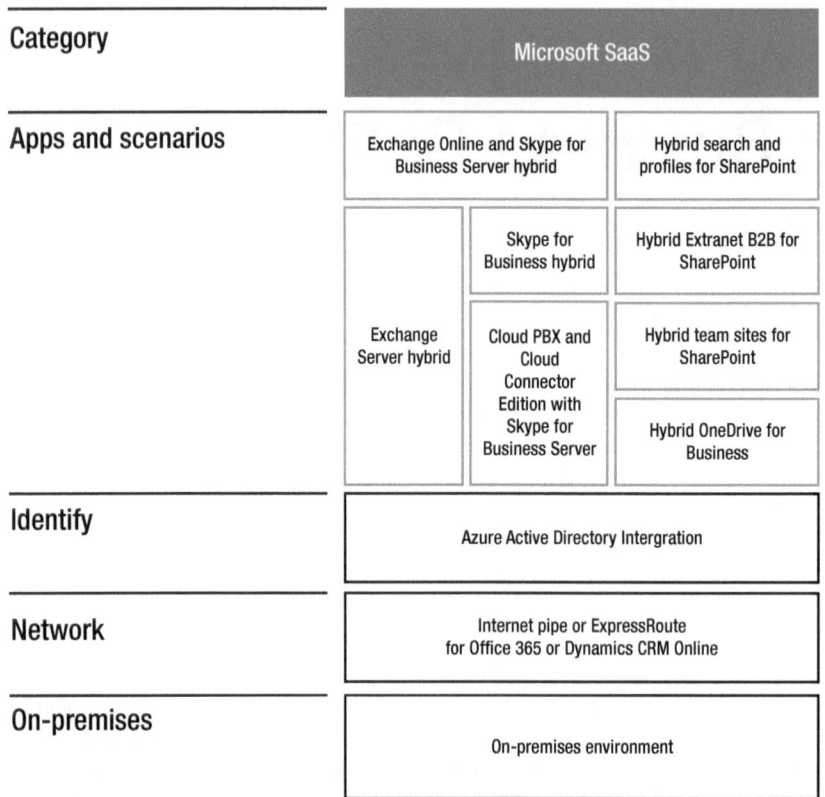

Figure 2-1. *Office 365 architecture components for hybrid configurations*

The other key focus will be on Hybrid Voice configurations. While there are plenty of strong feature sets in Skype for Business Online that justify the move to the cloud, such as conferencing, instant messaging, and federation, those are quite simple to understand and deploy when compared to the complexity of Hybrid Voice configurations. The user migration experience is also more complex, when you factor in the aspects of voice configurations such as dial plans, call flow, Public Switched Telephone Network (PSTN) connectivity, and the often-overlooked feature of voice mail.

You won't find me spending much time on the topic of PSTN Calling within Skype for Business Online, and let me start by saying that my lack of covering the topic is not because I think it unimportant. On the contrary, it is my strong feeling that PSTN Calling and cloud-based Voice over Internet Protocol (VoIP) are absolutely the future for universal communications. It transforms voice back into the technology service model where it belongs. And not just for the end users, but, more important, for the technology teams responsible for implementing and maintaining that service. However, the surprising ease with which PSTN Calling can be deployed via Office 365 means that it's something my customers, with their strong experience and knowledge of technology, tend not to require much assistance with. Also, PSTN Calling is not currently available in every country and region[1] for customers using Office 365. The service is expanding rapidly, but

---

[1]Microsoft, "Countries and regions that are supported for Skype for Business Online PSTN Services," https://support.office.com/en-us/article/Countries-and-regions-that-are-supported-for-Skype-for-Business-Online-PSTN-Services-6ba72f37-d303-4795-aa8f-7e1845078ed7?ui=en-US&rs=en-US&ad=US, 2017.

by focusing on that topic, I'm limiting my audience quite significantly. Case in point: I'm based in Canada, as are all the customers I typically do work with, and as of the writing of this book, PSTN Calling is not yet available for Office 365 tenants hosted in the Canadian data centers. Last, I have seen that most customers end up in either a permanent or very long-term Skype hybrid configuration, so it makes sense to focus most of our time on the technical challenges with implementing Hybrid Voice.

With that said, let me clarify more fully what will be covered in this chapter and what knowledge you, the reader, should take away in the end.

What will be covered is

- Overview of the Skype for Business Online service

- Overview of Skype for Business hybrid configuration and topology considerations

- A comparison of the differences between Cloud Voice versus Hybrid Voice

- Deep technical dive on Hybrid Voice configuration and user-migration considerations and challenges

- Service Administration tips pertinent to the Hybrid Voice configuration

- Network performance and connectivity considerations

What will not be covered is

- Non-Skype for Business Online–specific configurations in Office 365, such as identity management, directory synchronization, and Single Sign-On

- General feature set descriptions for the Skype for Business Online service, such as Web and Dial-in conferencing features, etc.

What you will learn is

- Deep technical configuration considerations for deploying Skype for Business hybrid

- The supported topology and design considerations for deploying Hybrid Voice with on-premises PSTN connectivity

- Guidance on provisioning and migrating Enterprise Voice users in a Hybrid Voice deployment

Skype for Business Online Overview

As a universal communications platform, Skype for Business Online provides many different types of communication features or modalities. While you may be familiar with these core components from a Lync or Skype for Business server deployment on-premises, it's worthwhile to clarify how those components relate to the online service in Office 365.

Skype for Business Core Modalities: On-Premises vs. Office 365

Most of the core modalities between on-premises Lync Server 2013 or Skype for Business Server 2015 and Skype for Business Online are the same. However, there are several that are specific either only on-premises deployments or Skype for Business Online.

Figure 2-2 shows all the core components of the Skype for Business Online service.

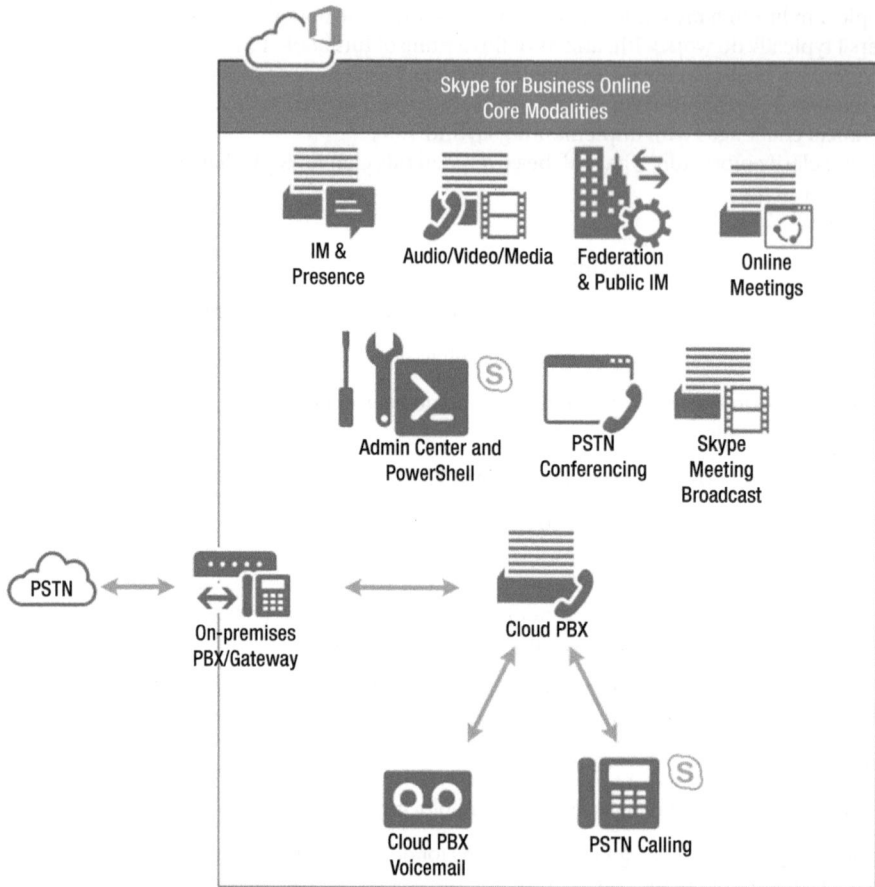

Figure 2-2. *Skype for Business Online core modalities*

I'll describe each in turn and discuss how they may differ from their on-premises equivalent. Microsoft has also recently released Microsoft Teams. Teams doesn't specifically fit into a single workload within Office 365 but instead pulls in various features from the entire Office 365 suite.

Instant Messaging and Presence (IM&P)

This is the core of the Skype for Business product suite. Most customers and users are very familiar with the functionality provided within IM&P. Although understanding the feature set differences between the various client versions is often a little more difficult, they are well-documented here:https://technet.microsoft.com/en-us/library/dn933896.aspx.

Key feature set differences follow:

- Features unavailable in Skype for Business Online

    - *My Picture: URL Photo Experience*: The option to point the Skype for Business client to pull your photo from a public Internet site. This is only available with on-premises deployments.

- Address book synchronization between Skype for Business Server 2015 on-premises and Skype for Business Online is not supported.

- *Persistent Chat*: While there is no direct equivalent to the Persistent Chat role in Skype for Business Online, Microsoft Teams accounts for most of this functionality plus even further integrations with SharePoint Online and Office 365 Groups.

- Feature similar to on-premises deployments

  - *Unified Contact Store*: This behaves as it does with on-premises deployments of UCS with Exchange Server 2013 or newer versions. However, it only integrates with mailboxes hosted within Exchange Online.

Audio, Video, and Media

Before diving into this topic, let's make an important clarification in terminology, specifically the difference between the Skype for Business product (the successor to Lync Server) and the Skype consumer product. While most people reading this book will be clear on the differences between those two, I want to ensure that the shorthand usage of "Skype" is always clear. Unless I specifically make reference to "Skype consumer," assume that any references to Skype for SfB are in relation to the Skype for Business product suite.

So, with that out of the way, let's discuss the core of Skype for Business audio and video, which are Skype-to-Skype audio and video calls. There is no specific difference in functionality here between on-premises and Skype for Business Online.

Features include

- One-to-one audio and video calls to users

  - within your Office 365 tenant

  - Homed on-premises as part of a hybrid configuration

  - Federated users running Lync or Skype for Business

  - High-definition video (1920 × 1080) for peer-to-peer calls

  - Media also includes

  - File Transfer

  - Skype-to-Skype desktop and application sharing

These also do not differ in any significant way from the Skype for Business Server 2015 feature set.

Federation and Public IM

Federation allows for external connectivity to other organizations running Skype for Business or previous Microsoft universal communications platforms. Those supported with Skype for Business Online are

- Skype for Business Server 2015

- Lync Server 2013

- Lync Server 2010

- Office Communications Server 2007 R2

Federation is also used to facilitate the hybrid configuration for Skype for Business Online. Through a Federation connection between your on-premises deployment and Skype for Business Online, along with the configuration of a Shared SIP Namespace, you can split users between both environments.

Online Meetings

Skype for Business Online provides a rich multipart meeting experience, but it's important to break down the unique components that make up Skype online meetings. I typically break these into two main categories.

- Meeting modalities

- Accessibility options (the different client options for connecting to online meetings)

While the accessibility options are essentially the same as the on-premises options, the Meeting modalities vary slightly.

I break them down as follows:

- Web conferencing

  - Group Instant Messaging & Presence

  - Content sharing

    - Desktop sharing

    - Application sharing

    - Enhanced PowerPoint presentation

  - Collaborative tools

    - Whiteboarding

    - Polls

    - Q&A

  - Audio Conference Bridge

    - Refers to the audio bridge for PC audio for client application access (Skype for Business client, Skype for Business Web App, Skype for Business Mobile app)

  - Dial-in Conference Bridge

    - A dial-in conference bridge that is integrated with the audio conference bridge

    - Provides dial-in access numbers for PSTN dial-in

    - Allows for dial-out capabilities to bring other PSTN attendees into the meeting

- Video conferencing

  - Soft client-based video end points (Skype for Business client, Web App, and Mobile app)

  - Skype Room System (SRS) end points

  - Interoperability with non-SRS end points

So, what are some of the differences in these conferencing modalities between on-premises deployments and Skype for Business Online?

- Dial-in conferencing is easy to deploy via Office 365, with appropriate licensing.

- Dial in conferencing can only be provided by the infrastructure that homes the user.

    - On-premises users must use dial-in conferencing provided by Skype for Business Server 2015 with PSTN connectivity for dial-in access numbers.

    - Skype for Business Online users must use Microsoft PSTN conferencing or one of the Audio Conferencing Providers (ACPs) that integrate with Office 365.

    - *No cross-functionality*. An on-premises user cannot be enabled for PSTN conferencing in Skype for Business Online.

- Non-SRS interoperability currently has more flexibility with on-premises Skype for Business Server 2015, but this gap is being closed quickly.

- SRS support is equal across on-premises and Skype for Business Online configurations.

Security and Archiving

In both the on-premises and Skype for Business Online scenarios, IM and media encryption is facilitated by use of a Transport Layer Security (TLS) protocol. However, with on-premises deployment, administrators can control the client versions, which are allowed to connect to the back-end servers. This ability for client version control or filtering is not currently available in Office 365.

From an archiving perspective, this is not controlled explicitly from within Skype for Business Online but, rather, by the user's associated Exchange mailbox, via In-Place Hold. For an on-premises deployment of Skype for Business, archiving is possible, whether the mailbox is home on-premises or in Exchange Online.

However, for Skype for Business Online users, archiving is only possible currently if the mailbox is homed in Exchange Online.

Admin Center and PowerShell

Historically, the on-premises functionality within the Skype for Business Control Panel and Management Shell was deeper than what was found in the Skype for Business Online Admin Center and PowerShell module. This was mainly due to the on-premises product having functionality that wasn't available within Skype for Business Online.

- Persistent Chat

- Enterprise Voice

- Response Groups

- Skype for Business Monitoring Reports

- Skype for Business Call Quality Dashboard

This feature parity continues to be closed between on-premises and Office 365, and with it, an ever-increasing amount of functionality within Skype for Business Online.

Examples of functionality that has already been added include the following:

- Skype for Business usage reports (covers the appropriate functionality provided by on-premises Monitoring reports)

- Skype for Business Call Quality Dashboard in Office 365

- Cloud PBX, PSTN Calling, and PSTN Conferencing (provides much of the functionality found within Enterprise Voice in Skype for Business Server 2015)

Features that are in preview or on the roadmap are

- Microsoft Teams (provides similar functionality to Persistent Chat)

- Cloud PBX Call Queues (provides Response Group functionality)

- Cloud PBX Auto Attendants (provides AA functionality previously provided by Exchange Unified Messaging)

These are all configured and managed through the Skype for Business Online Admin Center and PowerShell module.

PSTN Conferencing

This is an easy win for most customers. One of the biggest conferencing experience issues is when the web conferencing and PC audio bridge is not integrated with the dial-in or PSTN conferencing bridge. It's a confusing and poor end-user experience, connecting to the web conference via the PC and dialing into the audio bridge on the phone. This is easily solved, deployed, and managed by using PSTN Conferencing within Skype for Business Online.

PSTN Conferencing is easily managed via the Skype for Business Online Admin Center, and it integrates the dial-in conferencing details into the Skype Meeting invite via integration with Outlook. Microsoft has also added functionality to PSTN Conferencing, which now allows users to customize the dial-in access numbers, as follows:

- Use a toll-free number.

- Assign a service number.

- Port a DID and use it for the dial-in access number.

- PSTN Calling is required to facilitate this.

The configuration literally takes minutes for a huge improvement in conferencing experience and, frankly, ease of management.

Skype Meeting Broadcast (SMB)

Skype Meeting Broadcast provides capabilities for large meetings...very large meetings! This has long been a challenge on-premises, with the normal attendee limit for a Skype for Business Server 2015 being 250 attendees. While you could deploy a dedicated Enterprise Pool to facilitate very large meetings, it was still limited by the resources that could be made available within a single Enterprise Edition pool and the network connectivity on-premises.

The reality is that very large meetings, or town hall–style meetings, don't tend to be highly interactive. This is just a logistical constraint. You can't have 10,000 attendees IM'ing or presenting video and audio streams or content and have that be at all manageable. They are handled more like events, with presenters and event admin staff providing the content for the meeting, with a much larger audience consuming that content and usually providing feedback via polls or Q&As.

Skype Meeting Broadcast is designed specifically for this type of scenario and leverages the Office 365 data centers to provide the streaming of that content to up to 10,000 users! This requires having to deploy on-premises infrastructure with enough resources to host the meeting and network connectivity to stream out that content.

Cloud PBX, PSTN Calling, and Hybrid Voice

This is where we will spend most of our time. Understanding the differences between these and the supported topologies that can be deployed with them is critical to planning the voice capabilities you intend to use with Skype for Business Online. Much of this chapter is dedicated to this topic alone, so I won't try to tackle it here.

What I will say is that we continue to close the gap in feature parity between on-premises Enterprise Voice and the voice capabilities available with Skype for Business Online. The end goal is to have feature sets available that will allow most customers to use Cloud PBX in combination with PSTN Calling and remove their reliance on on-premises voice infrastructure and PSTN connectivity. But for most, Hybrid Voice will be the intermediate step to providing that functionality today.

Skype for Business Hybrid

Skype for Business hybrid allows you to maintain a set of users with the same SIP domain between your on-premises deployment and Office 365 tenant. It is strictly a one-to-one relationship of an on-premises Skype for Business topology with a single Office 365 tenant.

Before I go further, I'd like to recommend that readers look at the Microsoft Cloud IT architecture resources. These are excellent materials that are kept up to date with visual representations of all the important IT architecture considerations with Microsoft's cloud services (https://aka.ms/clouditarch).

Most pertinent to a discussion about Skype for Business Online are

- Microsoft Cloud Networking for Enterprise Architects

- Microsoft Hybrid Cloud for Enterprise Architects

I'd also recommend becoming deeply familiar with the architectural model diagrams for the Office 365 workloads that can be found at https://technet.microsoft.com/en-us/library/dn782272.aspx.

As with all hybrid configurations for Office 365 workloads, the key component is identity. Where are the user and group objects managed, or, in other words, what is the source of authority for those objects: on-premises Active Directory or Azure Active Directory? In the case of hybrid configurations, the source of authority sits with the on-premises Active Directory objects, hence the requirement for directory synchronization to Azure AD (see Figure 2-3).

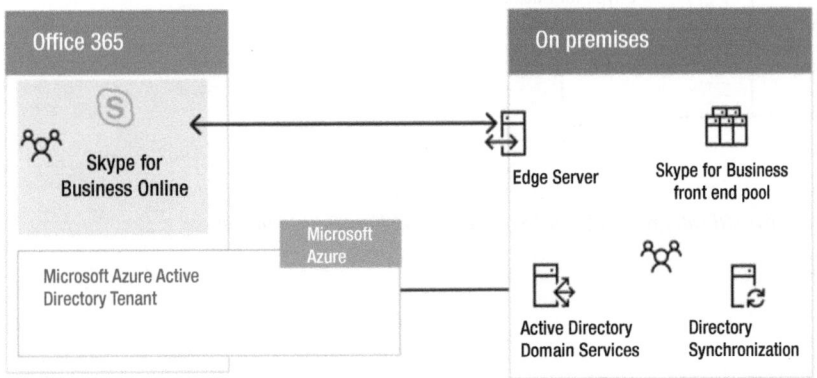

Figure 2-3. *Skype for Business Hybrid and Identity integration*

Hybrid configuration also allows for on-premises PSTN connectivity for Enterprise Voice (Cloud PBX) enabled users within Skype for Business Online (Figure 2-4 and Figure 2-5). I'll be expanding on this in more detail later in the chapter.

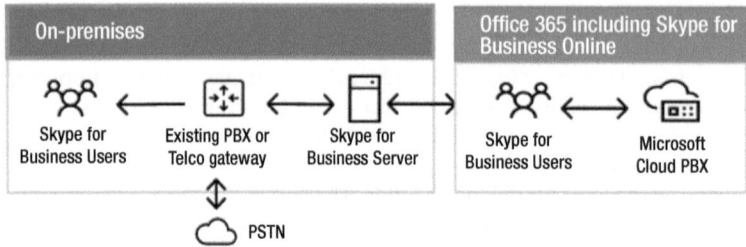

Figure 2-4. *On-premises PSTN connectivity via Skype for Business Server 2015*

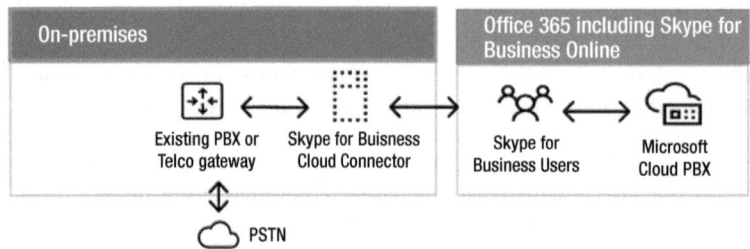

Figure 2-5. *On-premises PSTN connectivity via Cloud Connector Edition (CCE)*

Hybrid configuration also allows you deeper integrations with the other Office 365 workloads, Exchange Online and SharePoint Online in particular (Figure 2-6).

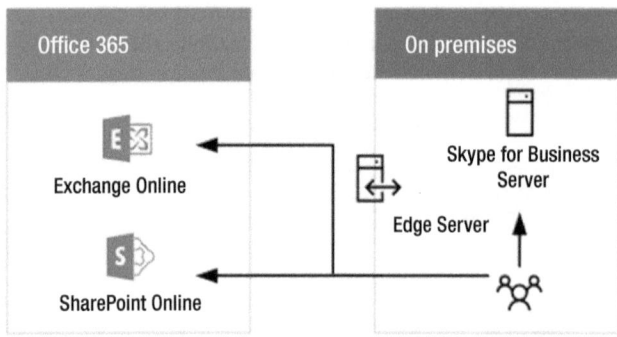

Figure 2-6. *Skype for Business hybrid integration with Exchange and SharePoint Online*

Topology Considerations

Following are the key topology considerations when looking at Skype for Business hybrid:

- *On-premises infrastructure*: This relates to the required on-premises infrastructure to establish Skype for Business hybrid configuration. It consists, at minimum, of

  - *Skype for Business Edge*: This is a single Skype for Business Edge server, although an Edge pool is recommended for high availability.

  - *Skype for Business Front End*: This can be a standard edition server or an enterprise pool. A three-server enterprise pool is the recommended minimum configuration to provide high availability.

  - *Reverse Proxy*: The existing reverse proxy solution used on-premises. Again, the recommendation is that this solution has high availability factored in.

  - *Active Directory Forest*: A supported Active Directory Forest topology. I will discuss this in more detail following.

  - *Directory Synchronization*: The recommended tool is Azure AD Connect.

  - *Authentication*: Synchronized or Federated authentication

    - *Synchronized*: Requires configuration of Password Synchronization within Azure AD Connect

    - *Federated*: Requires the deployment of a supported federated identity provider, such as Active Directory Federation Services (AD FS)

  - *Client End Points*: This covers the desktop and mobile clients, along with supported video end points, such as Skype Room Systems.

- *Office 365 Tenant*: This concerns the single tenant used to establish Skype for Business hybrid configuration with the on-premises deployment. The key point here is that this is a one-to-one ratio. You cannot have multiple on-premises deployments of Skype for Business or Lync Server 2013 federated with a single Office 365 tenant using hybrid configuration.

  - *Custom Domains*: You must add and verify all the appropriate SIP domains on-premises that will be used for shared SIP address configuration. You must also determine what authentication method those domains are going to use: Managed or Federated.

  - *Managed*: Office 365 is the source of authority for authentication, and so, typically, password synchronization is used via Azure AD Connect.

  - *Federated*: Office 365 custom domains are configured to redirect authentication to a supported identity provider, such as AD FS.

Supported Topologies

Supported topologies for Skype for Business fall into two categories

- Supported on-premises topologies

- Supported on-premises topologies that are also supported for hybrid configurations

The biggest impact on the on-premises topology is the design or layout of the Active Directory forests. A single forest with a single Skype for Business topology is the easiest topology to support. But most enterprise customers have complex Active Directory forest designs, and these can become a blocker for hybrid configurations.

The supported Active Directory topologies for Skype for Business Server 2015 are

- Single forest with single domain

- Single forest with a single tree and multiple domains

- Single forest with multiple trees and disjoint namespaces

- Multiple forests in a central forest topology

- Multiple forests in a resource forest topology

- Multiple forests in a Skype for Business resource forest topology with Exchange Online

- Multiple forests in a resource forest topology with Skype for Business Online and Azure Active Directory Connect

Reference URL: `https://technet.microsoft.com/en-us/library/dn933910.aspx`.

All the single-forest topologies are supported for hybrid configurations. However, when multiple forests are introduced, there is only a single, very specific topology that is supported for hybrid configuration (see Figure 2-7). It is detailed in the "Configure a Multi-Forest Environment for Hybrid Skype for Business" TechNet article found here: `https://technet.microsoft.com/en-us/library/mt603995.aspx`.

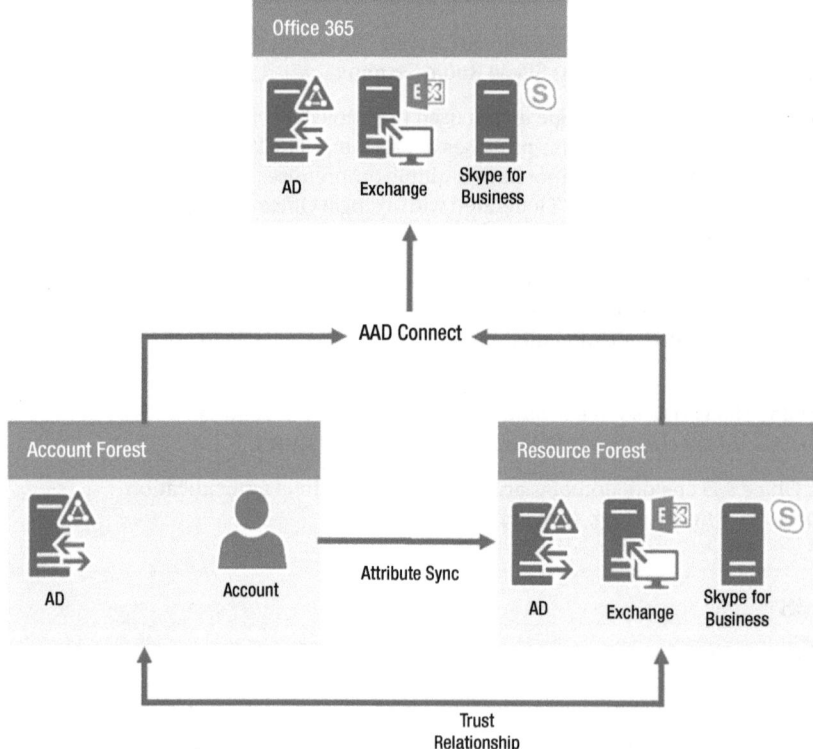

Figure 2-7. Multi-forest environment for Skype for Business hybrid

Even though the validation for the forest topology is covered in the TechNet article, I want to reiterate them here. Multiple user forests are supported. Keep the following in mind:

- For either a single-user forest or multiple-user forest deployment, there must be a single deployment of Skype for Business Server. You cannot have multiple deployments of Skype for Business Server using hybrid configurations to a single Office 365 tenant.

- Exchange Server can be deployed in the same resource forest as Skype for Business Server or in a different forest. You can also utilize Exchange Online.

Configuring Skype for Business Server in a central forest topology is not supported when hybrid mode is enabled. The main differentiator between a central and resource forest topology is over the objects used.

- Central forest topology utilizes contact objects.

- Resource forest topology utilizes disabled user objects.

While not explicitly stated, enabling users for Cloud PBX in this topology is supported. The article also discusses the issues of AD FS authentication and single-sign-on behavior in this type of resource forest topology. Its recommendations often get lost in the deep technical guidance on how to configure AD FS to support this topology, so I want to highlight it here, as it's critically important.

To avoid having a broken single-sign-on experience or AD FS authentication failures in a multi-forest topology with hybrid, the SIP/SMTP/UPN attributes for users from each forest *must* be unique, and not synchronized between forests (Figure 2-8).

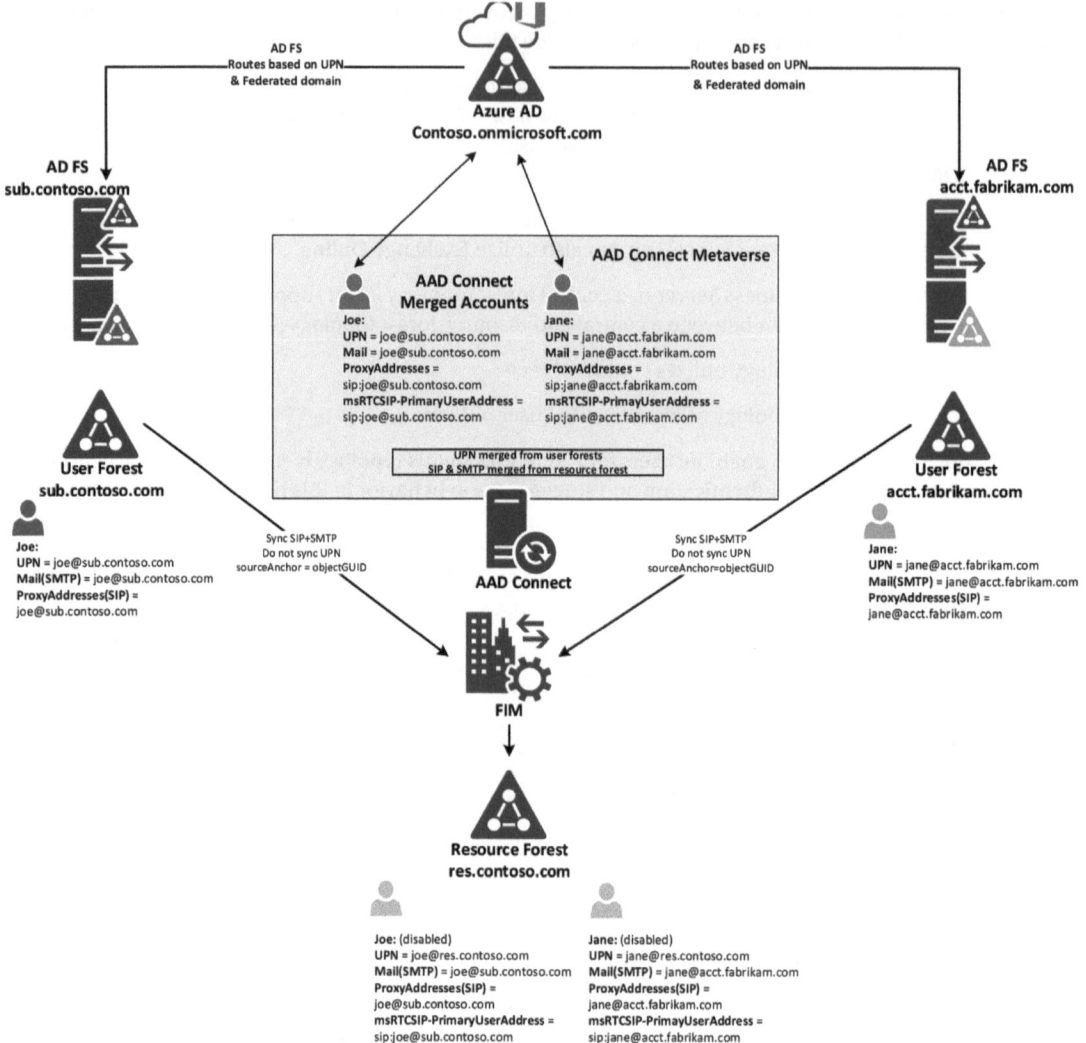

Figure 2-8. *Sample configuration for user attribute synchronization to support multi-forest hybrid for Skype for Business*

The key points are as follows:

- Have a unique SIP/SMTP/UPN domain for each forest.

- Do not synchronize the UPN between forests, as this breaks the single-sign-on via AD FS.

- Deploy AD FS in each user forest, to facilitate federated authentication and single-sign-on for the SIP/SMTP/UPN domains hosted by that user forest.

- FIM can be used to synchronize the required attributes between forests.

- Azure AD Connect will be used to create a merged user account, made up of attributes from the user and resource forests, that will then be synchronized to Azure AD.

- Custom domains added to the Office 356 tenant should be configured for Federated authentication, with references to the AD FS proxy in the user forest hosting that domain. AD FS is optional in this scenario. Managed authentication via password synchronization can also be used.

On-Premises Edge Considerations

A common scenario with many customers is to have only a single Skype for Business Edge server deployed. This is often the result of a phased rollout approach for Skype for Business, whereby, initially, high availability and capacity for external users are not a critical driver, and so a single Edge is deployed in an Edge Pool. This is essentially a pool with one Edge server.

While this technically fits the bill, it doesn't provide any high availability or proper capacity for the increased traffic that deploying Skype for Business hybrid puts on the Edge server. The recommendation is to deploy one of the scaled consolidated Edge pool configurations. Those are highlighted here: `https://technet.microsoft.com/en-us/library/mt346416.aspx`.

One of the more common scenarios is the "Scaled consolidated Edge pool with DNS load balancing and private IP addresses and NAT." This particular scenario has a requirement that is not explicitly called out in the TechNet documentation. That is, in this scenario, with private IPs and NAT, you are required to enable hairpinning on the network edge firewalls, to facilitate Edge-to-Edge media relay within an Edge pool.

Unlike Front End pools that utilized Windows Fabric to communicate and be aware of other nodes in the pool, Edge servers within an Edge pool really aren't "aware" of each other. So, when they are required to do media relay between Edge servers (picture a user connected to each Edge server, trying to establish a media session; the Edge servers essentially must proxy this between themselves), the only reference the Edge servers have to each other is the NAT'd public IP defined for the A/V Edge service (see Figure 2-9). When using private IPs with NAT, this is not allowed, unless hairpinning on the firewalls is allowed. If you are using Public IPs, this isn't an issue.

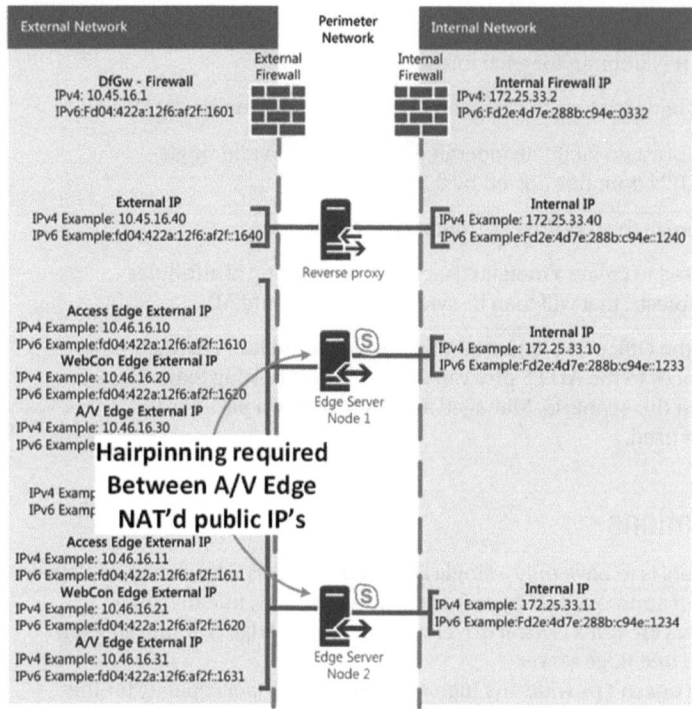

Figure 2-9. *Network hairpinning requirement for Edge Server communication within an Edge Pool with NAT'd IPs*

This is the main reason why you must state the Public IP for the A/V Edge service, if you configure your topology to not use Public IPs (Figure 2-10 and Figure 2-11).

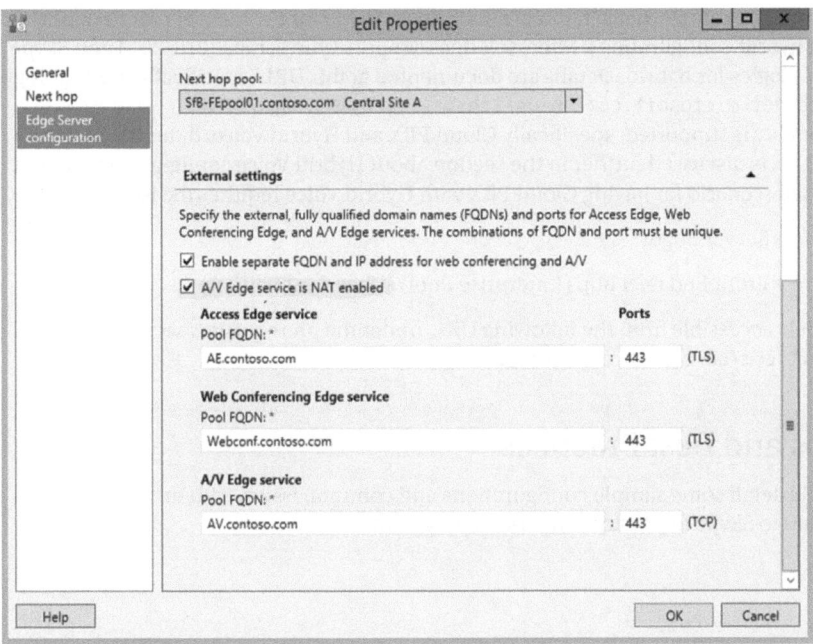

Figure 2-10. *Enabling NAT'd IP for the A/V Edge service*

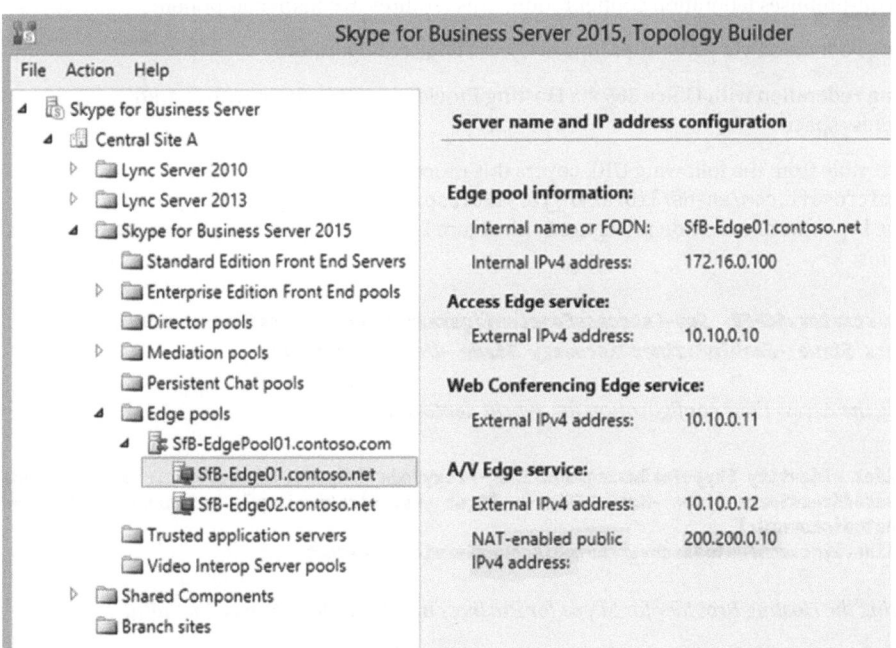

Figure 2-11. *Sample configuration showing the Public IP for a NAT-enabled A/V Edge configuration*

The other consideration is regarding what version of Lync Server/Skype for Business Server to deploy for the Edge role to support hybrid configurations. Microsoft does support Lync Server 2010/2013 and Skype for Business Server 2015 topologies for hybrid. Details are documented at this URL (specifically the Topology requirements): https://technet.microsoft.com/en-us/library/jj205403.aspx.

However, what functionality is supported, specifically Cloud PBX and Hybrid Voice, differs, based on the on-premises topology. This is discussed further in the section about Hybrid Voice configuration, but the key point is that the supported scenario for having Cloud PBX with Hybrid Voice requires the following:

- Skype for Business Server Edge

- Skype for Business Front End next hop (Enterprise Pool or Standard Edition)

That is listed in the article accessible from the following URL, under the prerequisites section: https://technet.microsoft.com/en-us/library/mt455212.aspx.

Configuration Tips and Best Practices

Through this next section, I'll detail some sample configurations and common issues with the on-premises Edge configuration in relation to Skype for Business hybrid deployments.

Edge Configuration

There are several key pieces of the on-premises Skype for Business Edge configuration that must be validated to implement Skype for Business hybrid. This is also tied to some resulting configurations that must take place in the Office 365 tenant configuration.

Let's start with on-premises federation configuration. This requires two main components.

- Enabling Federation via your on-premises Access Edge configuration

- Enabling Federation with Office 365 via Hosting Provider configuration with shared SIP address space

The article accessible from the following URL covers this process in detail: https://technet.microsoft.com/en-us/library/jj205126.aspx.

But here are the key PowerShell cmdlets (Figure 2-12, Figure 2-13, and Figure 2-14) for configuring each of the preceding items:

```
PS C:\Users\Administrator.SCPFE> Set-CsAccessEdgeConfiguration -AllowOutsideUsers $true -
AllowFederatedUsers $true -EnablePartnerDiscovery $true -UseDnsSrvRouting
```

Figure 2-12. *Setting the Access Edge configuration for hybrid deployment*

```
New-CsHostingProvider -Identity SkypeforBusinessOnline -ProxyFqdn "sipfed.online.lync.com" -Enabled
$true -EnabledSharedAddressSpace $true -HostsOCSUsers $true -VerificationLevel UseSourceVerification
-IsLocal $false -AutodiscoverUrl
https://webdir.online.lync.com/Autodiscover/AutodiscoverService.svc/root
```

Figure 2-13. *Creating the Hosting Provider for Skype for Business hybrid configurations, including the Autodiscover URL*

New-CsHostingProvider : There is a duplicate key sequence 'SIPFED.ONLINE.LYNC.COM' for the 'urn:schema:Microsoft.Rtc.Management.Settings.Edge.2008:ProviderProxyFqdn' key or unique identity constraint.

Figure 2-14. *Error presented when multiple Hosting Provider configurations reference the same* ProxyFqdn

You may receive an error regarding a "duplicate key sequence":

This is typically related to a hosting provider with the -ProxyFqdn already specified. Using Get-CsHostingProvider will list all existing hosting provider configurations. You can either

- Remove the existing hosting provider (often referenced as Lync Online, if you've upgraded from Lync Server 2010 or 2013), or

- Set the existing hosting provider configuration with the new configuration

I typically recommend just removing the existing hosting provider and rerunning the preceding New-CsHostingProvider cmdlet again, as advised in the support article available from the following URL: https://support.microsoft.com/en-us/help/3108403/-there-is-a-duplicate-key-sequence-error-in-lync-or-skype-for-business-after-you-run-the-new-cshostingprovider-powershell-cmdlet.

Remove-CSHostingProvider -Identity LyncOnline.

The identity may also be listed as SkypeforBusinessOnline, as follows: Remove-CSHostingProvider -Identity "Skype for Business Online".

Either way, the desired output from the cmdlet should be the same as what is shown in Figure 2-15.

```
Identity                   : SkypeforBusinessOnline
Name                       : SkypeforBusinessOnline
ProxyFqdn                  : sipfed.online.lync.com
VerificationLevel          : UseSourceVerification
Enabled                    : True
EnabledSharedAddressSpace  : True
HostsOCSUsers              : True
IsLocal                    : False
AutodiscoverUrl            : https://webdir.online.lync.com/Autodiscover/AutodiscoverService.svc/root
```

Figure 2-15. *Removing CSHostingProvider with PowerShell*

Do not confuse the Access Edge configuration for Federation with the external access policy. This is viewed by running Get-CsExternalAccessPolicy. This controls if and to whom external Skype for Business users can communicate when outside an on-premises network. This is not required for hybrid configuration to be implemented, but it is often confused with the Access Edge configuration policy. The only parameter that would have an impact on hybrid usability would be the -EnableFederationAccess parameter defined by Set-CsExternalAccessPolicy. This dictates whether external users can communicate with federated users. All hybrid users homed in Skype for Business Online would be considered federated users in this instance. So, this would have to be enabled to allow external on-premises users to communicate with hybrid users in Skype for Business Online.

All the preceding can also be leveraged via the Skype for Business Control Panel. This will evaluate your existing hybrid configuration, both on-premises and in Office 365, and then apply the appropriate configurations I've highlighted in the preceding paragraph. Figure 2-16 shows the hybrid Configuration Wizard screens that list configuration errors, whereas Figure 2-17 shows the same Wizard without any errors identified.

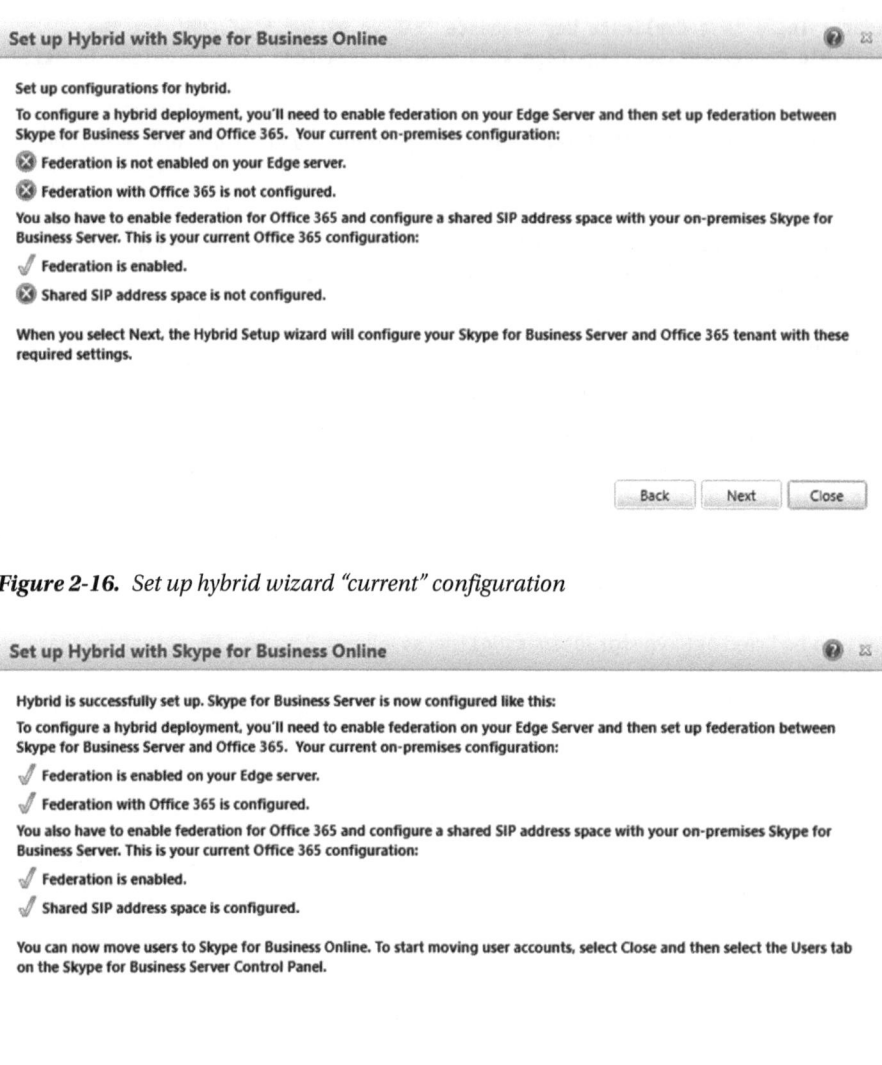

Figure 2-16. *Set up hybrid wizard "current" configuration*

Figure 2-17. *Set up hybrid "wizard" remediation configuration*

Before you can complete this wizard, however, you must sign in to Office 365 with a global administrator account. Most customers keep a cloud-only account in their tenant space with the global administrator role. This ensures that if you are using federated authentication, say, via AD FS, and AD FS becomes unavailable, you still have a cloud-only account that can be used to administer the Office 365 tenant.

In regard to the Skype for Business hybrid setup in Control Panel, you must use a cloud-only account tied to the <tenant>.onmicrosoft.com default domain. If you attempt to use a synchronized account that has been given the global administrator role in your tenant, and which is using a custom domain, the logon will fail. This is due to the login here leveraging Autodiscover (lyncdiscover.contoso.com) to find its way to Office 365 to log on.

For Office 365 <tenant>.onmicrosoft.com domains, this record exists and will point to Office 365 and allow the sign-in to work as expected (Figure 2-18).

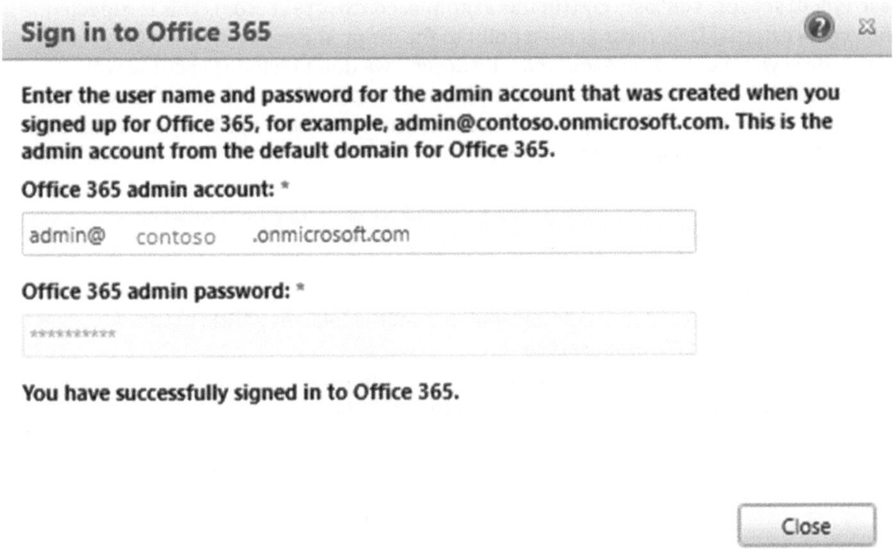

Sign in to Office 365　　　　　　　　　　　　　　　 ② ☒

Enter the user name and password for the admin account that was created when you signed up for Office 365, for example, admin@contoso.onmicrosoft.com. This is the admin account from the default domain for Office 365.

Office 365 admin account: *

admin@　contoso　.onmicrosoft.com

Office 365 admin password: *

****

You have successfully signed in to Office 365.

[Close]

Figure 2-18. *Authenticating to Office 365 to manage hybrid configuration via the Skype for Business Control Panel*

If you use a synchronized account, you'll typically see an error similar to that shown in Figure 2-19.

Sign in to Office 365　　　　　　　　　　　　　　　 ② ☒

Enter the user name and password for the admin account that was created when you signed up for Office 365, for example, admin@contoso.onmicrosoft.com. This is the admin account from the default domain for Office 365.

Office 365 admin account: *

admin@contosotest.com

Office 365 admin password: *

****

We couldn't log in to your Office 365 account. Please check the errors and then select OK to try again:
Get-CsPowerShellEndpoint : The remote name could not be resolved: 'lyncdiscover.contosotest.com'

Note: If your organization is using manual proxy settings, please see the Help for more information.

[OK]　　[Cancel]

Figure 2-19. *Error presented when authenticating with a synchronized account within the Skype for Business Control Panel*

It fails to discover `lyncdiscover.contoso.com` (in this example, `contosotest.com`). This is expected. In a hybrid configuration, all external DNS records must point to the on-premises deployment (Edge and reverse proxy). This includes `Lyncdiscover.contoso.com`. By design, we don't include `Lyncdiscover.contoso.com` on the internal DNS zones for the SIP domain. Instead, `Lyncdiscoverinternal.contoso.com` is used. So, when the front end server goes to look up `Lyncdiscover.contoso.com` in this instance, it does not find it in the internal DNS zone and gives the preceding error.

Office 365 Tenant Configuration

While configuring the Office 365 tenant configuration is most simple via the Control Panel wizard, you can also do it manually. This is detailed in TechNet article accessible from the following URL: `https://technet.microsoft.com/en-us/library/jj205126.aspx#Anchor_1`.

It requires the Skype for Business Online connector module for Windows PowerShell, which can be downloaded here: `https://go.microsoft.com/fwlink/p/?LinkId=391911`.

The following screenshot shows the cmdlets required to connect to Skype for Business Online PowerShell and the cmdlet for enabling shared SIP address space for your tenant (Figure 2-20).

```
PS C:\Users\Administrator.SCPFE> Import-Module SkypeOnlineConnector
PS C:\Users\Administrator.SCPFE> $cred = Get-Credential
PS C:\Users\Administrator.SCPFE> $CSSession = New-CsOnlineSession -Credential $cred
PS C:\Users\Administrator.SCPFE> Import-PSSession $CSSession -AllowClobber

ModuleType Version    Name                         ExportedCommands
---------- -------    ----                         ----------------
Script     1.0        tmp_4jgom4z4.wx4             {Clear-CsOnlineTelephoneNumberReservation

PS C:\Users\Administrator.SCPFE> Set-CsTenantFederationConfiguration -SharedSipAddressSpace $true
```

Figure 2-20. *Connecting to Skype for Business Online via remote PowerShell and enabling Shared SIP Address Space*

Multiple Edge Pools and Federation Route

The last Edge configuration consideration I'll discuss involves the Federation Route. You must configure all your Central Sites in the Skype for Business Topology to use a single Federation Route. Again, this isn't very clearly stated, but it is implied. Under Topology requirements, it doesn't state it explicitly for Skype for Business Server 2015; however, it does make the point when a mixed environment is listed. This is likely because an assumption is made that in a mixed environment, there may be multiple sites with multiple Edge pools.

The clarification is made that *the Edge Pool is associated with SIP federation* (`https://technet.microsoft.com/en-us/library/jj205403.aspx#Anchor_5`).

The key points are

- A single Edge Pool is assigned the Federation Route for all Central Sites in the topology.

- The Edge servers in that pool must be able to resolve `_sipfederationtls._tcp.<SIP domain>` for each SIP domain that is split between on-premises and online (`https://technet.microsoft.com/en-us/library/jj205403.aspx#Anchor_7`).

- Hybrid configuration is a one-to-one relationship between a single on-premises Edge Pool and an Office 365 tenant.

This is easily configured in the Skype for Business Topology Builder by configuring the site federation route assignment. Edit the properties of any Central Site and configure as displayed in Figure 2-21.

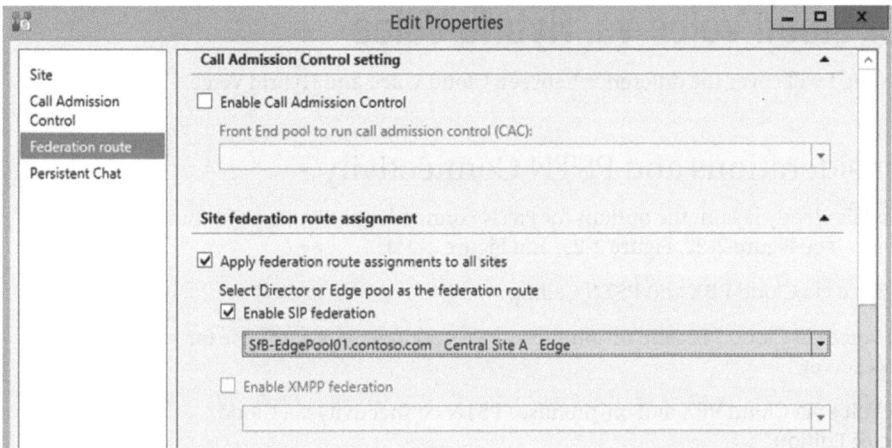

Figure 2-21. Configuring a global federation route across all Skype for Business Central Sites

Firewall Port and URL Configuration

The IPs and URLs for Office 365 workloads are clearly documented in information available at the following URL: `https://support.office.com/en-us/article/Office-365-URLs-and-IP-address-ranges-8548a211-3fe7-47cb-abb1-355ea5aa88a2`.

Read the list carefully, paying attention to FQDNs that are listed as required vs. optional. For full functionality, ensure that there are no content filters blocking the FQDNs or IP ranges. If you selectively start blocking or disabling these, you will impact individual feature sets within Skype for Business Online, and it can be very tricky to troubleshoot.

Outside of those requirements, there are port requirements that are specific to Skype for Business Online hybrid configurations (Table 2-1). They are detailed in a document accessible from the following URL: `https://technet.microsoft.com/en-us/library/jj205403.aspx#Anchor_9`.

Table 2-1. Port Requirements for Skype for Business Online Hybrid Configuration

Protocol	TCP or UDP	Source IP	Destination IP	Source Port	Destination Port	Notes
SIP (MTLS)	TCP	Access Edge	Office 365	Any	5061	Signaling
SIP (MTLS)	TCP	Office 365	Access Edge	Any	5061	Signaling
STUN	TCP	A/V Edge	Office 365	50000-59999	443, 50000-59999	Open for audio, video, application sharing sessions
STUN	TCP	Office 365	A/V Edge	443	50000-59999	Open for audio, video, application sharing sessions
STUN	UDP	A/V Edge	Office 365	3478	3478	Open for audio, video sessions
STUN	UDP	Office 365	A/V Edge	3478	3478	Open for audio, video sessions

Overview of Cloud Voice vs. Hybrid Voice

In the following section, I will cover the difference between Cloud Voice and Hybrid Voice.

Topology Considerations and PSTN Connectivity

The architecture models clearly lay out the options for PSTN connectivity with Skype for Business Online. There are three options (see Figure 2-22, Figure 2-23, and Figure 2-24).

- Cloud Voice via Cloud PBX and PSTN Calling

- Hybrid Voice via Cloud PBX and on-premises PSTN connectivity via Skype for Business Server

- Hybrid Voice via Cloud PBX and on-premises PSTN connectivity via Cloud Connector Edition

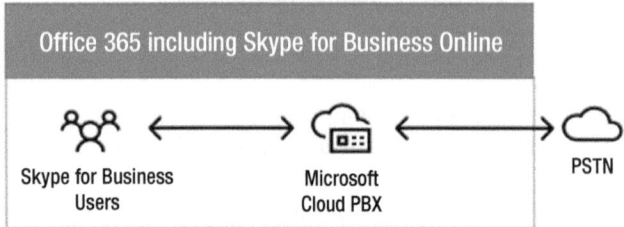

Figure 2-22. *Cloud PBX with PSTN Calling*

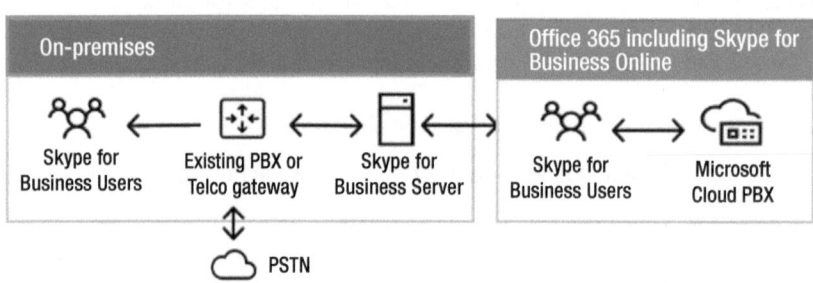

Figure 2-23. *Cloud PBX with on-premises PSTN connectivity via Skype for Business Server*

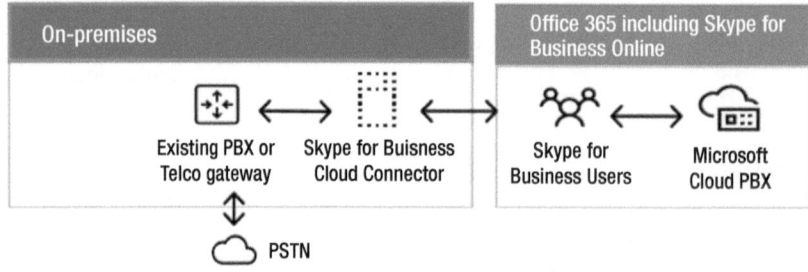

Figure 2-24. *Cloud PBX with on-premises PSTN connectivity via Cloud Connector Edition*

Laid out in the diagrams, it's much easier to understand the different topologies. Customers often confuse the functionality of Cloud PBX with PSTN connectivity. This leads to a lot of confusion about the topologies for deploying Hybrid Voice.

Cloud Connector Edition is for those environments that do not already have Skype for Business Server deployed on-premises and have no specific requirements for an on-premises deployment. Such requirements for an on-premises deployment, at the time this is being written, might be the following:

- Persistent Chat

- Response Groups

- VTC end-point interoperability for video conferencing

However, all the following features are on the roadmap and in preview at this time:

- Microsoft Teams as an answer to Persistent Chat

- Call Queues and Cloud PBX Auto Attendants as a replacement for Response Groups

- Polycom RealConnect Service for registering on-premises VTCs to Skype for Business Online

I won't be discussing Cloud Connector Edition here, but there are excellent resources and training materials for CCE found in the Skype Operations Framework (SOF) and the Skype Academy. The following resources are available to anyone who signs up with a Microsoft account and are highly recommended for hybrid configurations of Skype for Business Online:

- www.skypeoperationsframework.com/

- www.skypeoperationsframework.com/Academy?SOFTrainings

My focus is on Hybrid Voice with Cloud PBX via Skype for Business Server. The planning considerations and prerequisites are clearly defined in documentation accessible from the following URL: https://technet.microsoft.com/en-us/library/mt455212.aspx.

But one key clarification is needed regarding the supported on-premises server versions, which are discussed in detail in the next section.

On-Premises Server Versions

The article lists the following table (Table 2-2) of supported server versions for Cloud PBX with on-premises PSTN connectivity.

Table 2-2. Supported Server Versions for Cloud PBX with On-Premises PSTN Connectivity

Server Role	Supported Versions
Front End Server	Skype for Business Server 2015 Lync Server 2013
Edge Server	Skype for Business Server 2015
Mediation Server	Skype for Business Server 2015 Lync Server 2013

It's important to clarify that Skype for Business Server 2015 Edge, Front End, and Mediation server roles are required. You cannot mix Skype for Business 2015 and Lync Server 2013 server roles in a supported configuration.

Essentially, you must have a fully deployed Skype for Business topology. You may then have a Lync Server 2013 Front End and Mediation server deployment alongside it. But the Edge server and its associated next hop must be Skype for Business Server 2015.

There are several other key on-premises configurations that must be in place to facilitate Hybrid Voice.

- Skype for Business Edge server must be able to resolve _sipfederationtls._tcp.<SIP domain> for every SIP domain split between on-premises and Office 365.

- Strict DNS match for _sipfederationtls._tcp.<SIP domain> is required.

  - *Valid*: _sipfederationtls._tcp.contoso.com points to sip.contoso.com

  - *Invalid*: _sipfederationtls._tcp.fabrikam.com points to sip.contoso.com

- Sip.<sipdomain> must be in the SAN of the external Edge certificate for all supported SIP domains.

- Lync Phone Edition (LPE) must be updated to minimum required firmware before moving to SfB Online.

- Enterprise voice is configured and tested for on-premises users.

- Cloud PBX license and Exchange Plan 2 are assigned to the users in Office 365.

Cloud Voice Mail and Unified Messaging

Another topic that causes a lot of confusion is how voice mail is provided to Skype for Business Online users. In the on-premises world, there are two options:

- Voice mail provide by on-premises Exchange Unified Messaging (UM)

- Voice mail provided by hosted voice mail in Exchange Online

Either way, the voice mail functionality is provided exclusively by Exchange UM. In Skype for Business Online, this is slightly different. For any user hosted in Skype for Business Online

- Voice mail functionality is provided by Cloud PBX voice mail (also referred to as Azure Voicemail).

- The voice mail is deposited into the user's mailbox (on-premises or in Exchange Online).

- Voice mail deposit does *not* utilize the Exchange UM role either in Exchange Online or on-premises. Instead, it is deposited via Exchange EWS with SMTP as a failback.

- Exchange UM is still required to be enabled for the user to provide certain client-side UM features.

The main consideration here is the order of operations of a customer's move to Office 365. Where is the user's mailbox hosted at the time of their migration to Skype for Business Online with Hybrid Voice?

It is recommended that the mailbox be moved first. One of the main reasons for this regards the Meeting Migration Service. This service updates users' web and dial-in conferencing ID's for any scheduled Skype Meetings automatically, on the condition the mailbox is hosted in Exchange Online. If the mailbox is on-premises, the Skype Meeting Migration tool must be used instead.

With all the combinations of Skype for Business and Exchange both on-premises and in Office 365, a table (Table 2-3) is worth a thousand words!

Table 2-3. *Comparison of Exchange On-Premises and Exchange Online*

	Exchange On-Premises	Exchange Online
Skype for Business Server	On-prem OAuth config	OAuth configuration to Exchange Online
	Integration to on-prem OWA	Integration to Exchange Online OWA
	Voice mail integration with Exchange UM	Voice mail policy defined by hosted voice mail policy in Skype for Business, which points to Exchange Online UM
	Subscriber Access and Auto Attendants via Exchange UM	
	Voice mail policy defined via the Exchange UM dial plan and mailbox policy	Subscriber Access and Auto Attendants via Exchange Online UM
Skype for Business Online	OAuth configuration to on-premises Exchange	No on-prem OAuth required in this scenario
	Integration to on-prem OWA	Full online integration to OWA
	Voice mail service via Cloud PBX voice mail	Subscriber Access and Auto Attendants via Exchange Online UM
	Voice mail deposit to on-prem Exchange mailbox	User licensed for Exchange Online
	User not licensed for Exchange Online	

So, what does this look like in PowerShell for the various user scenarios? Again, pictures speak louder than words. Figures 2-25 to 2-28 show the PowerShell output of the various Skype for Business configurations.

```
SipAddress              : sip:sfb.onprem01@contoso.com
EnterpriseVoiceEnabled  : True
LineURI                 : tel:+14038889999
VoicePolicy             : On-Prem Voice Policy
VoiceRoutingPolicy      :
HostedVoiceMail         :
HostedVoicemailPolicy   :
HostingProvider         : SRV:
RegistrarPool           : SfBPool.contoso.net
ExUmEnabled             : True
```

Figure 2-25. *Skype for Business on-premises with Exchange UM on-premises*

```
SipAddress              : sip:sfb.onprem01@contoso.com
EnterpriseVoiceEnabled  : True
LineURI                 : tel:+14038889999
VoicePolicy             : On-Prem Voice Policy
VoiceRoutingPolicy      :
HostedVoiceMail         : True
HostedVoicemailPolicy   : EXOUM
HostingProvider         : SRV:
RegistrarPool           : SfBPool.contoso.net
ExUmEnabled             : True
```

Figure 2-26. *Skype for Business on-premises with Exchange UM online*

```
SipAddress                 : sip:EmilyB@contoso.onmicrosoft.com
EnterpriseVoiceEnabled     : True
VoicePolicy                : BusinessVoice
HostedVoiceMail            : True
HostedVoicemailPolicy      : BusinessVoice
OnPremLineURI              :
OnPremLineURIManuallySet   : False
LineURI                    : tel:+1206xxxxxxx
HostingProvider            : SRV:
RegistrarPool              : sippoolblu2a05.infra.lync.com
```

Figure 2-27. *Skype for Business Online & PSTN Calling with Exchange UM on-premises*

```
SipAddress                 : sip:AdeleV@contoso.onmicrosoft.com
EnterpriseVoiceEnabled     : True
VoicePolicy                : BusinessVoice
HostedVoiceMail            : True
HostedVoicemailPolicy      : BusinessVoice
OnPremLineURI              :
OnPremLineURIManuallySet   : False
LineURI                    : tel:+1206xxxxxxx
HostingProvider            : SRV:
RegistrarPool              : sippoolblu2a05.infra.lync.com
```

Figure 2-28. *Skype for Business Online and PSTN Calling with Exchange UM online*

The key attributes here are

- HostedVoiceMail: Enables or disables the user for hosted voice mail service, both on-premises and in Office 365

- HostedVoiceMailPolicy: Defines the configuration for hosted voice mail

  - *On-premises*: There is an example following of what an on-premises hosted voice mail policy looks like. The key configuration is the destination and organization parameters that tell the policy where to redirect voice mail and for what domains (organizations).

  - *Online*: All users are labeled as BusinessVoice. There is no option to create custom HostedVoiceMailPolicy in Office 365. The configuration of this policy essentially redirects voice mail to Exchange Online mailboxes.

You'll also notice that Figures 2-27 and 2-28 look identical. It's important to point out that the HostedVoiceMail and HostedVoiceMailPolicy parameters have no impact on the call flow of Azure Voicemail to depositing into an Exchange mailbox.

The main reason for this is that Skype for Business Online users have voice mail service and processing supplied exclusively via Cloud PBX voice mail. Cloud PBX voice mail does not leverage any Exchange UM roles to deposit voice mail into users' mailboxes.

Here's a clear breakdown of voice mail scenarios, including those that leverage Exchange UM for voice mail depositing:

- On-Premises SfB to EXO mailbox

  - Utilizes Exchange UM in EXO as the destination in the HostedMailboxPolicy that points to exap.um.outlook.com

  - SfBO to EXO mailbox

- Processing handled completely by Azure Voicemail

- Utilizes the default BusinessVoice HostedMailboxPolicy that points to
  sipedgeXXXX.infra.sfb.com to deposit into the mailbox

- EXO UM isn't utilized for depositing of voice mail, but it is for client-side
  features

- SfBO to on-premises mailbox

  - Processing handled completely by Azure VoiceMail

  - Looks for EXO licensed/enabled mailbox. If one isn't found, it uses Exchange
    hybrid and autodiscover/EWS/SMTP to deposit into the mailbox.

  - Only leverages UM Dial Plan for client-side features

Assuming that we are discussing environments with Skype for Business or Lync Server 2013 on-premises, and Enterprise voice is deployed, that Exchange UM is also leveraged for voice mail services. This is quite typical. It's also very typical for Exchange mailboxes to be migrated to Office 365 prior to Skype for Business users. To that end, knowing how to set up the hosted voice mail policy on-premises is an important configuration for that migration period between moving users' mailboxes and sending them over to Skype for Business Online.

Essentially, you must ensure the Enterprise Voice users are properly reconfigured to use the new hosted voice mail policy, once their mailboxes are migrated to Exchange Online. The prerequisite to configure the hosted voice mail policy for on-premises Enterprise Voice users prior to migrating them to Skype for Business Online are covered here: https://technet.microsoft.com/en-us/library/gg425807(v=ocs.15).aspx.

But following is a high-level summary:

- Create a DNS SRV record for integration with hosted Exchange UM.

  - Create a _sipfederationtls._tcp.<SIP domain> DNS SRV record. This should
    already exist as part of your Skype for Business hybrid configuration.

- Configure Edge Server integration with hosted Exchange UM.

  - Configure Federation via Set-CsAccessEdgeConfiguration. This should
    already exist as part of your Skype for Business hybrid configuration.

- Create a hosting provider for hosted Exchange UM:

- New-CsHostingProvider -Identity "Hosted UM" -Enabled $True
  -EnabledSharedAddressSpace $True -HostsOCSUsers $False -ProxyFqdn
  "exap.um.outlook.com" -IsLocal $False -VerificationLevel
  UseSourceVerification.

- Create a hosted voice mail policy via one of the following methods:

  - Modify the global hosted voice mail policy.

  - Create a site or user level hosted voice mail policy, as follows:

  - New-CsHostedVoicemailPolicy -Identity EXOUM -Destination exap.
    um.outlook.com -Description "Hosted voice mail policy for Exchange
    Online users." -Organization contoso.onmicrosoft.com.

- Assign the hosted voice mail policy.

- For global or site level policies, this happens automatically.

- For user level policies, it must be assigned per user, as follows:

  ```
  Grant-CsHostedVoicemailPolicy -Identity "Ken Myer" -PolicyName EXOUM.
  ```

- Create contact objects for hosted Exchange UM: Contact objects for both Subscriber Access and Auto Attendants are required.

- Subscriber Access contact:

  ```
  New-CsExUmContact -SipAddress "sip:exumsa1@contoso.com" -RegistrarPool
  "RedmondPool.contoso.com" -OU "HostedExUM Integration" -DisplayNumber
  "+14255550101"
  ```

- Auto Attendant contact:

  ```
  New-CsExUmContact -SipAddress "sip:exumaa1@contoso.com" -RegistrarPool
  "RedmondPool.contoso.com" -OU "HostedExUM Integration" -DisplayNumber
  "+14255550101" -AutoAttendant $True
  ```

- Enable users for hosted voice mail, as follows:

  ```
  Set-CsUser -HostedVoiceMail $True -Identity "contoso\kenmyer"
  ```

- Ensure that users are licensed for Exchange Online and enabled for Exchange UM in Office 365.

- Test and validate voice mail services against Exchange Online UM.

Migrating Enterprise Voice Users

I've just covered the voice mail impacts of users in various scenarios split between on-premises and Office 365. As mentioned, this was covered first, as users' mailboxes are often moved to Office 365 prior to users being migrated to Skype for Business Online.

Next, we must look at what is involved in migrating on-premises Skype for Business users, Enterprise Voice users in particular, to Office 365. I'm going to focus specifically on Enterprise Voice users. The process for moving Enterprise Voice and Non-Enterprise Voice users is the same. There are simply a few extra considerations with moving Enterprise Voice users, so I'll focus on that process.

Here are the high-level considerations for moving Enterprise Voice (EV) users:

- Ensure users are correctly enabled for EV on-premises.

- Document which users are enabled for dial-in conferencing on-premises.

- Document, as has been discussed, which users are enabled for voice mail services via Exchange UM.

- Understand all syntax involved with the Move-CsUser PowerShell cmdlet.

- Review web conferencing and dial-in conferencing ID changes and Skype Meeting invite updating.

- Review post-move commands (enabling user for EV in SfBO).

- Review Voice Policy vs. Voice Routing Policy considerations.

Enable Users for Enterprise Voice On-Premises

I won't spend any time on this. Configuration of Enterprise Voice on-premises is a complex topic and has been covered extensively elsewhere. For the purposes of our discussion about hybrid configurations, we must simply ensure that

- The on-premises user is enabled for Enterprise Voice

- The Enterprise Voice user has a valid Line URI

- A Voice Routing Policy is assigned.

- This is only used by Skype for Business Online.

- It can be scoped via the Global policy or via a user-level policy.

I'll discuss details of the Voice Routing Policy further in a following section.

Dial-in Conferencing Considerations

The main consideration here is that Skype for Business Online users cannot leverage on-premises dial-in conferencing services. When a user is migrated to Skype for Business Online, they must be enabled for PSTN Conferencing within Office 365 or one of the other Audio Conferencing Providers supported by Office 365.

Because of this, their dial-in conferencing numbers and ID will change. This also means that any future scheduled Skype Meetings in Exchange must also be updated with their new PSTN Conferencing details. How this updating is done will be covered when I discuss web conferencing.

Voice Mail Considerations

These were covered extensively in the previous section. Suffice to say, it is strongly recommended to document the various voice mail configurations and how they apply to where users' mailboxes are homed, or will be homed, in relation to the timing around migrating them to Skype for Business Online.

The Move-CsUser cmdlet

While users can be moved via the Skype for Business Control Panel, there are certain topology scenarios and reasons why you may be unable to use the Control Panel to move users. You may also want a scripted way of doing mass user migrations. As such, it is important to understand the syntax of the Move-CsUser PowerShell cmdlet.

Before we get into the syntax, though, what are the prerequisites for the workstation or server that you run the move cmdlet from? Ask and you shall receive!

- Skype for Business Management Shell (Install Admin Tools from the Skype Deployment wizard)

- Latest version of Skype for Business Online PowerShell Module:

  www.microsoft.com/en-us/download/details.aspx?id=39366

The key reason for this is that the Move-CsUser cmdlet modifies numerous attributes on the Skype for Business user, both on-premises and in Office 365. The PowerShell session you are in must have access to both Skype for Business Server on-premises and Skype for Business Online.

The recommendation is to open the Skype for Business Management Shell and then connect to Skype for Business Online, via a PowerShell session (see Figure 2-29). The latter process was shown before when I discussed implementing the hybrid configuration, but here it is again, for reference.

```
PS C:\Users\Administrator.SCPFE> Import-Module SkypeOnlineConnector
PS C:\Users\Administrator.SCPFE> $cred = Get-Credential
PS C:\Users\Administrator.SCPFE> $CSSession = New-CsOnlineSession -Credential $cred
PS C:\Users\Administrator.SCPFE> Import-PSSession $CSSession -AllowClobber

ModuleType Version    Name                            ExportedCommands
---------- -------    ----                            ----------------
Script     1.0        tmp_4jgom4z4.wx4                {Clear-CsOnlineTelephoneNumberReservat
```

Figure 2-29. *Connecting to Skype for Business Online via remote PowerShell*

When prompted for credentials, you must enter in Office 365 a UPN that has Global Administrator privileges.

If you are using the default `<tenant>.onmicrosoft.com` domain for the user, there are no additional considerations. However, if you are using a synchronized account using a custom domain (i.e., admin@ contoso.com), you must specify the `-OverrideAdminDomain` parameter with the `New-CsOnlineSession` cmdlet, for example: `$CSSession = New-CsOnlineSession -Credential $cred -OverrideAdminDomain "contoso.onmicrosoft.com"`.

With your PowerShell session now in place, you are ready to run the `Move-CsUser` cmdlet. Here is an example of a typical user move being executed via `Move-CsUser`.

```
Move-CsUser -Identity sfbuser@contoso.com -Target sipfed.online.lync.com -Credential
$cred -HostedMigrationOverrideUrl https://admin0a.online.lync.com/HostedMigration/
hostedmigrationService.svc -ProxyPool fepool.contoso.com
```

Let's break down the key pieces here.

- `-Identity`: The identity of the user being moved. Typically referenced by the user's UPN or SIP address value

- `-Target`: Where the user is to be moved. In this instance, Skype for Business Online (sipfed.online.lync.com)

- `-Credential`: The credentials required for the move. In this instance, the credentials for the admin user in Office 365

- `-HostedMigrationOverrideUrl`: This is a reference to the URL of your tenant's Skype for Business Online Admin Center. This URL shouldn't change once your tenant is provisioned. However, there are numerous URLs representing many different Office 365 data centers. So, where your tenant is located will impact what URL it is using. The easiest way to determine your URL is to simply open the Skype for Business Online Admin Center and look at the URL. The key piece of the URL is at the start. In the preceding example, it is admin0a.

- `-ProxyPool`: This parameter is optional. It is required when you have multiple Central Sites, with multiple Edge Pools on-premises. This tells the `Move-CsUser` cmdlet explicitly which pool you'd like to proxy the move against. This would be the FQDN of the pool, associated with the Edge Pool that is identified as the Federation Route, which I discussed earlier. If you have configured all your Central Sites to use a single Edge Pool for the Federation Route, then you shouldn't require this parameter.

Web Conferencing and Dial-in Conferencing ID Changes

When a user is moved from on-premises to Skype for Business Online, their contact list is moved with them (there is a limitation of 200 contacts in Skype for Business Online, so take that into consideration as well). However, as when you move users between pools on-premises, moving users online causes them to receive a new web conferencing ID and, if enabled for PSTN Conferencing, a new dial-in conferencing ID and numbers.

This is done automatically. However, references to these IDs inside a user's Exchange calendar may not be based on where the user's mailbox is homed, as has been discussed.

If the user's mailbox is homed in Exchange Online, the Meeting Migration Service will do the following:

- Find all old references to Skype Meeting ID occurrences in the user's mailbox

- Replace them with the user's new web conferencing and PSTN conferencing IDs

- Send out meeting updates to all attendees with the updated IDs

If the user's mailbox is homed on-premises, the user must either

- Manually update their Skype Meeting invites

- Use the Skype Meeting Update Tool to update them automatically

To use the tool, users must have open Outlook, Skype for Business or Lync Server 2013 client, and the tool to update their Skype Meeting invites.

Post-Move Commands and Configuration

When you move an Enterprise Voice user, you might assume that the user is going to be automatically enabled for Enterprise Voice in Skype for Business Online. This is not the case. There is likely a good reason for this, but I've not found a scenario in which you wouldn't want the user enabled automatically after being moved.

It's just a simple PowerShell cmdlet that is required to enable the user appropriately for Enterprise Voice and Hosted Voicemail in Skype for Business Online. With your PowerShell session still connected to Skype for Business Online, the following cmdlet must be run to finish enabling the user:

```
Set-CsUser -Identity "<User ID>" -EnterpriseVoiceEnabled $True -HostedVoiceMail$True
```

There also used to be a requirement to enable the user's mailbox for Exchange UM, if it hadn't been explicitly done so as part of the mailbox migration to Exchange Online. This was facilitated by use of the `Enable-CsOnlineUMMailbox` cmdlet. However, this is no longer required, as it is now done automatically. The first time Cloud PBX voice mail processes a voice mail for a Skype for Business Online user, it checks to see if they are enabled for Exchange Online, and have an active mailbox present. If they do, it will automatically enable the mailbox for UM. Again, this isn't required for depositing of the voice mail into the mailbox. But it is required for certain UM features to be available client-side.

Voice Policy vs. Voice Routing Policy

Voice policies in Skype for Business control the features that are available to Enterprise Voice users. While voice policies exist both on-premises and in Skype for Business Online, only on-premises voice policies can be customized. This is an important consideration when moving users online. Users migrated to Skype for Business Online who are enabled for Cloud PBX will all be assigned a predefined voice policy called HybridVoice. Again, this defines the voice features available to Skype for Business Online users. What it does not define, however, is what routes for PSTN connectivity are available to those users. For Hybrid Voice users, this PSTN connectivity is provided by on-premises infrastructure. As such, there must be on-premises policies within Skype for Business Server that define the routes and PSTN usages for Hybrid Voice users. This is where voice routing policies come into play.

Voice routing policies define the PSTN usages for Hybrid Voice users. This dictates the voice routes and trunks on-premises for PSTN connectivity. It is used exclusively for Hybrid Voice users and does not impact on-premises users. There are two scope levels for defining the voice routing policy, modifying the global policy, or creating a user level policy.

Typically, a user-level policy is used, so that users can be assigned the policy as they are moved over in migration groups. Following is an example of creating a user-level voice routing policy in PowerShell (Figure 2-30):

```
New-CSVoiceRoutingPolicy -Identity HybridVoice -Name Hybrid -PSTNUsages "Local", "Long Distance"
```

```
PS C:\Users\Administrator.SCPFE> New-CsVoiceRoutingPolicy -Identity HybridVoice -Name Hybrid -PstnUsages "Local","Long Distance"
```

Figure 2-30. *Creating an on-premises voice routing policy as part of a Hybrid Voice configuration*

You then need to grant the policy to users. I'll take you on a complete walk-through of how to migrate a user over to Skype for Business Online in the "User Provisioning and Migration Tips" section of this chapter.

Service Administration

Now that we've gone through configuring hybrid, looking at all the prerequisites for Hybrid Voice and understanding the supported topologies that we can deploy hybrid within, let us step through the process and order of operations of moving a user to Skype for Business Online.

User Provisioning and Migration Tips

When we talk about user provisioning, there are two scenarios that we will encounter:

- Moving of an existing Skype for Business on-premises user

- Provisioning of a brand-new user account on-premises

The biggest consideration is understanding which object is the source of authority for modifying attributes. In a hybrid configuration, the source of authority is the on-premises user object. As such, even after the hybrid configuration is in place, Active Directory user objects and initial Skype for Business enablement still has to take place on-premises, to populate the appropriate attribute values that we want to synchronize to Office 365.

Let's break down the order of operations for each of the scenarios.

- Move existing user order of operations.

  - Validate Enterprise Voice functionality.

  - Assign user the Voice Routing Policy.

  - Ensure user object is synchronized to Office 365.

  - Apply appropriate license to user in Office 365.

  - Confirm license provisioning status.

  - Use `Move-CsUser` PowerShell cmdlet to migrate user online.

  - Enable user for `HybridVoice` and `HostedVoiceMail` in Skype for Business Online.

- Validate user functionality

    - Instant Messaging and Presence

    - Web conferencing

    - Dial-in conferencing

    - Inbound/outbound PSTN calls

- New user order of operations

    - Create user object in Active Directory with the appropriate UPN suffix, or alternate ID attribute, to synchronize to Office 365.

    - Enable user for Skype for Business and Enterprise Voice on-premises.

    - Complete all the same steps listed previously for an existing user.

    - So, here is an example of moving an on-premises user to Office 365.

On-premises user enabled for Enterprise Voice with hosted voice mail in Exchange Online (Figure 2-31):

```
SipAddress            : sip:sfb.onprem01@contoso.com
EnterpriseVoiceEnabled : True
LineURI               : tel:+14038889999
VoicePolicy           : On-Prem Voice Policy
VoiceRoutingPolicy    :
HostedVoiceMail       : True
HostedVoicemailPolicy : EXOUM
HostingProvider       : SRV:
RegistrarPool         : SfBPool.contoso.net
ExUmEnabled           : True
```

Figure 2-31. *Output of* Get-CsUser *for an on-premises user enabled for Enterprise Voice with hosted voice mail*

Take note of the HostingProvider and RegistrarPool indicating that the user is still homed on-premises. We then assign it the newly created voice routing policy (Figure 2-32).

```
PS C:\Users\Administrator.SCPFE> Grant-CsVoiceRoutingPolicy -PolicyName HybridVoice -Identity sfb.onprem01@contoso.com
PS C:\Users\Administrator.SCPFE> get-csuser sfb.onprem01@contoso.com | select
sipaddress,enterprisevoiceenabled,lineuri,voicepolicy,voiceroutingpolicy,hosted*,hosting*,registrar*,exumenabled


SipAddress            : sip:sfb.onprem01@contoso.com
EnterpriseVoiceEnabled : True
LineURI               : tel:+14038889999
VoicePolicy           : On-Prem Voice Policy
VoiceRoutingPolicy    : HybridVoice
HostedVoiceMail       : True
HostedVoicemailPolicy : EXOUM
HostingProvider       : SRV:
RegistrarPool         : O365-SfB.scpfe.lab
ExUmEnabled           : False
```

Figure 2-32. *Granting the voice routing policy for Hybrid Voice to the on-premises user*

The user object is synchronized to Office 365 (Figure 2-33).

```
SipAddress            : sip:sfb.onprem01@contoso.com
OnPremHostingProvider : SRV:
HostingProvider       : SRV:
RegistrarPool         :
EnterpriseVoiceEnabled : False
VoicePolicy           : HybridVoice
HostedVoiceMail       : False
HostedVoicemailPolicy : BusinessVoice
OnPremLineURI         : tel:+14038889999
```

Figure 2-33. *Output of the* Get-CsOnlineUser *cmdlet for an on-premises Enterprise Voice user synchronized to Skype for Business Online*

Notice that the hosting providers are set to SRV, indicating that it should be doing an SRV lookup for the on-premises Skype for Business Edge server to contact this user. The RegistrarPool is also blank, as the user is not homed in Skype for Business Online. We then license the user for Skype for Business Online, in this instance, as part of the E5 license SKU (see Figure 2-34).

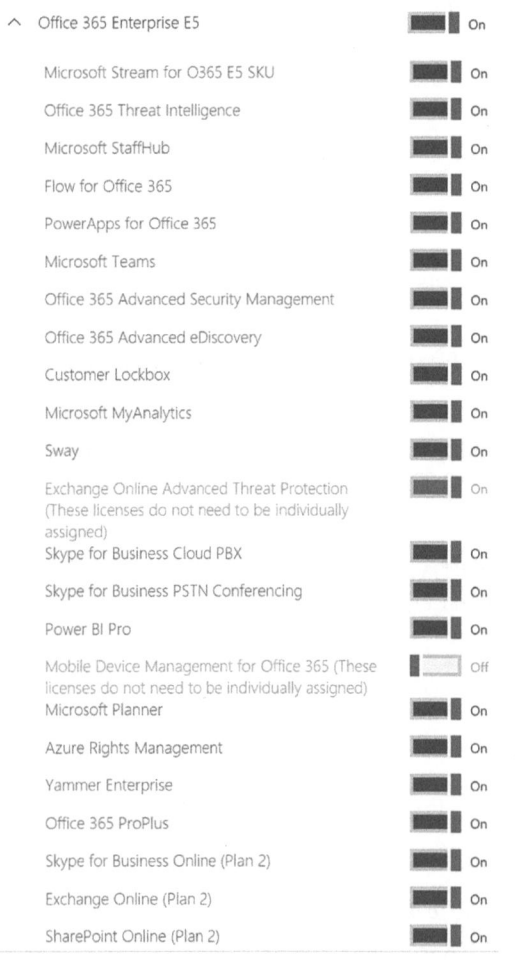

Figure 2-34. *Service included as part of the E5 license SKU in Office 365*

The licensing provisioning typically happens quickly, within a few minutes. But it can take as long as 10–15 minutes. And on occasion there may be issues with a synchronized object that prevents the provisioning from completing successfully. You can either look in the Skype for Business Online Admin Center, refreshing it until the user displays in the enabled users list, or you can use a PowerShell cmdlet to check the provisioning status.

```
(Get-MsolUser -UserPrincipalName user@domain.com).Licenses[0].ServiceStatus
```

You'll be looking for the MCOSTANDARD SKU in this instance for Skype for Business Online Plan 2. The user has now been synchronized, and licensed, and we can now move them to Skype for Business Online (Figure 2-35).

```
PS C:\Users\Administrator.SCPFE> Move-CsUser sfb.onprem01@contoso.com -target sipfed.online.lync.com –Credential $cred –HostedMigrationOverrideURL
https://admin2a.online.lync.com/HostedMigration/hostedmigrationservice.svc

Confirm
Move-CsUser
[Y] Yes  [A] Yes to All  [N] No  [L] No to All  [S] Suspend  [?] Help (default is "Y"): y
Results from this operation can be found at "C:\Users\Administrator.SCPFE\AppData\Local\Temp\MoveResults-066b50aa-738e-45ab-8870-52c16efe7691.csv".
PS C:\Users\Administrator.SCPFE>
```

Figure 2-35. *Sample* Move-CsUser *cmdlet for moving an on-premises user to Skype for Business Online*

If we then look at the on-premises attributes for our user, we see the following (Figure 2-36).

```
SipAddress             : sip:sfb.onprem01@contoso.com
EnterpriseVoiceEnabled : True
LineURI                : tel:+14038889999
VoicePolicy            : On-Prem Voice Policy
VoiceRoutingPolicy     : HybridVoice
HostedVoiceMail        : True
HostedVoicemailPolicy  : EXOUM
HostingProvider        : sipfed.online.lync.com
RegistrarPool          :
ExUmEnabled            : False
```

Figure 2-36. *Output from* Get-CsUser *for an on-premises user moved to Skype for Business Online*

Notice the HostingProvider is now listed as sipfed.online.lync.com and the RegistrarPool is blank, as they are no longer homed on the on-premises pool.

Now, let's see what our user object looks like in Skype for Business Online after the move. We can see this by using the Get-CsOnlineUser cmdlet (Figure 2-37).

```
SipAddress             : sip:sfb.onprem01@contoso.com
OnPremHostingProvider  : sipfed.online.lync.com
HostingProvider        : sipfed.online.lync.com
RegistrarPool          : sippoolblu2a05.infra.lync.com
EnterpriseVoiceEnabled : False
VoicePolicy            : HybridVoice
HostedVoiceMail        : False
HostedVoicemailPolicy  : BusinessVoice
OnPremLineURI          : tel:+14038889999
```

Figure 2-37. *Output of* Get-CsOnlineUser *cmdlet for an online user after running* Move-CsUser

You now see the HostingProvider attributes show sipfed.online.lync.com. But EnterpriseVoiceEnabled and HostedVoicemail by default are still set to False. As I discussed earlier, you must still enable the user for Enterprise Voice in Skype for Business Online after you move them. That is done with the following PowerShell cmdlet.

```
Set-CsUser -Identity <user's SIP address> -EnterpriseVoiceEnabled $True -HostedVoicemail $True
```

Once that is done, our user is now fully enabled for Hybrid Voice and will be able to make calls via the on-premises PSTN connectivity, by the PSTN Usages and trunks in Skype for Business Server on-premises (Figure 2-38).

```
SipAddress               : sip:sfb.onprem01@contoso.com
OnPremHostingProvider    : sipfed.online.lync.com
HostingProvider          : sipfed.online.lync.com
RegistrarPool            : sippoolblu2a05.infra.lync.com
EnterpriseVoiceEnabled   : True
VoicePolicy              : HybridVoice
HostedVoiceMail          : True
HostedVoicemailPolicy    : BusinessVoice
OnPremLineURI            : tel:+14038889999
```

Figure 2-38. Output of Get-CsOnlineUser for Hybrid Voice user migrated from on-premises and enabled for Enterprise Voice in Skype for Business Online

Summary

In this chapter, I covered the core components and modalities of the Skype for Business UC platform and how they differed from the on-premises product and that in Office 365. I clarified common misconceptions about how Cloud PBX, in combination with the type of PSTN Connectivity, define the types of deployments that can be supported by hybrid configurations. I also discussed infrastructure and configuration considerations in deploying hybrid configurations and various scenarios and examples of how to migrate users from on-premises Skype for Business to Skype for Business Online.

I hope it was enlightening for you, reader, and gave you a stronger sense of how to practically approach deploying Skype for Business Online and hybrid configurations within your environments.

CHAPTER 3

■ ■ ■

Introducing and Preparing for Exchange Hybrid

BY RHODERICK MILNE

This chapter will cover the underpinning aspects of an Exchange hybrid deployment. A brief overview of the alternative Exchange Online (EXO) migration methods will be provided, to demonstrate why enterprises will chose to deploy Hybrid. This is required, as there is perceived complexity with Hybrid. Typically, this is not the case, as existing issues in a given environment are what will cause most of the issues.

Introduction

Exchange Online is a critical and highly valuable component of Office 365. As part of their digital transformation, many businesses want to integrate on-premises Exchange deployments with Office 365. Drivers include the increased feature set and associated productivity benefits that a new version of Exchange can deliver. IT departments may be able to leverage cost savings by moving mailboxes to Office 365, because it provides very predictable scale.

One of Microsoft's great strengths is that Exchange provides a deployment model for customers of all types and sizes. Exchange can be deployed as follows:

- Cloud only

- On-premises only

- Exchange Hybrid melding the cloud and on-premises

It is the latter that we will focus on primarily in this chapter, because it is the one most commonly leveraged by enterprises as they transition to the cloud. This is because it provides the most functionality, eases the migration, and allows for mailboxes to be moved back on-premises using native tools, should there ever be a reason. Staged and cutover migration options do not provide a mechanism to off-board mailboxes without using third-party tools.

In this chapter, we will review the planning, deployment, and troubleshooting steps that are required for Exchange hybrid. It is an exciting time for Exchange administrators, because there are different tasks and issues that must be reviewed and addressed.

As part of the planning, we must consider the current Exchange on-premises deployment and potentially remediate any existing issues. In addition to the Exchange servers themselves, considerable time must also be spent working with the network team. Not only must we ensure Exchange is correctly published to the Internet, there will also be increased network consumption, owing to Outlook connecting over the Internet.

© Nikolas Charlebois-Laprade et al. 2017
N. Charlebois-Laprade et al., *Expert Office 365*, DOI 10.1007/978-1-4842-2991-0_3

Planning the mailbox migration will be a large project milestone. There are many considerations we will look at to ensure that mailboxes are moved correctly. This is owing to the way permissions currently function in an Exchange hybrid deployment. While there is some planning work in crafting out the order to move mailboxes, PowerShell will take the stress out of the actual move process. No one wants to move mailboxes by hand, one by one. Using PowerShell, we can automate the move process into convenient chunks called a migration batch. Finally, because customers never just call me to say hello, we must also review some of the common issues and challenges.

Planning and Preparations

Before diving into Exchange hybrid, we have to take a step back and ensure that some common Office 365 tasks have been completed. This is critical for larger organizations, in which multiple teams must work together to have a successful deployment. If this is not done, there will be many issues that will negatively impact the project.

Directory Synchronization

Ensure that directory synchronization to Azure Active Directory has been deployed and configured. The previous sentence greatly simplifies the work that is required to successfully deploy directory synchronization. There are many aspects, which include the following:

- Customer security team review and approval to deploy Azure AD Connect

- Azure AD Connect sizing

- Azure AD Connect filtering

- Azure AD Connect monitoring

- Azure AD Connect recovery

- Azure AD Connect Documentation

- Update to latest build of Azure AD Connect

Microsoft documents the sizing aspects for the solution, so be sure to review the limits, especially when running at scale. Note that the documentation discusses the number of objects in the source directory, not the number of carbon-based life units. Depending on the organization, this may be a significant difference.

Ensure that you consider the impact of filtering in Azure AD Connect for the Exchange hybrid deployment. Do not just assume that whoever set up Azure AD Connect has done all the work or deployed a configuration that will allow you to successfully deploy Exchange hybrid. There have been numerous projects burnt by this assumption. Exchange hybrid requires Azure AD Connect to function. One core aspect is the unified Global Address List (GAL). Azure AD Connect is the mechanism that makes this happen. For a mailbox or mail-enabled user from on-premises Exchange to be visible to Office 365–based mailboxes, Azure AD Connect must be synchronizing those on-premises objects. This will happen by default; however, it is common for enterprises to filter the OUs, or objects that are being synchronized, to Azure AD. If an on-premises mailbox object is not within the scope of Azure AD Connect, then it will not be synchronized.

This is a common issue when starting up a proof of concept in which only a test OU in on-premises AD is set to synchronize. Another issue is that all the relevant mail objects must be synchronized. Some customers have designed their AD so that mail-enabled distribution groups are stored in OUs separate from the user objects. For these distribution groups to be visible to Office 365–based mailboxes, they must be within the scope of synchronization. If not, the Office 365 mailboxes will not see those resources in their GAL. This will generate negative feedback.

The Azure AD Connect deployment and its recovery must be fully documented, so that the entire team understands the solution. In many cases, this is simply not done. One of the great things with Azure AD Connect is that it offers a very simple express deployment. One of the bad things with Azure AD Connect is that it offers a very simple express deployment. Because of the next, next, next clicking, many deployments are never documented. This is true for the initial installation and any subsequent modifications of customizations. Ensure that all aspects of the deployment are fully understood by the relevant teams. If you have deployed Azure AD Connect as a VM, this then needs to extend to the hypervisor administrators. One customer requested that I come on-site to help them, as their Office 365 tenant had become corrupt. Why did they think it was corrupt? Well, because when they modified user objects in on-premises AD, the changes never showed up in Exchange or SharePoint Online. Thus, their entire tenant must have been corrupted, right? Well, not so much. Turns out the hypervisor admin was doing some housekeeping and decided that the Azure AD Connect VM was no longer needed, so it was compressed to zero bytes by deleting it.

This leads to the point of ensuring that enterprises deploy at least their standard OS monitoring on the Azure AD Connect server. This ensures that notifications are sent if the machine goes offline or services that should be running are not. All too often, this is overlooked.

Why is monitoring skipped? Reasons given include the statement that Azure AD Connect is an appliance, and that it does not contain any state. If there is an issue, and we need to recover, will we just create a new VM and run the install again? That may fly for small organizations, but if you have tens of thousands, or even hundreds of thousands, of objects in the directory, that will take hours—in some cases, days. Will business stakeholders really be happy with such latency? If a change or new user must be created, are they willing to wait days? Thus, it is prudent to review the recovery options and define a written SLA. That way, the correct expectations are set on all sides.

Additionally, we must ensure that Azure AD Connect was deployed with the option to synchronize the required attributes for Exchange. In the days of ye olde DirSync, it was an all or nothing affair. All attributes that were required for all the Office 365 components were synchronized to Azure AD. Today, the installation of Azure AD Connect can be customized to only synchronize the attributes for the workloads that are to be used in Office 365. For example, if only Office 365 Profession Plus is to be used, then only the attributes that are required may be synchronized by checking the appropriate products. It is possible that the option to synchronize the Exchange attributes may not have been selected. Check the installation documentation. This is another reason why we require documentation.

Another issue that may arise is with the Exchange Hybrid writeback option in Azure AD Connect. As I will discuss later, the attribute flow is mainly from on-premises AD to Azure AD. Only a very small subset of attributes flows from Azure AD back to on-premises AD. To enable the writeback, the option to enable Exchange Hybrid must be selected (Figure 3-1).

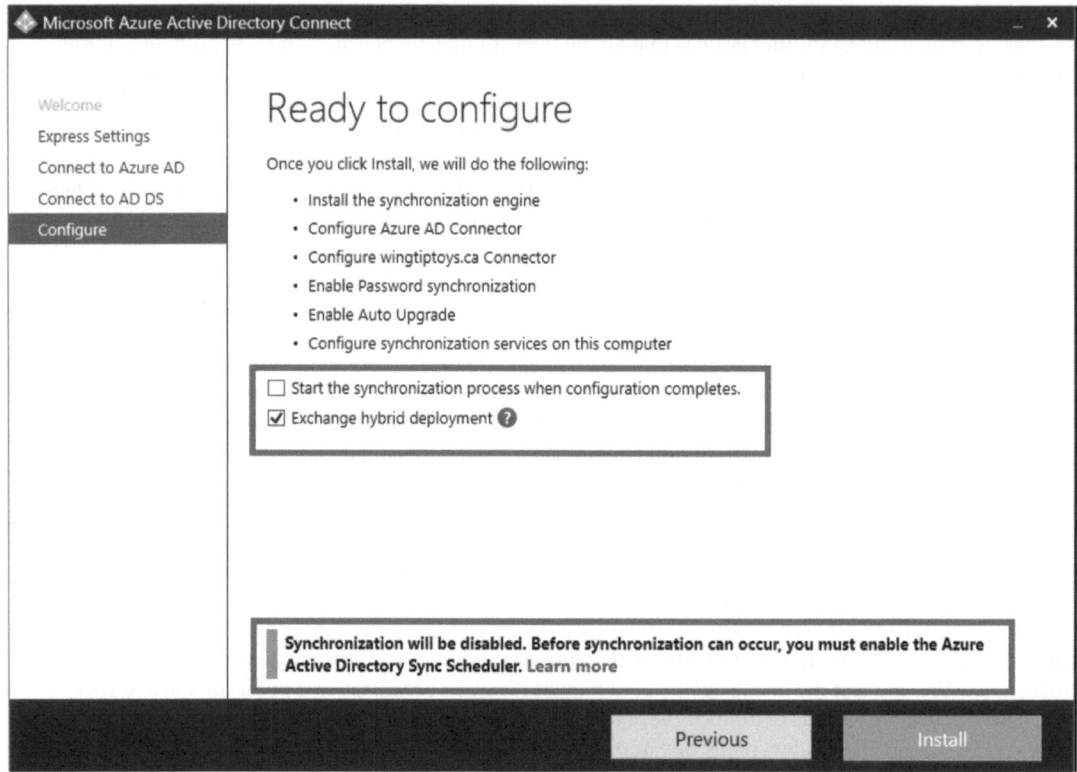

Figure 3-1. *Configuring Azure Active Directory for Exchange Hybrid*

Note that two areas are highlighted by red boxes in the preceding image. This is to indicate the option for Exchange Hybrid attribute writeback and to disable the synchronization process. If the synchronization process was disabled, please review "How To Enable AAD Connect Sync Cycle," accessible from `https://blogs.technet.microsoft.com/rmilne/2017/04/06/how-to-enable-aad-connect-sync-cycle/`.

As you embrace the cloud, it quickly becomes apparent that the rate of change is far greater than in many on-premises deployments. Office 365 is considered evergreen and is constantly changing and deploying new functionality. In order to keep up, the on-premises components must also be kept up to date. With regard to Azure AD Connect, this happens by installing a new release of Azure AD Connect. Depending on how you deployed Azure AD Connect and the version, you may already have the auto update feature that allows Azure AD Connect to automatically update itself. Should you have disabled this feature or deployed a custom install, you must manually update Azure AD Connect. At the time of writing in early 2017, customers must be on a 1.1 or newer build of Azure AD Connect. This brings many benefits. Multiple issues having been resolved, it is currently the latest supported version, and the synchronization cycle is now much quicker. In older builds, the synchronization used to occur every three hours. In the current builds, this now occurs every 30 minutes. This is a great improvement. If necessary, Azure AD Connect administrators may still initiate a manual sync, and this process is documented here: `https://blogs.technet.microsoft.com/rmilne/2014/10/01/how-to-run-manual-dirsync-azure-active-directory-sync-updates/`.

Office Client

As noted in the previous section, Office 365 is evergreen and designed to work with the latest versions of Office. This means that a version of Office that is in mainstream support is to be deployed. Ideally, Office 365 Profession Plus 2016 will be used. This will provide the most effective way to leverage new features and receive security fixes. Note that Office 365 Professional Plus 2013 will be out of support by the time this book is released. The support life cycle for the Office 365 Professional Plus products is much shorter than traditional MSI products. Note that the preceding comments do not apply to MSI builds. The support requirements are now much better documented with the upcoming announcement that, come 2020, specific versions of Office will be supported. Please factor this into your planning. The full details of the announcement are available here: `https://blogs.office.com/2017/04/20/office-365-proplus-updates/`.

While not directly within the control of the messaging team, it is critical that the version of Office is updated. This refers not only to the version but to ensure that it is fully patched. Numerous issues are resolved by proactively updating Outlook. This is especially important when MSI versions of Office are deployed, as history has shown that enterprises do not always update Outlook. This is one of the reasons for looking to deploy Office 365 Professional Plus, because it uses Click to Run (C2R). The application is packaged and updated differently from MSI software. Office 365 Professional Plus provides a great deal of control of the update process, so that customers can test updates from Microsoft to ensure that all their code, plug-ins, and line of business applications function and still receive security updates separately from the functionality updates. Please see the following for more information of this topic.

To obtain the best user experience, it is strongly recommended that customers deploy the latest version of Office, which will provide Outlook 2016. For customers running Office 2007, note that this version of Office will exit out of Extended support on the October 10, 2017. Microsoft has stated that Outlook Anywhere will be removed from Office 365 on October 31, 2017. This means that Outlook 2007 will be unable to connect to Exchange Online. Only newer versions of Outlook support the current client connectivity protocol, which is called MAPI/HTTP. If Office 365 Professional Plus 2016 is deployed, it supports MAPI/HTTP by default.

Verify Domain Ownership

When creating your Office 365 tenant, you will have been informed that you can now send and receive e-mail to the domain called `<tenantname>.onmicrosoft.com`. While that may be acceptable for certain organizations, enterprises must also be able to send and receive e-mail using their own DNS names.

In order to use a custom domain, it must be added and verified in your Office 365 tenant. This is not normally an issue when discussing the domains that are commonly used. But what about the domain marketing used five years ago for a campaign that is still stamped onto some mailboxes? Those mailboxes cannot be migrated to Office 365 unless all the domains on the mailbox's e-mail addresses have been added and verified.

It just may be that this is a good time for some spring cleaning. Review all the domains that have been used in the on-premises Exchange organization and remove those that are no longer required. Removing accepted domains is easy. Removing entries from Email Address Policies (EAPs) is also easy, but this will not delete e-mail addresses from the mailbox objects. The simplest method is to write a quick PowerShell script to run in the Exchange Management Shell, which will remove the unwanted addresses. If you do not want to write the script yourself, there are many examples on the Internet.

This issue is common when a separate team has performed the initial Office 365 deployment. They may only have added the domains that are used for User Principle Names (UPN) and not reviewed additional domains that are present in Exchange. It is recommended to align UPN, SMTP, and SIP addresses, to provide the smoothest user experience. This is to be done before the object is replicated to Azure AD by Azure AD Connect.

Take time to review your configuration and do not make assumptions. A good starting point is to review the EAP and Accepted Domains in your on-premises Exchange deployment. These findings should key you in to the SMTP domains that are being used. Also, be sure to review the Receive and Send Connectors. Sometimes, you may find that some interesting domains have been used. In recent engagements, domains such as user@internal.email were noted. This was a construct the customer created more than 15 years ago. This is not valid for Internet usage and must be removed. Such tasks must be a discrete item on the Office 365 project plan and will require executive sponsorship, because business processes must be refined and adapted.

Authentication

One of the biggest migration issues with regard to moving mailboxes to Office 365 was the user experience after the person's mailbox was moved. They were used to logging on to the workstation and opening Outlook. However, once the mailbox was moved to Office 365, they got a big fat authentication prompt. Users could hit the "save password" option, and the password would be saved inside the Credential Manager. You can see these entries in Control Panel. This would be fine until the user changed the password of Credential Manager which then went a little squirrely and required that the saved credential be deleted.

To solve this issue, we can deploy Modern Authentication. In a scenario wherein the user is logged on to their corporate machine on the corporate network, they can open up Outlook without being prompted for authentication. Some configuration is required if AD FS has been deployed to allow the browser to authenticate to AD FS without prompting for credentials. In the default configuration, the AD FS end point must be added to the local intranet security zone in Internet Explorer. This can be done using a Group Policy Object.

Office 2016 natively supports Modern Authentication. Office 2013 will require updates to be installed and for registry keys to be set on the client. Office 2010 will not support Modern Authentication, as Office 2010 was already in extended support when this feature was released. Again, life is better when the latest version is deployed, especially if this is Office 365 Professional Plus 2016.

Determine Migration Method

The introduction to this chapter noted that there are multiple methods to migrate mailboxes from on-premises mail servers to Office 365. Figure 3-2 outlines the different options.

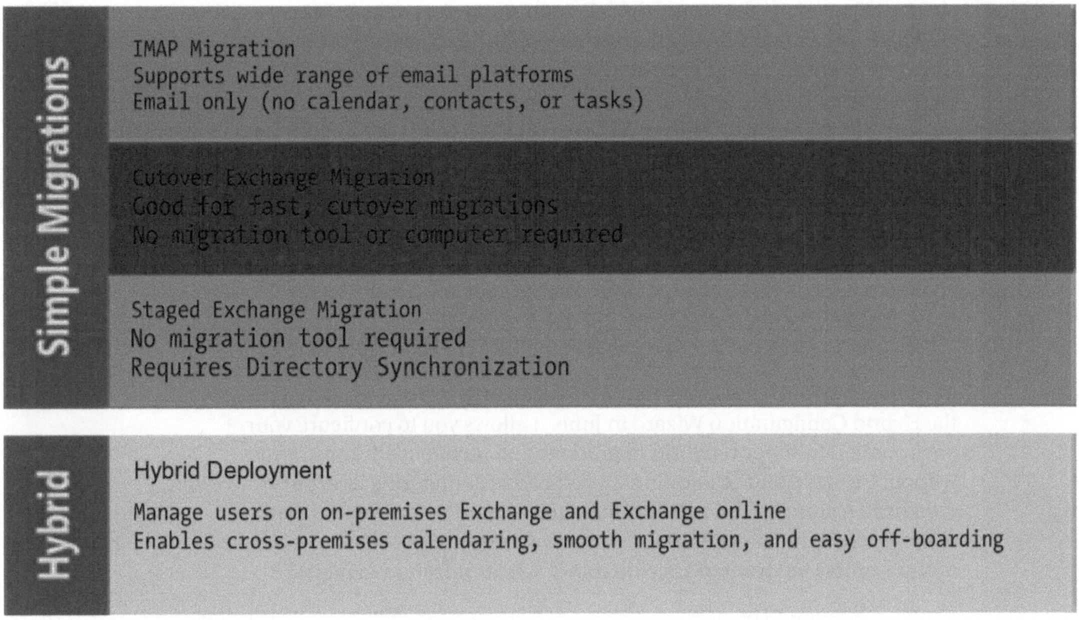

	IMAP Migration Supports wide range of email platforms Email only (no calendar, contacts, or tasks)
Simple Migrations	Cutover Exchange Migration Good for fast, cutover migrations No migration tool or computer required
	Staged Exchange Migration No migration tool required Requires Directory Synchronization
Hybrid	Hybrid Deployment Manage users on on-premises Exchange and Exchange online Enables cross-premises calendaring, smooth migration, and easy off-boarding

Figure 3-2. Migration options for Exchange

Multi-forest Exchange hybrid is supported today for

- Exchange 2010
- Exchange 2013
- Exchange 2016

Which Flavor of Hybrid?

IMAP allows for mailboxes to be migrated from just about any mail system. For the absolute corner cases in which this may not be possible, third-party migration tools may be required. Note that not all content will be migrated from the source system using the native Microsoft IMAP migration tool.

Cutover and staged migration are similar in that they both connect to an Outlook Anywhere end point on an on-premises Exchange server to pull data from the assigned mailboxes to Office 365. Cutover is a big-bang approach, which means *ALL* mailboxes are moved in the *SAME* migration window. This is great for small organizations but not for those with more than 2,000 mailboxes. Staged migration requires that Azure AD Connect is deployed, and this allows users to be grouped into multiple migration windows. Because we can slice and dice the overall user base, more than 2,000 mailboxes may be moved.

Do not rejoice at this. Because Outlook Anywhere is used to move the mailbox data, it does not perform all of the steps that are required. In addition to moving the data using Outlook Anywhere, we must

- Convert on-premises mailbox to mail enabled user
- Reconfigure all Outlook profiles
- Re-download all mail content to new OST files
- Re-download OAB
- Redo any customizations that may have been lost in Outlook

That is not a pretty scenario for enterprises. Do you want users to have to create a new Outlook profile? Absolutely not! All the issues mentioned are addressed in the Exchange Hybrid scenario. Therefore, enterprises focus on Exchange hybrid and eschew the staged and cutover approaches.

Today, there are also multiple options available when running Exchange hybrid. Not all customers wish to deploy the full hybrid experience. Typically, these are the smaller customers who previously would have used the staged or cutover migration option. Now they can avoid some of the aforementioned issues. Yay!

Please review the options outlined in New Exchange Online migration options.

Full Hybrid: This is a common configuration for customers that are larger in size and will take some time to migrate for customers that will not be able to move all their mailboxes to Exchange Online in the short to medium term. This is the most complex option to configure, though it will give you enhanced features, such as cross-premises free/busy and enhanced mail flow options.

Minimal Hybrid: This is a recently introduced option that was added to the Hybrid Configuration Wizard in June. It allows you to configure your environment to support hybrid migrations and recipient administration without the need for the additional overhead of configuring free/busy and other enhanced features of full hybrid. Often, this is used for customers that want to move all their mailboxes to Exchange Online over the course of a couple of months or less but want to keep directory synchronization in place.

Express Migration: The newest option added is Express Migration. This is the path in the Hybrid Configuration Wizard that will benefit smaller customers or a customer that truly wants to move to Exchange Online over the course of a couple of weeks or less. If you have to keep directory synchronization in place, this is not the option for you. This option will configure your users and walk you through the new migration experience, to get the mailboxes to Exchange Online with minimal disruption for your users.

The Minimal Hybrid and Express Migration options may be suitable for some organizations, though larger enterprises will most likely still pursue the Full Hybrid option. This is the one that will provide the most features and enhanced options. Typically, large enterprises will take a very long time to migrate to office 365, or they may fully intend to leave some mailboxes on-premises and not move them to Office 365. This may be owing to business requirements that are unique to their organization.

The remainder of this chapter will focus on Full Hybrid deployment. However, before we jump right in and run the wizard that will create the hybrid deployment, we must cover some prerequisites.

What Servers Will Provide Hybrid Services

One item to address immediately is that there is no such thing as a "hybrid Exchange server." There is no hybrid server. There is no special hybrid media. There is no /Hybrid install switch. There is no Hybrid server.

What we do have is an Exchange server that will provide Hybrid services. This means that the Exchange server(s) that will provide the link between on-premises and Office 365 must be deployed as if there were a regular Exchanger server. This means that CAS namespace planning, certificate planning, and dealing with self-signed certificates is no different than deploying a regular Exchange server. Exchange will consider all valid Exchange servers in an Active Directory site as valid servers to include in an Autodiscover response. This means that if you deploy additional Exchange servers, you must ensure that they are properly configured, as per the CAS namespace design. This leads us to the question: Are additional Exchange servers required? This is the consultant's answer: It depends!

If the current environment is already properly published to the Internet and has sufficient capacity to perform mailbox moves and respond to free/busy requests, it may be possible to leverage the current infrastructure. In other cases, this may not be possible. As noted previously, in order get the best experience with Office 365, the latest version of the Office suite must be used. The same is true with Exchange hybrid. There are features that are not present if Exchange 2010 is used as the hybrid solution. In such cases, it may be desired to deploy a newer version of Exchange. However, there is no specific sizing guidance for a server that is used for hybrid purposes, and it must be sized as a regular Exchange server in the environment. Additionally, owing to the migration methodology of moving from Exchange 2010, the new environment must be fully sized and deployed at the time of cutover. This is because all the HTTP namespaces will be moved from Exchange 2010 to Exchange 2013/2016 in a single operation. The new Exchange 2013/2016 servers must be able to handle the workload of these connections. For details on Exchange 2010 migration, please review the Exchange Deployment Assistant.

If the current environment is able to provide the required features and can meet the load requirements, it generally makes sense to leverage the investment made in the current deployment. Some customers have deployed Hybrid with the existing infrastructure and moved a large percentage of mailboxes to Office 365. Once they have migrated mailboxes and thinned out the on-premises environment, they then deployed a new version of Exchange.

CAS Namespace Planning

As in previous on-premises-only Exchange deployments, CAS namespace planning is a critical phase of the project that is often overlooked. A sage Microsoft program manager once said that CAS is 95% planning and 5% implementation. This is so very true. This was also the program manager who provided the elephant's bottom analogy for Outlook Anywhere...

As mentioned in the preceding section with regard to additional Exchange servers, the same may also be true for CAS Namespaces. If your current Exchange servers are correctly published to the Internet, you may be able to leverage the existing infrastructure and move forward. If this is the case, it typically makes sense to do so. Generally, you will be moving mailboxes from on-premises servers to Office 365 and, as a result, thin out or remove some of the on-premises infrastructure.

Some drivers to deploy additional Exchange servers may be to address issues with an existing on-premises Exchange deployment. For example, some customers may have published Exchange to the Internet with certain pre-authentication solutions. This worked well when only Outlook clients were connecting to the published infrastructure. However, now that Office 365 also must connect to the on-premises Exchange servers in a hybrid deployment, this is an issue. For example, Autodiscover must be published without pre-authentication. Pre-authentication is not supported for the Autodiscover end points that Office 365 will use. This is covered in more detail in the next section.

Autodiscover must point on on-premises Exchange servers in a hybrid deployment. Do not let the Office 365 portal goad or cajole you into prematurely moving Autodiscover to Office 365. See Office 365 Exchange Hybrid Deployments Busting the Autodiscover Myth, for more details on this issue.

In some cases, it may be desirable to create additional CAS namespaces for Office 365 mailbox migration. This may be to account for regional, publishing, or performance issues. Assume that you have a multinational on-premises Exchange deployment that spans North America, EMEA, and APAC. If you only create a mailbox migration end point in one location, that means that you will be pulling data over a WAN link from the other locations. If the migration end point was created in London, consider how Office 365 will obtain access to mailbox content. If the mailbox to be migrated resides in London, the content is locally available, and no WAN traffic is created. However, if the mailbox is in APAC, the content must be retrieved over the customer's internal WAN from APAC. To avoid this situation, additional migration end points can be created. It is the Exchange Mailbox Replication Service (MRS), specifically the MRS proxy, that is the component used with Office 365. If we take the previous example, additional MRS end points can be created in North America and APAC. We will require an additional name on a certificate, public DNS records, and for Exchange servers to be published correctly to the Internet.

For example, we could create multiple MRS end points (Table 3-1). The following example illustrates the creation of an MRS end point per region, so that content is pulled from the region over the Internet, rather than having to backhaul over the customer's internal WAN circuits.

Table 3-1. *MRS End Point Example*

Location	MRS End Point DNS Name
EMEA	mrs-emea.tailspintoys.com
North America	mrs-na.tailspintoys.com
APAC	mrs-apac.tailspintoys.com

Typically, each of these DNS entries will resolve to a load-balanced VIP that contains multiple Exchange servers.

In some cases, issues have arisen when trying to migrate mailboxes to Office 365. This is often owing to misconfigured on-premises network equipment. Common examples are low-level packet inspection devices, misconfigured load balancers, or problems with other on-premises network equipment. To move the migration forward, a separate migration end point can be created that is separate from the existing publishing mechanism. One customer example stands out: they spent four months trying to migrate mailboxes to Office 365 and could not even migrate a 200KB test mailbox with nothing in it. Because the customer was trying to get the mailbox content to Office 365, then surely was that not where the issue was? After spending four fruitless months, they contacted Premier support. The issue was immediately noted and a solution provided. We could immediately migrate mailboxes by creating a new MRS namespace. The new MRS namespace was not published via the security team's standard practices; they were bypassed. A new external IP address was added and mapped to Exchange. The external firewall ACLs only allowed Office 365 to connect, so this did not present any security issues. This does require additional work to deploy, as a new external IP, public DNS record, and name on a certificate are required. But those things do not take four months.

Network Prerequisites

This is what North Americans will call the elephant in the room, in other words, a large issue that some people may wish to gloss over but must be addressed head-on. Because Office 365 resides in a Microsoft-operated data center, we require connectivity to this data center. This connectivity will take many forms as we deploy, migrate, and use the hybrid solution. Initially, we will create the hybrid relationship with the on-premises Exchange servers to Office 365. The next step is typically moving some test mailboxes over, to validate the solution from a functional perspective. When in run-state, connectivity is required between Exchange servers on-premises to Office 365, to look up the availability web service that will provide free/busy information. Note that this will work both ways. An on-premises mailbox will look up a cloud mailbox's free/busy and vice versa.

In addition to the server-to-server free/busy lookups, we must also factor in SMTP mail flow. For a given user, their mailbox will not exist simultaneously in Office 365 and on-premises. For users to send and receive e-mail, it must flow between on-premises and Office 365. This will consume bandwidth. If the MX continues to point to an on-premises appliance/device/Exchange server, the incoming e-mail will consume bandwidth as it is handed off to the on-premises device. Should a recipient of this e-mail be located in Office 365, the message will have to be delivered to Office 365. Typically, this will mean that Internet bandwidth is used a second time for the same e-mail.

Client connectivity will also consume bandwidth. This has typically not been a major concern for most on-premises Exchange customers, if their users and mailboxes resided in the same location. The local LAN would be used for connectivity. Should the on-premises Exchange organization span multiple locations or even continents, then on-premises Outlook connectivity would have been carefully planned. The same is true for Office 365. Clients will now connect via proxy servers and firewalls to access their Office 365 mailbox that is on the Internet.

This paradigm shift in connectivity from on-premises to Office 365 created many issues for proxy server administrators. Often, the proxy administrator was not involved in the planning or was not allocated additional funding to scale the proxy infrastructure to deal with the increase in Office 365 traffic. Consider the extra volume of connections, SMTP e-mail, Outlook data, and OneDrive for Business data. Other unfortunate side effects can also be caused if the proxy servers require authentication. In many cases, NTLM authentication is used to authenticate the end users who are trying to browse the Internet. This is not the most scalable protocol and will cause NTLM bottlenecks. The issue is made worse if only a single Active Directory domain controller has been specified to authenticate the proxy requests. For this reason, Office 365 URLs should not be authenticated, as we do not want to add additional latency or potential issues.

There are multiple tools to help determine what the uptick in bandwidth consumption will be. They can be obtained from `http://aka.ms/tune`, along with another detailed network guidance.

In addition to the client connectivity requirements, also ensure that the necessary server connectivity requirements have been met. For details, please see the Office 365 IP and URL documentation. There are specific requirements for publishing Exchange with Office 365 that are covered in the publishing requirements for Exchange 2010 hybrid. The documentation provides details on why pre-authentication is not possible for certain Exchange on-premises URLs when Office 365 hybrid is deployed.

We are almost ready to discuss running the Exchange hybrid wizard. To recap some of the items we have discussed,

- IDFix has been executed and issues remediated.

- All Accepted domains have been reviewed and legacy/unwanted domains removed.

- All Email Address Polices have been reviewed and legacy/unwanted policies or addresses removed.

- Mailboxes have been updated to remove unwanted e-mail addresses, such as `contoso.local`.

- All domains have been added and verified in Office 365.

- Unwanted and legacy mailbox permissions have been documented and removed.

- Permission assignments have been reviewed to determine how users will be grouped into migration batches, to accommodate the current cross-premises permission support.

- Office clients are running a version of Office that is in mainstream support, and it is fully updated.

- The latest version of browser(s) is deployed onto all machines. This is IE11 for Windows clients. Note that Windows XP and Windows Vista are no longer supported.

- Exchange servers have been fully patched to install all Windows updates.

- Exchange servers have been updated to the latest Exchange update. This may be a Rollup Update (RU) or Cumulative Update (CU), depending if you have Exchange 2010 or 2013/32016, respectively.

Identity and authentication requirements have been discussed and documented. This may mean that AD FS is deployed. If this is the case, it is expected that a high-availability deployment of both AD FS and WAP is present. This will require load balancers in both the corporate network and the DMZ (Figure 3-3).

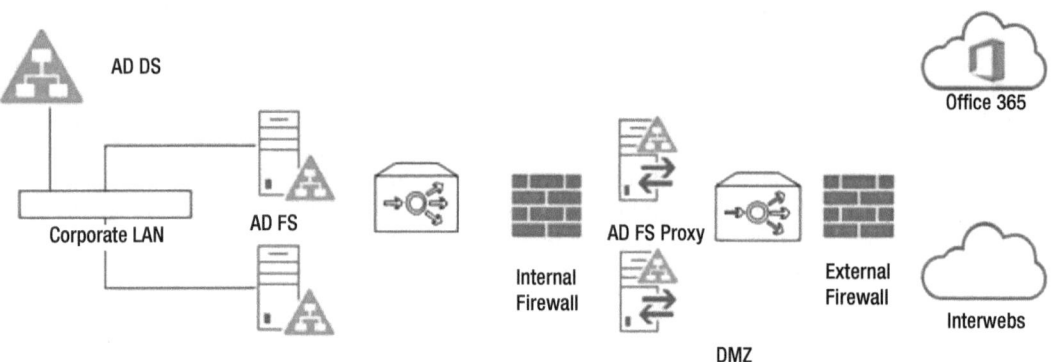

Figure 3-3. Network diagram showing network load balancers

A new authentication option is currently in preview. This is the Azure AD Connect Pass Through feature. AD FS–like authentication experience can be provided for domain-joined machines when they are on the corporate network and able to contact a DC.

The password hash synchronization option will also be a valid authentication mechanism for some customers. It provides the capability to use the same username and password on-premises and with Office 365.

Now that the on-premises infrastructure has been updated and legacy items removed, we can move forward with the actual Exchange hybrid deployment.

Exchange Hybrid Deployment

At the time of writing, Exchange 2003 and 2007 have already exited out of extended support. They will not be mentioned here, as customers should have already migrated off these platforms.

Regardless of the Exchange version in which the hybrid wizard is to be executed, the downloadable wizard must be used. Exchange 2010 and early Exchange 2013 builds included the hybrid wizard in the product. This was not ideal, owing to the different cadence of Exchange on-premises and Office 365 updates. By decoupling the hybrid wizard from Exchange RU and CU updates, it allows for it to be rapidly updated. Telemetry data is also provided so that if there is an issue, it is detected and can be proactively corrected. There is the opportunity to provide feedback at each stage with the new wizard. Do not use the built-in hybrid wizard on Exchange 2010, it is no longer supported. All new iterations must use the new wizard. The new Exchange hybrid wizard can be obtained from http://aka.ms/HybridWizard.

The new wizard is downloaded and installed onto the machine. Note that Internet access is required to download the wizard. This is documented in the Office 365 IP and URL article, specifically in the Exchange Online section.

Note that you will require credentials for both the on-premises and Office 365 environment. The hybrid wizard does not do anything secret. It automates the cmdlets that are already available to you on-premises and in Office 365. It is required to run the hybrid wizard to create a supported deployment. Manually creating the components is very error-prone and is no longer supported. The wizard will make the required changes to the on-premises and Office 365 environment. Some of the changes include the following:

- Disabling tiny tenant mode

- Creating coexistence mail domain—`tenant.mail.onmicrosoft.com`

- Creating additional send connector

- Creating additional receive connector

- Updating default Email Address Policy

- Creating trust relationship with Azure trust system—previously known as MFG (Microsoft Federation Gateway)

- Creating organization relationship between on-premises Exchange and Exchange Online

The wizard will prompt you with a series of questions, so that it can understand the environment and make the necessary configuration changes.

If the hybrid wizard encounters an issue, do not worry, as it is not the end of the world! Review the hybrid wizard log file on the servers where it was executed. Every iteration of the hybrid wizard will create a new log file. The logs are detailed and should normally allow you to isolate the issue. Once you have identified and corrected the issue, just rerun the wizard. It will verify that each configuration item was done and pick up at the point where the previous iteration failed. It is possible that there might be two separate issues. This is fine. Identify and correct the issue and then retry the wizard.

Note that blindly rerunning the wizard without making any configuration corrections will not provide a solution. In fact, if you run the wizard too many times in a given period, you will be blocked from running it until the period has elapsed.

Once the wizard has completed successfully, you should now be the owner of a shiny new Exchange hybrid deployment! Congratulations! The next step will be to run a series of functionality checks and verifications. Typically, at this point, I would suggest the following, as a minimum:

- Migrate a test mailbox to Office 365.

- Migrate a batch of test mailboxes to Office 365 that contain a reasonable amount of data.

- Review the mailbox migration statistics for these mailboxes, so that you have an initial baseline for mailbox migration performance.

- Migrate one test mailbox back to on-premises.

- Verify that AutoDiscover correctly updates the Outlook profile of a mailbox moved to Exchange Online. There should be no need of manual intervention.

- If Modern Authentication was enabled for Exchange Online, and Office 365 Professional Plus 2016 is used, the authentication experience should be smooth for AD FS and Azure AD Connect Pass through Authentication deployments.

- Verify that free/busy and calendar data is visible between on-premises and Exchange Online mailbox.

- Assuming you previously remediated AD objects and replicated them to Office 365, verify that the Global Address List is correct. There may be a little delay for it to be updated after a mailbox move.

- Test that the external mailtip is not displayed for the cross-premises mailbox.

- Send test e-mail between the on-premises and Exchange Online test mailbox.

- Review the X-Headers, to ensure that the message was treated as from a trusted source.

- Verify that OOF messages are visible cross-premises.

Once the base functionality checks have completed, you can now start to migrate some of the pilot users to Exchange Online. The pilot users must be a representative mix of your organization's user base. These people should be willing to work with IT through any possible issues that may arise. While it is perfectly fine to include the IT team as part of the pilot group, additional business staff must also be added. If there is an issue or behavior change, the typical IT person will take it in stride and just address or fix the issue, with minimal impact. If the same challenge were presented to a standard user, they might be sidelined by this change. By adding such people to the pilot group, feedback and learning can take place, so that issues can be corrected for the mass migrations that will follow.

Note that permissions to shared resources must be considered when selecting the pilot group. Do not move people who have a dependency on resources that are still on premises where they require send-as and receive-as permissions on those resources. The considerations for a hybrid deployment are outlined here, as is the current stance on cross-premises permissions.

Exchange Server Hybrid Deployments

As the pilot users are migrated to Office 365, it is critical that you continue to monitor performance on the on-premises Exchange infrastructure. The act of moving a mailbox will require the mailbox content to be read, serialized, and then transferred to Office 365. Additionally, there will be cross-premises Exchange Web Services (EWS) calls between Exchange Online and Exchange on-premises. A prime example is for calendar and free/busy data. Users will have to continue to book meetings and review calendar data, and EWS requests are used in modern versions on Exchange.

It is also required that you plan and manage the subsequent mailbox migrations to Office 365. As noted earlier, ensure that you consider the permission implications and map out how people interact with others within the business. While the UI is great for moving some test mailboxes and a limited number of pilot users, we really need to script and automate the mass migrations. PowerShell can be used to do all of this, and TechNet documents the cmdlets, for example, `New-MigrationBatch`.

It is also critical that you have an initial network performance baseline, taken before migrating users to Office 365. As the migrations continue, the statics from your network devices must be collected and reviewed. The CPU load and connection count on firewalls is one of the items your network team must review. There have been issues in larger deployments wherein there were issues with NAT scalability. Troubleshooting such connections from the client side is ineffective, as the symptoms are sporadic. It is much more efficient to track from the network infrastructure. The network team should already have the tooling and process to report and analyze their devices.

In addition to the performance of specific network devices, the available network bandwidth must also be monitored. Planning for an increase in connections, firewall resources, and bandwidth is a core task of successfully deploying any cloud service. Microsoft provides tools to help with this process. Please review the available documentation and tools at `http://aka.ms/tune`.

As part of the bandwidth planning, there are two distinct elements to this. Bandwidth consumed while migration is in progress and bandwidth consumed once the new steady state is obtained. For example, the bandwidth to move 10TB of mailbox content is not the same as the bandwidth required once all content has been migrated. At this point, the bandwidth will be consumed by SMTP, client connectivity, and cross-premises web services requests. Probably, it will be less than what was used to migrate the content.

The network team must be engaged right at the start of any Office 365 project. Most likely, an increase in bandwidth is required. This could take months to procure, and the lead time factored into the project. Service providers may have to lay new fiber, and this could take even longer. In extreme cases, when the additional load of the Office 365 connections was factored in, the network team reported back that they needed brand-new egress firewalls. The cost for this was projected at $1.5 million. This was a larger enterprise customer, and the firewalls were already due for replacement. They wanted to get the Office 365 project to pay for their new gear. The lead Office 365 project manager said absolutely not! The meeting in which that was discussed was "interesting," to say the least...

As you continue to move mailboxes, there may come a point where you are able to consolidate and shrink the on-premises messaging footprint. The degree to which you will be able to do this will vary by organization. Some will move 99% of mailboxes to Office 365, others will move less. If you can move 100% of mailboxes, currently it is still expected that you maintain at least one Exchange server on-premises. This is to provide the following two capabilities:

- Ability to manage Exchange attributes in a supported manner

- Mail flow from printers/scanners/LOB applications

Once the on-premises footprint and the number of mailboxes located there have been reduced, some customers then chose to update Exchange to the next version, if this has not already been done. If you recall, some customers may use Exchange 2010 as the hybrid solution, if it was correctly published to the Internet and there are no performance concerns. Once the number of on-premises mailboxes has been reduced, they deploy Exchange 2016. The CAS namespaces are cut over to Exchange 2016, and the hybrid wizard is then executed on Exchange 2016, to update the configuration. The remaining mailboxes can then be moved over to Exchange 2016, if desired, and the legacy Exchange 2010 servers are retired. Note that this assumes the Exchange 2016 deployment was correctly planned and implemented. Because any migration takes time and resources, some customers do not have the appetite to do both an Exchange on-premises and Office 365 migration at the same time. By performing them in a serial fashion, the Exchange 2016 on-premises migration is simplified, because there are fewer mailboxes to move to the destination Exchange 2016 infrastructure.

Public Folders can be migrated to Office 365. Typically, this is done after all users who use them have been moved to Office 365. Prior to migrating the content to Office 365, the on-premises public folders can be made available to Office 365 mailboxes.

See the following links for details on coexistence and migration of Public Folders from legacy Exchange servers to Office 365.

- **Public Folder Coexistence with Office 365**

  `https://technet.microsoft.com/en-us/library/dn249373(v=exchg.150).aspx`

- **Public Folder Migration to Office 365**

  `https://technet.microsoft.com/en-us/library/dn874017(v=exchg.150).aspx`

Summary

Migrating to Exchange Online is a migration. Just as when you have migrated to a previous version of Exchange on-premises, you must plan and prepare for this migration, for it to be successful. I reviewed some of the common issues and considerations to deploy Exchange hybrid. Do not underestimate the criticality of network planning with regard to any aspect of an Office 365 project. Ensure that the network and security team are fully engaged right from the initial planning stages, so that all parties are aligned on your deployment strategy. This will set you up for a successful digital transformation!

CHAPTER 4

■ ■ ■

SharePoint Hybrid Team Sites

BY ROGER CORMIER

As anybody working in the enterprise space can tell you, there's no avoiding the cloud. Whether your organization is looking to reduce its data center footprint, simplify its operations model, or simply achieve that fabled "evergreen state," some form of public or private cloud will be part of that future landscape. When organizations are moving services and workloads to the cloud, it is often required that these services and workloads continue to exist on-premises for a certain amount of time. One of the most significant challenges faced by many organizations is managing the experience for users during that bridge state. Managing user impact and creating a single unified and cohesive collaboration experience are considered key success factors when migrating from SharePoint on-premises to SharePoint Online (Office 365).

Getting Started

In this chapter, we will be taking an in-depth look at a key product enhancement that aims to tackle this very issue head-on: Hybrid Team Sites. Hybrid Team Sites—also referenced as hybrid sites in some documentation—is available in both SharePoint 2013 and SharePoint 2016 on-premises and is designed to work with your Office 365 Enterprise subscription. We will review how Hybrid Team Sites will change your collaboration experience and dive into what must be done for any organization to start taking advantage of the value that Hybrid Team Sites brings.

As the objective of this chapter is to truly explain how Hybrid Team Sites works in depth, we will also be taking a closer look at some of the underlying technologies that make this possible, such as Office Graph.

Exploring Office Graph

One of the key elements that makes it possible to have a cohesive SharePoint hybrid sites experience is Office Graph. The features and capabilities provided by Office Graph really serve as the fabric that unifies the SharePoint 2013/2016 on-premises and SharePoint Online experiences. Before delving into how Office Graph influences the SharePoint hybrid sites experience, it is important for us to take a closer look at Office Graph.

What's in a Name?

The name *Graph*, in the context of computing, is derived from mathematical graph theory. In mathematics, a graph is effectively a representation of a collection of objects in which some pairs of objects are connected by various links. Think, for example, User A and User B are both contributing to the same document (document.docx). These two users do not know each other but may share a skip-level manager. A very simplified view of that section of the graph may look like the following (see Figure 4-1).

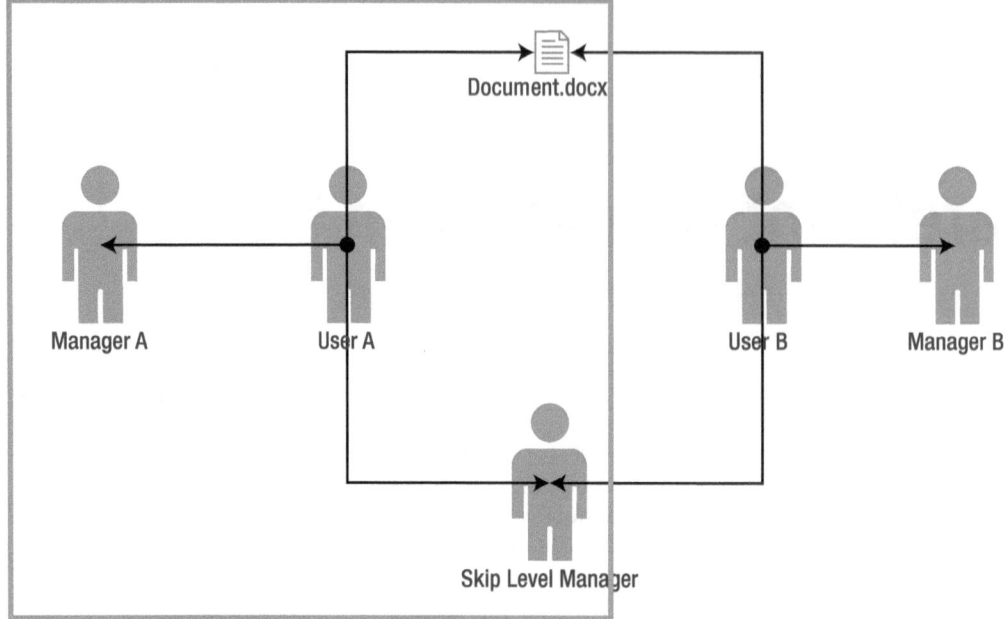

Figure 4-1. *Abstract representation of a Graph*

What About the Other Graph?

Yes, you've heard that right. There are, in fact, both an Office Graph and a Microsoft Graph. Although conceptually they both provide the same type of functionality—that is, to identify relationships between various types of objects/entities—they are not the same, and the terms should not be used interchangeably.

You can think of the Office Graph as being user-centric. As a user collaborates on documents and interacts with colleagues, connections are made. Leveraging machine learning algorithms, using these data points as well as knowledge of the user's organization, Office Graph can bubble up information that is most relevant in the context of the user. Microsoft Graph expands on this by connecting the individual user-centric networks across a variety of services and is frequently described as the "one endpoint to rule them all" (https://graph.microsoft.io/). In effect, the Office Graph computes insights across Office 365 and makes those insights available through Microsoft Graph.

How Can You Use Graph?

I would like to preface this section by stating that at the time of this writing, many features of the Office Graph API were still in pre-release. As a result, some of the features described may change and/or not be available after general availability.

As of this writing, there are two types of insights that can be queried from the Office Graph: the first being TrendingAround and the second being People. TrendingAround will return items that the user has access to, and People will return people that the user interacts with.

Graph Query Language (GQL) is the primary method used to query the Office Graph via the SharePoint Online search REST API. As such, we can simply issue HTTP requests with appropriate syntax, in order to query the Office Graph.

What Syntax Do I Use?

Let's start by looking at an example.

```
https://SPOTenant.sharepoint.com/_api/search/query?Querytext='*'&Properties='GraphQuery:
ACTOR(17593168896770)'
```

This URL is composed of three distinct sections.

```
https://spotenant.sharepoint.com/_api/search/query?
```

This section of the URL represents the address of the service, and the question mark (?) indicates that there are additional query parameters.

```
Querytext='*'
```

This section of the URL is a wildcard search, which effectively says "return everything."

```
&Properties='GraphQuery:ACTOR(17593168896770)
```

This section indicates that this is an Office Graph query, and it supplies a filter for the ACTOR. The ACTOR, in this case, means the user with ID 17593168896770 in SharePoint. ACTOR can be either the ID of a user, or "ME." To obtain the ID of a specific user, we can query the SharePoint search service directly. The following example will search for a user with the login `spfarm`:

```
https://SPOTenant.sharepoint.com/_api/search/query?Querytext='Username:spfarm'&SourceId=
'b09a7990-05ea-4af9-81ef-edfab16c4e31'
```

This example, again, is composed of three distinct sections. The first two sections are easily explained using the same logic as before. In this case, the SourceID represents the ID of the "local people results" result source.

How Do I Query for Specific Actions?

The Office Graph API describes several "Action Types," which can be used to filter the returned results. Table 4-1 describes the available action types.

Table 4-1. Available Action Types

Action Type	Description	Visibility	ID	Weight	Timestamp
PersonalFeed	The actor's personal feed, as shown on their Home view in Delve	Private	1021	A sequence number	When the item was added to the feed on the Home view in Delve
Modified	Items that the actor has modified in the last three months	Public	1003	The number of modifications	Last modified
OrgColleague	Everyone who reports to the same manager as the actor	Public	1015	Always 1	-
OrgDirect	The actor's direct reports	Public	1014	Always 1	-
OrgManager	The person to whom the actor reports	Public	1013	Always 1	-
OrgSkipLevelManager	The actor's skip-level manager	Public	1016	Always 1	-
WorkingWith	People with whom the actor frequently communicates or works	Private	1019	A relevance score	-
TrendingAround	Items popular with people with whom the actor frequently works or communicates	Public	1020	A relevance score	-
Viewed	Items viewed by the actor in the last three months	Private	1001	The number of views	Last viewed
WorkingWithPublic	A public version of the WorkingWith edge	Public	1033	A sequence number	-

Using this table, we could execute the following request, to return all items that have been "Viewed" or "Modified" by a specific user:

```
https://SPOTenant.sharepoint.com/_api/search/query?Querytext='*'&Properties='GraphQuery:ACTOR
(17593168896770, OR(action:1001,action:1003))'
```

Note that in this case, two actions are being passed. We encapsulate the OR'd conditions in parentheses. Therefore, OR(action:1001,action:1003) can actually be read literally as either action 1001 (viewed) or action 1003 (modified)."

So, What Does All of This Have to Do with SharePoint Hybrid Sites?

As I was explaining earlier in the chapter, Office Graph really is the fabric that unifies the user experience in a hybrid SharePoint configuration. Although we do configure both the on-premises farm and the SharePoint Online tenant to be aware of and trust each other, the contents of each site is distinctly in a single environment. As such, so are the interactions of a user within the context of that site.

This is where the concept of a "signal" comes into the picture. There are several types of signals to identify various types of actions, such as viewing an item, sharing an item, following an item, modifying an item, etc. A signal will include an "actor," an "action," and an "object." For example, "User A" shared Document X. When we configure SharePoint hybrid sites, we are actually allowing SharePoint on-premises to send these "signals" into the Office Graph. This way, when a user encounters a feature that leverages Office Graph, the experience presented to the user will represent activities performed in the on-premises SharePoint environment and in Office 365.

In the case of hybrid sites, when you follow a site in SharePoint 2013 or 2016 on-premises, an entry will be populated in the "followed" list in both the on-premises environment but also to SharePoint Online, via the Office Graph API. Links that point to the followed sites (via the "sites" link and the Extensible App Launcher) will redirect users to the "followed" list in SharePoint Online.

It is also important to note that this functionality applies only to followed sites. Followed documents and followed people do not have this same characteristic presently. It is also important to note that any existing sites that were followed will not automatically be ported over to SharePoint Online; therefore, users will have to follow their sites again to populate their existing followed sites in the "followed" list in SharePoint Online.

Getting Back to SharePoint Hybrid Sites

Now that we have covered the basics of Office Graph, we are ready to move on to SharePoint hybrid sites. Any time an organization transitions a workload into the cloud, there is a real potential to disrupt the way people work. If there is too much disruption, adoption of the new solution could be hindered. In the case of SharePoint, or any other workload in Office 365, this could impact the productivity of the organization, and, in turn, that could impact the morale of their business users. Therefore, how change is managed and how the impact of such a change is reduced becomes a critical success factor in such a transition.

When we talk about hybrid workloads in SharePoint 2013/2016—whether it's SharePoint hybrid sites, Hybrid OneDrive, Hybrid Search, Hybrid Taxonomy, etc.—we're really talking about concepts that are designed to make the transition from SharePoint on-premises to SharePoint Online less disruptive. The objective of a successful SharePoint hybrid implementation is to create a seamless experience for end users, such that the location where the user collaborates is completely transparent. Configuring SharePoint hybrid sites will also configure Hybrid OneDrive redirection, hybrid user profiles, hybrid site following, and the hybrid app launcher.

Before You Get Started

This section assumes that the Office 365 tenant has already been configured to a certain standard, primarily, that the following prerequisites have been met:

- All necessary domains have been registered with your tenant.

- UPN suffixes have been assigned for user accounts.

- User accounts have been synchronized to Azure Active Directory.

- Required licenses have been assigned to users.

As of this writing, the primary method used to deploy SharePoint hybrid sites for SharePoint 2013 and SharePoint 2016 is Hybrid Picker. The Hybrid Picker tool must be run from a SharePoint server that is joined to a farm and will help to automate some of the configuration steps that are needed to connect your on-premises SharePoint farm with your SharePoint Online tenant. Hybrid Picker is accessed via the SharePoint Admin Center in Office 365 (Figure 4-2).

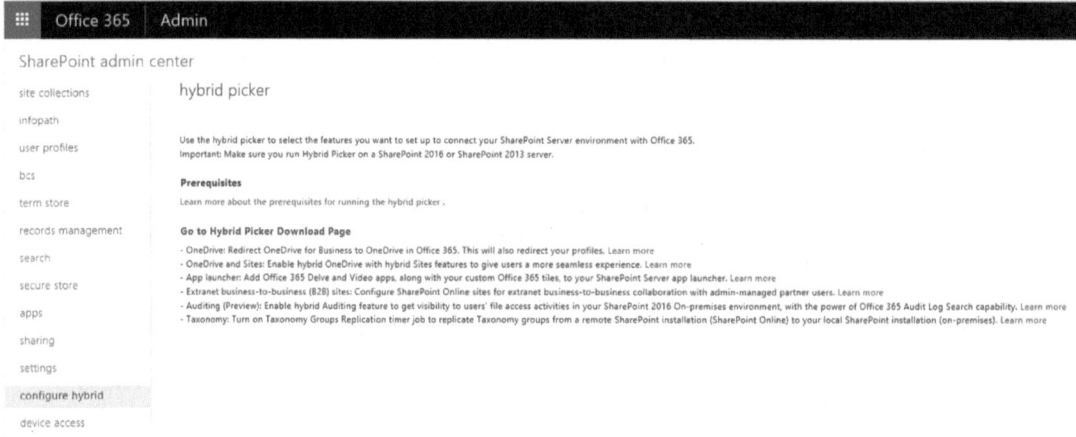

Figure 4-2. *Hybrid Picker in Office 365*

The account that you use to run Hybrid Picker will also have to meet the following requirements:

- A member of the Farm Administrators group

- A service application administrator (Full Control) for the User Profile Service

- An Office 365 Global Administrator or a SharePoint Online Administrator

- Logged into Office 365 and SharePoint Server from a server in your SharePoint Server farm

- Ability to launch Hybrid Picker as a Farm Administrator with elevated permissions

Familiarizing Yourself with Hybrid Picker

Although we use Hybrid Picker to set up Hybrid OneDrive and Sites, and will focus on that application in this chapter, Hybrid Picker continues to be developed to support more hybrid scenarios. As of this writing, the following workloads are supported by Hybrid Picker:

- OneDrive

- OneDrive and Sites

- App Launcher

- Extranet Business-to-Business Sites

- Auditing

- Taxonomy

Installing Hybrid Picker

Hybrid Picker itself should be launched from a server that has SharePoint 2013 or SharePoint 2016 installed and is joined to a farm. The basic sequence of the steps you will take are as follows (see Figure 4-3):

1. Log on to a SharePoint 2013/2016 Server using an account that meets the requirements outlined in the preceding text.

2. Navigate to your SharePoint Admin Center (in Office 365), again using the same credentials you used to log on to the server.

3. Click Configure Hybrid in the left navigation.

4. Click Go to Hybrid Picker Download Page.

5. Click click here. This will launch an Application Install—Security Warning.

6. Click Install to proceed.

SharePoint Hybrid Picker

To Enable or Modify SharePoint Hybrid Configuration you need to first initiate Hybrid Picker, to get started click here

(SharePoint Hybrid Picker should be launched at SharePoint On-Premise Servers where SharePoint 2013 or SharePoint 2016 was installed

Learn more about the Office 365 Support Assistant and how we use your data

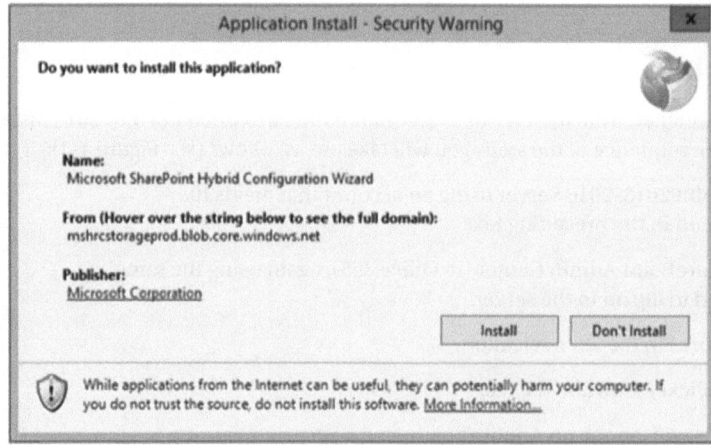

***Figure 4-3.** Installing Hybrid Picker application*

Execution of Hybrid Picker

Immediately after installing Hybrid Picker, a wizard experience will be launched (Figure 4-4).

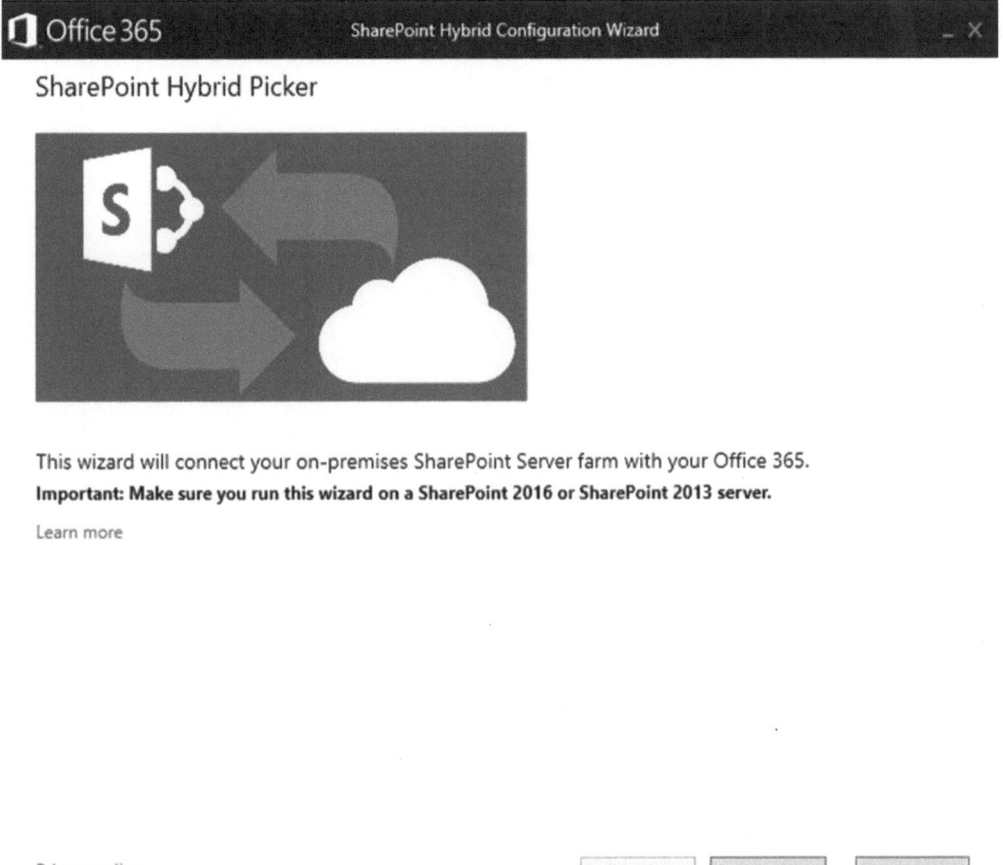

Figure 4-4. *Hybrid wizard in Office 365*

Once we click Next, we will be asked for credentials for the account that will be used for on-premises activities, as well as credentials for a global administrator account. We click Validate credentials, in order to validate that the credentials supplied meet the expected requirements (Figure 4-5).

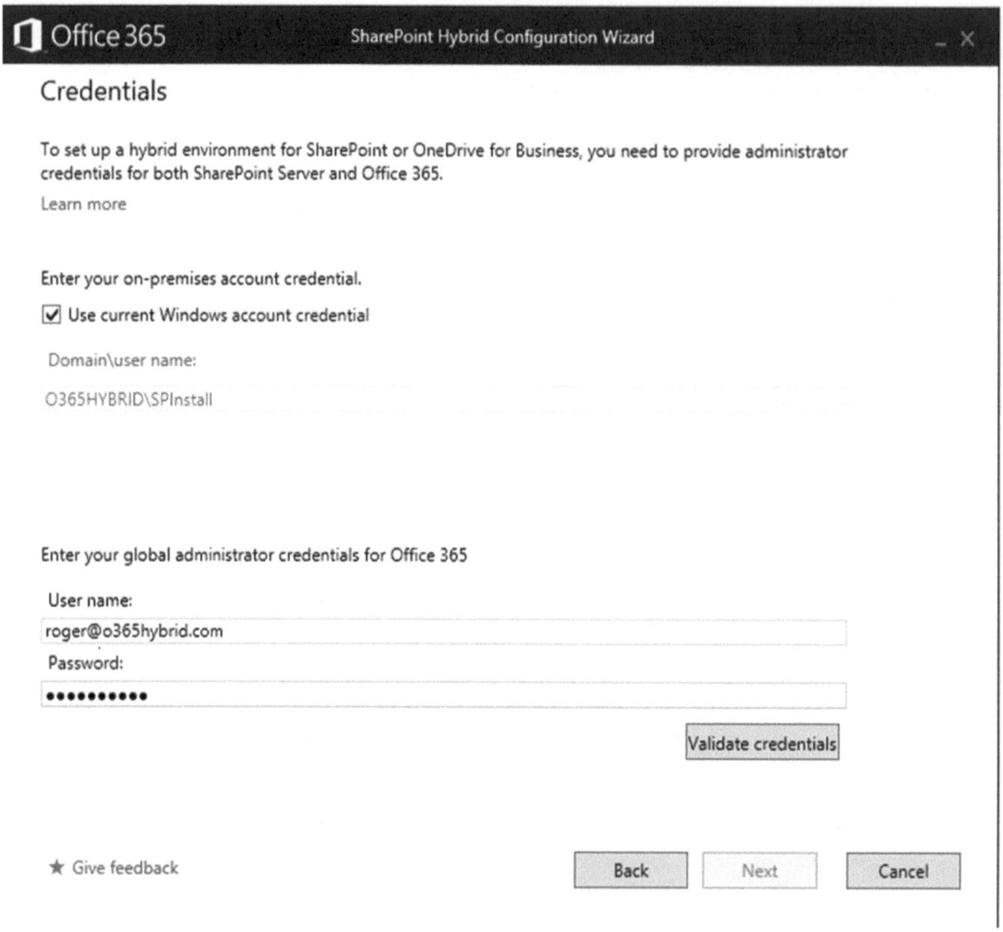

Figure 4-5. *Hybrid Configuration Wizard Credentials screen*

If you happen to enter valid credentials that do not meet the requirements to complete the configuration, Hybrid Picker will provide you with a very clear message, such as the message in the following screenshot. In this example, credentials for a valid SharePoint Online Administrator that is not a global administrator were entered (Figure 4-6).

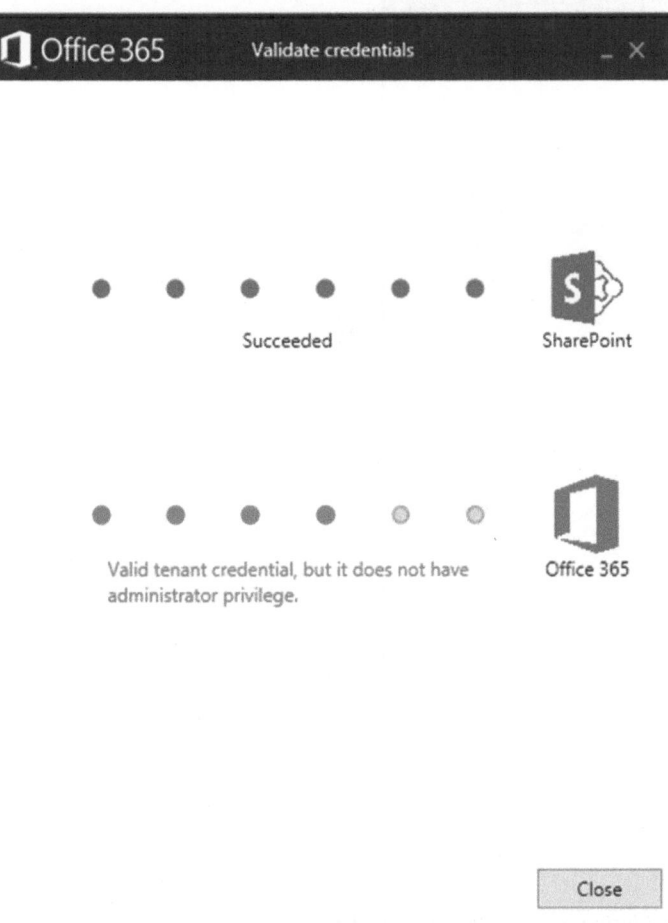

Figure 4-6. *Hybrid wizard credentials validation screen with no administrator privileges*

Once we have supplied credentials that meet the expected requirements, validation will return a message, as seen in the following screenshot (Figure 4-7).

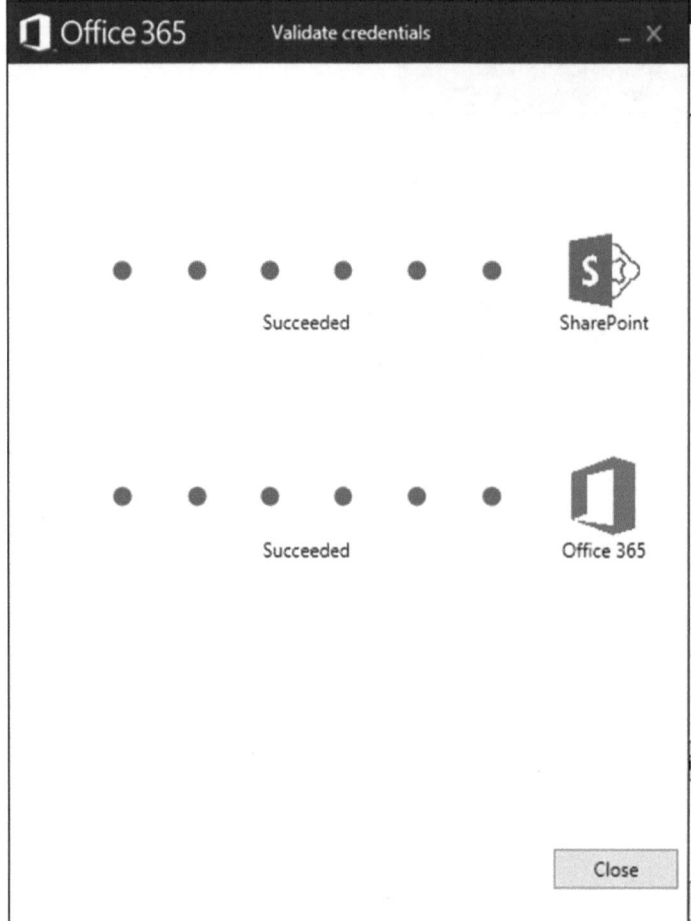

Figure 4-7. *Hybrid wizard credentials validation screen with valid privileges*

Upon closing the validation screen, the Next button in the main window will become visible, and we can proceed. At this point, we are going to validate that the local SharePoint environment also meets the expected configuration. If you happen to fail any of the local validations, Hybrid Picker will notify you, so that you can remediate any issues that would prevent you from being successful with a hybrid configuration (Figure 4-8).

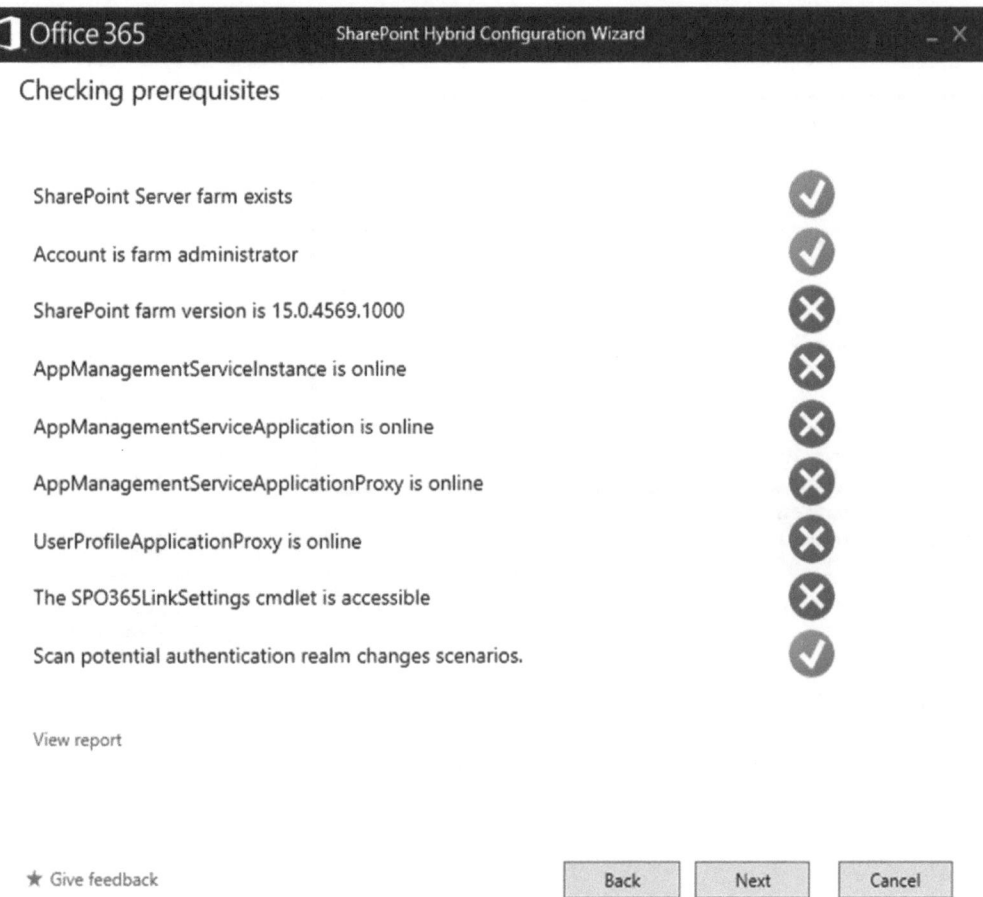

Figure 4-8. *Hybrid Configuration Wizard missing prerequisites*

Clicking View report will give you detailed information about why specific validation steps failed (Figure 4-9).

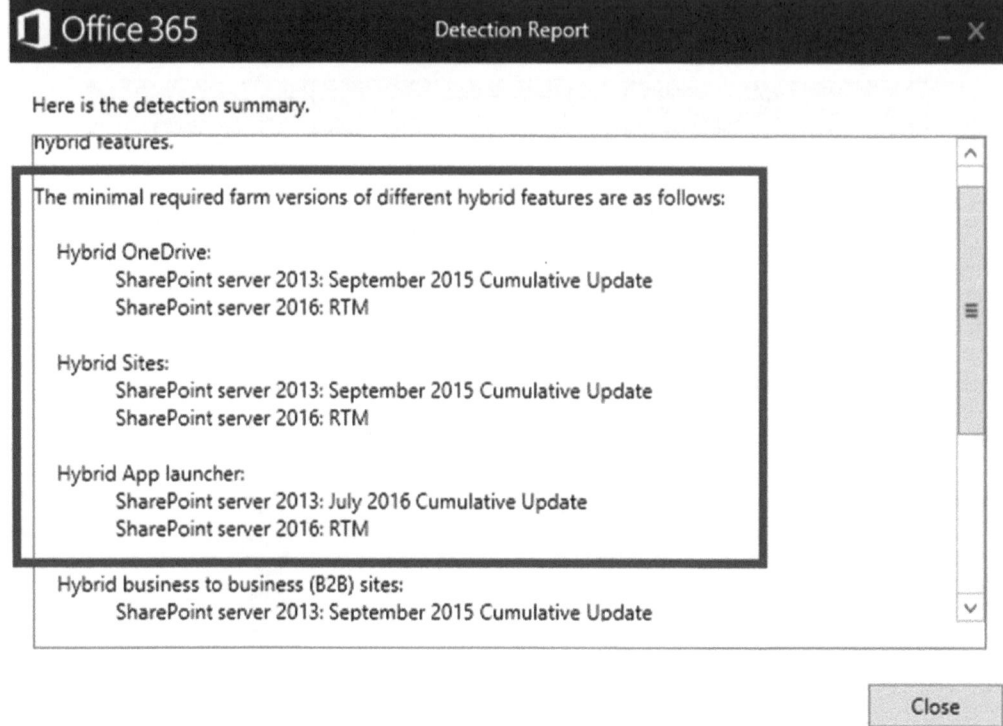

Figure 4-9. Hybrid Configuration Wizard Detection Report

Once we have performed all necessary remediation, Hybrid Picker should return a validation message that looks like the following screenshot (Figure 4-10).

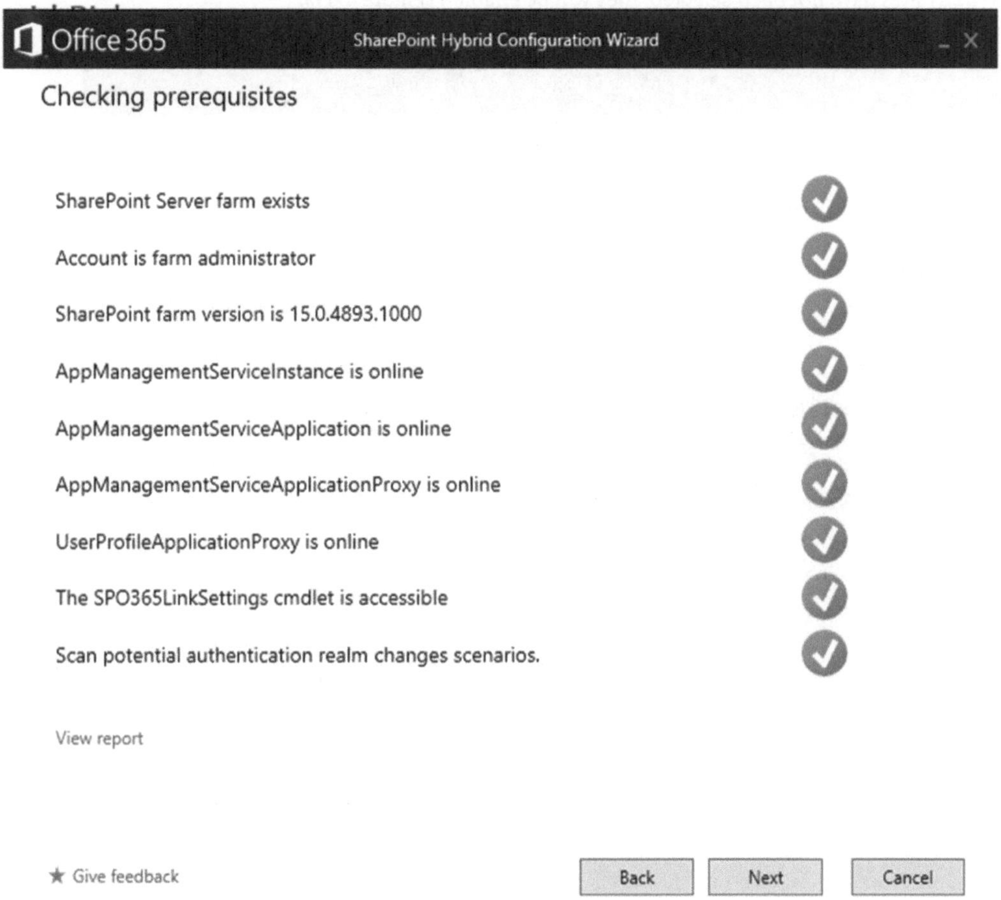

Figure 4-10. *Hybrid Configuration Wizard with all prerequisites*

Clicking Next will move you along to the hybrid feature selection screen, from which you can choose the hybrid features you would like to configure. Selecting one feature may require additional features to be enabled, as we see in the following screenshot. As you can see, even though App Launcher and Business to Business (B2B) sites have not been selected, they will be enabled (Figure 4-11).

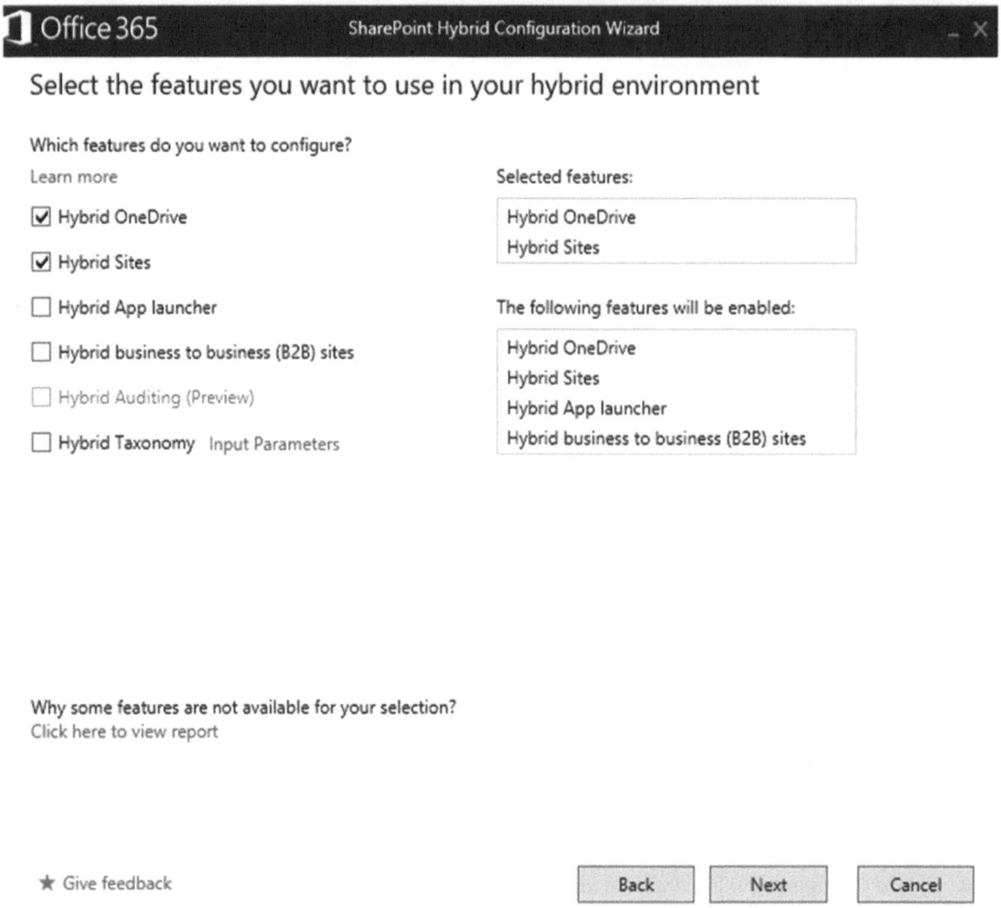

Figure 4-11. *Features selection for Hybrid environment*

As a general practice, I personally select to configure all services that will be enabled, such that my selected features match the features that will be enabled, as illustrated in Figure 4-12.

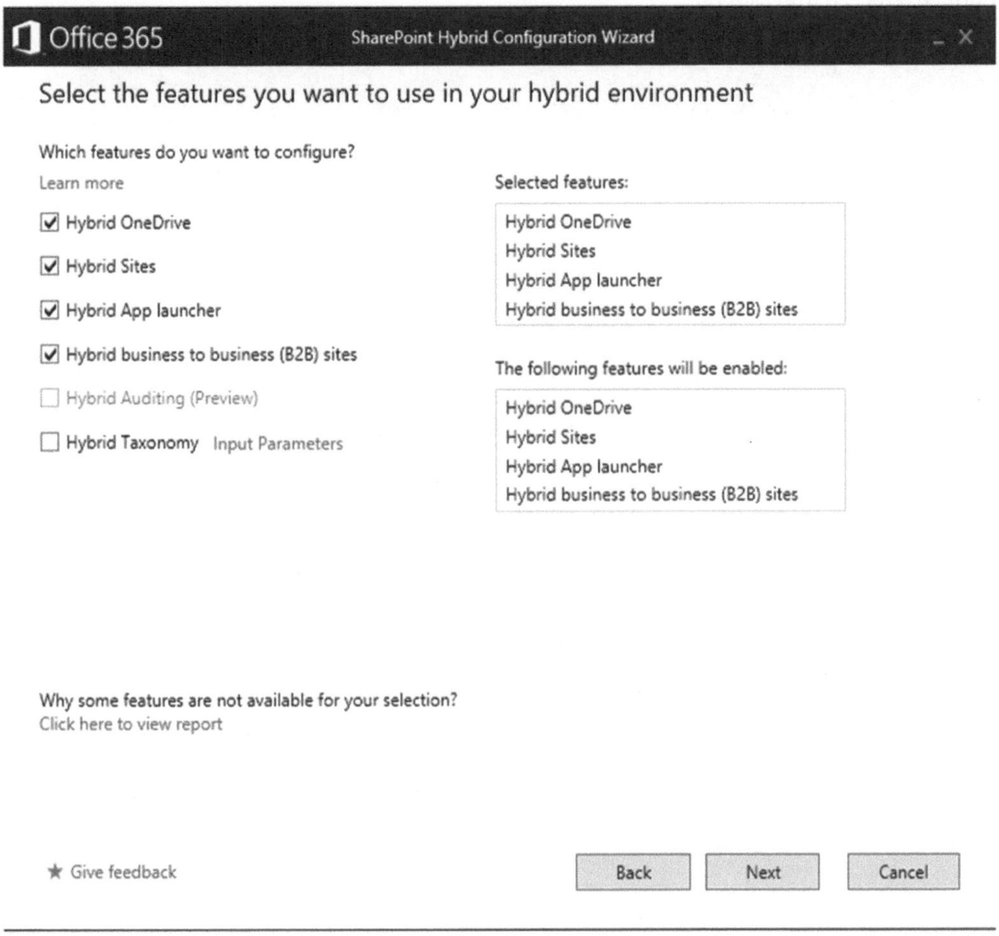

Figure 4-12. Recommended features selection for Hybrid environment

Clicking Next brings us into the configuration phase, and Hybrid Picker begins to configure the environment, based on the chosen configuration (Figure 4-13). As noted in the following screenshot, clicking Stop will prevent the configuration from continuing but will not roll back any changes that have been performed. Proceed with caution.

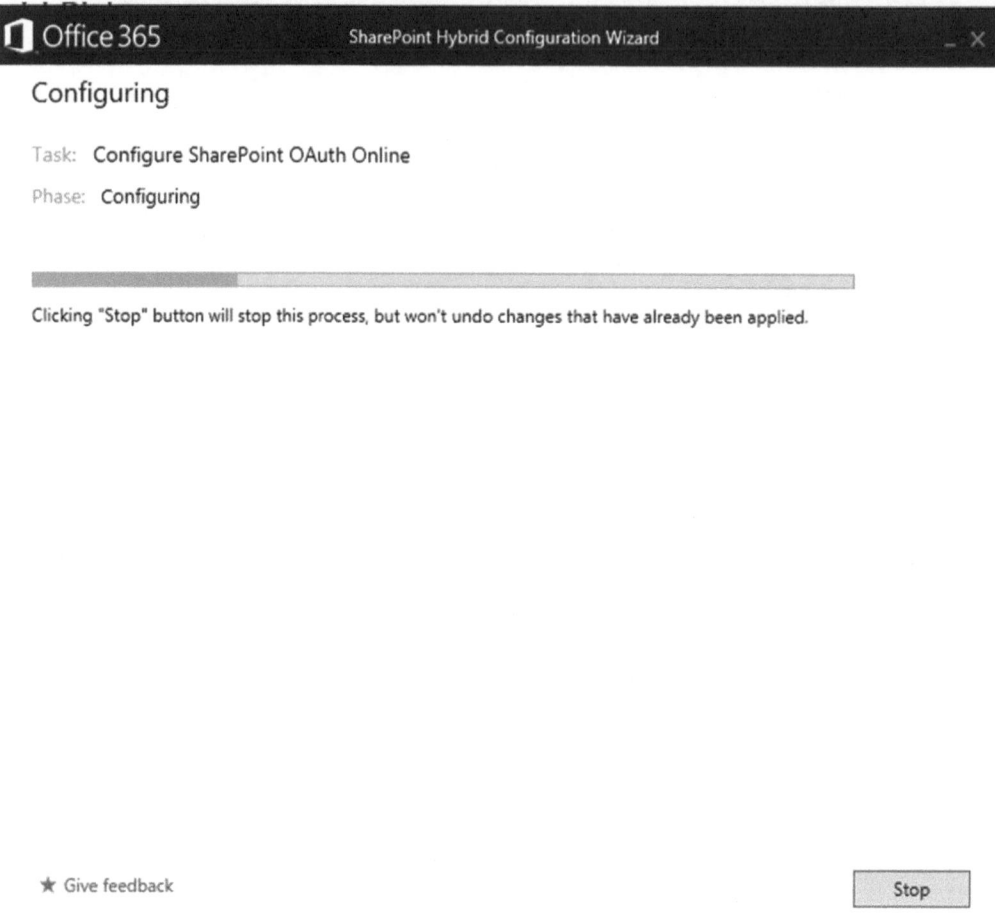

Figure 4-13. *Hybrid configuration progress*

Once this has been completed, a configuration summary page will be displayed. Assuming all remediation was performed before continuing with the configuration, the configuration will be successful, and the output will be similar to that shown in Figure 4-14.

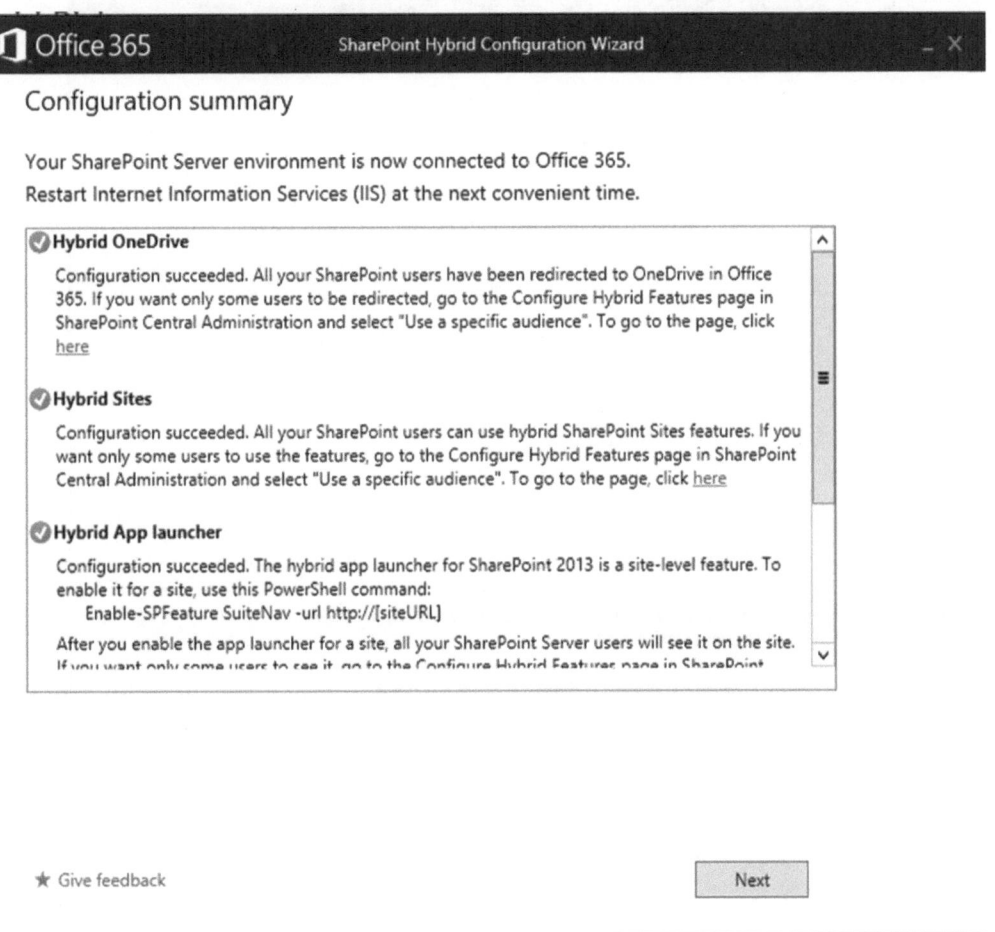

Figure 4-14. Hybrid configuration summary screen

Clicking Next will allow you an opportunity to submit feedback regarding your experience, which will be used to improve the experience in the future (Figure 4-15).

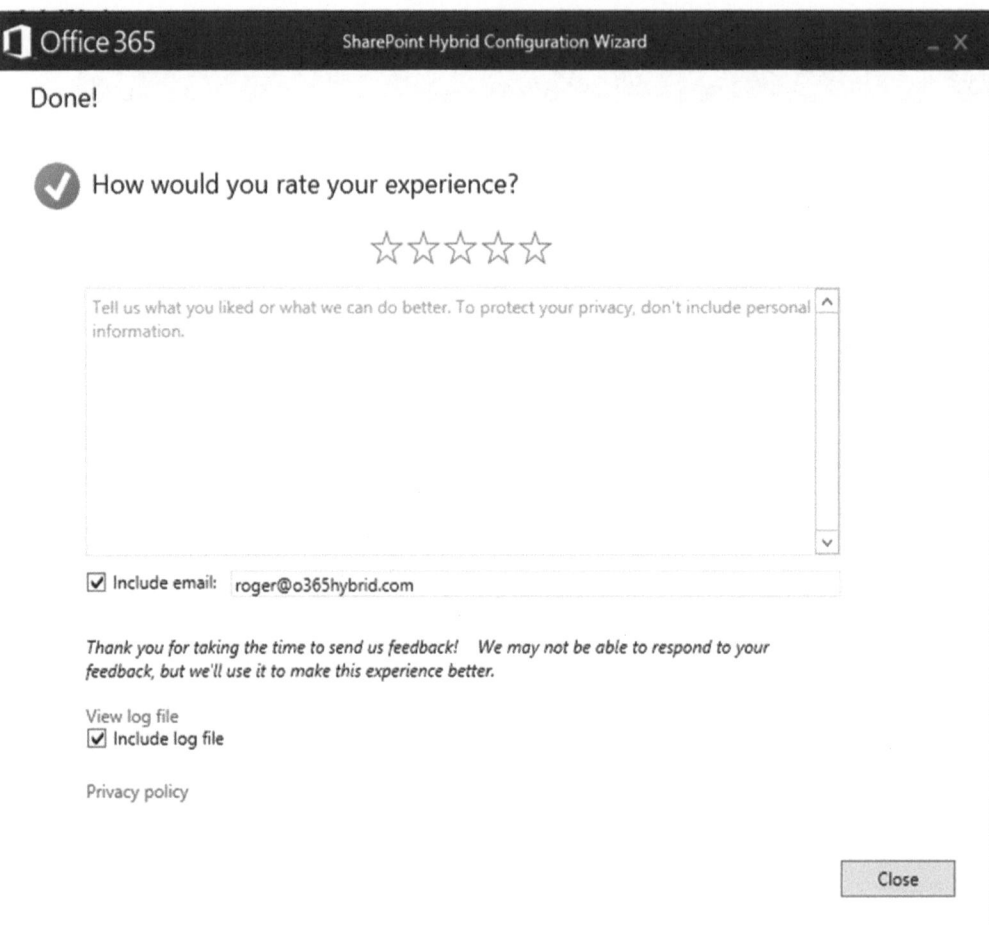

Figure 4-15. *Hybrid configuration successful completion screen*

Clicking Close concludes the Hybrid Picker configuration, and you are ready to validate that your hybrid features have been successfully configured.

Validating Extensible App Launcher, SharePoint Hybrid Sites, and Hybrid OneDrive Configuration

One of the primary requirements for a working SharePoint Hybrid environment is that a trust must exist between your local farm and your SharePoint Online tenant. After having run Hybrid Picker, you should see some additional trusts present in your on-premises environment. There may be a slight difference if you are comparing a SharePoint 2013 and a SharePoint 2016 environment. In SharePoint 2013, trusts will only be registered for the ACS STS, and in SharePoint 2016, you will see both the ACS STS and the EVOSTS entries. In SharePoint 2013, the screen will look like that shown in Figure 4-16.

Figure 4-16. *Trusted service consumers in SharePoint 2013*

In SharePoint 2016, it will look rather like Figure 4-17.

Figure 4-17. *Trusted service consumers in SharePoint 2016*

You can also validate that the additional trusts have been added in PowerShell by issuing the
Get-SPTrustedSecurityTokenIssuerPowerSell cmdlet. Each trust will be represented by the certificate
entry and will contain information similar to that shown in Figure 4-18.

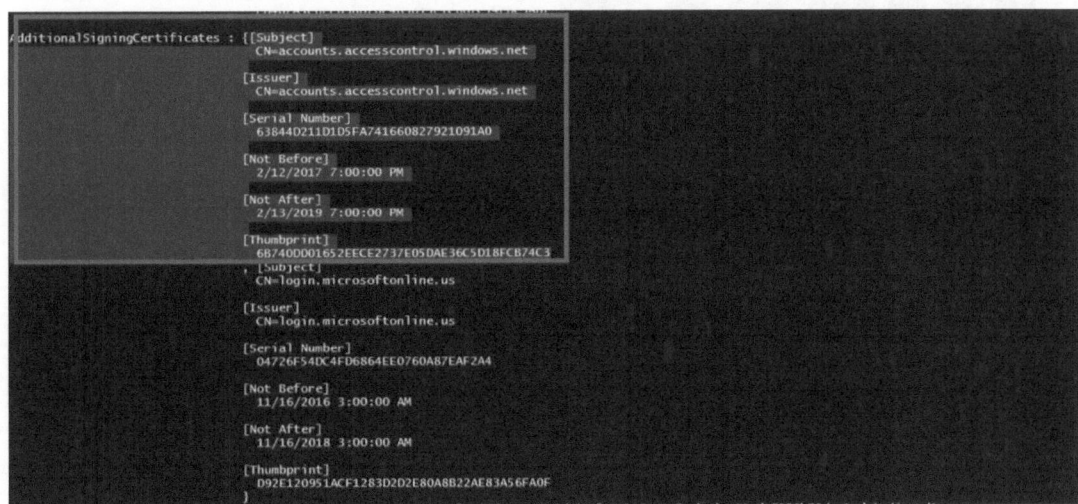

Figure 4-18. *Listing trusted service consumers with PowerShell*

Extensible App Launcher Validation

Once we have verified that all necessary trusts are in place, we should be able to move on to other validation steps. When it comes to validating the successful configuration of the Extensible App Launcher, the steps are slightly different, depending on the version of SharePoint you are using. In SharePoint 2013, Hybrid Picker will install the SuiteNav feature but will not activate the feature on your sites. This feature can be enabled on your sites by using the following PowerShell cmdlet:

```
Enable-SPFeature SuiteNav -url <SiteCollectionURL>
```

If you prefer to activate this feature on all sites in your environment at once, you could use the following cmdlet:

```
Get-SPSite | %{Enable-SPFeature SuiteNav -url $_.url -ErrorAction 0}
```

After having performed this action, you may have to wait for the application pool that hosts your SharePoint site to recycle. You could also force this action, or perform an IISReset. Each SharePoint 2013 site for which the SuiteNav feature has been activated will then include the Extensible App Launcher, as seen in Figure 4-19.

Figure 4-19. *App launcher in SharePoint 2013*

In SharePoint 2016, there will be no visual change, as the app launcher is already present and remains unchanged (see Figure 4-20).

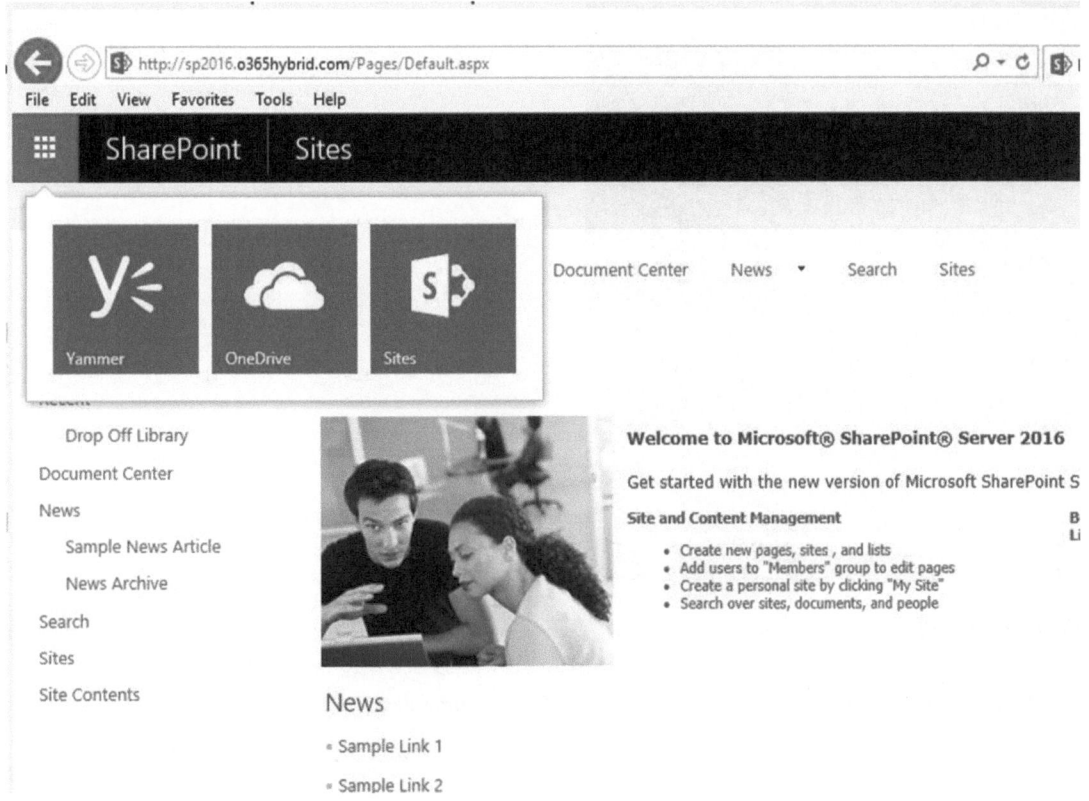

Figure 4-20. *App launcher in SharePoint 2016*

You can then add custom tiles to your Extensible App Launcher by using the Office 365 Admin Center. Expand Settings and click Organization profile (Figure 4-21).

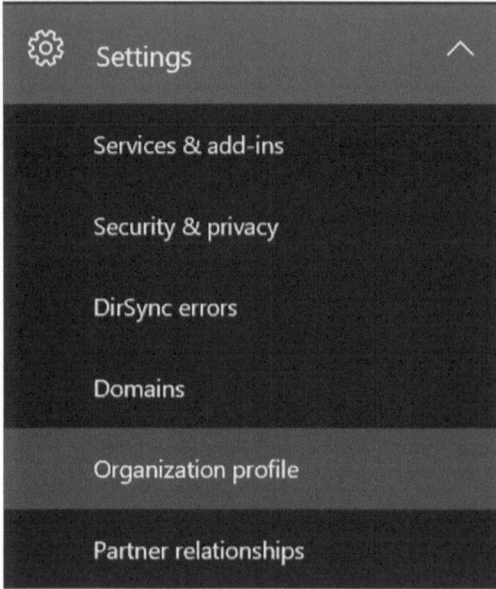

Figure 4-21. *Office 365 admin center*

In here, you will see a section to add custom tiles for your organization (Figure 4-22).

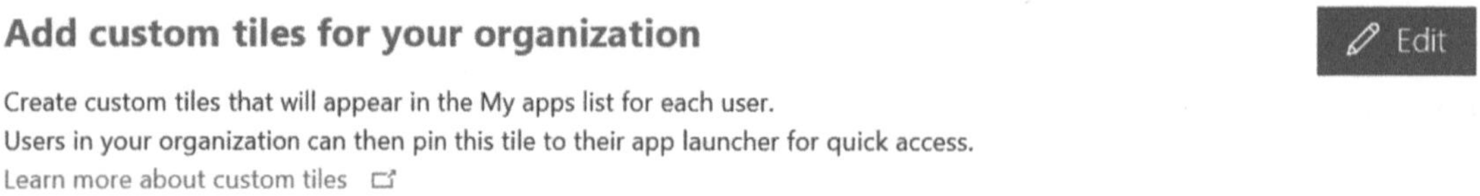

Add custom tiles for your organization

Create custom tiles that will appear in the My apps list for each user.
Users in your organization can then pin this tile to their app launcher for quick access.
Learn more about custom tiles

Figure 4-22. *Organizational tiles screen*

Click Edit and complete the requested details (Figure 4-23).

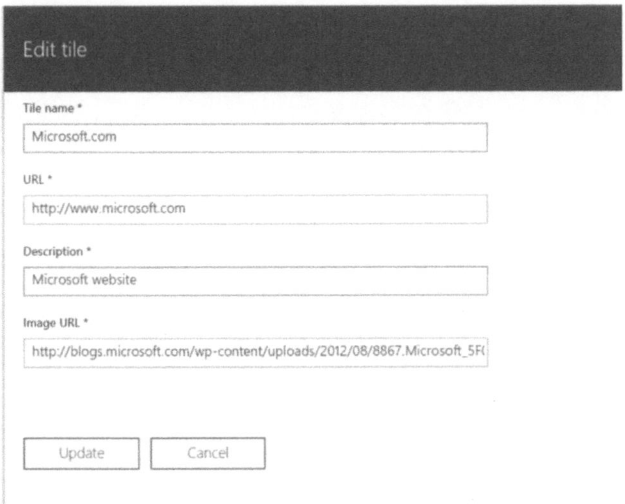

Figure 4-23. *Edit tile screen*

New or modified tiles may take up to a day to appear in SharePoint 2013 and SharePoint 2016 on-premises environments.

Hybrid OneDrive Validation

Validating Hybrid OneDrive configuration is relatively similar, regardless of whether you are completing these steps in SharePoint 2013 or SharePoint 2016. The first place we would look is in SharePoint Central Administration. As of this writing, in a fully patched environment, SharePoint central administration will have an "Office 365" link in the left navigation. Clicking this item will take you to a page with a link to "Configure hybrid OneDrive and Sites features." Clicking this link should show you your OneDrive for Business Hybrid configuration options, as displayed in Figure 4-24.

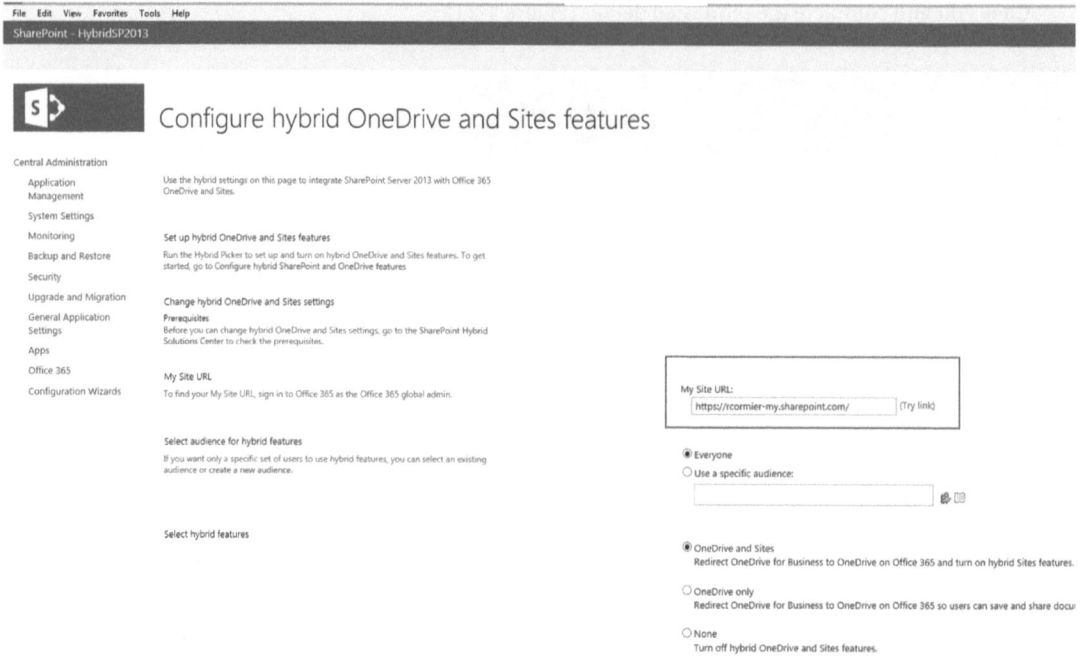

Figure 4-24. *Hybrid OneDrive and Sites features screen*

You should note that the URL of the `my-site` host in your tenant has been configured. It should be formatted as `https://<tenant>-my.sharepoint.com`.

You will also notice some additional options, such as the ability to choose between both hybrid OneDrive and Sites, just OneDrive, or to disable this hybrid functionality. In addition, you can also choose to limit the hybrid functionality to a select audience of users or enable this functionality to everyone in your organization.

Once the configuration has been validated, we can validate the functionality. This is quite simple. All you do is access OneDrive the way you would normally access OneDrive from your on-premises environment, with a user to whom this feature has been made available.

In SharePoint 2013, it will look like what is depicted in Figure 4-25 and Figure 4-26.

Figure 4-25. *OneDrive option in the SharePoint 2013 suite bar*

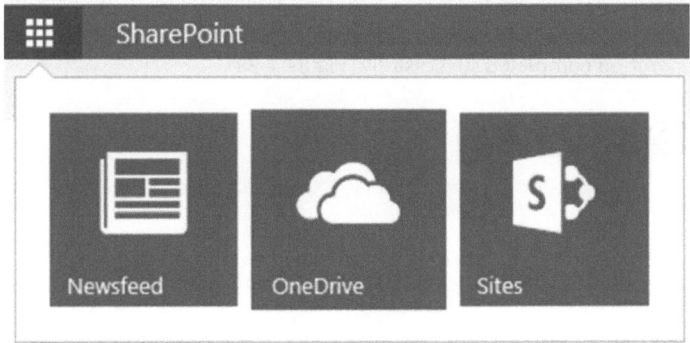

Figure 4-26. *OneDrive Option in the SharePoint 2013 app launcher*

And in SharePoint 2016, it will look like what is shown in Figure 4-27.

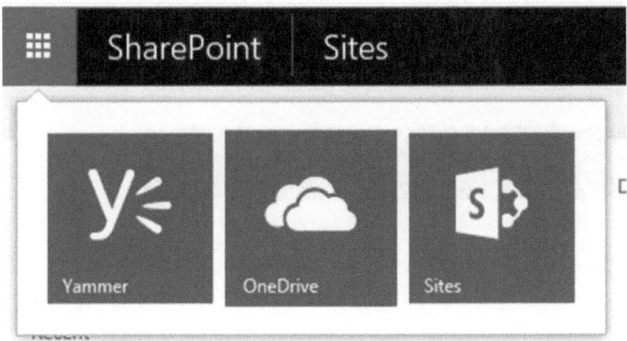

Figure 4-27. *OneDrive Option in the Sharepoint 2016 app launcher*

The hyperlink itself should point to a URL such as `https://<tenant>-my.sharepoint.com/_layouts/15/MySite.aspx?MySiteRedirect=AllDocuments&Source=SP2016`.

Validating Hybrid Sites

The first time you try to follow a site after you have configured hybrid sites, you may be prompted with the following message, if your OneDrive hasn't already been configured in SharePoint Online (Figure 4-28).

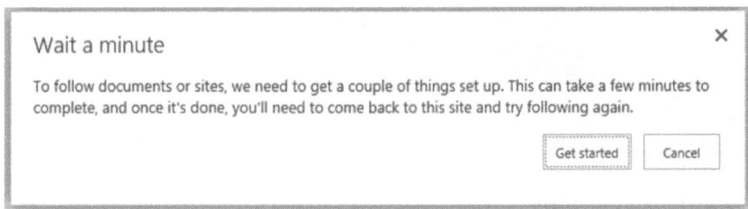

Figure 4-28. *Hybrid sites configuration wait screen*

Clicking Get Started will take you to your OneDrive for Business site in Office 365 and bring you through a quick introduction to OneDrive. Once everything has been set up, following a site will return a simple message to the user indicating that the operation completed successfully (Figure 4-29).

Figure 4-29. *Document Center notification*

Then, clicking on the Sites tile in the Extensible App Launcher will take you to your "followed" list in your OneDrive for Business site in SharePoint Online. Sites the user has followed in both the on-premises environment and the SharePoint Online tenant will be displayed (see Figure 4-30).

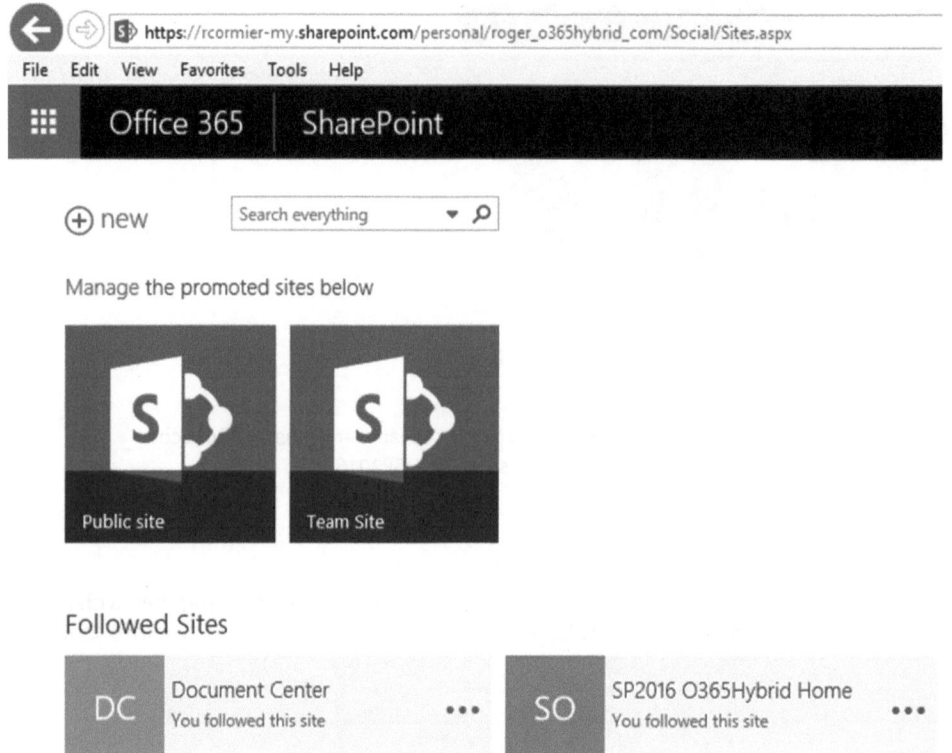

Figure 4-30. *Sites you are following in SharePoint 2016*

Summary

The purpose of these hybrid features is to help users have a seamless experience while their services are distributed among multiple premises, such as SharePoint on-premises and SharePoint Online. In the instance of the services discussed in this chapter, SharePoint online becomes the authoritative source, and SharePoint on-premises becomes a consumer of data stored in SharePoint Online.

Hybrid Picker is the most common method used when configuring SharePoint hybrid sites, hybrid OneDrive for Business, and the hybrid app launcher; however, you can still find many resources that illustrate that this process can also be performed via PowerShell. The main benefits of Hybrid Picker are the time savings and the accuracy of the solution. Using Hybrid Picker, SharePoint administrators can be confident that all the necessary environment and access prerequisites are met before beginning making any changes to their SharePoint environment. This helps to ensure that the environment is never left in an unknown state, which could result in a negative experience for end users.

Although not discussed in this chapter, there are other hybrid services available today in SharePoint 2013 and SharePoint 2016 that further improve the user experience across multiple premises. These hybrid services include multiple flavors of Search and Taxonomy (managed metadata).

CHAPTER 5

■ ■ ■

Hybrid Search

BY COLIN HUGHES-JONES

One of the most popular features in SharePoint is its search functionality. The service has been evolving with each version of SharePoint, incorporating new functionality and improving performance and relevance of results. The search service is responsible for crawling, indexing, and returning results from the index.

As organizations start to migrate workloads from SharePoint on-premises to SharePoint online contents, URLs will change. These location changes will create some user confusion. However, teaching users how to search the center with one of the hybrid search models can allow them to quickly locate the files they are looking for. In some cases, workloads will remain on-premise and never migrate to SharePoint online. In such cases, a hybrid search center can help users that heavily employ online services to locate on-premises files. Both SharePoint 2013 and 2016 support the two types of hybrid models: query-based and crawl-based.

The query-based hybrid model is considered the classic model and has been around for a few years. These hybrid solutions utilize a federated query model. Federated queries are issued to a remote search provider for content that is not directly indexed by the associated Search Service Application. Federated query results will also utilize a second result source, which will be displayed in a second result block separate from the primary result block on your results page. In these hybrid models, one result block would be for the on-premises results; the second result block would be for the SharePoint online results.

In the outbound hybrid model, a user issues a search query to an on-premises search center, and the results page from the on-premises search center returns two results blocks: one for the native on-premise results and the other federated from SharePoint online results.

The second model is the inbound hybrid model. By this model, users employ a search center hosted on SharePoint online. The online results page has a native result block from the SharePoint online content and a federated result block for the SharePoint on-premises results. The third hybrid model, known as two-way hybrid, is a combination of the outbound and inbound models. In other words, search centers both on-premises and in SharePoint online have result blocks for the other environment.

The crawl-based hybrid model was introduced in late 2015. This is a hybrid model that uses the Cloud Search Service Application. The Cloud Search Service Application will crawl content from the on-premises SharePoint farm and feed the files to SharePoint online, for indexing into a unified index with online content. Like the Enterprise Search Service Application, content sources can be configured to crawl the local SharePoint farm, remote SharePoint farms, file shares, web sites, and line-of-business applications. This service application allows for both on-premises and SharePoint online search centers to return mixed search results for on-premises and SharePoint Online in a single result block.

In the test screenshots, the on-premises farm has a document library with a series of text files with different animal names. SharePoint Online has a document library with a service of text files of various color names. In this chapter, we will walk through the advantages, disadvantages, and process of setting up the four hybrid search models.

© Nikolas Charlebois-Laprade et al. 2017
N. Charlebois-Laprade et al., *Expert Office 365*, DOI 10.1007/978-1-4842-2991-0_5

Prerequisites

Azure Active Directory Connect—This is a product designed to synchronize your user's identities between your on-premises environment and Office 365. It is deployed on a member server in the on-premises environment.

Active Directory Federation Services (AD FS)—This is an infrastructure service that allows for federated authentication across environments. Between on-premises and Office 365, it can be used as a single sign-on solution, requiring users to authenticate once to all the Office 365 services. On-premises users can be configured to be authenticated silently, without prompting for credentials. AD FS is not required if Azure Active Directory Connect has been configured with `Password sync`.

Azure Access Control Service—As its name states, it is a service based in Azure. It is a federated service used to authenticate users against identity providers such as Windows Azure Active Directory and others. A server to server (S2S) trust has to be set up between an Azure Access Control Service Application Proxy on the on-premises farm and Azure Active Directory. This will act as a trust broker service to authorize on-premises requests. The Cloud Search Service On-boarding script will configure this. This must be manually configured for the query Hybrid scenarios.

User Profile Service Application—This is SharePoint's local repository of user information synced from Active Directory. It can determine what right, group member, and claims a user has. In Hybrid scenarios, SharePoint resolves the querying UPN that is passed along with the query. The remote SharePoint farm (on-premises or SharePoint Online) will use the UPN, e-mail, or SIP address to resolve the user against its local User Profile Service and generate a claim.

Subscription Setting Service Application—Originally introduced in SharePoint 2010 to support multiple tenant environments, this is also used in SharePoint 2013 and 2016, to support app permissions.

App Management Service Application—This is used to support the app model in SharePoint and in Hybrid environments to register SharePoint as a high-trust app on-premises.

Query-Based Hybrid

The query-based hybrid system utilizes two different indexes: the on-premise's index and the SharePoint Online index. These solutions use two results source and query rules to trigger the additional results source to be displayed.

Outbound Hybrid Search

This allows your on-premises SharePoint farm to display query results from SharePoint Online. The process uses a result source to federate queries to SharePoint Online and a query rule to trigger that result source to be displayed when the result source has results. Outbound Hybrid Search can also be used in conjunction with the Cloud Search Service Application to display results on-premises.

Result Source

1. Select the search service application, site collection, or site you wish to create the result source on (Figure 5-1).

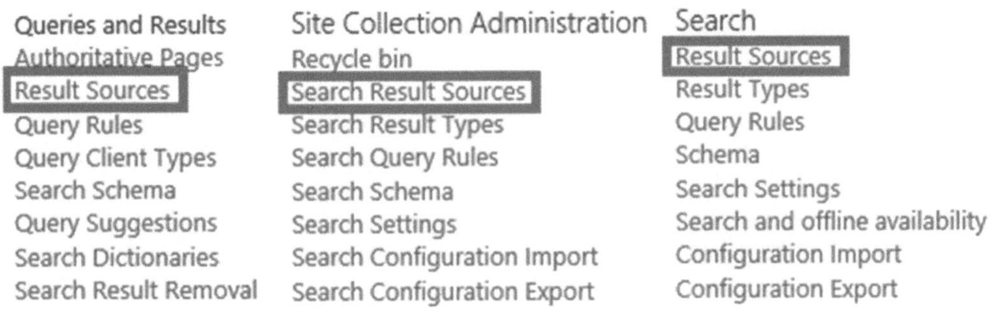

Queries and Results   Site Collection Administration   Search
Authoritative Pages   Recycle bin   Result Sources
Result Sources   Search Result Sources   Result Types
Query Rules   Search Result Types   Query Rules
Query Client Types   Search Query Rules   Schema
Search Schema   Search Schema   Search Settings
Query Suggestions   Search Settings   Search and offline availability
Search Dictionaries   Search Configuration Import   Configuration Import
Search Result Removal   Search Configuration Export   Configuration Export

Figure 5-1. Result source—service application (left), site collection (center), site (right)

2. On the Manage Source page, click New Result Source.

3. On the Add Result Source page (Figure 5-2), complete the following:

    a. In the Name text box, enter a name of your choice for the result source (example: Office 365).

    b. For the Protocol, select Remote SharePoint.

    c. For the Remote Service URL, type the address of the root site collection of the Office 365 SharePoint Online tenant whose results should be included (example: `https://Contoso.SharePoint.com`).

    d. For Credentials Information, ensure that the Default Authentication option is selected. This will pass the user's UPN as a claim, along with the query for the result source.

    e. Leave the remainder of the option with their default settings.

Enterprise Search Service Application: Add Result Source

ⓘ **Note:** This result source will be available to all sites. To make one for just a specific site, use the query rules page in its Site Settings.

General Information

Names must be unique at each administrative level. For example, two result sources in a site cannot share a name, but one in a site and one provided by the site collection can.

Descriptions are shown as tooltips when selecting result sources in other configuration pages.

Name

Office 365

Description

Protocol

Select Local SharePoint for results from the index of this Search Service.

Select OpenSearch 1.0/1.1 for results from a search engine that uses that protocol.

Select Exchange for results from an exchange source.

Select Remote SharePoint for results from the index of a search service hosted in another farm.

○ Local SharePoint
◉ Remote SharePoint
○ OpenSearch 1.0/1.1
○ Exchange

Remote Service URL

Type the address of the root site collection of the remote SharePoint farm.

https://Contoso.SharePoint.com

Type

Select SharePoint Search Results to search over the entire index.

Select People Search Results to enable query processing specific to People Search, such as phonetic name matching or nickname matching. Only people profiles will be returned from a People Search source.

◉ SharePoint Search Results
○ People Search Results

Query Transform

Change incoming queries to use this new query text instead. Include the incoming query in the new text by using the query variable "{searchTerms}".

Use this to scope results. For example, to only return OneNote items, set the new text to "{searchTerms} fileextension=one". Then, an incoming query "sharepoint" becomes "sharepoint fileextension=one". Launch the Query Builder for additional options.

{searchTerms} | Launch Query Builder |

Learn more about query transforms.

Credentials Information

If you are connecting to your intranet through a reverse proxy, please select and enter the SSO Id of the Single Sign On entry which stores the certificate used to authenticate against the reverse proxy. Else use the Default Authentication to authenticate against the remote SharePoint location.

◉ Default Authentication
○ SSO Id

| Save | Cancel |

Figure 5-2. *Outbound query result source*

4. Click Save to save the new result source.

Query Rule

Triggering parallel queries for one, multiple, or all result sources allows you to promote results, add additional result locks, and change the results ranking.

1. Select the search service application, site collection, or site your wish to create the Query Rule on. If the result source was created at the Search Service Application, it can be created there or on a site collection or site (Figure 5-3).

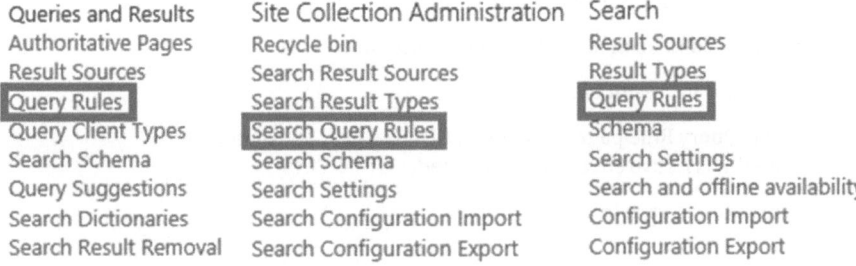

Figure 5-3. *Result source—service application (left), site collection (center), site (right)*

2. On the Manage Query Rules page, in the For what context do you want to configure rules? list box, select Local SharePoint Results (Figure 5-4).

Figure 5-4. *For what context do you want to configure rules?*

3. Click New Query Rule.

4. On the Add Query Rule page, do the following:

    a. In the General Information section, in the Rule Name box, type a name for the new query rule (example: Office 365).

    b. If you would like the Query Rule to trigger for additional contexts, click the Context link to expand it.

        •   After the Query is performed on these sources you can select All Sources, or add additional Context source with the Add Source Link

        •   Leave the remainder of the settings in this section set to their defaults.

    c. In the Query Condition section, click the Remove Condition, to have the query rule run for every query.

    d. In the Action section, under Result Blocks, click Add Result Block.

    e.   In the Add Result Block dialog box, complete the following:

- In the Query section, in the Search this Source list box, select the name of the result source that you created earlier (example: Office 365). In the items list box section, the default number of items that will be displayed is 2. You can increase or decrease this value to control the number of items that will be displayed.

- Click the Settings link to expand the section.

- Ensure that This block is always shown above core results is selected.

- No changes need to be made in the Routing section.

- Click OK to add the result block.

    f.   Back on the Add Query Rule page, click the Publishing link, to expand the section. Ensure the Is Active check box is selected.

    g.   Click the Save button to save the result source.

Testing

To test this setup, be sure that you are using a user account that has permissions to the on-premises content and is licensed and permissioned on content in SharePoint Online and take the following steps:

1. Using this account, go to the site collection or search center that you configured your query rule on and issue a query (Figure 5-5).

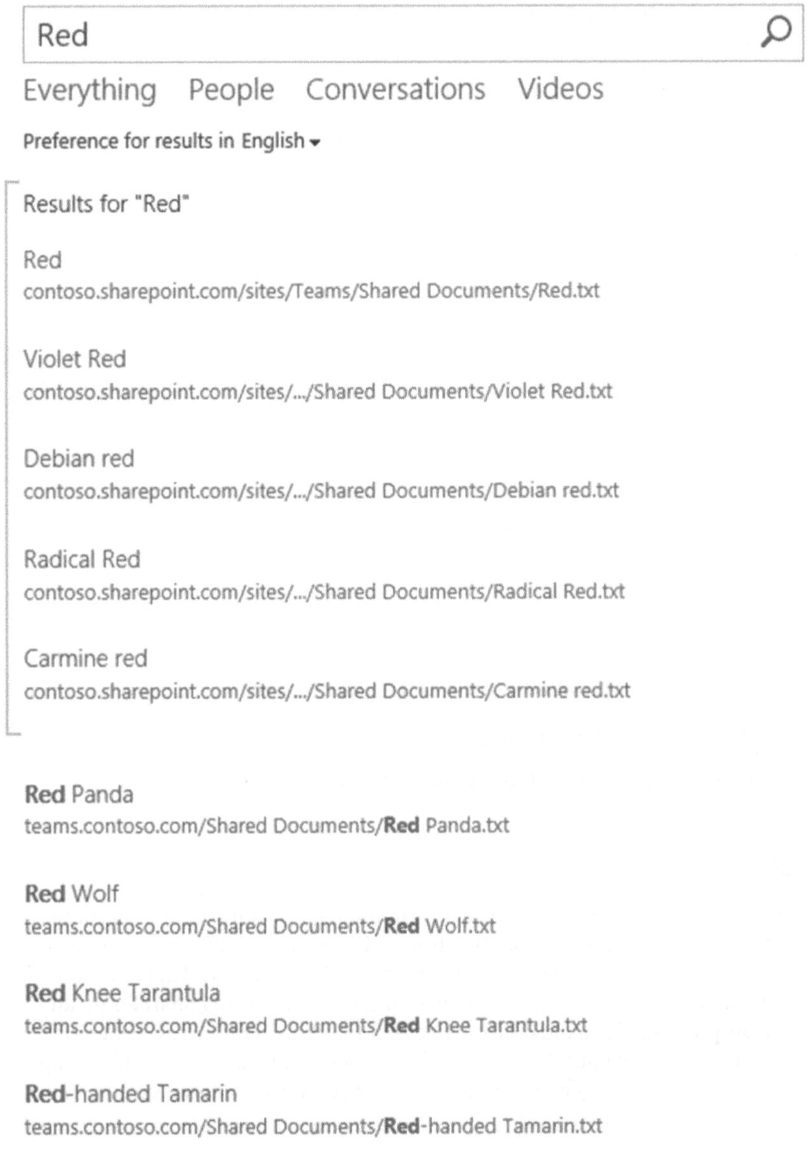

Red	🔍

Everything   People   Conversations   Videos

Preference for results in English ▾

Results for "Red"

Red
contoso.sharepoint.com/sites/Teams/Shared Documents/Red.txt

Violet Red
contoso.sharepoint.com/sites/.../Shared Documents/Violet Red.txt

Debian red
contoso.sharepoint.com/sites/.../Shared Documents/Debian red.txt

Radical Red
contoso.sharepoint.com/sites/.../Shared Documents/Radical Red.txt

Carmine red
contoso.sharepoint.com/sites/.../Shared Documents/Carmine red.txt

Red Panda
teams.contoso.com/Shared Documents/**Red** Panda.txt

Red Wolf
teams.contoso.com/Shared Documents/**Red** Wolf.txt

Red Knee Tarantula
teams.contoso.com/Shared Documents/**Red** Knee Tarantula.txt

Red-handed Tamarin
teams.contoso.com/Shared Documents/**Red**-handed Tamarin.txt

Figure 5-5. *Outbound query results*

    a.   If you receive results for on-premises content and SharePoint Online content, you have set everything up successfully.

    b.   If no results return for SharePoint Online, proceed to the next step.

2.   Browse to a SharePoint Online search center and confirm that you get results.

    a.   If you don't get any results, be sure you have permissions on the content you are trying to query. If you don't, update the permissions and wait a while for the content to be re-indexed.

    b.   If do you do get results, proceed to the next step.

3. Navigate back to your result source page and from the result source context menu, click the test button (Figure 5-6).

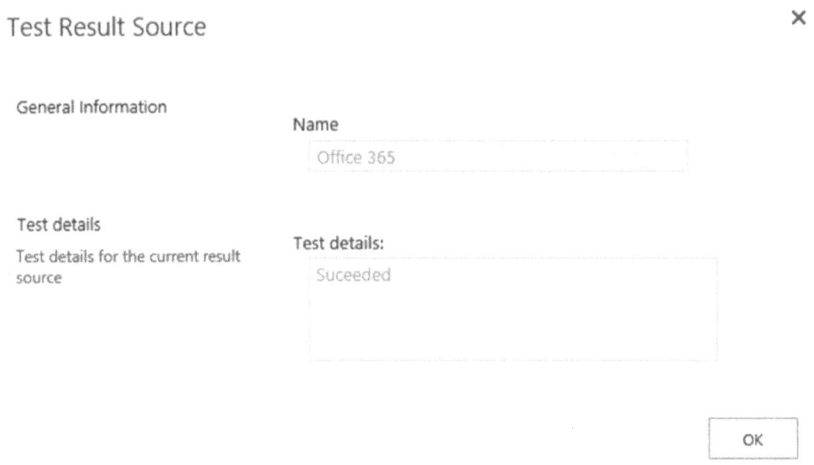

Test Result Source   ✕

General Information

Name

Office 365

Test details

Test details for the current result source

Test details:

Suceeded

OK

Figure 5-6. Outbound result source test

    a. If the test fails, troubleshoot the contents of the Test details section.

    b. If the test succeeds, proceed to the next step.

4. Navigate to your query rule and ensure that the settings are correct.

Inbound Hybrid Search

The Inbound Hybrid Search model is much like the Outbound Hybrid model. The difference is this time, instead of setting up the Results Source and Query Rule on the on-premises SharePoint farm, it will be set up in SharePoint Online. This setup is more complex than the Inbound Query Hybrid. This is because SharePoint Online must authenticate to the on-premises farm. In addition to configuring SharePoint, an Internet-facing end point for the on-premises farm must be created for SharePoint Online to be able to connect. A SharePoint Web Application must be published through a reverse application proxy. If you are using AD FS you can reuse the same Reverse Application Proxy server. A Secure Store Target Application will also be needed.

Publish On-Premises SharePoint Web Application with Client Certificate

You have the option of using one certificate or two for configuring your Web Application Proxy. The advantage of using a second certificate is that it authenticates that the incoming connect is not publicly accessible, unlike the External certificate.

Both certificates will have to be issued from a third-party Certificate Authority, to ensure that they are trusted both by the end user devices and Office 365. For this setup, we will use the two-certificate model.

Configure Claim Rule Mapping

When the user's query reaches the on-premises SharePoint farm, the Identity Claim must be rehydrated into a user claim for permission trimming the query. These steps are required for any build of SharePoint 2016 and SharePoint 2013 post April 2014 CU (build 15.0.4605.1000). These SharePoint builds are missing the OrgID rule claim mapping, which allows the on-premises farm to resolve the incoming user identity claim. This can easily be configured by opening the SharePoint Management Shell on any one of the SharePoint server's inbound query farm, by executing the following:

```
$config = Get-SPSecurityTokenServiceConfig
$config.AuthenticationPipelineClaimMappingRules.AddIdentityProviderNameMappingRule("OrgId
Rule", [Microsoft.SharePoint.Administration.Claims.SPIdentityProviderTypes]::Forms,
"membership", "urn:federation:microsoftonline")
$config.Update()
```

The change in behavior has been documented in the Microsoft Knowledge Base Article 3000380.

Configure Web Application Proxy

Windows 2012 has a Web Application Proxy. We will walk through the steps to configure the application proxy. We will be using Windows Server 2012 Web Application Proxy as a Reverse Proxy. The same Web Application Proxy server can be used to publish AD FS and the Inbound SharePoint Web Application.

To configure Windows Web Application Proxy to use Client Certificate Authentication, we must employ PowerShell. The following script will prompt for passwords for each certificate. It will then import both to the local computer personal certificate store, then set up the new application proxy.

```
$ExternalCertPath = "c:\Certs\SharePoint.Contoso.com.pfx"
$ClientCertPath = "c:\Certs\userauth.Contoso.com.pfx"
$ExternalURL = "https://SharePoint.Contoso.com"

<# If External and Internal URLs Please change the URL below
   are different please add
   -DisableTranslateUrlInRequestHeaders:$False and
   -DisableTranslateUrlInResponseHeaders:$False to the
   Add-WebApplicationProxyApplication cmdlet
 #>

$InteranlURL = $ExternalURL

#Get the thumbprint of the External URL Certificate

# Prompt for Certicate passwords
$ExternalCertPassword = Read-Host -Prompt "External Certificate Password" -AsSecureString
$ClientCertPassword = Read-Host -Prompt "Client Certificate Password" -AsSecureString

# Imports Certificates to the Local Computer Personal store
Import-PfxCertificate -FilePath $ExternalCertPath -Password $ExternalCertPassword -
CertStoreLocation Cert:\LocalMachine\My
Import-PfxCertificate -FilePath $ClientCertPath -Password $ClientCertPassword -
CertStoreLocation Cert:\LocalMachine\My
```

```
#Publish the Web Application
Add-WebApplicationProxyApplication `
-Name "Hybrid Inbound Rule" `
-BackendServerUrl $InteranlURL `
-ExternalUrl $ExternalURL `
-ExternalCertificateThumbprint $ExternalCert.Thumbprint `
-ExternalPreauthentication "ClientCertificate" `
-ClientCertificatePreauthenticationThumbprint $ClientCert.Thumbprint
```

To verify that the Web Application Proxy has been set up properly, you can use the following PowerShell command.

```
Get-WebApplicationProxyApplication -Name "Hybrid Inbound Rule" | fl
```

The output should resemble the following table (Table 5-1).

Table 5-1. *Output of the Get-WebApplicationProxyApplication PowerShell Command*

Property	Value
ADFSRelyingPartyID	Null
ADFSRelyingPartyName	Null
BackendServerAuthenticationMode	NoAuthentication
BackendServerAuthenticationSPN	Null
BackendServerCertificateValidation	None
BackendServerUrl	https://sharepoint.Contoso.com/
ClientCertificateAuthenticationBindingMode	None
ClientCertificatePreauthenticationThumbprint	5613187F8484BF8BAB21A679C4AFAD83B772177F
DisableHttpOnlyCookieProtection	FALSE
DisableTranslateUrlInRequestHeaders	FALSE
DisableTranslateUrlInResponseHeaders	FALSE
ExternalCertificateThumbprint	7FB20F1669386671F17C6ECA77FF691EBA3CAAF5
ExternalPreauthentication	ClientCertificate
ExternalUrl	https://sharepoint.Contoso.com/
ID	E0B88B55-9F6A-4677-0992-F1717702EE27
InactiveTransactionsTimeoutSec	300
Name	Hybrid Inbound Rule
UseOAuthAuthentication	FALSE
PSComputerName	Null

Configure Secure Store Target Application

The next step is to set up a secure store application, to attach the certificate's authentication to queries made to the on-premises farm.

1. Sign into your Office 365 tenant with a Global Admin account.

2. Click the App Launcher and select the Admin tile.

3. From the Admin Center, expand Admin Centers and click SharePoint.

4. On the SharePoint Admin Center, click Secure Store on the quick launch.

5. On the Secure Store page, click New in the Manage Target Application section of the ribbon.

6. On the Manage Target Application page, complete the following steps:

   a. In the Target Application Settings section, fill in the Target Application ID, Display Name, and Contact Email.

   b. In the Credentials Fields section,

      • Rename Windows User Name to Certificate and set the field type of Certificate.

      • Rename Windows Password to Certificate Password and set the field to Certificate Password.

   c. In Target Application Administrators, enter the user accounts you want to be able to administrate in the Secure Store Target Application.

   d. In the Member field, enter the user accounts you would like to be able to query the on-premises farm from SharePoint Online.

   e. Click OK to save the Target Application.

7. On the Manage Target Application page, select your new Target Application and in the Credentials, click Set.

8. In the Set credentials for secure store target Application dialog,

   a. Click Browse in the fields section.

   b. Navigate to your client certificate and upload it.

   c. Enter the password in both the certificate password fields. Be careful when entering the password, as it is not validated on this page.

SharePoint Online Result Source

To complete the setup of the inbound query, we will create a result source and query similar to the Outbound Query Rule. As it can on-premises, your result source can be created at three levels: Tenant Administration, Site Collection, and Site. Two changes must be made in this process.

The first is to the Remote Service URL. Instead of using the Office 365 root URL, you will use the URL of the externally published SharePoint Web Application (Figure 5-7).

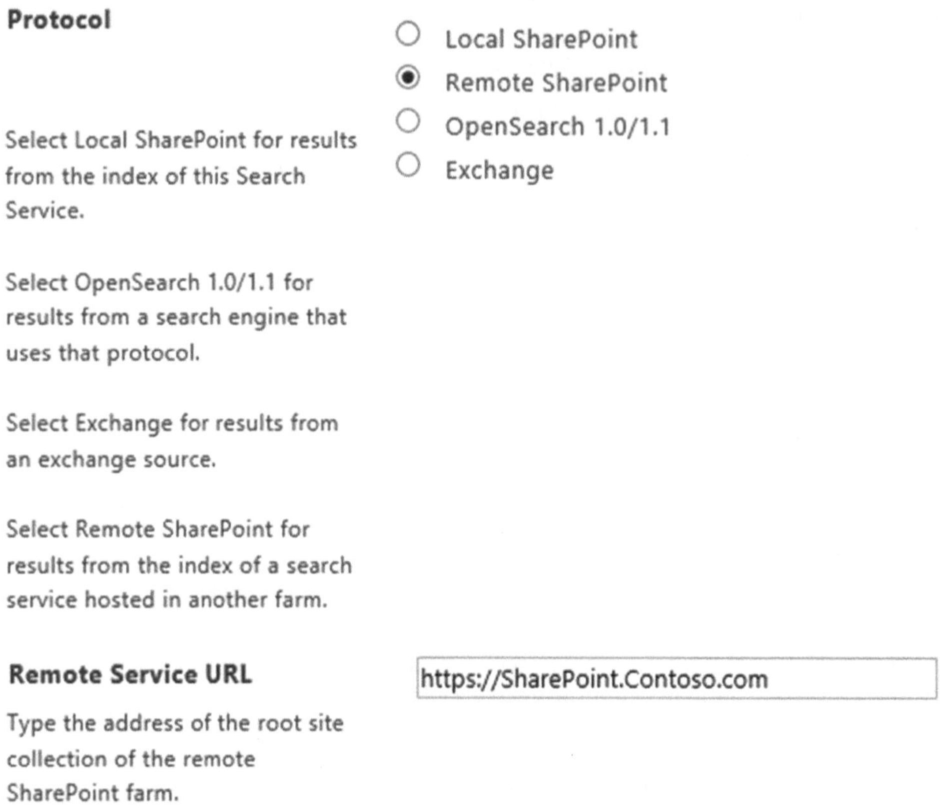

Protocol

    ○ Local SharePoint

    ◉ Remote SharePoint

Select Local SharePoint for results
from the index of this Search
Service.

    ○ OpenSearch 1.0/1.1

    ○ Exchange

Select OpenSearch 1.0/1.1 for
results from a search engine that
uses that protocol.

Select Exchange for results from
an exchange source.

Select Remote SharePoint for
results from the index of a search
service hosted in another farm.

Remote Service URL

https://SharePoint.Contoso.com

Type the address of the root site
collection of the remote
SharePoint farm.

Figure 5-7. SharePoint Online result source protocol

The second change required is to the Credentials Information section. Select the SSO Id radio button and in the Reverse proxy certificate (Secure Store Id) enter the ID of the secure store target application created in the preceding step (see Figure 5-8).

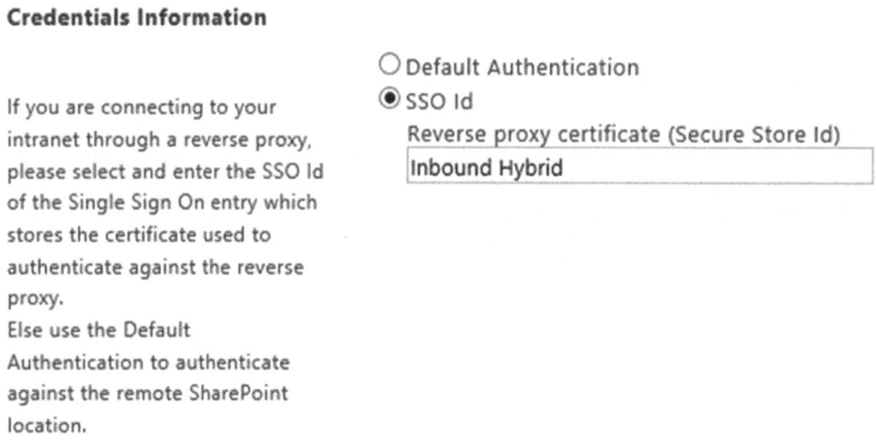

Credentials Information

    ○ Default Authentication

    ◉ SSO Id

If you are connecting to your
intranet through a reverse proxy,
please select and enter the SSO Id
of the Single Sign On entry which
stores the certificate used to
authenticate against the reverse
proxy.
Else use the Default
Authentication to authenticate
against the remote SharePoint
location.

    Reverse proxy certificate (Secure Store Id)

    Inbound Hybrid

Figure 5-8. SharePoint Online result source credentials

SharePoint Online Query Rule

Again, as it can on-premises, the query rule can be created at the same or lower level than the result source. The only change to the query rule will be to use the result source created in Office 365 to display the contents from the on-premises Search Service Application.

Testing

To test this setup, be sure that you are using a user account that has permissions to on-premises content and is licensed and permissioned on content in SharePoint Online and take the following steps:

1. Using this account, go to the site collection or search center that you configured your query rule on and issue a query (Figure 5-9).

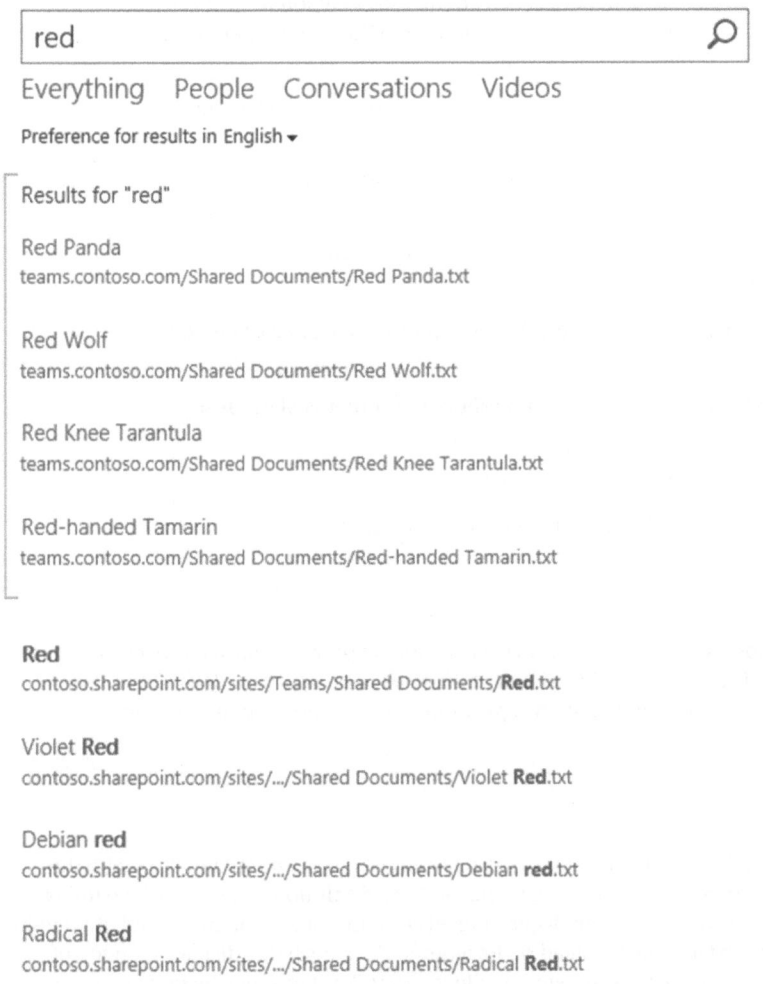

Figure 5-9. Inbound query results

    a.   If you receive results for SharePoint Online and on-premises content, you have set everything up successfully.

    b.   If no results return for SharePoint on-premises, proceed to the next step.

2.   Browse to a SharePoint on-premises search center and confirm that you get results.

    a.   If you don't get any results, ensure that you have permissions on the content you are trying to query. If you don't, update the permissions and start an incremental crawl on Cloud Search Service Application Content Source. Wait for the content to be re-indexed and try again.

    b.   If do you do get results, proceed to the next step.

3.   Copy the Client Certificate to a computer on an external network not connected to your corporate network. Install the Certificate to the user's personal certificate store. Open a browser, navigate to the publish SharePoint URL, and authenticate to the site with corporate credentials, if prompted.

    a.   If the SharePoint Site renders or you get an access denied proceed, to the next step.

    b.   If you are unable to connect, review your Reverses Application Proxy Configuration.

4.   Navigate back to your Result Source page and from the result source context menu, click the test button.

    a.   If the test fails with a 401 error, review the Security Token Service Claim Rule Mapping.

    b.   If the test fails with any other error, troubleshoot the contents of the Test Details section.

    c.   If the test succeeds, proceed to the next step.

5.   Navigate to your query rule and ensure the settings are correct.

Two-Way Hybrid Search

The Two-Way Hybrid Search model is a simplified way of seeing your on-premises farm has been configured with Outbound Query to SharePoint online and SharePoint Online has been configured with Inbound Queries to your on-premises farm. By completing the two previous configuration sections, you have set up Two-Way Hybrid Search.

Crawl-Based Hybrid

Hybrid crawl was introduced with SharePoint 2016. It was also backported into SharePoint 2013 with the August 2015 public update for SharePoint 2013. The crawl-braced hybrid solution creates a unified index. This allows the use of a single result source that can display mixed content from on-premises and SharePoint online. The unified results are ranked together, instead of the federated results being displayed on top of the local results. The unified results can be ranked together allows SharePoint to show the most relevant results, regardless of the source. This display helps reduce the user's confusion about what results are more important. As content is migrated from on-premises to SharePoint online, the search service detects the removal of the site from the on-premises environment and removes those results from the index. It also detects the creation of the site in SharePoint Online and indexes the content accordingly. Users see the same search results from one day to the next, minus the change in the URL of the items.

Crawl components of your on-premises SharePoint farm are used to retrieve content for indexing by Azure. SharePoint will be the first content source that will start crawling with the Hybrid Search Service application. However, the Cloud Search Service Application has all the same content source types as the Enterprise Search Service Application. Those sources are

- SharePoint sites
- Web sites
- File shares
- Exchange public folders
- Line-of-business data
- Custom repositories

SharePoint environments have a large corpus of data that they crawl and index. These indexes take up disk space on our SharePoint servers. To have a highly available Search Service Application, multiple copies (two to three) of each index partition must be spread across multiple servers in the SharePoint farm. With the Cloud Search Service Application, the index is stored in the cloud, removing the need for the storage required to support the indexing.

Create Cloud Search Service Application

A Cloud Search Service is created in a similar manner to an Enterprise Search Service Application. The first change is when creating the Search Service Application: the CloudIndex property must be set to true. This property disables the ContentPlugin in the Crawler component that is responsible for routing items to the Content Processing component for indexing. After the Search Service is created, the IsHybrid property of the Search Service Application must be initialized. The initialization process will activate AzurePlugin to replace ContentPlugin. AzurePlugin batches crawled content and prepares it to be pushed to Azure.

Because content processing is done in the cloud, and the index is stored there as well, there is no reason to scale out the Content Processing and Index components in the Search Service Application. However, you must have one of each of these components in the Search Service topology. You have the option to scale out the Crawling, Query, Admin, and Analytics Processing components. You must have one of each of these components. Scaling them out to different servers in the on-premises farm will create high availability for their services.

The following script creates a Cloud Search Service Application with one of each component required for a Search Service topology. The script assumes the Service Application pool already exists.

```
# Ensure SharePoint PowerShell Snapin is loaded
Add-PSSnapin Microsoft.SharePoint.PowerShell -ErrorAction SilentlyContinue

# Set varabiles up for Service Application

$SSAName = "Cloud Search Service Application"
$SVCAcct = "Contoso\SP_Farm"
$indexLocation = "E:\CloudSearch"
$AppPoolName = "ServiceApplicationPool"
$DatabaseName = "SP2016_CloudSearch"

# Get the Service Application pool
$AppPool = Get-SPServiceApplicationPool -Identity $AppPoolName

# Get the local Search Service Instance for additional servers can be set to other vaiables
$SSI = get-spenterprisesearchserviceinstance -local
```

```
# Create the directory to store the index
New-Item $indexLocation -ItemType Directory

# Create Cloud Search Service Application
$SearchApp = New-SPEnterpriseSearchServiceApplication -Name $SSAName -applicationpool
$AppPool -databasename $DatabaseName  -CloudIndex $true

# Create Service Application Proxy for Search Service Application
$SSAProxy = new-spenterprisesearchserviceapplicationproxy -name $SSAName -SearchApplication
$SSAName

# Get the default Topology Object and create a new Topology object
$initialSearchTopology = $searchApp | Get-SPEnterpriseSearchTopology -Active
$newSearchTopology = $searchApp | New-SPEnterpriseSearchTopology

# Create Admin component, more then one component can be deployed to additional servers
New-SPEnterpriseSearchAdminComponent -SearchTopology $newSearchTopology
-SearchServiceInstance $SSI

# Create Analytics component
New-SPEnterpriseSearchAnalyticsProcessingComponent -SearchTopology $newSearchTopology -
SearchServiceInstance $SSI

# Create Crawl component , more then one component can be deployed to additional servers
New-SPEnterpriseSearchCrawlComponent -SearchTopology $newSearchTopology -
SearchServiceInstance $SSI

# Create Content Processing Component
New-SPEnterpriseSearchContentProcessingComponent -SearchTopology $newSearchTopology -
SearchServiceInstance $SSI

# Create Query Processing Component, more then one component can be deployed to additional servers
New-SPEnterpriseSearchQueryProcessingComponent -SearchTopology $newSearchTopology -
SearchServiceInstance $SSI

# Create Index Component
New-SPEnterpriseSearchIndexComponent -SearchTopology $newSearchTopology -
SearchServiceInstance $SSI -RootDirectory $indexLocation -IndexPartition 0

# Active the new Topology Object
Set-SPEnterpriseSearchTopology $newSearchTopology

# Default Topology Object
Remove-SPEnterpriseSearchTopology -Identity $initialSearchTopology
```

Onboarding the Search Service to SharePoint Online

Microsoft has made the onboarding process to connect a Cloud Search Service Application to your
SharePoint Online service very simple. The script Onboard-CloudHybridSearch.ps1 is available on the
Microsoft download site. Before you run this script, you must install two additional components on that
server. If they are not present, the script will fail, requesting that the components be downloaded and

installed. Most administrators will install these modules on their Central Administration Server(s), as these are the servers that do most of the administration of the farm. The prerequires, which can be downloaded from the Microsoft download site, are

1. Microsoft Online Services Sign-In Assistant

2. Microsoft Online Services Module

The file name you will want to search for on the Microsoft download site is `CloudHybridSearchScripts.zip`. It contains the `Onboard-CloudHybridSearch.ps1`, along with the `CreateCloudSSA.ps1` script. The `CreateCloudSSA.ps1` is another way to create a single server Cloud Search Service Application.

To complete the onboarding process, open a new PowerShell console and set the location to the directory containing the `Onboard-CloudHybridSearch.ps1` script. You will have to provide the SharePoint Online portal URL or the Cloud Search Service Application name or GUID, if the farm has more than one Search Service Application.

The script starts by determining if a Search Service Application was provided. If not, and the service has only one Search Service Application, it will use it. The selected Search Service Application `CloudIndex` property will be confirmed, and the `IsHybrid` property will be set to `true`.

The tenant admin credentials are requested, if not provided at execution, and a connection is made to Microsoft Online. The tenant information and Azure Active Directory ID are retrieved from Microsoft Online.

The local SharePoint farm is configured next. The script determines if the Azure Access Control Service Application Proxy exists, and the script exits if it does, prompting for it to be manually removed. If it does not exist, the Azure Access Control Service Application will be created with the name ACS, and it is added to the default proxy group. The ACS Service Application Proxy is required to be in the default proxy group for authentication to work. The S2S Trust Broker is configured between the proxy and Azure Active Directory. A SharePoint Online Application Principal Management Service Application Proxy, named SPO App Management Proxy, is created, with a connection to the tenant SharePoint portal.

The security token local login certificate is uploaded to the Microsoft Online tenant as a new service principal credential for SharePoint Online. The Azure Search Connector Service URLs are added to a new Service Principal name in the Microsoft Online tenant as well. Then, the on-premises farm is connected to SharePoint Online.

The Microsoft Online Tenant is prepared for the Cloud Hybrid Search Service. This process can take up to four minutes. Service information is collected and validated and then configured on the Cloud Search Service Application. Finally, the SharePoint Timer Service is restarted.

On-Premises Content Source

The configuration of the content sources in a Cloud Search Service Application is the same as for a regular Enterprise Search Service Application. When crawling large start addresses, the status polling for the batches that have been submitted to Azure can be overly aggressive and trigger throttling responses from Azure. Setting the `EnableNoGetStatusFlight` property on the Search Service Application will stop the pooling and prevent you from getting throttled. This can be done with the following code. You must restart the SharePoint Host Controller for this property change to take effect.

```
$ssa=Get-SPEnterpriseSearchServiceApplication
$ssa.SetProperty("EnableNoGetStatusFlight",1)
$ssa.update()
```

The Search Gatherer Azure Plugin performance object in Performance Monitor can also be used to monitor the progress of your crawls. Another common bottleneck that can reduce crawl performance is the server's uplink to the Internet. An example of this would be the web front end rendering the content for the crawler.

Testing

Once your first full crawl has completed, you are ready to test SharePoint Online. As in the case of federated query hybrid tests, you must ensure that you employ a user account with permission for on-premises content and that is licensed and has permissions for content in SharePoint Online. Navigate to your SharePoint Online Search Center and issue a query. You should see a mix of on-premises and SharePoint Online content returned (Figure 5-10).

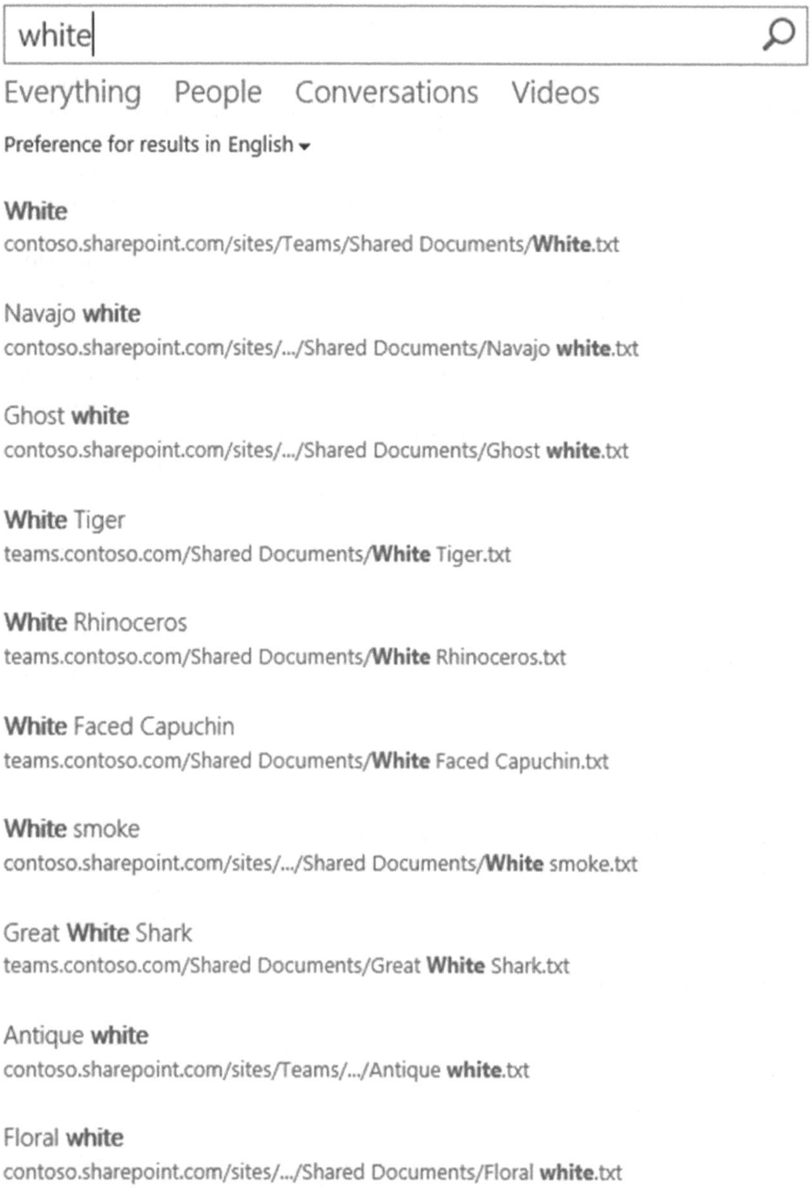

white   🔍

Everything   People   Conversations   Videos

Preference for results in English ▾

White
contoso.sharepoint.com/sites/Teams/Shared Documents/**White**.txt

Navajo **white**
contoso.sharepoint.com/sites/.../Shared Documents/Navajo **white**.txt

Ghost **white**
contoso.sharepoint.com/sites/.../Shared Documents/Ghost **white**.txt

White Tiger
teams.contoso.com/Shared Documents/**White** Tiger.txt

White Rhinoceros
teams.contoso.com/Shared Documents/**White** Rhinoceros.txt

White Faced Capuchin
teams.contoso.com/Shared Documents/**White** Faced Capuchin.txt

White smoke
contoso.sharepoint.com/sites/.../Shared Documents/**White** smoke.txt

Great **White** Shark
teams.contoso.com/Shared Documents/Great **White** Shark.txt

Antique **white**
contoso.sharepoint.com/sites/Teams/.../Antique **white**.txt

Floral **white**
contoso.sharepoint.com/sites/.../Shared Documents/Floral **white**.txt

Figure 5-10. *Cloud Search Service query results*

Document Previews

In SharePoint 2013, with the Office Web Application Server, and in SharePoint 2016, with the Office Online Server, the query result page will show document previews for Office documents. These previews are available for results from SharePoint Online. However, for on-premises content, they are not displayed, unless the Office Web Application Server or Office Online Server are published externally to the Internet. The proper steps to publish these servers has been published on Microsoft's TechNet site, in the article "Plan to Publish Applications through Web Application Proxy."

On-Premises Query Options for Cloud Hybrid Search

The Enterprise Search Service Application, with the *CloudIndex* property set to true, will switch the plug-ins used by the crawl components to redirect the parsed content to Azure. No changes are made to the query process for these Service Applications; they are still directed to the local index, which will have no content. The parsed content that is directed to Azure is stored in the same index locations that are used by SharePoint Online for its query process. No further changes are needed to allow it to return cloud and on-premises content.

In terms of queries issues on on-premises sites, there are a few configuration changes that can be made to ensure that your user's queries are processed by SharePoint Online. The first option can be used independently or in conjunction with one or both the other options. This option is to set up the outbound federated hybrid query result source as described earlier in this chapter. After the result source is saved, I recommend creating the result source at the Search Service Application level and making it the default result source from its context menu on the result sources page, after it has been saved. Look for the local SharePoint results. Each result source and query rule should also be duplicated and targeted at SharePoint Online. You will also require multiple query components on different servers, if you want high availability for your search queries.

The second option you can configure is to set the Global Search Center URL in the Cloud Search Service Application to a search center site collection in SharePoint Online. You can use this in conjunction with the first or third options. This will redirect the Everything, People, and Conversations search box option to the SharePoint Online Search Center. This can be set up by browsing to the Search Service Administration page and clicking the URL to the right of Global Search Center URL. The contextual options of This Site and This List will still be directed to the site's current default result sources (Figure 5-11).

System Status

Administrative status	Running
Crawler background activity	None
Recent crawl rate	0.00 items per second
Recent query rate	0.00 queries per minute
Default content access account	Contoso\SP_Services
Contact e-mail address for crawls	Crawler@Contoso.com
Proxy server for crawling and federation	None
Search alerts status	On Disable
Query logging	On Disable
Global Search Center URL	https://Contoso.SharePoint.com/search/pages

Figure 5-11. *Global Search Center URL*

The third option is to redirect the Contextual Search result page on a site-by-site level to SharePoint Online. It is a good idea to use this in conjunction with the second option. It can be manually set or confirmed with the following steps.

1. From an on-premises site collection, navigate to Site Settings.

2. On the Site Settings page, click Search Settings, under Site Collection Administration (Figure 5-12).

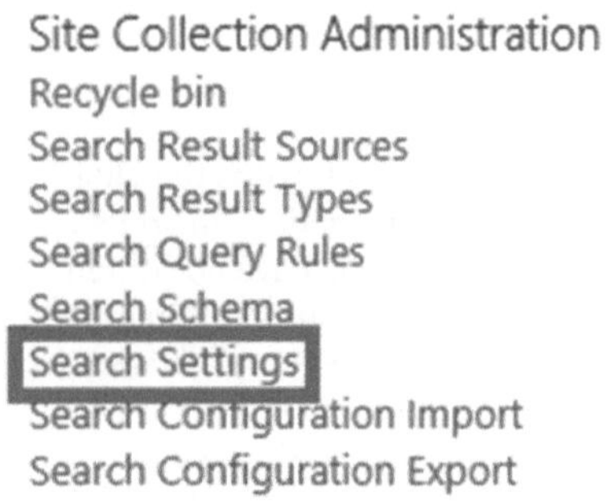

Site Collection Administration
Recycle bin
Search Result Sources
Search Result Types
Search Query Rules
Search Schema
Search Settings
Search Configuration Import
Search Configuration Export

Figure 5-12. *Site collection search settings*

3. On the Site Collection Administration Search Settings page, under Which search results page should queries be sent to? (see Figure 5-13),

   a. Disable Use the same Results Page Setting as my Parent.

   b. Send queries to a custom results page.

   c. In the results page URL, enter the following text: {SearchCenterURL} /Results.aspx.

   d. * {SearchCenterURL} is a token that can use the value of Search Center URL from the top section of the page. If that value is null, it will inherent the Global Search Center URL for the Search Service Application.

   e. Click OK to save the settings.

Site Collection Administration Search Settings

Use this page to configure how Search behaves in this site collection. The shared Search Box at the top of most pages will use these settings. Note: A change to these settings may take up to 30 minutes to take effect.
Changes made here will affect this site collection and all sites within it.

Enter a Search Center URL

When you've specified a search center, the search system displays a message to all users offering them the ability to try their search again from that Search Center.

Search Center URL:

[   ]

Example: /SearchCenter/Pages or http://server/sites/SearchCenter/Pages

Which search results page should queries be sent to?

Custom results page URLs can be relative or absolute.

URLs can also include special tokens, such as {SearchCenterURL}. This token will be replaced by the value in the "Search Center URL" property. If the value in this property ever changes, any URL using the token will update automatically.

Example:
{SearchCenterURL}/results.aspx

☐ Use the same results page settings as my parent.

⦿ Send queries to a custom results page URL.

Results page URL:

[{SearchCenterURL}/results.aspx   ]

Example: /SearchCenter/Pages/results.aspx or http://server/sites/SearchCenter/Pages/results.aspx

◯ Turn on the drop-down menu inside the search box, and use the first Search Navigation node as the destination results page.

[OK]   [Cancel]

Figure 5-13. *Site collection search settings page*

4. It can take up to 30 minutes for this setting change to take effect.

The following PowerShell code can also be used to update a site collection. It can be nested in a foreach loop for all site collection.

```
$Site = Get-SPSite <URL>
$Web = $Site.RootWeb
$Web.SetProperty("SRCH_SB_SET_SITE", "{`"Inherit`":false,`"ResultsPageAddress`":`"{Search
CenterURL}/results.aspx`",`"ShowNavigation`":false}")
$Web.Update()
```

Search Schema Changes

SharePoint 2013 introduced local search schemas at the site and site collection levels. These are present in SharePoint 2016 as well. However, when using a Cloud Search Service Application, it's access is limited to the crawled properties. It cannot update any of the mappings between crawled and managed properties. Any modifications you make must be updated from the SharePoint Online Tenant Manage Search Schema page in the Search section.

The Cloud Search Service Application has also brought a new crawled and managed property, both called `IsExternalContent`. This is a Boolean property and is set to `true` for all content crawled from the Cloud Search Service Application, as it is external to the index location of SharePoint Online. This property can be used in a query or result source, to filter between SharePoint Online content and on-premises content.

People Search

SharePoint Online is configured to automatically import your users' information from Azure Active Directory into the SharePoint Online User Profile Service. The User Profile server is also crawled by SharePoint Online and can present that information in the People Search results. If your organization has used line-of-business applications to augment your users' profiles, you will most likely want to index the on-premises User Profile Service. This can be done by adding the URL of a web application connected to the User Profile Service Application Proxy replacing `http` with `sps3` or `https` with `sps3s`.

Indexing this content will have duplicate profiles displayed in results. A new Results Source will be created that uses the `IsExternalContent` property set to `1` or `true`, to filter results to on-premises users only, with a query transformation of

```
{?{searchTerms} ContentClass=urn:content-class:SPSPeople IsExternalcontent:1}
```

SharePoint Online profiles can be displayed with a similar query transformation that has a `NOT` before the `IsExternalContent`, as shown following:

```
{?{searchTerms} ContentClass=urn:content-class:SPSPeople NOT IsExternalcontent:1}
```

Removing On-Premises Content from SharePoint Online

Special consideration needs to be taken when removing content indexed through the Cloud Search Service Application. You should ***never use the Reset Index*** option in the service application. This will orphan the on-premises content in the cloud index. When using incremental crawls, the Cloud Search Service Application can remove content from the index, by deleting it on-premises and waiting for the next incremental crawl. You can set the `NoCrawl` flag at the list or site level and wait for the next incremental crawl. You can also create a crawl rule to exclude the content and then start a full crawl of just that URL from the crawl log. The final option to remove all content is to delete the start address from the content source. When a start address is removed from a content source, SharePoint automatically starts a delete crawl and removes all content from the index that was crawled because of that start address. If you plan on deleting the content source, you should allow the delete crawl to finish before removing the content source.

Summary

By introducing the hybrid search functionality within the SharePoint product, Microsoft has opened the door to new, robust enterprise search scenarios. Today, Hybrid is still one of the top areas of investment the company continues to focus on within the business productivity tool that is SharePoint. As iterated many times by the Product Group during events such as the SharePoint Virtual Summit, which took place on May 16, 2017, SharePoint on-premises is far from being dead, and it is making it easier than ever to access and consume your content, wherever it resides.

CHAPTER 6

■ ■ ■

SharePoint Recovery

BY DANIEL BRUNET

In this chapter, you will learn everything that you need to be aware of concerning recovery for SharePoint. This book has a lot of great technical content, produced by some of my excellent colleagues, and while this chapter will probably be the least technical, its subject is one of the most difficult to implement. The challenge with recovery is rarely due to the technical aspect but mainly processes and expectations.

In all my years at Microsoft, working on support, knowledge transfer, or program assessment, data recovery has continuously been an area in which opportunities for improvement with SharePoint exist. While this book focuses on Office 365 (O365), in this chapter, I will also cover SharePoint infrastructure recovery on-premises.

I will cover many aspects of recovery that you may have to discuss with business/application owners and backup and/or storage groups and that you may have to implement. I will also discuss the different capabilities (or lack thereof) between recovery on-premises and on a Software as a service (Saas) such as SharePoint Online.

As most of you know, SharePoint is a multilayered platform, and like many Microsoft products, there are multiple ways to achieve the same goal. Depending on implementation and complexity, many methods can be employed. I will provide the right approach, in general, but will focus on large enterprise scenarios. I will give you the other options available and their pros and cons.

Note that some reference will be made to disaster recovery (DR), but this chapter is not about that. The only DR scenario will be that of a failure of the farm, and not the underlying infrastructure. I will not cover high availability or data center issues.

Infrastructure

One of the key statements that I make in workshops that you can also find in TechNet articles is that the best infrastructure recovery process is a strong automated build process. Owing to the stateless nature of most SharePoint servers, there are many scenarios wherein build automation can offer clear advantages over other forms of troubleshooting and/or recovery. With that said, the most critical and most complex recovery scenario is, of course, the SharePoint farm. Fortunately, in O365, this is something you don't have to worry about. The patching process at Microsoft is very mature and has improved with the lessons learned from deployments at this scale. This is one of the benefits that you see in SharePoint 2016, with which you can now have zero downtime patching and a much more robust update process (PSconfig/Wizard). This comes from our own experience at upgrading SharePoint in such a large scale as O365.

Many factors may also impact the degree of difficulty you will face when recovering other SharePoint components, for example, recovering a faulty SharePoint server. I have seen many issues with customers trying to restore a server from a virtual machine snapshot, and while this should be very simple, it is unsupported and can lead to more problems.

© Nikolas Charlebois-Laprade et al. 2017
N. Charlebois-Laprade et al., *Expert Office 365*, DOI 10.1007/978-1-4842-2991-0_6

We then have the services. While they can all be restored using the SharePoint backup method, it is not necessarily the preferred approach for many of them. We will look at this in detail later in this chapter. As you can see in Figure 6-1, you have a single point of failure, which is the configuration database that is the core of a SharePoint farm. It is well known that restoring the configuration database is unsupported, and I will explain this in greater detail later. Every infrastructure layer that will be discussed in this chapter is represented in this diagram.

- The farm

- The servers

- The services and their databases (including any server dependencies)

- The web application and its databases

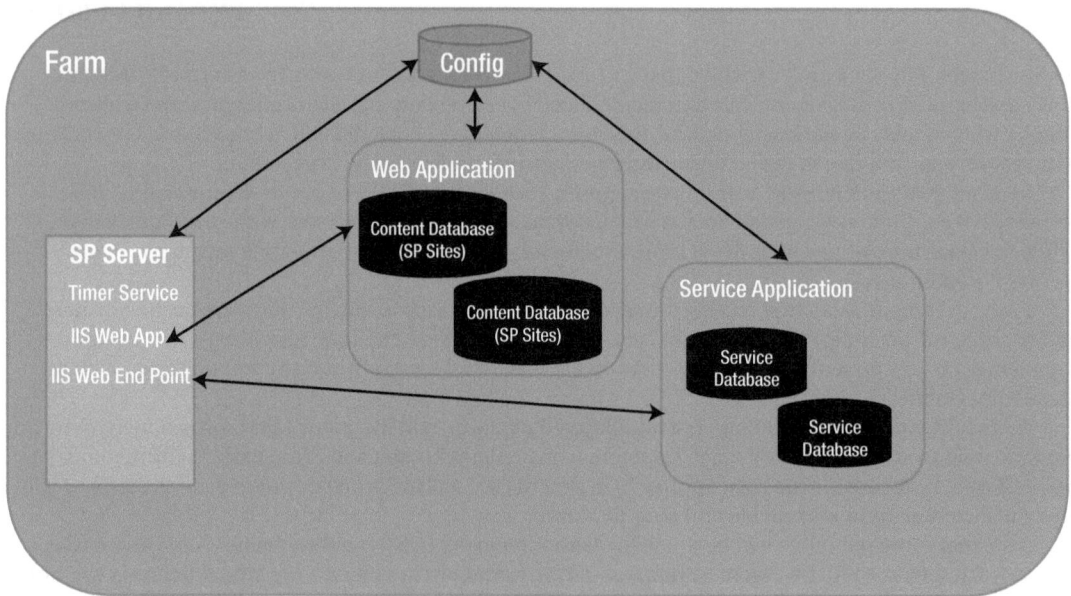

Figure 6-1. *SharePoint logical architecture—infrastructure points of recovery*

Content

While you can consider many services as actual content, such as the Managed Metadata Service, "content," in this chapter, refers to everything authored within a site collection and stored in a content database. This is where processes can differ, based on business Service Level Agreements (SLAs). Recovery Point Objective, Recovery Level Objective, and Recovery Time Objective may all have a financial impact on your recovery solution. Figure 6-2 represents the content hierarchy in SharePoint.

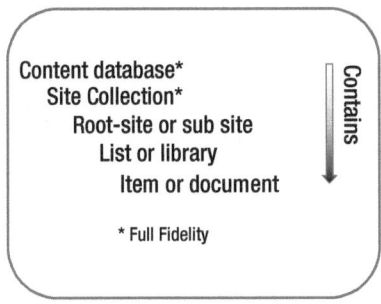

Figure 6-2. *Content hierarchy*

As you can see, every layer is part of a larger container, and what's important to understand is that they do not all offer the same recovery capabilities. One of the most important things to understand in SharePoint on-premises and Online is that the smallest native full-fidelity restore capability is the site collection (see Figure 6-3). I will discuss this further, later in the chapter.

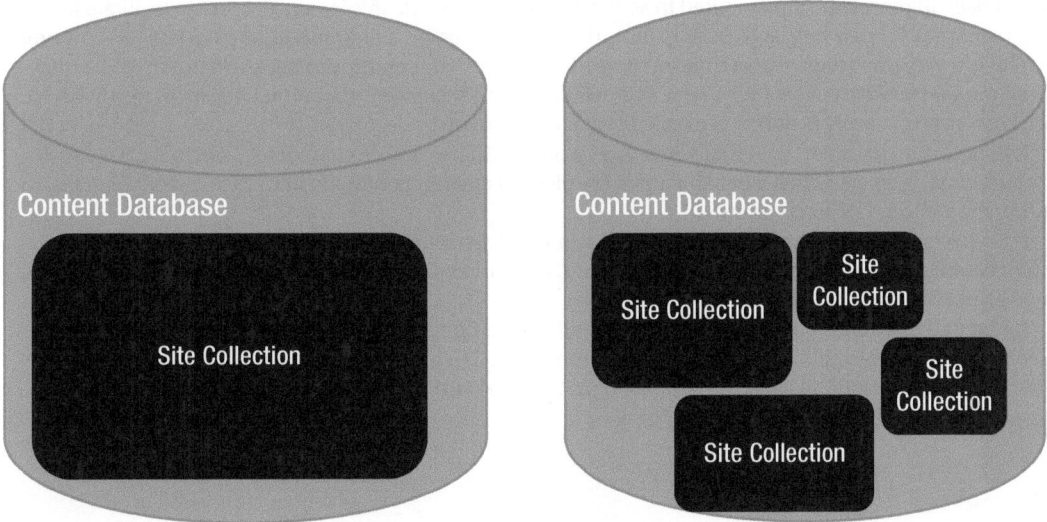

Figure 6-3. *Full-fidelity recoverable containers in SharePoint infrastructure with out-of-the-box functionalities*

Content Recovery

Let me start with this topic, as it covers both SharePoint on-premises and Online. SharePoint can be a one-stop shop for all your content, from your personal corporate documents to something like a critical business process form. As I mentioned previously, not all content may have the same restoration needs. Some organizations will have the same retention point-in-time recovery (PTR) for every item in SharePoint. Practically, while this simplifies the backup rules, it can have a much higher storage and manageability cost. It may also have a higher restoration overhead, depending on the backup approach. This is where it is very important to differentiate what you are accustomed to in SharePoint on-premises and what you can expect in SharePoint Online.

Point-in-Time Recovery

This is the concept of recovering content across time. While you might expect to be able to restore a piece of content from any time in the past, the reality is very different. Here are some points to consider in this regard:

- How long in the past do you really need to recover a piece of content, and from where?

- What type of content requires PTR?

- Differentiate data loss recovery type—deletion operation vs. alteration

- What is the PTR coverage you currently offer on your existing infrastructure?

- What are the current tool(s) and methods you use to achieve the different PTR objectives?

- What does O365 offer in terms of PTR?

As I mentioned in the introduction, in SharePoint, you must consider these specifications for every layer of content. On many occasions, I have seen backups duplicated for the sole purpose of recovering many layers. For example, to recover a document vs. a site collection vs. a content database, I would see three different backup processes implemented to achieve these goals. While this is very efficient to facilitate the recovery process, it has a very large backup footprint for both storage requirements and backup window time.

This is a very important aspect that you must discuss with your enterprise backup vendor. While they will tell you that you are covered for every layer, ask how the backup process is done. Basically, if you back up a database, can you easily restore a site collection or a document?

It is important to understand that when you back up a SharePoint content database, no matter which method you use, you are actually backing up every piece of content contained in it: site collections, sites, lists/libraries, and items/documents.

But a backup is only as good as the restoration process that comes with it. While all content is part of a content database, your expectations may not be met, as your recovery may require more granularity than can be achieved through content database recovery.

As I stated previously, out of the box, the smallest full-fidelity restoration in SharePoint is a site collection. And it is also bound to a supported limit of 100GB that may impact your backup and restore scenarios. Let me detail the capabilities, based on the level and service and the proper approach for large-site collections (Table 6-1).

Table 6-1. *Capabilities*

Restoration Point	Possible Backup Method(s)	Limitation	Scenarios	Point-in-Time On-Premises	Point-in-Time on O365
Database	SQL only SQL Agent with enterprise software SharePoint backup	None, but consider storage space	Database corruption Isolated site collection restoration (1 in database)	Based on your database retention policy	14-day overwrite, only with support request at Microsoft
Site Collection	SQL database restore if alone in database SharePoint backup-spsite/restore-spsite operation	100GB with SharePoint backup operation Consider disk space requirement where backup is executed	Site corruption Site duplication (test/dev) Granular recovery on copy of site	Based on your database retention policy or site collection retention, if applicable	14-day overwrite, only with support request at Microsoft
Site or subsite	Site without the site collection using content export (export/import-spweb)	Not full-fidelity	Content reorganization Faulty site	Based on database retention and/or tool limitation	Not available
List or library	Complete list or library using content export (export/import-spweb)	Not full-fidelity	Content reorganization Faulty library Granular recovery	Based on database retention and/or tool limitation	Not available
Item or document	Granular document recovery point in time	Not possible out of the box outside of recycle bin and versioning	Lost document Document change tracking	Based on database retention and/or tool limitation	Recycle bin (90-day default) Versioning based on library setting

14-Day SharePoint Online

This is an important aspect differentiating usual on-premises expectations and SharePoint Online. If you have to recover a faulty artifact in SharePoint, it can be restored for any point time in the preceding 14 days, as long as it's a database or a site collection. Outside of that scope, no official support is offered.

Let's look at some hypothetical scenarios in which the expectations of a user may not be met after transitioning to SharePoint Online.

1. I am looking for a document that I created three months ago, and it is not present in either

   a. My recycle bin

   b. My previous versions

2. I need to restore my site collection to the state it was in a month ago.

3. I want to restore a specific library on SharePoint Online.

4. I have a compliance that requires that I keep deleted and altered content for a specific period.

While this is not the subject of this chapter, it is important to differentiate between a restore requirement vs. compliance. There are many features in SharePoint Online and in the security and compliance center of Office 365 that are designed to address specific concerns about retention outside of a backup. Although activation and configuration of these features may result in content being retained indefinitely, this is not a one-size-fits-all solution.

If your compliance requires you to keep everything, altered or deleted, for, let's say, seven years, this is achievable with a retention rule in Office 365. Note that this will impact the size of your site and your tenant quota.

Alternatives on the Cloud

The 14-day PTR in the cloud is very similar to a well-balanced PTR on-premises. The difference is only in long-term recovery. On-premises, you will not have a full PTR. Instead, you will probably have a monthly PTR, and it is very possible that a piece of content will not exist on an archived tape, for example. If a document or a version was created/deleted within a month, chances are that it will not be captured. Because there is no equivalent of something like a tape retention, what are the other options available, if required?

The most popular are cloud-based enterprise tools. As you would probably do on-premises to an archiving area, the vendor will store your PTR content on the cloud. There are a few advantages to this approach.

- Much less storage requirement on-premises

- No archiving management

- No traffic from O365 to your network and much faster transfer time, especially if you are storing your PTR content on Azure, which can be in the same data center as O365

You can still back up the content to your data center, but that would defeat the benefits of using SharePoint Online, and you must manage bandwidth and storage requirements.

Limitations

You have to understand that these cloud backups are only for granular content. It will not do a database or a site collection backup. It is a limitation but, at the same time, a benefit. Let me explain.

At Microsoft, we will cover a recovery of a site collection or a database within 14 days. This is sufficient in any corruption scenarios in which your site is defective. The missing piece is granular PTR, and this is where we rely on great partners to provide a solution, if you require it.

Capabilities may differ from vendor to vendor, but you can at least expect the capability of recovering a document at a point in time based on your retention rules. But another benefit is that vendors can also provide more services, such as site reconstruction. Let me explain where site reconstruction/reorganization fits into a recovery requirement.

Site Reconstruction/Reorganization

Many times, when organizations start to use SharePoint, they do so without a proper governance and taxonomy (site and content structure). On top of this, they mix or aggregate too much content within a site collection, which becomes unmanageable over time. While this chapter does not cover site creation governance, you may have to reorganize content at some point, and this will require you to have a recovery strategy that is in line with our discussion.

Another scenario is when a site becomes defective owing to heavy customization or other issues, and you have to extract its content to a new site collection, so that you do not lose content but regain stability. On-premises, you can use the export feature of SharePoint (export-spweb), but it has limitations. It is bound to the version you are running and the site definition it was created with. But you can use an export to, well, export content to a new site collection. If you have a granular backup solution on O365, you could achieve the same goal of exporting content to a new site.

Just be aware that any exportation is not the same as a fidelity backup, and you may have to do some manual work to make your new site behave exactly as its predecessor. Typical limitations in exporting content are

- Last edited author and date replaced
- Workflow state lost and to be rerun
- List lookup relation lost
- Recycle bin content
- Alerts

Content Categorization

Content categorization is very important to help you define your recovery strategy, especially that we now know that, with SharePoint, we must deal with the content and/or the container. A simple strategy, such as what you may be used to with backing up a file share, or a database, may not be sufficient. Let me show you the type of content and high-level categorization that exist in SharePoint.

Whenever I work with information architecture (IA), no matter the size or how mature it is, I provide the basic pyramid that is the foundation of understanding content categorization in SharePoint. No matter how your IA is defined, you will probably find your content in one of these categories and can apply a basic SLA to it (see Figure 6-4).

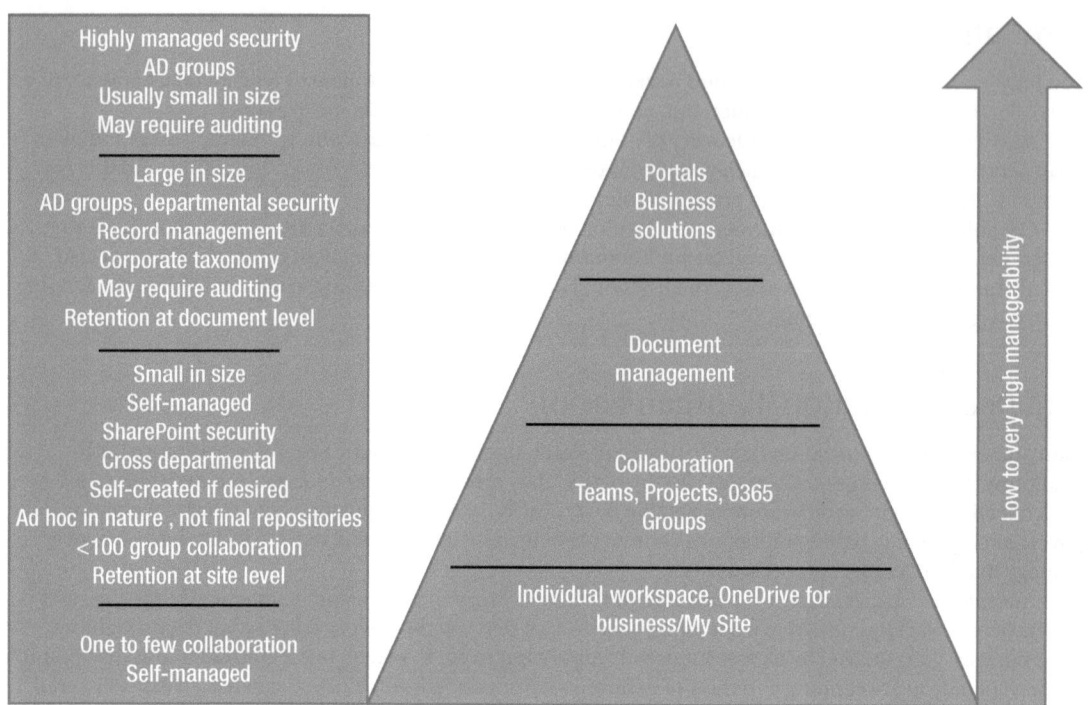

Figure 6-4. *My own extended version of the SharePoint content pyramid*

The top layer is the realm of any business-critical application. It may be identified as a portal, but in SharePoint, it defines something that is highly managed. It can be very small or mildly large, but it has a high impact and requires a specific recovery SLA. In any case, it should be isolated in a site collection and, many times, an isolated database.

The second layer is the most complex area to handle. Document management and record management are usually subject to well-defined retention policies, which vary from geography to geography, from industry to industry, and even among customers. It should have, by far, the largest containers and site collections. This is usually where you must decide if you need granular recovery capabilities.

The third layer, while it is the most puzzling category lately, should be the easiest to handle and has the most capabilities. This is the "team," "social," and "modern collaboration" category. The technologies used in this category of content extends outside just SharePoint! We now have Outlook groups that use both the best from SharePoint and Exchange, Yammer, and, more recently, Microsoft Teams. You may wonder which one to use, and this is a very hot topic right now, but not within the scope of this chapter. I will limit this layer to the typical SharePoint team site that is not meant for departmental usage. That means that security is not centralized in AD or Azure and that sites are typically small and have a limited lifespan.

Talking about lifespan, a departmental site is not meant to have an expiration. We will manage document retention instead. Collaborative sites, on the other hand, may have expiration and retention rules and can be ad hoc in nature.

Last, but not least, is personal storage—what used to be your personal drive on a network server or local My Documents. Many individuals have moved or are planning to move to either on-premises or O365 One Drive for Business. This can be small or very large and comes with many functionalities, such as versioning, sharing, compliance, and access from anywhere and on different devices. With a capability that can go up to 5TB per user, and even more on demand, compliance may be required, but what about recovery?

If we recapitulate, the following is what categorization and recovery can look like:

- A critical business application site collection has a very rapid SLA covering the site collection.

- A departmental or business unit site collection(s) has (have) a granular document SLA and a database SLA.

- An ad hoc project/team has a site collection SLA without granular level.

- A personal drive is an isolated storage without any SLA besides the Sync Client and/ or manager's retention.

You can now translate this to a basic service definition, as in Table 6-2.

Table 6-2. *Basic Service*

Type of Site	Requirement	Type of Backup On-Premises	Type of Backup on O365	Process On-Premises	Process on O365	PTR
Critical business application xyz, portal, etc....	Fast recovery Usually small in size	Database Duplicated site collection backup, if desired	Normal 14-day PTR	Recovery copy of database to extract site collection or overwrite database Site collection restore operation, if used	Call support to recover faulty site	Not required, granular recovery covered by recycle bin and versioning/ approval process
Collaboration Small teams Ad doc project-based	Site only recovery, no granular SLA	Database only Recycle bin Versioning	Database only Recycle bin Versioning	Recover only if site defective	Recover only if site defective	No granular PTR, users are responsible and can use local synced copies
My Site	Site only recovery, no granular SLA	Database only Recycle bin Versioning	Database only Recycle bin Versioning	Recover only if site defective	Recover only if site defective	No PTR, but may require management review and content retention if employee leaves company
Departmental, official corporate document management	Database and/or site collection Document PTR	Database Granular enterprise tool, if desired	Database Cloud granular enterprise tool if desired	Recovery site collection or database, if faulty PTR document based on policy	Recovery site collection or database, if faulty PTR document based on policy	Yes based on policy and type of content

148

Now that we have a minimal content categorization, we will be able to define a backup retention strategy. I will provide some examples, but this will depend on your policies. Be sure to validate the typical statement whereby an organization thinks it has to keep everything forever. This is where technicalities are important to understand, as they greatly affect the restoration process.

Database and Site Collection Storage Strategy

As I had mentioned before, you may at some point have to restore a site collection that exceeds the 100GB threshold for supportability. A site collection backup and restore operation is generated from a SharePoint server. A backup will consist of a massive amount of read statements in SQL, downloading the site content to the SharePoint server and saving it as a binary file. This operation is very costly in bandwidth and time, especially when it comes to large sites.

The restore operation is even worse, as you are now taking the contents of this binary file and uploading it to SQL, using many update and/or insert statements. You can imagine that for a 100GB site collection, this will take a very long time, be sensitive to any network disruption, and potentially fill your SQL transaction log file or drive. In a storage strategy, which is bound to your recovery strategy when you know you will have a site collection that is expected to be large, like a departmental site, a record management or archiving site collection, you want to isolate the site and store it alone in the database. SharePoint content databases can contain more than one site collection, but in the case of large ones, you will want to have a one-to-one ratio. That way, if you have to recover a large site collection, you will use an SQL restore operation.

Dealing with large site collections and databases, you may be tempted to look at RBS storage. I will not cover this subject in this book, but it is rarely recommended to customers, unless they have a very strong requirement for it and the proper maturity level to handle its recovery complexity, to prevent any mismatch between the database and external storage. When also using RBS with a third-party vendor, the recovery process will be tightly bound with this vendor, and you must ensure that you will have the proper support from the vendor, depending on the recovery issue. RBS also may not be suitable or have limitations, based on what you expect to achieve.

Fortunately, in SharePoint Online, we deal with how we store large site collections, so there is no need to worry or think about it. It is also one of the reasons Microsoft supports site collections up to 1TB in SharePoint Online, as opposed to the previous 100GB limit.

The GUID Story

Other important factors to understand when dealing with site restoration are globally unique identifiers (GUIDs). GUIDs are unique IDs that keep the consistency in the SharePoint structure, but they can lead to disconnected services and various additional issues. They are the relational aspect in SQL and, by doing some faulty operations, can lead to conflicting artifacts that you often see referenced as orphans. In dealing with recovery of databases and site collections, there are two important GUIDs: the site collection and the content database.

One operation that will lead to issues is the restoration and mounting to SharePoint of a copy of a database. In mount-spcontentdatabase, you have an optional parameter -AssignNewDatabaseId that allows you to have a new database GUID. Unfortunately, this command will not change the site collection's GUIDs, in it or its URL. So, if you do this, you will end up with orphaned site collections. A copy of a content database that contains site collections can only be restored in a different farm.

The other operation that may lead to some issues is restore-spsite. By default, if you restore and overwrite a site collection using the -force parameter, the site will get a new GUID. Great! That should prevent orphans—but it will cause a disconnection with your Managed Metadata Service (MMS), if you have local terms in that site collection. Local terms are stored in the MMS database and have the site collection GUID to reference them. Change your GUID, and you will have the metadata available in your site collection, as the content is also stored there, but you cannot edit it, as the MMS is now referring to the wrong GUID. If you plan to overwrite a site collection, you should delete it first and use the latest parameter in SharePoint 2013: -PreserveSiteId.

149

And last, one common restore request is to have a copy of a site collection, sometimes for parallel improvement or granular recovery of some content. Ideally, you want to restore a copy in a different farm. This provides better protection from any mistake by users or administrators. But if you must, you can restore a copy of a site collection, as long as it is in a different content database, has a different URL, and, of course, a different GUID.

Figure 6-5 shows a typical site collection and overwrite restoration process when the database contains more than one site.

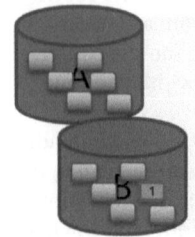

Issue with team site collection http://contoso/sites/project500
                    Missing content, broken functionality, etc...
Site owner open tickets
Issue is first handled by SharePoint team
                    Require to restore from most recent backup
SharePoint team open ticket with SQL team

SQL team restore a copy of the requested content database
SharePoint team extract site collection from copy of database
        Backup-Spsite OR
        Recover content from unattached database (Central Admin)

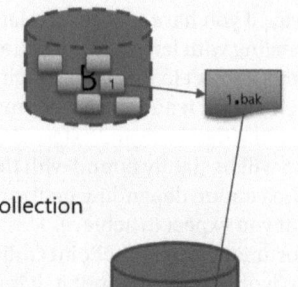
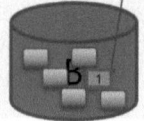

SharePoint team will restore and overwrite defective site collection
        Restore-spsite
        Cannot be done with Central Administration
SQL team deletes copy of database

Figure 6-5. *Site collection operation*

Figure 6-6 shows a typical restore operation when dealing with a large and isolated site collection.

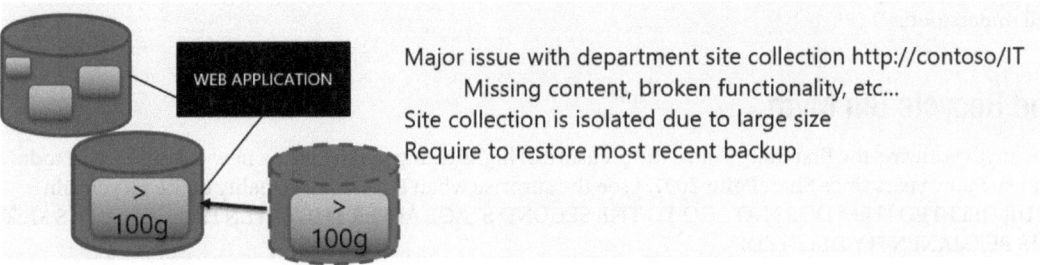

SharePoint team detach content database from the web application
    Dismount-spcontentdatabase OR
    Using Central Administration –Manage Content Databases
SharePoint team waits 5 minutes to let the unmount operation
complete before requesting any SQL operation
SharePoint team open ticket with SQL team
SQL team restore and overwrite full content database
SharePoint team re-attach content database to SharePoint
    Mount-spcontentdatabase OR
    Using Central Administration – Manage Content Databases

Figure 6-6. *Large site collection*

While Figure 6-6 shows a site larger than 100GB, I suggest that you proactively identify which sites are or will grow larger, isolate them right away, and use the database recovery process.

Another important point is when the SQL team overwrites the database, if any connections are still open, do not forcibly close them. The site may not be functional after restoration. It takes about five minutes for SharePoint to complete an unmount operation. This is the clean way of approaching a large site restoration and will ensure a successful process. And if the site does not respond after restoration (404 error or blank page), you may have to clear the Timer Job Cache and reset IIS.

As for database size, you probably saw the recommended 200GB. This is not a hard limit but a recommendation, owing to these backup/recovery processes. As you just read, in the case of an isolated site collection, all you must do is restore and overwrite a database. But imagine a scenario in which you must restore a copy for a more granular request. In this case, it would not be very practical to have a 2TB content database. The different database size recommendations, based on usage such as archiving and record management while dealing with capacity for IOPS (input/output operations per seconds) are well explained on TechNet. But, as I explained, they are bound by how content is managed in them for operational processes and SLAs.

For example, if you store all your archives in a very large database in one site collection, let's say, 4TB, you understand that you will not require the same performance access as active sites or will require much higher IOPS. You will also have a different SLA and backup schedule, as the content is, in theory, inactive and mainly for read access. And if granular recovery is necessary, you will require an enterprise backup tool that will capture document changes, as you will not really restore a copy of that database to capture one document.

Recycle Bin and Versioning

These two very important features of SharePoint are often overlooked and not managed. They are also not well understood.

The Recycle Bin Myth

This myth is always the first thing I have the pleasure of highlighting when I visit a new customer. Still today, after so many years since SharePoint 2007, I see the surprise when I explain the reality of the recycle bin. YOUR DELETED ITEM DOES NOT GO TO THE SECOND STAGE AFTER THE RETENTION PERIOD IS MET! IT IS PERMANENTLY DELETED!

I am sure many of you reading this will be surprised too. Here's how it works in only two sentences:

- It will go to the second stage only if you delete it a second time, meaning that you empty your own recycle bin.

- It will stay only in the second stage for the remaining time from the first deletion date, meaning that if you deleted a document and empty your recycle bin after ten days, that document has 20 days left in the second stage.

So, of course, the next question is, Can I change this? The answer is no for the process, but you can improve it.

Your first option is to change the retention period. You can extend the recycle bin life cycle to, let's say, 90 days. Now, while this will improve your PTR for accidental deletion, it will require more space. Also, note that the recycle bin handles deleted lists/libraries, sites/subsites, and even site collections. So, the longer the retention, the more space is required.

What about SharePoint Online? The retention period cannot be changed and is set at 93 days. For the folks who must manage either storage capabilities on-premises or quotas on O365, following is a little more technical information that may help.

The first stage recycle bin goes against a site collection quota. Unfortunately, in many cases on-premises, I see people not applying quotas and having site collections running large, without the knowledge of the administrator responsible for capacity planning. On O365, a site collection quota is mandatory and forces you to think about the goal of that site collection. For example, a project/team site would have a small quota, so it is not used to doing something different from its original purpose, and a departmental document management site collection will have a large quota.

No matter the quota, the first-stage recycle bin content counts toward it, which means that it has an impact on site collection, database, and storage size. The second-stage recycle bin does not count toward a site collection quota. So, let's say you are running low on site collection space. You could empty the first recycle bin and make some room.

While it doesn't count toward the site collection quota, it is still in the database, meaning that it counts toward your capacity planning and tenant storage allocation. Also, the second stage is not unlimited. It can grow up to 50% of the site collection storage quota. On SharePoint Online, the quota is set at 200%.

■ **Very Important Note**   What happens if the second stage reaches that 50% on-premises? All content in it will be purged and permanently deleted. You can increase it up to 100%.

New in SharePoint Online

In modern collaborations such as Outlook groups, a new trend in support calls began to appear concerning the first-stage recycle bin. Currently, in every version of SharePoint, when a user deletes a document, it is only visible in the recycle bin of the person who deleted the document. Only a site collection administrator has the capability of viewing every deleted document in the first stage and the second stage.

This can lead to a lack of functionality in small collaborations in which you may have to recover a document deleted by a colleague, if you are also an editor. In SharePoint Online, users with editing permission will now be able to see a document deleted by a colleague.

Versioning

One of the first reasons people move from File Share to SharePoint is, of course, versioning. While the recycle bin protects you from accidental deletion, versioning is your first line of defense against undesired change or history tracking. Good recovery planning will include a versioning strategy. Why a strategy? Because versioning has a certain impact on storage requirement, and not every type of content requires the same versioning setting. SharePoint provides not only versioning but also content-approval processes.

When you enable versioning, the default settings will probably not apply to all your content. Depending on the type of site you are working in, versioning may or may not be enabled by default in a specific library (Figure 6-7). As well, when enabled, limitations are optional and inactive by default, which will consume more storage than if you impose limits. Fortunately, since SharePoint 2013, shredded storage was introduced, and only the delta (differences) are saved in the SharePoint database when saving multiple versions of a document, reducing storage requirement quite dramatically, compared to SharePoint 2010 and earlier versions.

Settings · Versioning Settings

Content Approval

Specify whether new items or changes to existing items should remain in a draft state until they have been approved. Learn about requiring approval.

Require content approval for submitted items?
○ Yes ● No

Document Version History

Specify whether a version is created each time you edit a file in this document library. Learn about versions.

Create a version each time you edit a file in this document library?
● No versioning
○ Create major versions
  Example: 1, 2, 3, 4
○ Create major and minor (draft) versions
  Example: 1.0, 1.1, 1.2, 2.0

Optionally limit the number of versions to retain:
☐ Keep the following number of major versions:

☐ Keep drafts for the following number of major versions:

Draft Item Security

Drafts are minor versions or items which have not been approved. Specify which users should be able to view drafts in this document library. Learn about specifying who can view and edit drafts.

Who should see draft items in this document library?
● Any user who can read items
○ Only users who can edit items
○ Only users who can approve items (and the author of the item)

Figure 6-7. *Versioning settings in a SharePoint library*

As with the recycle bin second-stage myth I described previously, versioning also has a setting that is often misinterpreted. If you read the previous screen capture rapidly, you will assume that you can define the number of major and minor versions, basically, how many minor versions you can save between two major ones and how many majors. But go ahead and read again. The reality, and it is well explained in the setting page, is very different.

You should read how many major versions can be stored and how many of them will have minor versions. If I choose to keep five drafts, then only the last five major versions will have minor versions. The previous majors will not. But in these five majors, you can have up to 511 minor versions between each major.

This way of thinking assumes that once a major version is released, keeping track of changes with the last is not required permanently within the drafts. Basically, you will only have to keep track between two major versions. It also assumes that when working with versions, you will at some point publish that document and that you don't really have to put any limitation between majors.

The reality is that, sometimes, many people work with a minor, without ever publishing a major, version. And some customers will even have high expectations of SharePoint deals with minors, such as being available in a search result. This is not a good working plan, and it should be better defined, depending, again, on the type of content authored.

Versioning requirements will probably be very different in a publishing web site than a collaborative team site. They will also be very different in official document managed sites. For example, in a collaborative site, there may not be much requirement to enable minor versions. In a publishing web site or with a legal department's document management, where content approval is required, you will probably want to have draft versions enabled. But once a document is approved and final, the need for keeping the draft versions may be less important, at least for a certain time. If change tracking is required, it may be sufficient to keep drafts between two previous major versions.

Web Applications

A web application in SharePoint is in a very high level, an IIS site that exposes your site content from the database. While your content stored in site collection is backed up by the processes covered before, the web application is not.

Sometimes, I see people back up the web application, using SharePoint. To do so, you are, in fact, using the farm backup tool (or backup-spfarm) and selecting the web application. While this works, it is not very efficient, for many reasons that I will explain.

- Backing up the web application will also back up the content database.

- The SQL server will send a backup of the database to a Share on the SharePoint server.

- This tool is not really in line with your enterprise database backup strategy, process, and tools.

A web application is not that much different from the service application we will look at following. Also, the creation of a web application and its customization, like its settings but also its IIS counterpart, such as web.config, certificates, and network settings, should be part of the build process and very well documented and, ideally, automated. If your process is in place, it is more efficient to rebuild a web application and use or restore the content database.

It is very rare that a web application has to be restored. It is usually the content. We usually "restore" a web application in another environment, and this should be done with your build process. Some vendors will offer restoring web application and IIS settings or even transfer them to a different farm. These are probably very good secondary options but should not replace your build process.

Service Applications

Like web applications, service applications are IIS web services that can also have Windows services dependencies and, in most cases, databases. Like web applications, they can be backed up using the SharePoint backup function (`backup-spfarm`). But in many cases, like web applications, they are redundant of your SQL database backup and build process. But there are exceptions. In the following section, I will cover the different categories of services, based on their recovery process. Some of them are common, and other are more unusual.

Services That Fit a Database Strategy

These services, like web applications, can rely on your overall build and SQL backup processes. Basically, if a service must be restored, rebuild the service, using a restored database. Following is a list of services that can use this model:

- Managed Metadata Service

- BCS Service**

- User Profile Service *

- Secure Store *

- Subscription setting

- Apps *

- Machine Translation Service Application

- Performance Point**

Requires additional steps to complete the process and may depend on other services
*** May use Secure Store*

As explained in TechNet, you can simply overwrite a service database, but you need, at a minimum, to stop the timer services. You should also never forcibly close the connections when restoring in SQL. In some cases, this is insufficient, and deleting the service application and database(s) is the safest method to recover. In any case, if after a restore the service is not running as expected, you will probably have to reset the IIS service and, in some cases, clear the timer service cache.

Also, restoring only the content of a service application is probably very rare, unless you are copying the service to another farm. Usual restoration requests for a service would probably be due to instability or misconfiguration. In this case, it is preferable to rebuild the service application, using the restored database and reprovisioning the end points (Services on server Stop/Start). Note that deleting the database by removing the service application may not be possible, if it is part of a SQL availability group. Deleting a database may also create overhead on the SQL team.

Basic Steps

The following steps must be followed to restore your service applications:

1. Delete the service application and its databases.

2. **Note:** If the databases are part of an SQL availability group, you won't be able to delete them. You can decide to keep them, but you must restore it to all SQL instances.

3. Request an SQL restore operation from the SQL team and overwrite, if you did not delete in the previous step.

4. Create your service application using your known build and/or script process, using the same database name.

5. Your script should also include starting any services instances on the proper servers, unless you use the MinRole of SharePoint 2016.

Dependencies (Restore in Different Farm)

A common problem when restoring a service database to be used in another farm, such as refreshing your pre-production environment, is the GUID mismatch. In services such as Managed Metadata, there are references to GUID present in other databases, such as site collections. If the site collections did not come from the same environment and were also copied using the database process, their GUIDs will be different, and when you restore your service in that environment, your site collection local MMS columns will be grayed out, as the restored MMS database will point to a different site collection GUID. Similar issues can apply to the App Service application.

This chapter will not cover how to fix these scenarios, as it covers only restoration within the same farm, bypassing this issue, but it is important to understand how it affects your content and service staging and refreshing.

Additional Steps for Some Services

User Profile Service

In the case of the User Profile Service, you must also restore the Social database. If you are using the FIM engine to synchronize, you are also using the profile Sync database. This database contains encryption, and the key must be restored, if you plan to restore it.

The easiest method to restore the User Profile Service with FIM is to not restore that database.

1. Delete the service and the databases.

2. Restore the Profile and Social databases.

3. Re-create the service. A new Sync database will be created.

Secure Store

On TechNet, the documentation only offers the SharePoint backup as a recovery method, but you can still use the database method. There is one extra element that is very important to consider with this service. This is the Master key that you created originally by using a pass phrase at the service creation. You must store this pass phrase, as it will be required if you re-create your service application using the restored database (Figure 6-8). Note that if you did not delete the service application and only overwrote the database, you do not have to refresh the pass phrase (Figure 6-9).

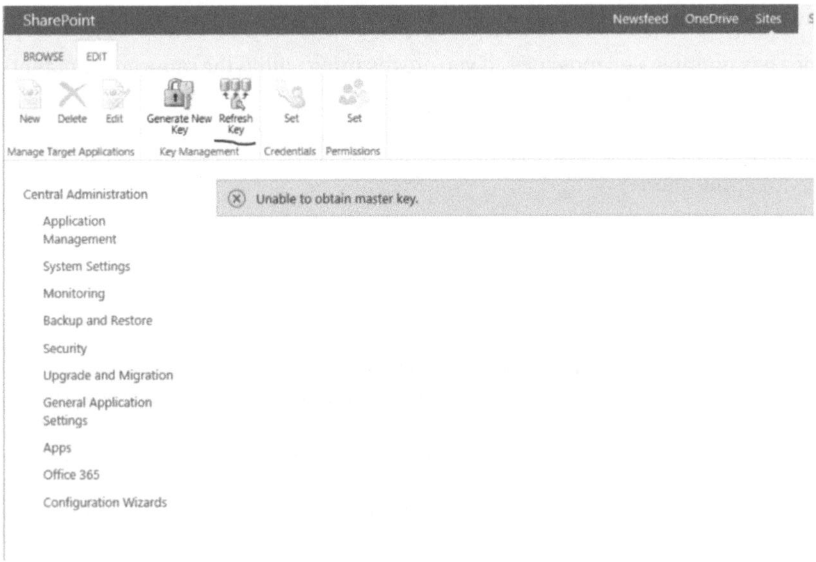

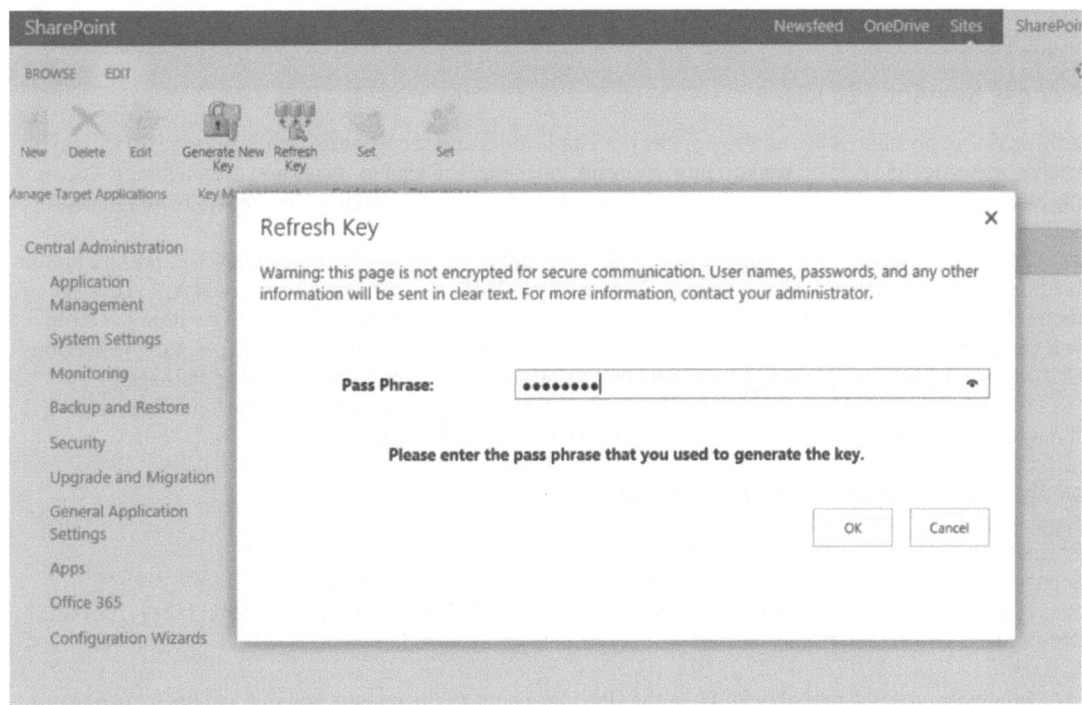

Figure 6-8. *Master key error after restore*

Figure 6-9. *Master key refresh*

App Management Service

The App Management Service has multiple dependencies. If you are restoring within the same environment, consider which component you want to restore.

- App Management Service

- Secure Store service application

- Subscription service application

- Apps Catalog Site Collection

- Any site collection with Apps/Add-in deployed

If you plan to restore the App Service in the same environment, you need only restore the service database. If, in the other end, you want to restore apps in the catalog, the site collection will also have to be restored.

It is also important to note that if you are restoring in another farm, every dependent artifact must also be restored. Otherwise, you may have to reinstall or configure some components, such as trusts, manifest, etc....

For this scenario, because we are only restoring the service application in our current environment, the same process as with the other service applies.

1. Delete the service application.

2. Restore the database.

3. Re-create the service application using the same database name.

Access Service (2013)

This service application relies on the App Service Application and secure store. While Access Service can be backed up using the SP-Farm backup process, restoring it may still lead to issues and errors. Also, re-creating the Access Service application causes the existing Access App to stop working. The newly created Access Service application will be OK.

The problem when re-creating the Access Service application is that it creates a new GUID entry for the hosting SQL server. Any new access apps will use the new GUID, and the previous one will try to connect to the one that does not exist anymore. In the case of a DR farm or recovery of the service within the farm, you will have to reconfigure the service to use the previous GUID. If you are not able to point to the previous GUID, you will have to export the Access data using the Access client, by creating an App Package.

To identify your SQL server reference ID, before any recovery attempt, execute the following script. It may be a good idea to keep this GUID documented in your build documentation.

```
$ASapp = Get-SPAccessServicesApplication
$app = $Null
if ($ASapp.length -ne $Null) { $app = $ASapp[0] } else { $app = $ASapp }
$context = [Microsoft.SharePoint.SPServiceContext]::GetContext($app.
ServiceApplicationProxyGroup, [Microsoft.SharePoint.SPSiteSubscriptionIdentifier]::Default)
Get-SPAccessServicesDatabaseServer -ServiceContext $context
```

Otherwise, you will probably find it in the ULS log, where after a restore, you may get the following error in the ULS log: "AccessServicesDatabaseServerGroupCollection.GetDatabaseServer: Could not find a server matching reference id..."

To add the previous server entry, you can execute the following script, by inserting the previous GUID in the $ServerRefID and your SQL Server Host Name variables.

```
$ServerRefID = "Your previous GUID here"
$SqlHost = "Your SQL Host Name"
########
$serverGroupName = 'DEFAULT'
$ASapp = Get-SPAccessServicesApplication
$app = $Null
if ($ASapp.length -ne $Null) { $app = $ASapp[0] } else { $app = $ASapp }
$context = [Microsoft.SharePoint.SPServiceContext]::GetContext($app.
ServiceApplicationProxyGroup, [Microsoft.SharePoint.SPSiteSubscriptionIdentifier]::Default)
$newdbserver = New-SPAccessServicesDatabaseServer -ServiceContext $context
-DatabaseServerName $SqlHost -DatabaseServerGroup $serverGroupName -ServerReferenceId
$ServerRefID -AvailableForCreate $true
```

Services That Do Not Have a Database

These services have only to be re-created if there are issues and do not possess any recovery steps.

- Excel Services

- Visio Services

- Word Automation

- Work Management

Search

Search is very different and has its own complexity. It contains not only databases but local indexes that need to be in sync. Therefore, there are no complete search database recovery processes. If your SLA requires that you back up search completely, in a scenario in which recovery would be faster than rebuilding the indexes and crawling the content, you will be required to use the SharePoint backup process (backup-spfarm).

```
Backup-spfarm -Item "Farm\Shared Services\Shared Services Applications\<SearchServiceApplic
ationName>"
```

If you desire only to keep the search configuration, your build process and documentation should have the automation and documentation for any configuration, such as custom result sources, content sources, etc. If automation/documentation is not present or not up to date, it is possible to reuse the Admin database to re-create your new Search Service Application, using the same process to create the service via the existing/restored Admin database. You must also ensure that you have a copy of the thesaurus files that you used to import into search, as they are not part of the SharePoint backup.

Server

One potential mistake I often see is the expectation to reuse a nightly snapshot of a VM as a restore method for a server. The only artifacts that should be backed up from a server are specific manual deployments that are not done by SharePoint.

- Web.Config entries

- Networking configuration

- IIS custom settings

- Certificates

- Any custom artifacts (Dll, resources, etc., not deployed by a SharePoint packaged solution)

If a server becomes unstable for unknown reasons, or is compromised by a disk corruption or bad update, it is very tempting to simply bring back a server from the previous snapshot.

This is a very risky operation, and while some people may achieve the expected result by clearing the timer cache, it may introduce unexpected results and even affect the integrity of the farm. Server recovery is only used in a full rollback scenario, including every other component from a point-in-time backup within minutes.

The proper method is to remove the server from the farm and rebuild and reintegrate it. If you have high availability implemented, this can be achieved during the production hour. The only impact would be a performance reduction on the services provided by the server.

Since SharePoint 2013, a new complexity appeared when removing a server from a farm, which caused some issues when not done properly. If a server is either part of a distributed cache cluster or a search topology, it must be removed from these before being disconnected from the farm. Skipping these steps will cause orphan entries, even if the server is reinserted with the same name.

The following script will prevent you from removing the server from any cluster and topology before being disconnected from the farm. If the server is available and running, always attempt to execute the script from it. If it is not healthy, or simply not available anymore, run the script from another server. It will force the removal of the entries.

```
$FqdnServerName = read-host ("What is the FQDN server name to remove?")
$servername = $FqdnServerName.split(".")[0]
Add-PSSnapin microsoft.sharepoint.powershell


#####Cleaning up distributed cache###############
$instanceName ="SPDistributedCacheService Name=AppFabricCachingService"
$serviceInstance = Get-SPServiceInstance | ? {($_.Service.Tostring()) -eq $instanceName -and
($_.Server.Name) -eq $ServerName}
if($serviceInstance)
{
    if ($servername -ne $env:COMPUTERNAME)
    {
        $notGraceful = $true
    }

    if(!$notGraceful)
    {
        $startTime = Get-Date
        $currentTime = $startTime
        $elapsedTime = $currentTime - $startTime
        $timeOut = 900

        try
        {
            Write-Host "Shutting down gracefuly distributed cache host. This can take a few
            minutes to transfer cached memory to other DC servers"
            $hostInfo = Stop-CacheHost -Graceful -CachePort 22233 -ComputerName $FqdnServerName
```

```
        while($elapsedTime.TotalSeconds -le $timeOut-and $hostInfo.Status -ne 'Down')
        {
            Write-Host "Host Status : [$($hostInfo.Status)]"
            Start-Sleep(5)
            $currentTime = Get-Date
            $elapsedTime = $currentTime - $startTime
            $hostInfo = Get-CacheHost -HostName $FQDNServerName -CachePort 22233
        }

        Write-Host "Stopping distributed cache host was successful. Stopping Service in
        SharePoint."
        Stop-SPDistributedCacheServiceInstance
        Write-Host "Removing from cluster."
        Remove-SPDistributedCacheServiceInstance
    }
    catch [System.Exception]
    {
        Write-Host "Unable to stop cache host within 15 minutes."
        $NotGraceful = $true
    }
}
if ($NotGraceful )
{
    if($env:COMPUTERNAME -EQ $servername)
    {
        try
        {
            write-host "Removing server without graceful"
            Remove-SPDistributedCacheServiceInstance
        }
        catch [System.Exception]
        {
            write-host "Unable to remove Server with remove-SPDistributedCacheServiceIns
            tance, forcing deletion"
            $forceDelete = $true
        }
    }
    else
    {$forceDelete = $true}
}

if ($forceDelete)
{
    $serviceInstance.Delete()
}
}

###############CLEANING UP SEARCH TOPOLOGY#####################
write-host ("Removing server from search topology")
$ssa = Get-SPEnterpriseSearchServiceApplication
$active = Get-SPEnterpriseSearchTopology -SearchApplication $ssa -Active
```

```
$clone = New-SPEnterpriseSearchTopology -SearchApplication $ssa -Clone -SearchTopology $active
$componenttoRemove = Get-SPEnterpriseSearchComponent -SearchTopology $clone | where-object
{$_.servername -like $ServerName}
if ($componenttoRemove)
{
    Foreach ($component in $componenttoRemove)
    {   $CId = $component.ComponentId
        write-host "Removing $cid"
        Remove-SPEnterpriseSearchComponent -searchtopology $clone -Identity $component
        -confirm:$false
    }

    Write-host ("Applying New Clone Search Topology. This can take a few minutes")
    Set-SPEnterpriseSearchTopology -Identity $clone
}

#########Disconnecting from the farm###############
if($env:COMPUTERNAME -EQ $servername)
{

    write-host ("Disconnecting server from the farm")
    try
    {
        disconnect-spconfigurationdatabase -Confirm:$false
    }
    catch
    {
        Write-host ("Unable to disconnect, remove server from Central Admin or try with
        Configuration Wizard")
    }

}
else
{
    try
    {
        $serverToDelete = get-spserver $servername
        $serverToDelete.delete()
    }
    catch
    {
        Write-host ("Unable to delete server, remove server from Central Admin")
    }
}
```

Farm

Configuration Database

By now, you should know that restoration of the configuration database is not supported. The only method by which you can reuse the configuration database is by some replication scenario in which every bit of SharePoint is guaranteed to be backed up at the same time, including VM and databases.

The other typical scenario in which a configuration database will be restored is when a complete backup is taken before a major update, while the farm is offline, and where, in the case of a major issue, it is part of a rollback plan whereby every component, server, and database is restored at the same point in time. This is an all-or-nothing scenario. You cannot restore a configuration database alone from a point in time different from that of any other of its components.

I always tell my customers that the best farm recovery process is a great build process. It is much easier to rebuild than fix. If it is not the case in your organization, you should prioritize testing your build process.

SharePoint Farm Backup

The SharePoint farm backup can be practical and useful in certain situations, but it may not be sufficient in many scenarios. It is also redundant of your actual SQL backup and build strategy. If your farm becomes unstable, unusable, or even if one of the servers is problematic, chances are that using the `restore-spfarm` operation will not fix your issue. I like to think of this backup as a setting backup that does not replace a good enterprise strategy. Remember that the configuration database is not really restored, and if it was damaged, chances are that the farm backup would not fix it.

The farm backup can be used to reapply settings to a new farm, if you don't have any automation in place. Also, the `backup-spfarm` configuration can only be useful to recuperate settings, without backing up other components, such as databases that are already taken by SQL backups.

Summary

As you may have noted by now, I am a firm believer in a great build automation, coupled with a good database backup strategy. The most common issue I faced is a lack of familiarity with these operations, with outdated build and deployment documentation and a lack of practice or priority regarding them.

As a general recommendation, to ensure that your organization's backup process is healthy, you should

- Practice your farm build process.

- Test your services recovery until you have the right recipe in your recovery cookbook.

- Ensure that you have all the customization sources and packages (WSP) up to date in a source controlled environment.

- Ensure that the custom application deployment documentation is up to date, with separated initial blank deployment vs. one that already has site artifacts implemented.

- Ensure that you have all the third-party installation and required keys available, including SharePoint binaries.

- Ensure that you have any certificate or other server manual artifacts available.

CHAPTER 7

■ ■ ■

Azure Rights Management for SharePoint

BY MIKE FARRAN

What's better than convenient access to data? *Secure* convenient access to data, and the ability to share that data with whomever you want, knowing it will be protected in its digital travels. Your company has a lot of data that it must protect. When everything was on-premise, securing data wasn't difficult to do. Users had to physically be on-site and have a computer that was physically connected to the network by network cable. Virtual private networks (VPNs) came in, and we had to extend that protection to home computers. Wireless networking came in with mobile devices, and the security perimeter had to be further extended, which, in turn, increased the scenarios in which we could leak data. Your users are already sharing this data via e-mail and uploading the data to cloud services. You have no control over how this data is protected, unless you implement rights management.

Sharing data is a good thing. It's fast and easy and encourages collaboration. It also creates a huge challenge: protecting that data after it leaves your company's secure infrastructure. With Azure Rights Management (RMS), you can share almost any file on almost any platform inside and outside of your company, and do it securely. RMS is built on modern encryption and authentication standards that protect your data both in motion and at rest. Implementing RMS will help to begin planning or solve questions such as

- How do I control access to this data?

- How do I control how they are used?

- What is my sensitive data?

- How do I track who has accessed them?

What Is Azure RMS?

Azure RMS is a cloud-based service that uses encryption, identity, and authorization policies to help secure your files and e-mail. This works across all the devices employees may use to complete their daily tasks: phones, tablets, and PCs. Your information will be protected within your organization and outside your organization, because that protection remains with the data, even when it leaves your organization's perimeter.

Following, you'll see Figure 7-1, which describes how Azure RMS protects your information for both Office 365 and on-premises servers and services. You'll also see that it supports the end-user devices that your company may allow through its "bring your own device policy": Windows, Mac OS, iOS, Android, and Windows Phone.

© Nikolas Charlebois-Laprade et al. 2017   165
N. Charlebois-Laprade et al., *Expert Office 365*, DOI 10.1007/978-1-4842-2991-0_7

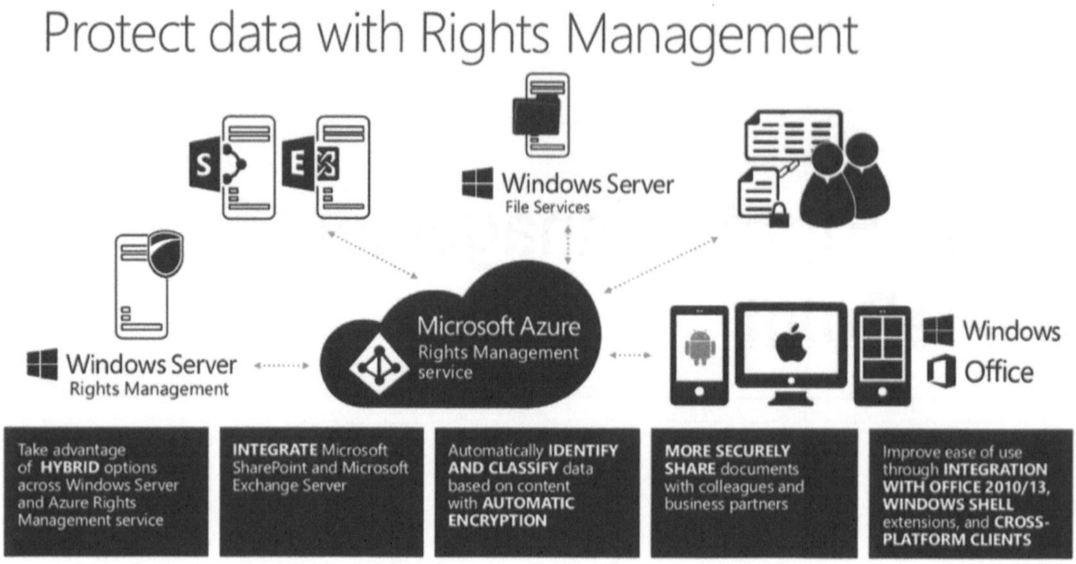

Protect data with Rights Management

Figure 7-1. *How Azure RMS protects your information*

How Do I Control Access to This Data?

Control access via the following steps.

How Does It Work?

Azure RMS is built around four core principles:

- *Identity*: Active Directory user identities are used to restrict or allow access to your documents.

- *Encryption*: Your documents are strongly encrypted at rest, in-motion, and in-use.

- *Authorization Policy*: This contains the actions users can enact on your documents, such as edit, print, and forward.

- *Access Logging*: Access to your documents is logged wherever and whenever it's used. This includes access by users and administrators.

Figure 7-2 shows our secret Cola formula, as perceived by Azure RMS, and the client application used to open the document. The ingredients are water, sugar, and a secret substance known as brown #16. This information is stored in documents all over your organization, and you want to keep that information protected, whether it's inside your perimeter or shared with an authorized external source.

Every document is protected with a content key (green key) that is generated by the client application used to open the document. A unique key is generated for every document protected. When the document is opened, a call is made to the Azure Information Protection tenant, where the root key is stored (red key, labeled "License protected by customer-owned RSA key"). Without having both keys, the contents (red box) is unreadable. Your tenant root key can be automatically generated by Microsoft, or you can manage your own key.

■ **Note** This process is handled at the client level. The secret formula document does not pass through any Microsoft service.

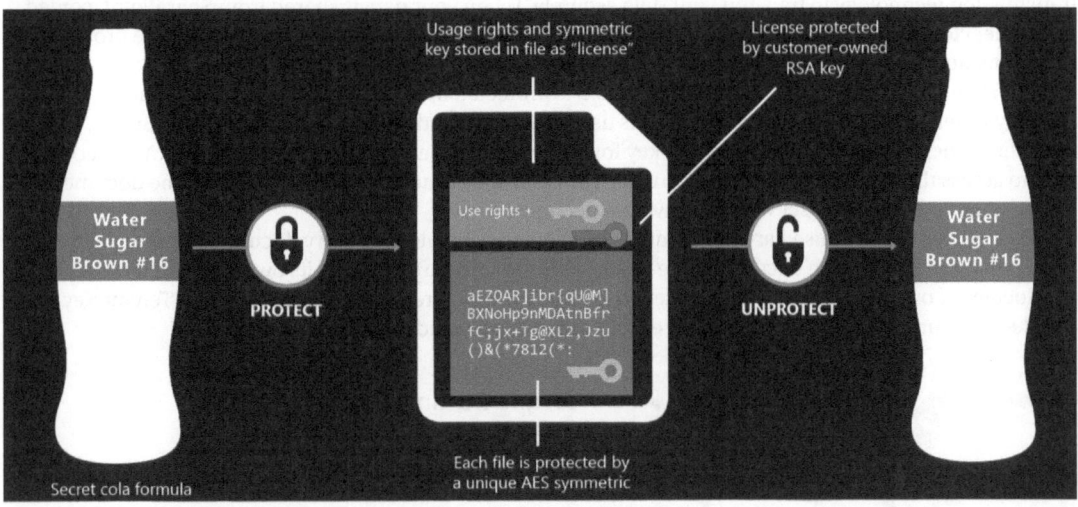

Figure 7-2. *Azure RMS encryption—high-level*

Identity

The first time a user opens a right-protected document on a new device, a call is made to Azure RMS. This is an automatic and invisible check of the user's identity, made against their Azure Active Directory. Once it's determined the user is authenticated and authorized to access the document, the connection is, again, automatically redirected to the organization's Azure Information Protection tenant. This will issue a certificate for the Azure RMS to retrieve the part of the document that has the authorization policy (green box in Figure 7-2). Azure RMS isn't concerned about the contents of the document, just the policy. Your data isn't passed through the service. Figure 7-3 shows the authentication flow.

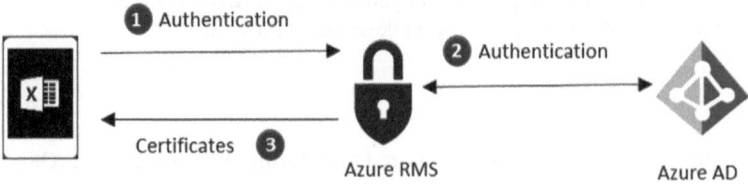

Figure 7-3. *Azure RMS Identity*

Encryption

At rest, in transit, on-premise, in the cloud, or a hybrid setup—no matter what configuration you use, you can be assured that Azure RMS will protect your data. Azure RMS uses industry-standard cryptography, has worked diligently to pass many security compliances around the world, and uses a wide array of secure transmission technology to transmit your data securely. When your data is shared from SharePoint, copied to another cloud service, and even if a document is e-mailed as an attachment, your files will be protected. The protection and instructions on how to access the file travel with it.

Referring to Figure 7-4, your content (red box) is protected by an Advanced Encryption Standard (AES) symmetric encryption algorithm. This is used to encrypt and decrypt your documents. Briefly, AES symmetric encryption algorithms use one key for encryption and another key for decryption. You need both keys to access the contents of the document. If a user fails the authorization to Azure RMS, the document will be unreadable, as the user won't receive the decryption key.

The encryption keys used are the unique keys that are generated for every document or e-mail you wish to protect (green key). Each document or e-mail protected by Azure RMS has its own key, and it travels with the document or e-mail. The decryption key (red key) is your Azure Information Protection Tenant Key. This key is common to all documents and e-mail that are protected by Azure RMS.

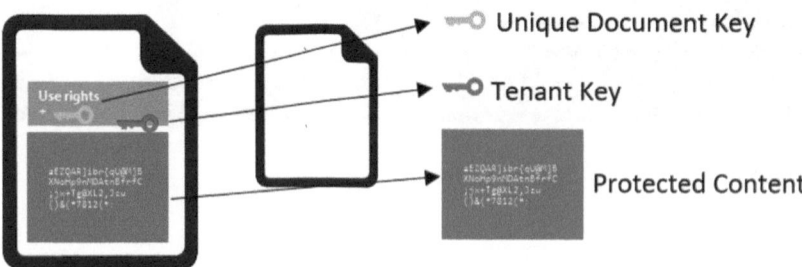

Figure 7-4. *Azure RMS encryption keys*

Microsoft Managed Tenant Key

By default, when you sign up for Azure Information Protection, Microsoft takes care of generating your tenant key. Microsoft can take care of generating your key and manage all aspects related to your key. Your key will be stored in Microsoft Online Services in a highly controlled and secure environment. Choosing Microsoft to manage your key is the simplest option. After you sign up for Azure Information Protection, you choose Microsoft to manage the key, and Microsoft takes care of the rest.

Bring Your Own Key

The other option is to choose to manage your own key, which is referred to as "bring your own key" (BYOK). This is handled through a service called the Azure Key Vault. You can use the Azure Key Vault not only for your Azure RMS Tenant key but also for other authentication keys, such as a custom application developed in Azure that requires keys, storage account keys, data encryption keys, .PFX files, and passwords. This process involves generating a tenant key on-premises from a Hardware Security Module (HSM). An HSM is an encryption device with functions that include generating keys and helping to encrypt or decrypt data. Once you generate a key from your HSM, you securely transfer your key from your HSM to Microsoft-owned and -managed HSMs. Your key is then stored in your Azure Key Vault.

Authorization Policy

After the identification and authorization step is completed and a user has their authorization policy, Azure RMS decrypts and evaluates the policy to determine the user's rights. The authorization policy is a wrapper around the document that details what can be done with the data and who can access it (see Figure 7-5).

Figure 7-5. *User rights*

The policy or policies for what can be done to the file can include whether it can be saved, edited, forwarded, or printed. Table 7-1 shows the rights that can be assigned and their descriptions.

Table 7-1. *User Rights*

User Right	Description
Edit Content, Edit Policy: DOCEDIT	Allows the user to modify, rearrange, format, or filter the content inside the application. It does not grant the right to save the edited copy.
Save Policy: EDIT	Allows the user to save the document in its current location. In Office applications, this right also allows the user to modify the document.
Comment Policy: COMMENT	Enables the option to add annotations or comments to the content. This right, available in the SDK, is also available as an ad-hoc policy in the Azure Information Protection and RMS Protection module for Windows PowerShell and has been implemented in some software vendor applications. However, it is not widely used and is not currently supported by Office applications.
Save As, Export Policy: EXPORT	Enables the option to save the content to a different file name (Save As). For Office documents and the Azure Information Protection client, the file can be saved without protection. This right also allows the user to perform other export options in applications, such as Send to OneNote. Note: If this right is not granted, Office applications let a user save a document to a new name, if the selected file format natively supports Rights Management protection.

(*continued*)

Table 7-1. (*continued*)

User Right	Description
Forward Policy: FORWARD	Enables the option to forward an e-mail message and to add recipients to the To and Cc lines. This right does not apply to documents; only e-mail messages. Does not allow the forwarder to grant rights to other users as part of the forward action. Note: When you send an e-mail to another organization, the recipient's Outlook client or Outlook web app requires the Edit Content, Edit right (common name), in addition to Forward.
Full Control Policy: OWNER	Grants all rights to the document, and all available actions can be performed. Includes the ability to remove protection and to re-protect a document.
Print Policy: PRINT	Enables the options to print the content.
Reply Policy: REPLY	Enables the Reply option in an e-mail client, without allowing changes in the To or Cc lines. Note: When you send an e-mail to another organization, the recipient's Outlook client or Outlook web app requires the Edit Content, Edit right (common name), in addition to Reply.
Reply All Policy: REPLYALL	Enables the Reply All option in an e-mail client but doesn't allow the user to add recipients to the To or Cc lines. Note: When you send an e-mail to another organization, the recipient's Outlook client or Outlook web app requires the Edit Content, Edit right (common name), in addition to Reply All.
View, Open, Read Policy: VIEW	Allows the user to open the document and see the content.
Copy Policy: EXTRACT	Enables options to copy data (including screen captures) from the document into the same or another document. In some applications, it also allows the whole document to be saved in unprotected form.
Allow Macros Policy: OBJMODEL	Enables the option to run macros or perform other programmatic or remote access to the content in a document.

Who can access the file is controlled by the permission polices. These policies can be assigned to an individual or group. Table 7-2 shows the permission polices that can be assigned and their operations.

Table 7-2. *Permissions Policies*

Permissions Level	Rights Included (Common Name)
Viewer	View, Open, Read; Reply; Reply All Note: Do not use this permission level for Reply or Reply All when you send an e-mail to another organization and the recipient uses Outlook or the Outlook web app. Instead, use Reviewer, which includes the **Edit Content, Edit** right (common name), which these e-mail clients require to reply.
Reviewer	View, Open, Read; Save; Edit Content, Edit; Reply; Reply All; Forward
Co-Author	View, Open, Read; Save; Edit Content, Edit; Copy; View Rights; Allow Macros; Save As, Export; Print; Reply; Reply All; Forward
Co-Owner	View, Open, Read; Save; Edit Content, Edit; Copy; View Rights; Allow Macros; Save As, Export; Print; Reply; Reply All; Forward; Full Control

RMS-Enlightened Applications

To access rights-protected documents, we must use RMS-enlightened applications. RMS-enlightened applications can process the encrypted file information and allow users to consume the content, according to the permissions that are defined in the authorization policy. Table 7-3 shows which client applications are RMS-enlightened.

Table 7-3. *RMS-Enlightened Applications*

Operating System	Word, Excel, PowerPoint	Protected PDF	E-mail	Other File Types
Windows	Office 2010 Office 2013 Office 2016 Office Mobile apps (Azure RMS only)[1] Office Online [2]	Azure Information Protection client for Windows Gaaiho Doc GigaTrust Desktop PDF Client for Adobe Foxit Reader Nitro PDF Reader RMS sharing app	Outlook 2010 Outlook 2013 Office 2016 Outlook Web App (OWA)[3] Windows Mail [4]	Azure Information Protection client for Windows: Text, images, pfile RMS sharing application for Windows: Text, images, pfile SealPath RMS plug-in for AutoCAD : .dwg
iOS	Office for iPad and iPhone [5] Office Online [2] TITUS Docs	Azure Information Protection app[1] Foxit Reader TITUS Docs	Azure Information Protection app [1] Citrix WorxMail NitroDesk [4] Outlook for iPad and iPhone [4] OWA for iOS [3] TITUS Mail	Azure Information Protection app[1]: Text, images TITUS Docs: Pfile
Android	GigaTrust App for Android Office Online [2] Office Mobile (Azure RMS only) [1]	Azure Information Protection app [1] GigaTrust App for Android Foxit Reader RMS sharing app [1]	9Folders [1] Azure Information Protection app [1] GigaTrust App for Android [4] Citrix WorxMail NitroDesk [4] Outlook for Android [4] OWA for Android [3] and Samsung Email (S3 and later) TITUS Classification for Mobile	Azure Information Protection app [1]: Text, images
OS X	Office 2011 (AD RMS only) Office 2016 for Mac Office Online [2]	Foxit Reader RMS sharing app [1]	Outlook 2011 (AD RMS only) Outlook 2016 for Mac Outlook for Mac	RMS sharing app [1]: Text, images, pfile
Windows 10 Mobile	Office Mobile apps (Azure RMS only) [1]	Not supported	Citrix WorxMail Outlook Mail	Not supported

(*continued*)

Table 7-3. (*continued*)

Operating System	Word, Excel, PowerPoint	Protected PDF	E-mail	Other File Types
Windows RT	Office 2013 RT Office Online [1]	Not supported	Outlook 2013 RT Mail app for Windows Windows Mail [4]	Siemens JT2Go: JT files
Windows Phone 8.1	Office Mobile (AD RMS only)	RMS sharing app [1]	Outlook Mobile [4]	RMS sharing app [1]: Text, images, pfile
Blackberry 10	Not supported	Not supported	Blackberry e-mail [4]	Not supported

[1]Supports viewing protected content.

[2]Supports viewing protected documents when an unprotected document is uploaded to a protected library in SharePoint Online and OneDrive for Business.

[3]If a recipient receives a protected e-mail and is not using Exchange as the mail server, or if the sender belongs to another organization, this content can be opened only in a rich e-mail client, such as Outlook. This content cannot be opened from Outlook Web Access.

[4]Uses Exchange ActiveSync IRM, which must be enabled by the Exchange administrator. Users can view, reply, and reply all for protected -mail messages but cannot protect new e-mail messages themselves. If a recipient receives a protected e-mail and is not using Exchange as the mail server, or if the sender belongs to another organization, this content can be opened only in a rich e-mail client, such as Outlook. This content cannot be opened from Outlook Web Access or from mobile mail clients using Exchange Active Sync IRM.

[5]Supports viewing and editing protected documents for iOS; supports viewing protected documents for Android. For more information, see the following post on the Office blog: "Azure Rights Management support comes to Office for iPad and iPhone" (`https://blogs.office.com/en-us/2015/07/22/azure-rights-management-support-comes-to-office-for-ipad-and-iphone-2/`).

How Do I Control How They Are Used?

In order to get Information Rights Management in SharePoint Online, you must activate Rights Management in Azure. Once Azure Rights Management is enabled, you'll have protection across your Azure services, as well as the offerings in Office 365: Exchange, Office, OneDrive, and SharePoint. There are some requirements that must be taken care of before we can activate RMS. These are listed in Table 7-4.

Table 7-4. *Rights ManagementRrequirements*

Requirement	Description
Subscription	Azure RMS requires a subscription for Enterprise Mobility Suite or an Azure Information Protection Premium subscription.
Azure Active Directory	This is the only identity provider Azure RMS authenticates against. If you want to use your on-premise accounts, Active Directory federation or AD DS must be in place.
Network	There are connection configurations that must to be implemented to allow access to Azure and O365 services. These can be found in the following article: `https://support.office.com/en-us/article/Office-365-URLs-and-IP-address-ranges-8548a211-3fe7-47cb-abb1-355ea5aa88a2?ui=en-US&rs=en-US&ad=US should I list out all these ports in another table?`.

Activating RMS

Here are the steps to activate the Rights Management Services (Figure 7-6).

1. Sign into the Azure Classic Portal or `https://manage.windowsazure.com`.

2. In the left pane, click ACTIVE DIRECTORY—near the bottom.

3. From the active directory page, click RIGHTS MANAGEMENT.

4. Select the directory to manage for Rights Management, click ACTIVATE, and then confirm your action.

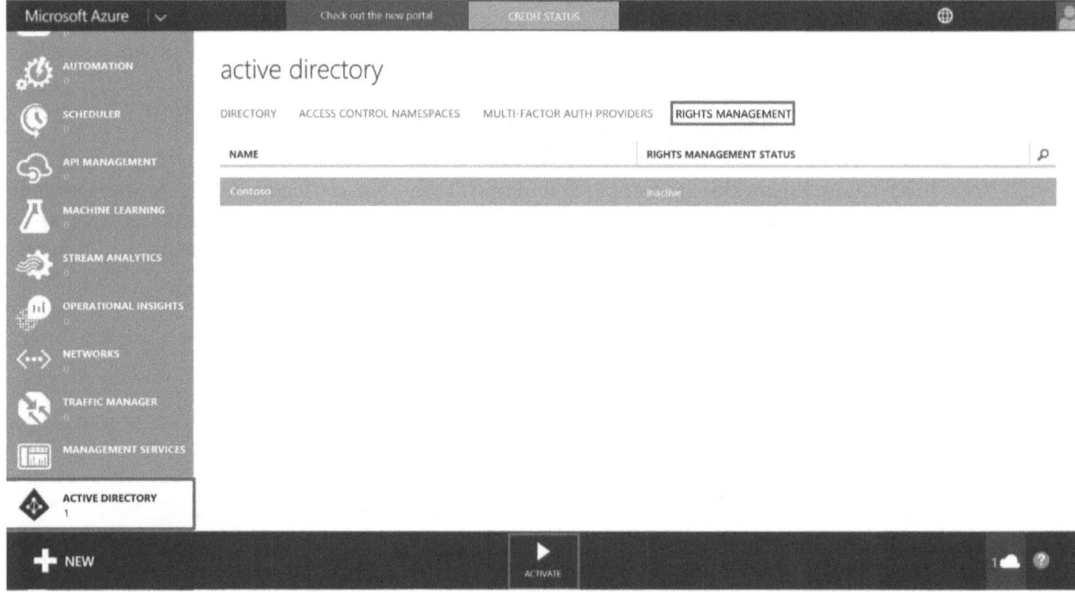

Figure 7-6. *Activate Azure Rights Management*

■ **Note**   If you haven't set up the above-mentioned subscriptions, you will see the error in Figure 7-7.

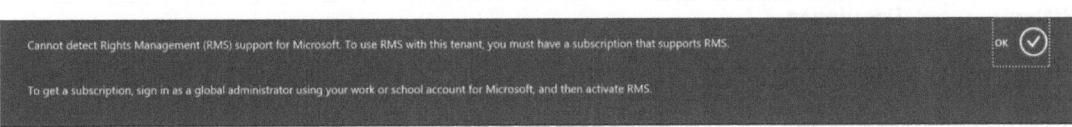

Figure 7-7. *Azure subscription error*

If the subscriptions are active, you'll see the activation page, such as that shown in Figure 7-8.

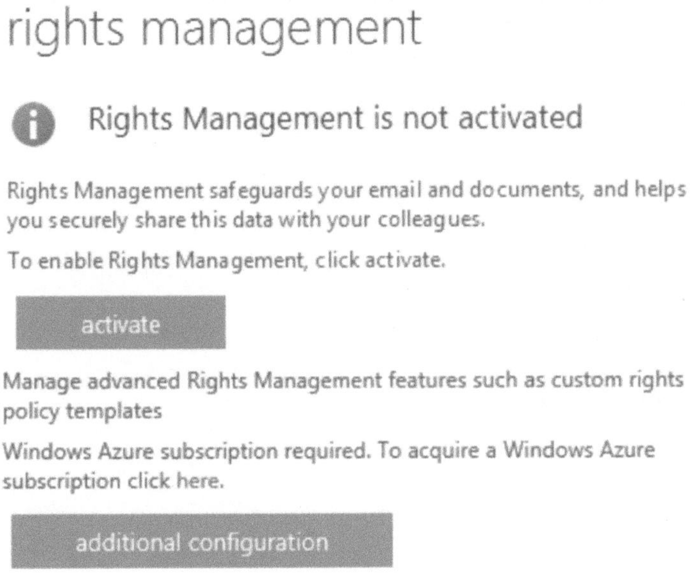

rights management

ⓘ   Rights Management is not activated

Rights Management safeguards your email and documents, and helps
you securely share this data with your colleagues.

To enable Rights Management, click activate.

    activate

Manage advanced Rights Management features such as custom rights
policy templates

Windows Azure subscription required. To acquire a Windows Azure
subscription click here.

    additional configuration

Figure 7-8. *Rights Management activation page*

Upon clicking the activate button, you'll see the *activate* button change to *deactivate*.
Back on the Rights Management page, you'll see the previously selected directory's Rights Management
status set to Active (see Figure 7-9).

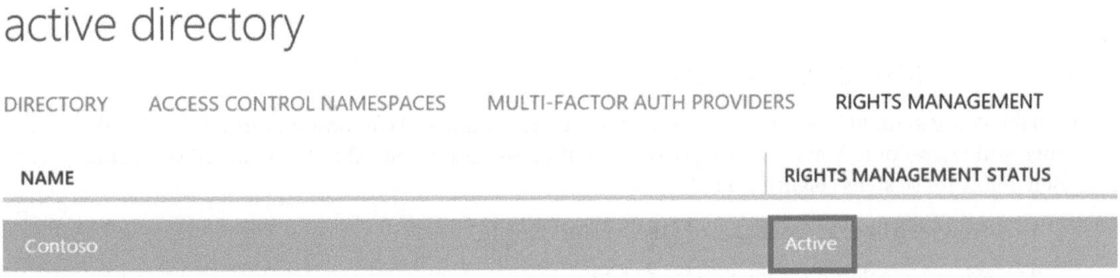

active directory

DIRECTORY   ACCESS CONTROL NAMESPACES   MULTI-FACTOR AUTH PROVIDERS   **RIGHTS MANAGEMENT**

NAME	RIGHTS MANAGEMENT STATUS
Contoso	Active

Figure 7-9. *Active Rights Management status*

There are four other Rights Management Statuses to be aware of, as shown in Table 7-5.

Table 7-5. *Rights Management Status*

Status	Description
Active	Rights Management is enabled.
Inactivate	Rights Management is disabled.
Unavailable	Rights Management services is down.
Unauthorized	You don't have permission to view the status of Rights Management. Your account may be locked out, or you're not the Global Administrator.

Clicking our recently activated Rights Management Directory, we're taken to the start page for Rights Management (see Figure 7-10).

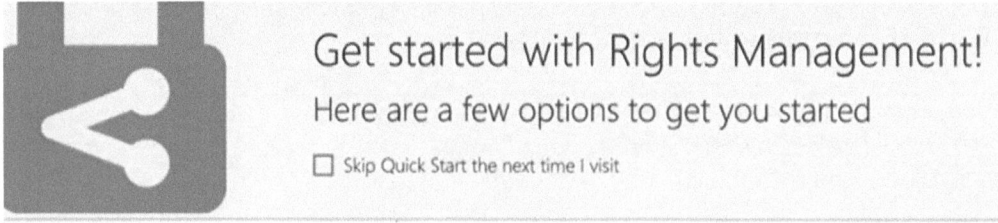

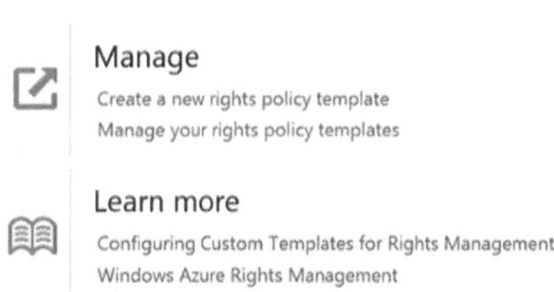

Figure 7-10. *Rights Management start page*

RMS Activation for Office 365

Azure Rights Management has been enabled in your Azure tenant and can now be turned on in both Exchange and SharePoint. You first must go to your Office 365 admin portal and activate IRM for Office 365 and then follow these steps (Figure 7-11):

1. Browse to `https://portal.office.com` and log in.

2. Navigate to Settings then Service & Add-ins.

3. Find and Select Microsoft Azure Information Protection.

4. Click Manage Microsoft Azure Information Protection Settings in the window that slides in.

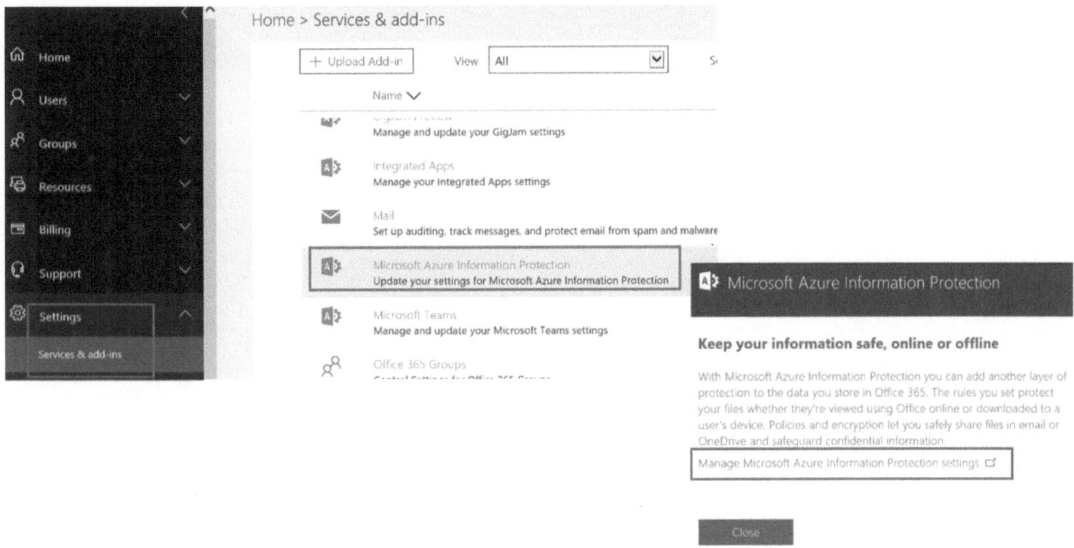

Figure 7-11. *Activate Azure RMS in Office 365*

5. Click activate on the next window, as shown in Figure 7-12 (it looks the same as the page in Azure Rights Management).

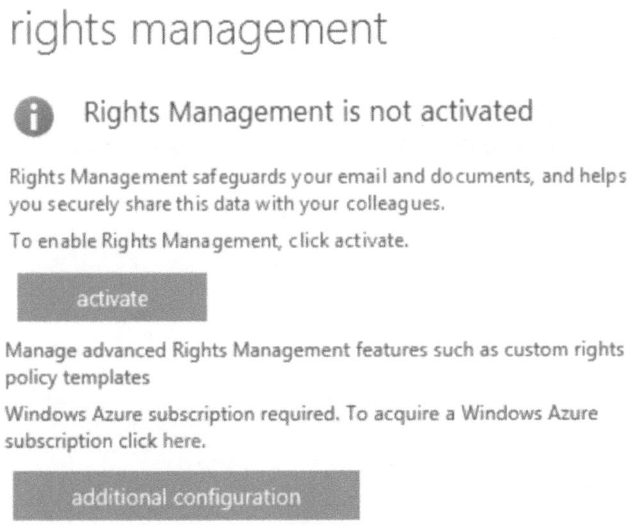

rights management

ℹ️ Rights Management is not activated

Rights Management safeguards your email and documents, and helps you securely share this data with your colleagues.

To enable Rights Management, click activate.

> activate

Manage advanced Rights Management features such as custom rights policy templates

Windows Azure subscription required. To acquire a Windows Azure subscription click here.

> additional configuration

Figure 7-12. *Azure RMS in Office 365 not activated*

You should see Rights Management as Activated, as in Figure 7-13.

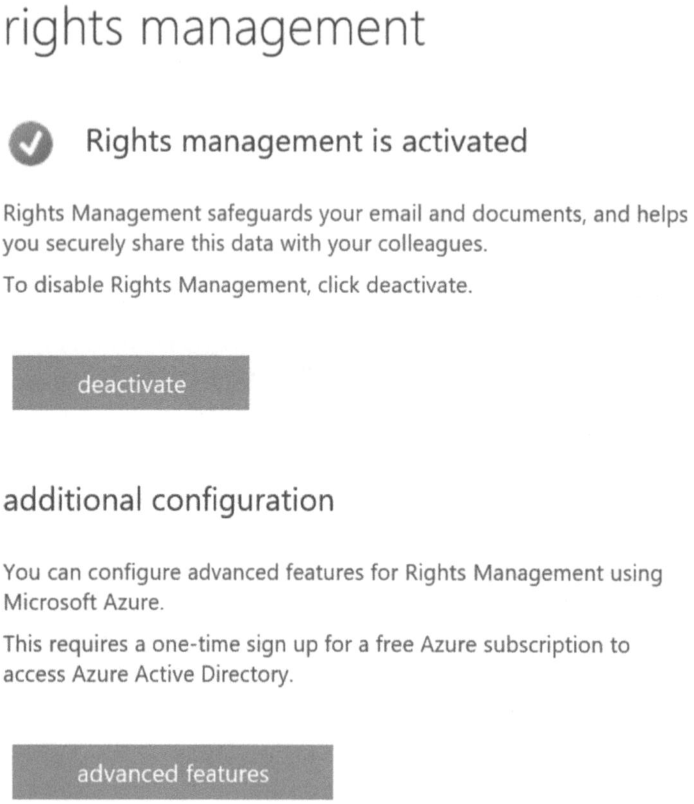

rights management

 ## Rights management is activated

Rights Management safeguards your email and documents, and helps you securely share this data with your colleagues.

To disable Rights Management, click deactivate.

deactivate

additional configuration

You can configure advanced features for Rights Management using Microsoft Azure.

This requires a one-time sign up for a free Azure subscription to access Azure Active Directory.

advanced features

Figure 7-13. *Azure RMS in Office 365 activated*

RMS Activation for SharePoint Online

SharePoint Online can require activation for RMS at the SharePoint Admin level for lists and libraries to inherit whatever policies are created in your Azure RMS.

Admin Activation

Here are the steps to activate the Admin features:

1. Browse to the SharePoint Admin page `https://domain-admin.sharepoint.com/_layouts/15/online/TenantSettings.aspx`.

2. Click settings on the left.

3. Select "Use the IRM service specified in your configuration."

4. Click the Refresh IRM Settings button.

If you don't click Refresh IRM Settings on activation (Figure 7-14), users won't see Information Rights Management configuration settings on lists or libraries.

Figure 7-14. *RMS in SharePoint Online*

Library Activation

Document libraries and lists have additional settings that can be configured. Here are the steps to follow to achieve this:

1. Browse to the library or list you wish to activate.

2. Click the cog ⚙ on the upper right of the library.

3. Click Library settings (Figure 7-15).

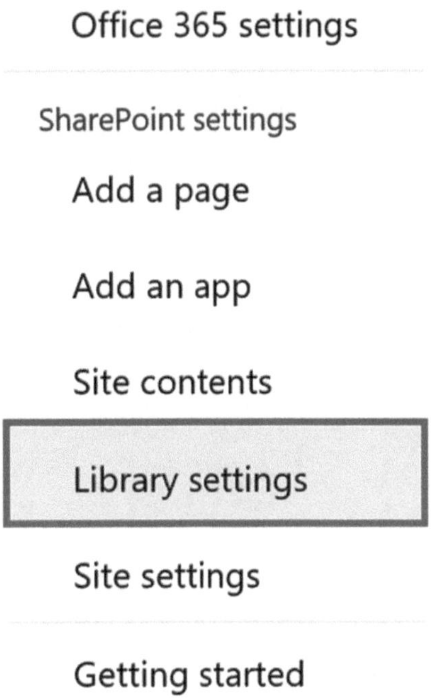

Office 365 settings

SharePoint settings

Add a page

Add an app

Site contents

Library settings

Site settings

Getting started

Figure 7-15. *Library settings options*

> 4. Under Permissions and Management, click Information Rights Management (Figure 7-16).

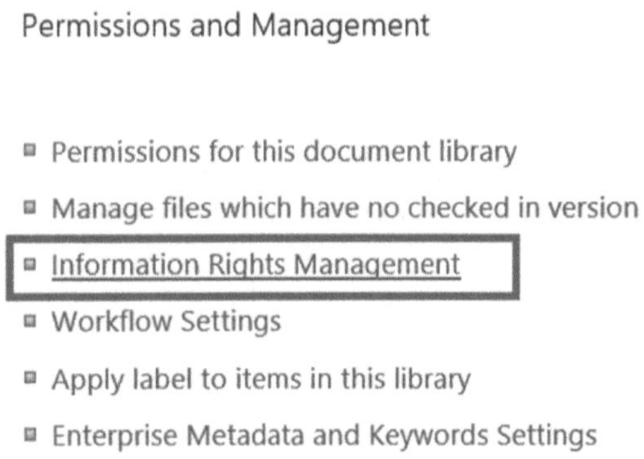

Permissions and Management

- Permissions for this document library
- Manage files which have no checked in version
- Information Rights Management
- Workflow Settings
- Apply label to items in this library
- Enterprise Metadata and Keywords Settings

Figure 7-16. *Information Rights Management settings*

> 5. On the Information Rights Management Settings page, select the Restrict permission to documents in this library on download check box (Figure 7-17).

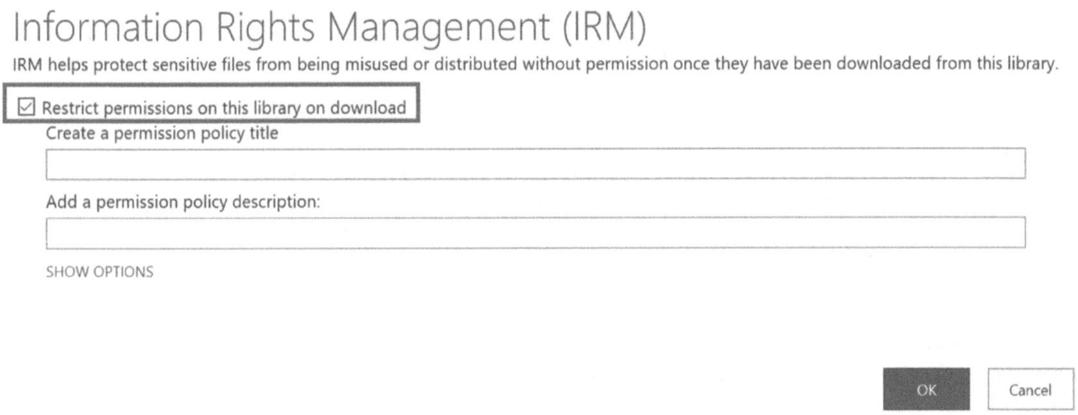

Information Rights Management (IRM)

IRM helps protect sensitive files from being misused or distributed without permission once they have been downloaded from this library.

☑ Restrict permissions on this library on download
    Create a permission policy title

    Add a permission policy description:

SHOW OPTIONS

                                         OK   Cancel

Figure 7-17. *Restrict permissions on library option*

    6.   Choose a descriptive name for the policy title that coincides with the purpose of the policy. For example: A document library has Word Docs that contain the latest schematics for a new product, we don't want our users to take screenshots of the document. We do not check the "Allow viewers to print" and name the policy "Newest Product no Print on Download" (Figure 7-18).

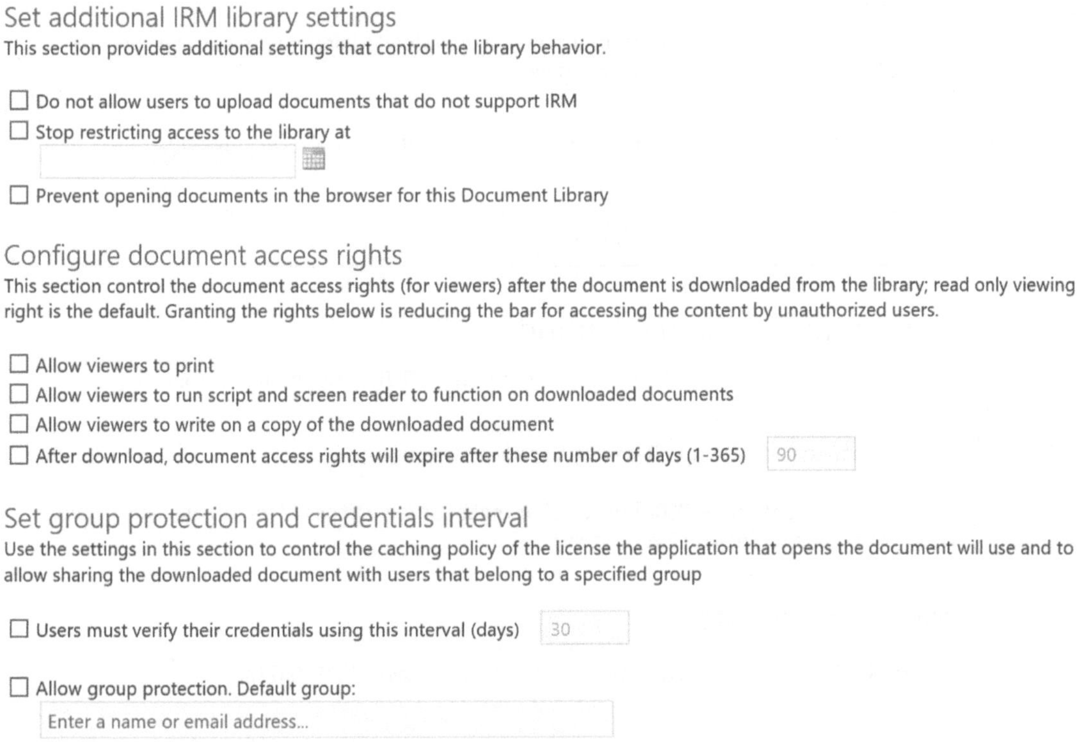

Set additional IRM library settings
This section provides additional settings that control the library behavior.

☐ Do not allow users to upload documents that do not support IRM
☐ Stop restricting access to the library at

☐ Prevent opening documents in the browser for this Document Library

Configure document access rights
This section control the document access rights (for viewers) after the document is downloaded from the library; read only viewing right is the default. Granting the rights below is reducing the bar for accessing the content by unauthorized users.

☐ Allow viewers to print
☐ Allow viewers to run script and screen reader to function on downloaded documents
☐ Allow viewers to write on a copy of the downloaded document
☐ After download, document access rights will expire after these number of days (1-365)   90

Set group protection and credentials interval
Use the settings in this section to control the caching policy of the license the application that opens the document will use and to allow sharing the downloaded document with users that belong to a specified group

☐ Users must verify their credentials using this interval (days)   30

☐ Allow group protection. Default group:
    Enter a name or email address...

Figure 7-18. *RMS in SharePoint Online Document Library Settings*

7. Click Show Options button to reveal what IRM protection can be applied. Options are listed in Table 7-6.

Table 7-6. *IRM Protection Options*

List Item	Description
Do not allow users to upload documents that do not support IRM	Requires users to upload documents from IRM-enlightened applications only.
Stop restricting access to the library at	Remove restricted permissions from this list or library on a specific date.
Prevent opening documents in the browser for this Document Library	If a user doesn't have a compatible application to view a document, Office Web Apps allows rendering of documents in the browser. Selecting this option renders the documents in the browser in Read Only Mode. Note: Screen capture prevention doesn't work for browsers.
Allow viewers to print	Enables printing of documents from the list or library.
Allow viewers to run script and screen reader to function on downloaded documents	Allow people with at least the View Items permission to run embedded code or macros on a document.
Allow viewers to write on a copy of the downloaded document	Allow users to edit the documents after download.
After download, document access rights will expire after these number of days (1-365)	Prevents access to a downloaded document after the specified number of days.
Users must verify their credentials using this interval (days)	Require users to re-authenticate at specific intervals.
Allow group protection	Allow group protection, so that users can share with members of the same group.

RMS Activation for Exchange Online

Exchange online IRM is enabled through PowerShell. There isn't a GUI component. The following commands must be run:

- Point Exchange to your Azure RMS Key Location by running

```
Set-IRMConfiguration -RMSOnlineKeySharingLocation https://sp-rms.na.aadrm.com/
TenantManagement/ServicePartner.svc
```

- Import the key by running

```
Import-RMSTrustedPublishingDomain -RMSOnline -name "RMS Online"
```

- Enable IRM Functionality by running

```
Set-IRMConfiguration -InternalLicensingEnabled $true
```

Protecting Your Files

Azure RMS allows the protection of documents and enforcement of user rights through Enlightened Applications (as discussed previously). We call this Native Protection. Azure RMS also provides protection to documents that don't have an RMS-enlightened application, such as an image file. This is called Generic Protection. With Generic Protection, we protect the files with encryption and authentication but can't enforce Authentication Policies (user rights and restrictions). To access these files, Microsoft provides a free downloadable application called the Rights Management Sharing Application (RMS Sharing App). The RMS Sharing App not only protects the generic files that are protected by your RMS but also allows you to access and edit files from other organizations that use Azure RMS.

Protecting E-mail with Outlook Client

In Outlook, start a new e-mail and click on the Options tab. Then, click the Permissions button and select the permission level you wish to protect the e-mail with (see Figure 7-19).

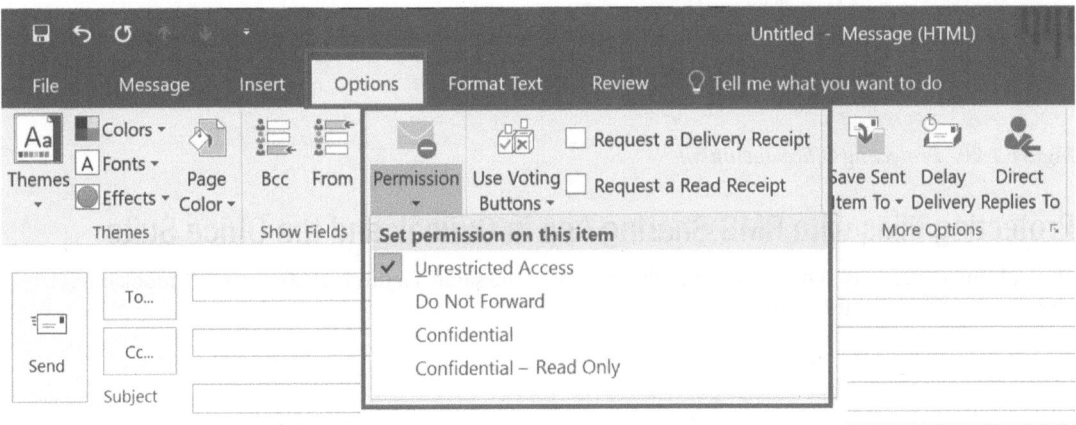

Figure 7-19. *Protecting Outlook e-mails*

Protecting a Document with Office Suite Client

In an MS Office Application, click the File Menu Option. Then click Protect Document and select the permission level you wish to protect the document with (Figure 7-20).

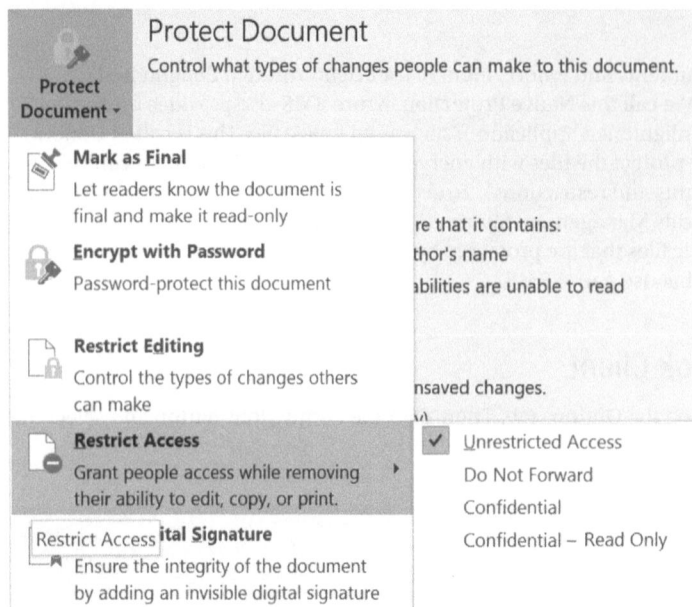

Figure 7-20. Protecting Office documents

Protecting Files with RMS Sharing App in Outlook and the Office Suite

Outlook and Office have different UIs, but the process is the same. Figure 7-21 shows the Outlook interface, and Figure 7-22 shows the Office interface.

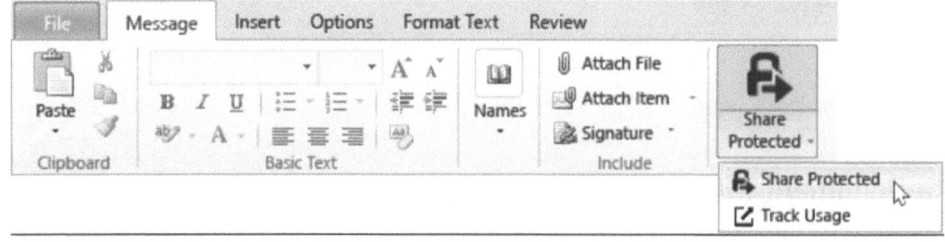

Figure 7-21. Outlook and RMS Sharing App

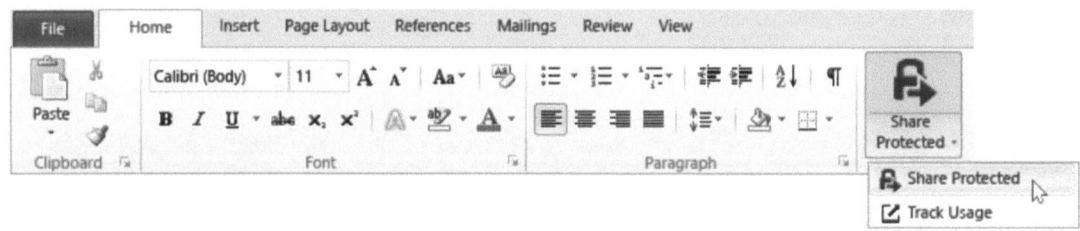

Figure 7-22. Office and RMS Sharing App

Selecting the Share Protected option will bring up a dialog box with options to protect the file (shown in Figure 7-23). Table 7-7 lists these options and their descriptions.

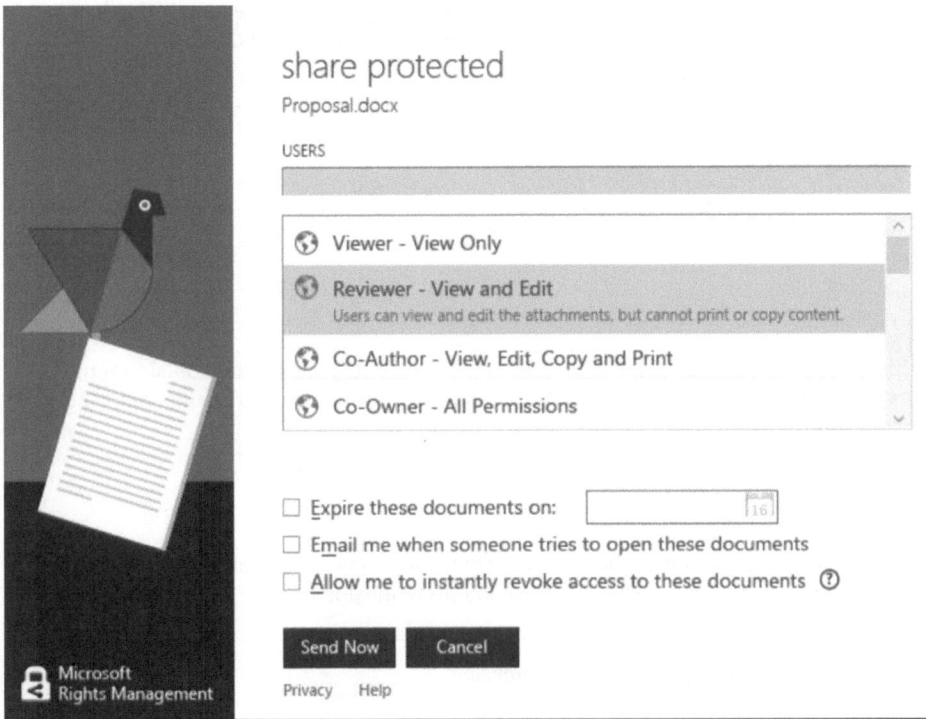

Figure 7-23. *RMS Sharing App dialog box*

Table 7-7. *Share Protected Options*

Option	Description
USERS	List of user e-mails intended to open the file. Note: Personal e-mail addresses are not currently supported by the RMS Sharing app.
Viewer—View Only **Reviewer—View and Edit** **Co-Author—View, Edit, Copy, and Print** **Co-Owner—All Permissions**	Select one of these options to define the rights of the protected document.
Expire these documents on	Prevents access to the file on the specified date.
Email me when somebody tries to open these documents	Receive e-mail notifications whenever somebody tries to open the document that you're protecting. The e-mail message will say who tried to open it, when, and whether they were successful.
Allow me to instantly revoke access to these documents	Revocation or "Remote Kill" allows you to revoke access to the documents later, by using the document tracking site. Note: If option isn't selected, you can revoke access later, by using the document tracking site.

PDDF File

When a Word, Excel, PowerPoint, or PDF file is protected through the RMS Sharing App in Outlook, a second file is added as an attachment with a .pddf extension. This is a read-only protected version of the document that can only be accessed by authorized users. In order for the intended user to read this file, they must be authorized and have the AMS Sharing App.

Azure RMS Templates

Templates are containers for assigning policy to your documents. When Azure RMS was activated, a few default templates were created automatically.

Confidential

When we assign this template to a document, the document will not be able to be shared outside your organization. Users have permission to interact with the file as they normally would; they just can't share the file outside the organization.

Confidential View Only

When we assign this template to a document, the document will not be able to be shared outside your organization, and users have permission view to only the contents of the document.

■ **Note**   The default templates cannot be deleted, only archived.

Custom Templates

If the default templates don't fulfill your organization's needs, or you want to build off of them, you can create custom templates.

You can access your templates from either the Office 365 portal or the Azure portal. I have discussed both methods previously. Whichever method you choose, you'll be taken to the same location: the Azure administration portal.

Adding New Template

Browse back to your active directory and select Rights Management (Figure 7-24).

active directory

DIRECTORY   ACCESS CONTROL NAMESPACES   MULTI-FACTOR AUTH PROVIDERS   RIGHTS MANAGEMENT

NAME	RIGHTS MANAGEMENT STATUS
Contoso	Inactive

Figure 7-24. *Azure RMS Rights Management*

From Manage, click Create a new rights policy template (Figure 7-25).

Manage

Create a new rights policy template

Manage your rights policy templates

Figure 7-25. *Create a new rights policy template*

On the next window, enter the language, name of the policy, and description, then click the check mark (Figure 7-26).

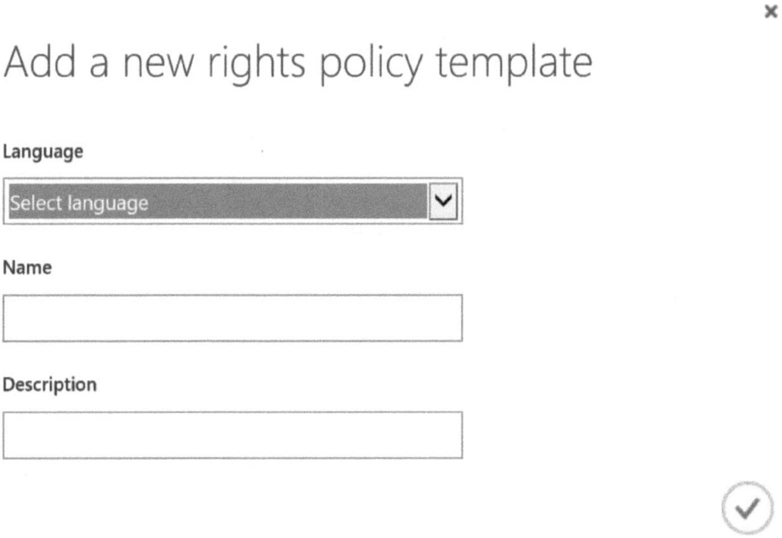

✕

Add a new rights policy template

Language

Select language ▾

Name

Description

✓

Figure 7-26. *Add a new rights policy template*

You'll see Azure working on creating your new template then take you back to the Azure RMS start screen. Click Manage your rights policy templates. The next screen, shown in Figure 7-27, shows the two default templates, as well as the custom template that was just created. Click the new Template.

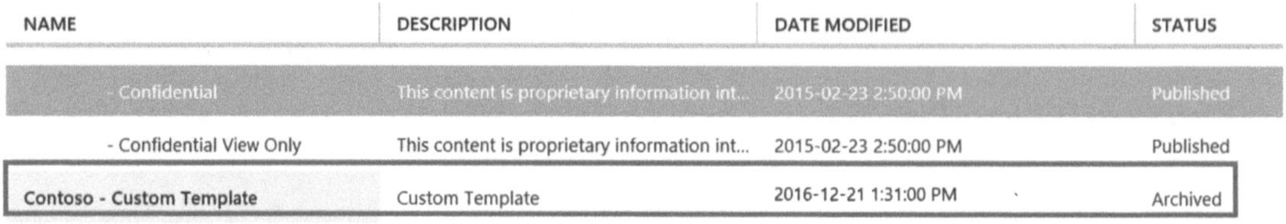

NAME	DESCRIPTION	DATE MODIFIED	STATUS
- Confidential	This content is proprietary information int...	2015-02-23 2:50:00 PM	Published
- Confidential View Only	This content is proprietary information int...	2015-02-23 2:50:00 PM	Published
Contoso - Custom Template	Custom Template	2016-12-21 1:31:00 PM	Archived

Figure 7-27. New template creation

You can then choose to continue with the wizard to complete the next three tasks of configuring the rights, publishing the template, and other configurations. For this example, I'll select Rights, at the top of the page (Figure 7-28).

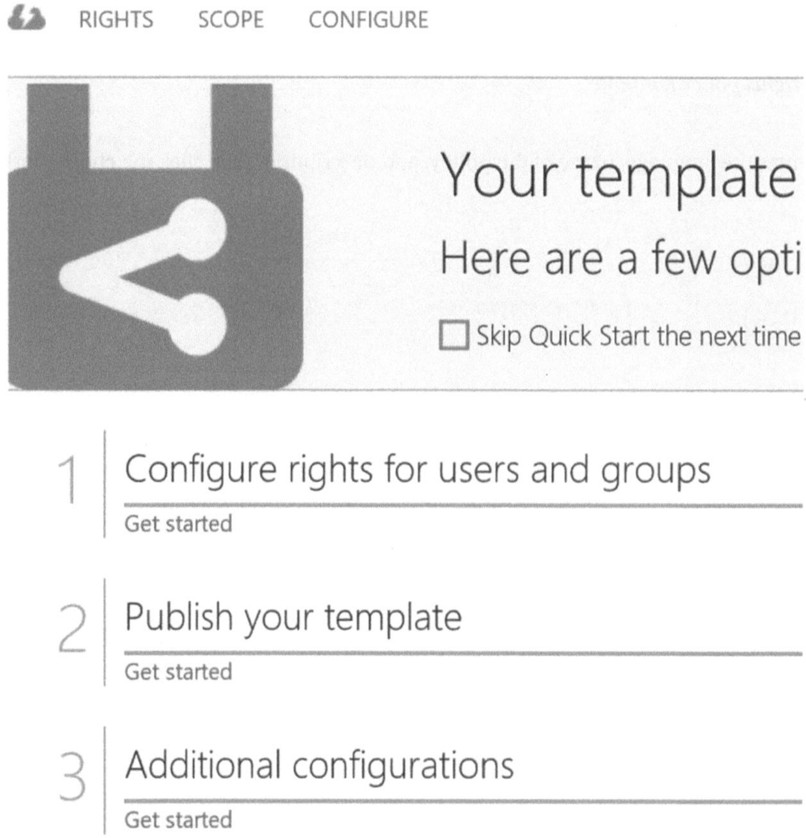

Figure 7-28. Configuring rights

Configure Rights and Scopes for Users and Groups

Let us go back to the start screen for user rights. Click the Get Started Now link. If you have set up AD Sync, you will see a list of users and groups that are syncing from your on-premise AD. If this list is empty, AD Sync has not been set up. Select the users and/or groups you wish to add to the policy then click the check mark (Figure 7-29).

CONFIGURE RIGHTS FOR USERS

Select users and groups

Groups must be email-enabled before they can be selected

SHOW	Groups ⌄		✓

NAME	DESCRIPTION 🔍	SELECTED
ⓘ admintest45 ⊕		None
ⓘ GroupShareGroup	GroupShareGroup	
ⓘ testingadmin ☒		
ⓘ TestingGroupDemo	TestingGroupDemo	
ⓘ TestingShareingGroup	dddd	

Figure 7-29. Selecting users and groups

■ **Note**   Groups will not be listed here unless they are e-mail-enabled groups. Groups that aren't e-mail-enabled will be displayed with an X (orange box).

Select the rights to the selected users and groups. You can mouse over the question mark to get more information about the right. Next, click the arrow at the lower right (Figure 7-30).

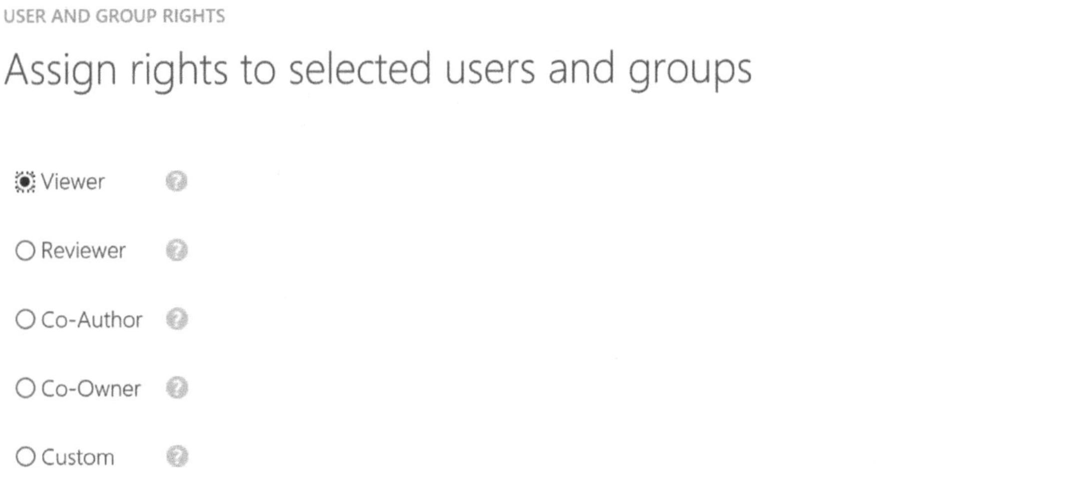

USER AND GROUP RIGHTS

Assign rights to selected users and groups

◉ Viewer   ❓

○ Reviewer   ❓

○ Co-Author   ❓

○ Co-Owner   ❓

○ Custom   ❓

Figure 7-30. Assigning rights to selected users and groups

Azure will create the custom template and take you back to the Rights page, to display what you previously configured. Clicking Scopes will take you to a similar page as Rights. In this screen, you select the users or groups that will be able to apply this template. By default, all users and groups in your organization can apply this template.

Additional Configurations and Publishing Your Template

Clicking Configure takes us to the screen where we can Publish and select other configurations. The top of the page is where we can choose to Publish the template, making it accessible to users and groups within our organization, or we can choose to Archive the template, removing it from view from our Office Applications, Azure, and Office 365 (Figure 7-31 and Table 7-8).

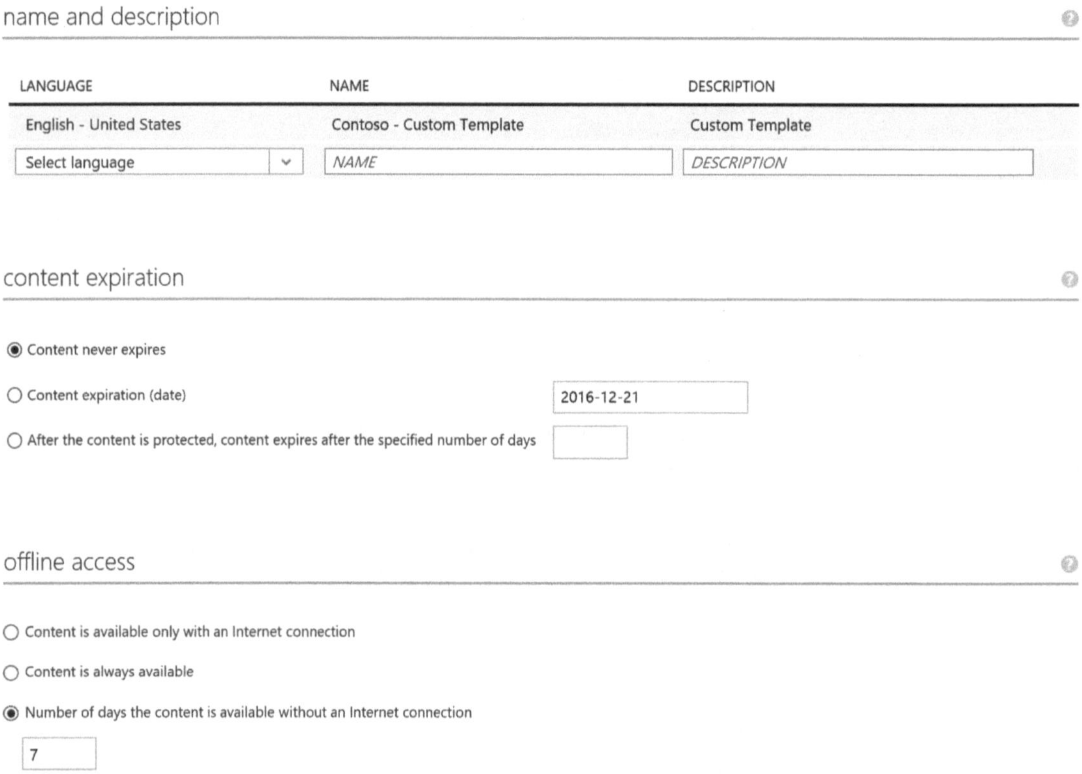

name and description

LANGUAGE	NAME	DESCRIPTION
English - United States	Contoso - Custom Template	Custom Template
Select language ⌄	NAME	DESCRIPTION

content expiration

◉ Content never expires

○ Content expiration (date)   2016-12-21

○ After the content is protected, content expires after the specified number of days

offline access

○ Content is available only with an Internet connection

○ Content is always available

◉ Number of days the content is available without an Internet connection

    7

Figure 7-31. *Publishing a template*

Table 7-8. *Publishing a Template*

Setting	More Information
Language	Make sure that you add each language that your company requires for the policy. Users with specific language configurations will see the language they've selected.
Content expiration	Number of days files that are protected by the template should not open. You can specify a date or the number of days, starting from the time that the protection is applied to the file.
Offline access	When a user reaches the limit of the specified number of days without Internet connection, or we choose Content is only available with an Internet Connection, the users will have to sign in again before they can open the file.

When all configuration items are set for the policy, scroll back to the top of the page and click Publish and then Click the Disk icon at the bottom of the page, to publish the template (Figure 7-32).

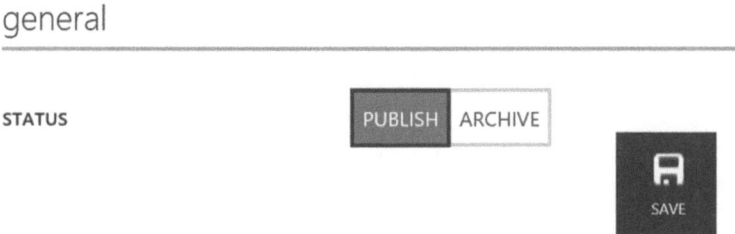

Figure 7-32. *Saving publishing options*

Once published, all users and groups selected during the template creation will now see this template (Figure 7-33).

Figure 7-33. *Template status shown as "Publish"*

Summary

Azure Rights Management is critical for every organization that is serious about protecting its sensitive information against unauthorized access. It is crucial for IT employees to take the time to learn how to properly configure and manage this service. By providing control to the administrator to monitor how this sensitive information is accessed and consumed, Azure RMS is a critical component of the success of any enterprise.

CHAPTER 8

■ ■ ■

Introduction to the SharePoint Framework

BY NIKOLAS CHARLEBOIS-LAPRADE

Recently announced by Microsoft, the SharePoint Framework is generating a lot of interest in the industry. Built around the latest web development trends, it allows organizations to leverage the skill set of their current developers to build rich SharePoint experiences. In this chapter, I will be introducing that new framework and will cover the various components that are involved in developing modern applications on top of SharePoint using it. Microsoft announced at the Virtual SharePoint Summit on May 16, 2017, the framework available on-premises via Feature Pack 2 for SharePoint 2016. While the chapter's example focuses mostly on Office 365, everything covered in it will also be applicable to on-premises SharePoint 2016 environments.

History of SharePoint Development

Anyone who's been involved with the SharePoint technology for the past few years has seen the platform's developer story evolve from simply supporting customization via C# to supporting a wide range of other, more modern web technologies. Back in the SharePoint 2007 days, the only way to customize and extend the platform was to create server-side solutions using C# and deploying them in the server's Global Assembly Cache (GAC), by packaging them as Windows SharePoint Package solutions (.wsp). These solutions were referred to as Full Trust Code and required a server administrator to connect to the SharePoint server and deploy the solution using a command line tool (STSadm.exe).

When SharePoint 2010 was released a few years later, it introduced two new development models: Sandboxed solutions and the client-side object model. Sandboxed solutions allowed for a limited set of the SharePoint Object Model to be used and limited the solutions' scopes to the site collection in which they were deployed. Users having site collection administrator permissions could deploy the solutions, still packaged as .wsp files, directly in the new solutions gallery. There was no longer a need to deploy packages by connecting directly to the server and running STSadm.exe to have them deployed; it could now be done remotely. The client-side object model built on that idea of remote solutions and allowed users to develop solutions that would either run directly on the client side (using the JavaScript flavor) or that could be hosted on a server hosted outside of the SharePoint farm (using the Silverlight or .NET flavor) and have them interact with SharePoint remotely.

Then SharePoint 2013 came along and introduced a completely new development model, called SharePoint Apps model at the time and later renamed SharePoint Add-ins model. The beauty of this model was that it allowed for an add-in to be developed once, and be deployed to either a SharePoint on-premises environment or to SharePoint Online in Office 365. This new model came with the premise that all the code interaction with SharePoint would be done either on the client side or outside of SharePoint. The main goal of that new model was to reduce the load on the SharePoint server itself and have the solution run outside of the SharePoint processes.

As part of this new development model, two deployment flavors where offered. (there were three in the beginning, but the Auto-hosted one was discontinued): SharePoint-hosted or Provider-hosted. The SharePoint-hosted model implied that the code would be hosted on the SharePoint server but would be contained in a web site running outside of the SharePoint processes' scope. All SharePoint-hosted add-ins would have to be written in JavaScript and either use CSOM or call the available REST APIs to interact back with SharePoint. On the other hand, Provider-hosted add-ins had to be hosted entirely outside of SharePoint, on a different server. They could be coded in any web language available (PHP, .NET, JavaScript, etc.) and would also be communicating back to the SharePoint server, using CSOM or REST API calls. Now, if you built some widget-like user interface components for these add-ins and wanted to include them directly in one of your SharePoint pages, you had to wrap them into what is called an add-in part. An add-in part is nothing more than an iframe that you add on your page and that loads the remote (SharePoint-hosted or Provider-hosted) add-in. While this provided an interesting way of creating rich dashboard within your SharePoint sites, it also introduced its share of problems, notably issues with Cross-Domain scripting. The add-in model came a long way from the traditional server-side way of doing SharePoint customization, but still there was room for improvements.

New Framework

At the "Future of SharePoint" event hosted on May 4, 2016, Microsoft introduced a new development framework for SharePoint 2016 named the SharePoint Framework. The SharePoint Framework, often referred to as SPFx, runs entirely on the client side, directly within a SharePoint page. While it is a new development model for SharePoint 2016, it really is considered an addition to the existing add-in model introduced with SharePoint 2013. The SharePoint Framework leverages the same skill set required to build SharePoint Hosted add-ins, which are all built using JavaScript. In the past, developers wanting to get around the restrictions imposed by the traditional add-in model were using a Script Editor web part to inject JavaScript components and mimic add-ins parts. The SPFx aims at providing more elegant ways for these developers to create rich and interactive interfaces in SharePoint, by having the code loaded directly within the page, without the use of an iframe.

The new framework is technology agnostic, in the sense that, while requiring developers to know JavaScript, it supports any flavors of the language. Most examples from Microsoft you will find on the Web use the React.js and TypeScript frameworks, but in reality, you could use whatever JavaScript variant you wish. This makes it easier for organizations to reuse the current skill sets of their employees. Another interesting aspect of the framework is that it doesn't lock you down to using Microsoft-specific development tools. One could very well be using a Mac Book with XCode on it and be coding SharePoint applications, using the new SharePoint Framework. Visual Studio does, however, remain a first-class citizen with the SPFx and provides all the required scaffolding for the framework's projects.

The SharePoint Framework really reveals its strengths when we start talking about web parts. It introduces a new concept called Client-Side Web Parts, which can be thought of as traditional web parts having no server components whatsoever. They are made available directly in the Web Part section of the SharePoint ribbon and can be inserted directly within a page, without generating an iframe in the background. As with all SharePoint Framework solutions, Client-Side Web Parts is packaged as a new file format, represented by the file extension .SPPKG, and is deployed to your SharePoint sites using the traditional Add-in Catalog that was introduced with SharePoint 2013.

Client-Side Web Parts are added to SharePoint pages by using the new SharePoint page canvas, which is almost the equivalent of what page layouts are for classic SharePoint pages. While a canvas acts the same way a regular web part zone would, it differs in a way that is it reactive by default. What we mean by reactive is that if you were to modify the web part's properties, these properties would automatically take effect without you having to save the properties' changes and wait for the page to post back. For example, imagine a dumb Client-Side Web Part that simply displays a square of a given color. If that color is controlled by a color picker in the web part's properties, the moment you change the selected value (e.g., change from blue to red), the web part will get updated, and the new color will show up, even if you didn't save the web part's changes (Figure 8-1).

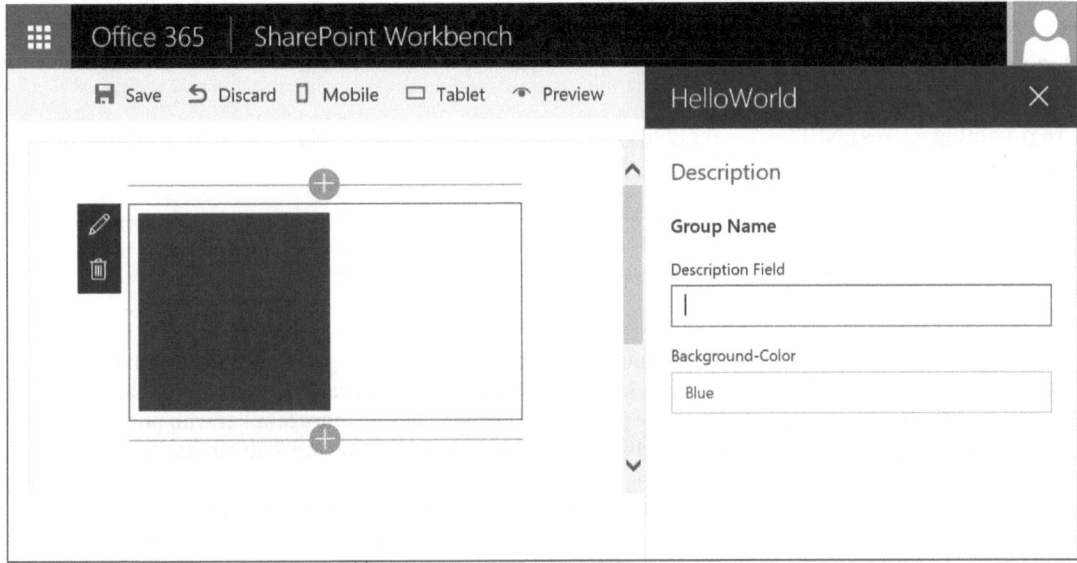

Figure 8-1. *Custom Client-Side Web Part showing properties panel*

If you pay close attention to Figure 8-1, you can clearly see that the Suite bar (top menu bar) wears the mention "SharePoint Workbench." We will be covering the SharePoint workbench in more depth in a later section of the current chapter, but for the moment all that is important is to understand that this new component of the SharePoint Framework is run locally and allows developers to easily test their Client-Side Web Parts. Not only does the SharePoint workbench run locally, it also doesn't require any SharePoint specific bits to be installed on the machine, and most of all doesn't require Visual Studio to be installed on the developer's workstation in order to let them interact with it. This is a huge step forward for Microsoft, who now truly allows anyone, running on any platform, to start developing on SharePoint.

With the evolution of the SharePoint developers' story, we've seen the requirements for a developer workstation be reduced to a minimum. Table 8-1 shows the evolution of the requirements for a SharePoint developer's workstation over the years, as new versions of the SharePoint product were released.

Table 8-1. *Development Model Comparisons*

	Full Trust Code	Sandboxed Solution	Client Side (JSOM, .NET, Silverlight)	Add-in Model	SharePoint Framework
Available in Product Version	2003, 2007, 2010, 2013, 2016	2010, 2013, 2016*, Online*	2010, 2013, 2016, Online	2013, 2016, Online	Online
Requires development to be done on Windows Server OS	Yes**	No	No	No	No
Requires Visual Studio	Yes	Yes	No	No	No
Programming language specific	Yes (.NET)	Yes (.NET)	Yes (.NET, JSOM, or Silverlight)	No***	No

*Only sandboxed solutions containing declarative elements (files and not code logic) are allowed.
**SharePoint 2010 is allowed for development to be done on Windows Operating System (e.g., Windows 7).
***SharePoint hosted add-ins require JavaScript.

While some may argue that the SharePoint Framework is not really language-agnostic, as shown in Table 8-1, because it fundamentally requires JavaScript to work, it is important to understand that it will support any flavors of libraries built on top of it. Some developers may be more familiar with pure Angular.js, while others may prefer to use Typescript (which is built on Angular.js 2), owing to its similarities to C# coding.

Additionally, if you pay close attention to the third data row of Table 8-1 , you'll see that the SharePoint Framework doesn't require you to use Visual Studio to build components. This is particularly interesting for developers who want to develop on Mac. Now that Microsoft has released both Visual Studio for Mac and Visual Studio code, Mac developers can now benefit from the advantages offered by one of the most popular integrated development environments (IDEs) out there. However, as specified in the table, you are not required to use Visual Studio to do development against the framework. One could very well decide to use any other IDE out there, or even use plain old Notepad to do so, if he/she wished. Most examples covered in the current chapter will be using Typescript to ease the transition between traditional SharePoint C# developers to SharePoint Framework developers, but know you can use whatever library you wish to follow along. The beauty of the SharePoint Framework is that this is totally up to the developer to choose what language and what tool set he/she wants to use.

An Evolutive Process

At the time of writing this chapter, the SharePoint Framework had just hit General Availability (GA), which means it had been rolled out to all Office 365 tenants. The SharePoint engineering team is continuously improving the framework's API and tools, and changes to the developers' components are being kept on GitHub as an open source project. You can get access to this project by browsing to the following URL: https://github.com/SharePoint/sp-dev-docs.

In order to ensure consistency across this chapter, and to avoid any confusion between various versions, we will be using the SharePoint Framework Release Candidate version 0 for all of our examples. While some components are likely to change slightly before the framework hits its production milestone, it is not expected that any breaking changes will be introduced, and, therefore, code written in this chapter should continue to work with future versions.

Major Components of the Framework

At a first glance, you may think that the SharePoint Framework is fairly simple to understand. After all, it is just JavaScript running inside a page, right? In reality, there is much more to the framework than meets the eye on the surface. Under its cover, the framework is made up of a mix of various components that are each essential to getting developers up and running. If you have been reading various articles on the Web about the SharePoint Framework, you've probably stumbled on some of these components but don't quite understand their roles within the begin scheme of things. Software components such as Node.js, Yeoman, NVM/NPM, and Gulp may not mean much to you at this point, but fear not, we will be covering each one of these in greater details in this section.

Node.js

This component is probably the most important of them all when it comes to the internal mechanics of the SharePoint Framework. By definition, Node.js is an event-driven, non-blocking IO model built on top of Chrome's JavaScript engine, but in order to simplify and keep things within the context of the SharePoint Framework, let me provide you with my own tuned-down explanation of what Node.js really does. In a nutshell, Node.js allows a developer to run JavaScript code server side; it is a server-side JavaScript engine. At its core, Node.js is made up of three main components:

- libuv: Cross-Platform I/O library

- Chrome V8: Google Chrome's JavaScript engine

- Js/C++ code: core of the tool

Because this chapter is not about making you become a Node.js expert, it is not important for you to fully understand how Node.js's internals work. What is important for you to grasp, though, is that even if Node.js allows you to run JavaScript on the server, it is not itself built in JavaScript (at least, not entirely). In order to leverage Node.js on your machine, you have to download the installer and properly install it. In my case, I will be doing development directly from my Windows 10 machine. Therefore, I will have to go and download Node.js and install it on my client-operating system directly. The latest version of the Node.js installer can be obtained at https://nodejs.org/en/download/. It currently supports installation on Linux, Mac, and Windows.

In the context of the SharePoint Framework, Node.js is used to properly render the components of the framework's workbench (covered in a later section). If you really want to dumb it down, you can almost compare Node.js to what IIS Express is for Visual Studio. It is a lightweight software component that quickly allows us to run streamlined server-side code and test our applications. It doesn't require much configuration to get started. Figure 8-2 is an evolutive graph that shows where Node.js fits in the SharePoint Framework ecosystem. We will build upon this graph, as I cover additional components of the framework.

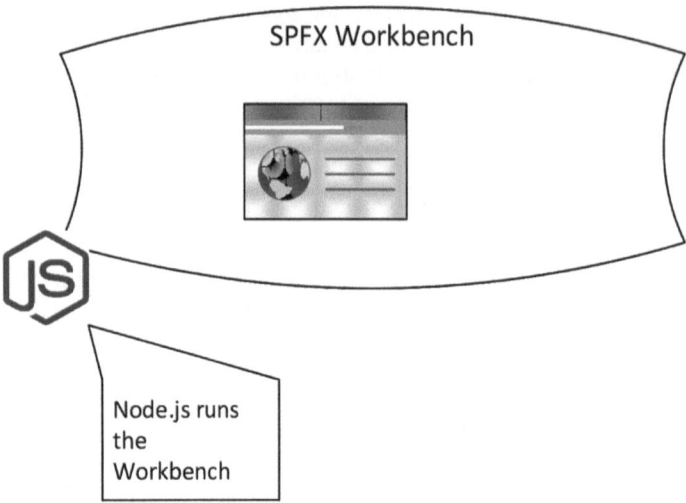

Figure 8-2. *Overview of how Node.js fits in the SPFx ecosystem*

Installing Node.js

The following steps must be initiated if you wish to install Node.js on your Windows machine:

1. Browse to `https://nodejs.org/en/download/` and download the distribution that is supported by your machine (`.msi` or `.exe`). I used the Windows 64-bit distribution for my Windows 10 machine.

2. Execute the download setup. On the main screen, click Next (Figure 8-3).

Figure 8-3. *Main Node.js installation screen*

3. On the second screen, check the "I accept the terms in the License Agreement" and click Next (Figure 8-4).

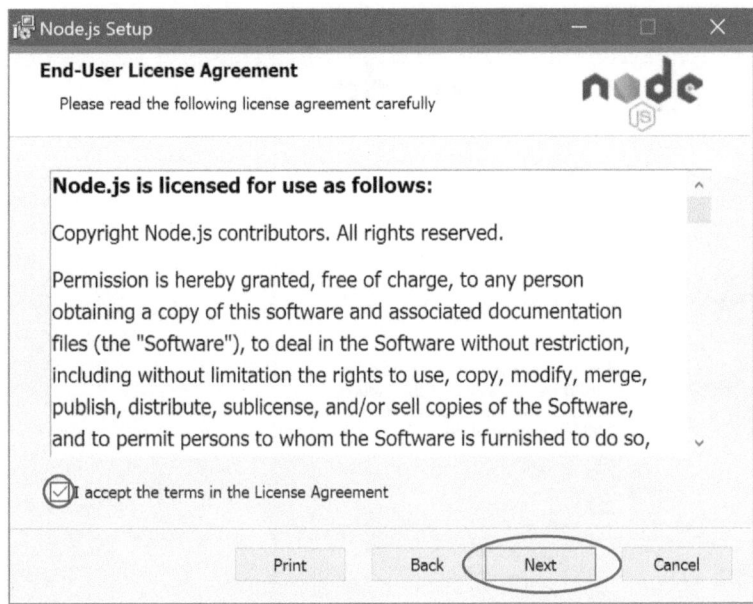

Figure 8-4. *Node.js License Agreement*

4. On the next screen, keep the default path and click Next (Figure 8-5).

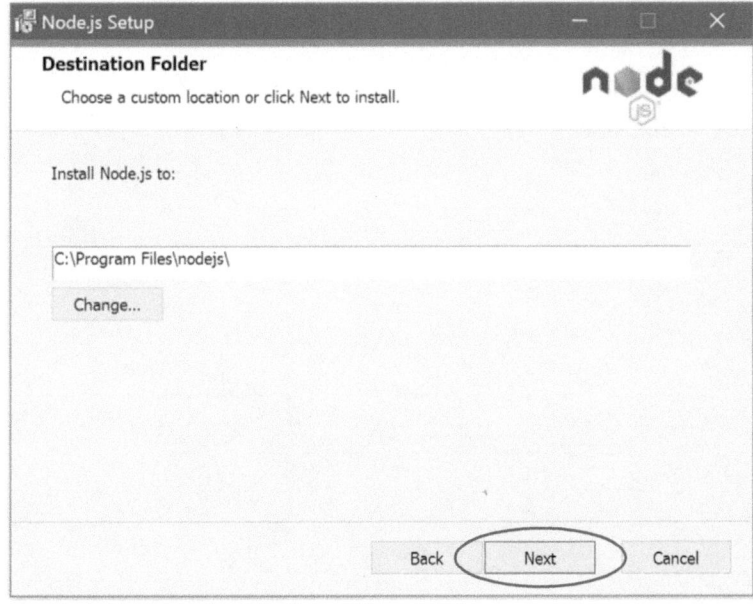

Figure 8-5. *Node.js installation path*

5. On the Custom Setup screen, keep all default options by default and click Next (Figure 8-6).

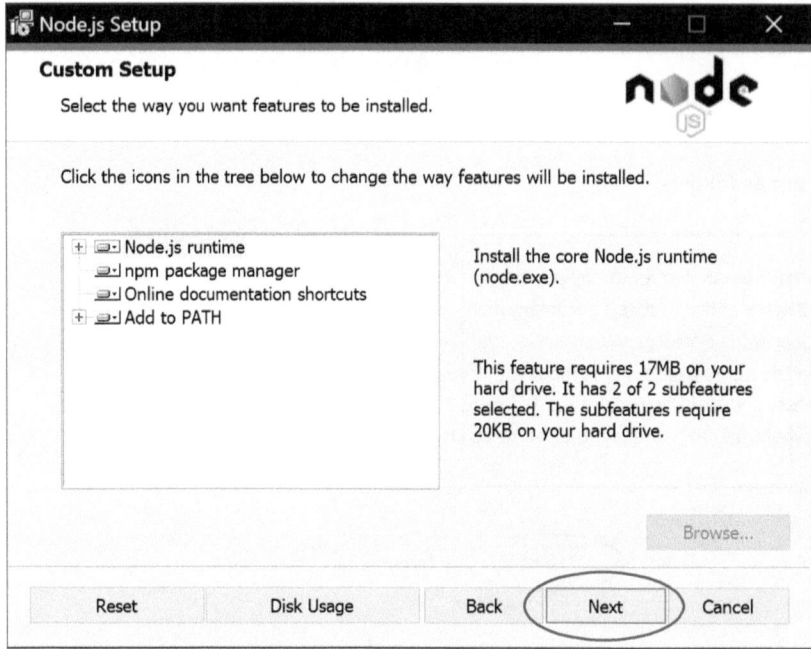

Figure 8-6. *Node.js Custom Setup screen*

6. On the next screen, click the Install button and accept any confirmation from the User Account Control (UAC) (Figure 8-7).

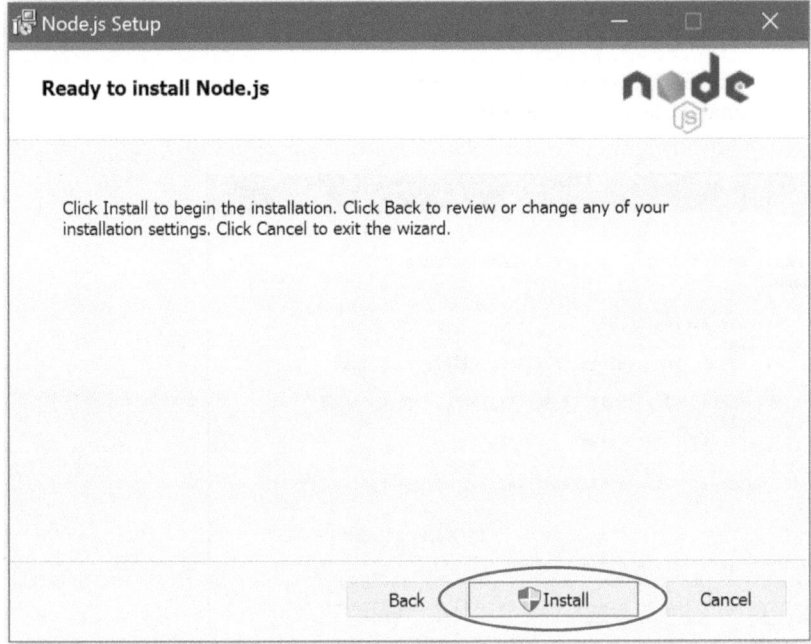

Figure 8-7. *Node.js Initiate installation screen*

7. Wait for the installation process to finish and click Finish (Figure 8-8).

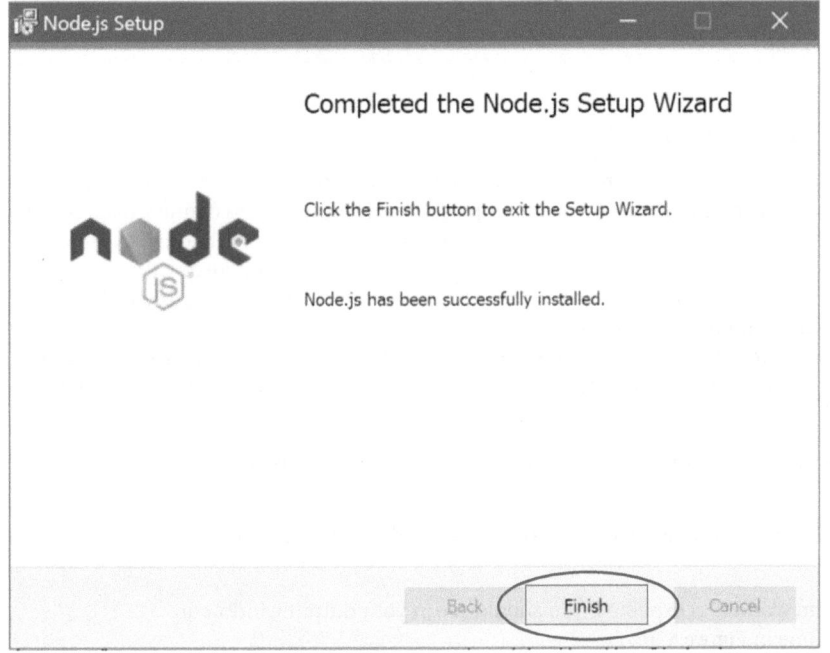

Figure 8-8. *Node.js completed installation*

8. To confirm the installation, launch a new command prompt window and type in the following command: `node -help`.

9. If the installation was successful, you should now see an exhaustive list of all available Node.js commands, as shown in Figure 8-9.

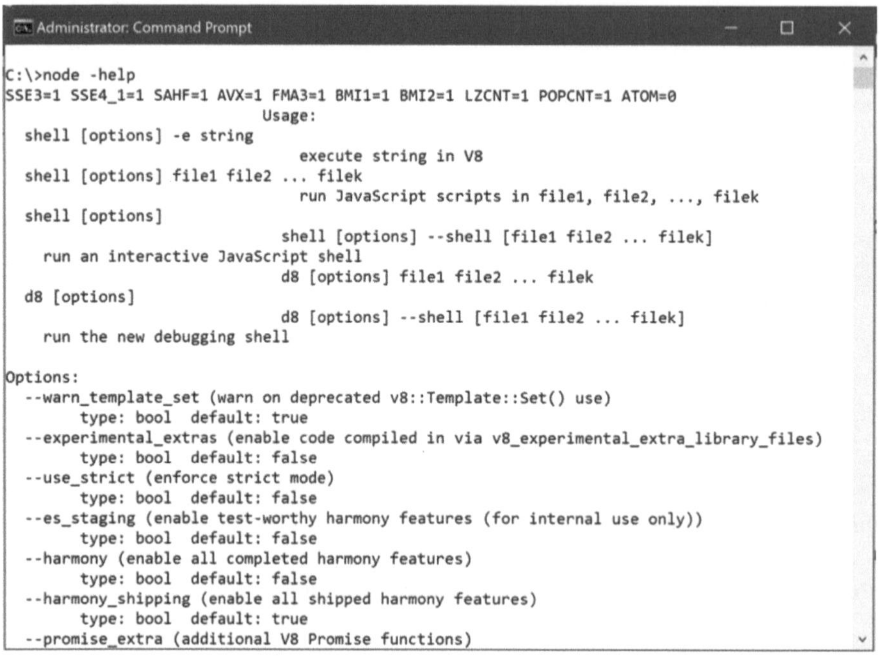

Figure 8-9. Node.js help content

Node Package Manager (NPM)

While the Node Package Manager itself is not directly involved in the SharePoint Framework, you'll see it being referenced enough times throughout our various examples that it is important to define what it is used for. NPM allows developers to manage various JavaScript packages (and their various versions), by allowing them to be acquired from various central repositories. As a comparison, we can compare it to the NuGet engine for the JavaScript world. NPM comes preinstalled with Node.js, and it is used to acquire the latest version of the SPFx workbench from official Microsoft repositories.

For example, one of the prerequisites for our workbench to properly run is to have the Visual C++ Build Tools 2015 installed on our machine. Using the Node Package Manager, these can easily be obtained and installed, using the following easy steps:

1. Launch a new command prompt window (or a PowerShell session) as an administrator.

2. Type in the following command: `npm install -g --production windows-build-tools`.

3. If the installation worked as expected, you should see in your output window an output like the one in Figure 8-10.

```
> node ./lib/index.js

Downloading BuildTools_Full.exe
Downloading python-2.7.11.msi
[>                                      ] 0.0% (0 B/s)
Downloaded python-2.7.11.msi. Saved to C:\Users\▓▓▓▓\.windows-build-tools\python-2.7.11.msi.
Starting installation...
Launched installers, now waiting for them to finish.
This will likely take some time - please be patient!
Waiting for installers... \Successfully installed Visual Studio Build Tools.
Successfully installed Python 2.7
```

Figure 8-10. *Installing Visual C++ Build Tools 2015 with Node Package Manager*

Yeoman

This component is responsible for doing what we call the scaffolding of our SharePoint Framework components. As an analogy, Yeoman is taking care of the same job the Visual Studio "New Project" wizard is doing. Scaffolding is the process of setting up all the various files and components that together make up a solution. To better help you understand what scaffolding really is about, let us consider an example in which you would open Visual Studio and create a new SharePoint Full Trust Code solution. Figure 8-11 shows you the Visual Studio New Project wizard that allows us to perform this task.

Upon clicking the OK button in the Visual Studio New Project wizard, the scaffolding process will be automatically initiated, and Visual Studio will go ahead and create all the required components that make up a SharePoint 2016 Empty solution, as in the example shown in Figure 8-11. This includes a Features folder, a Package folder, and a signing key (as shown in Figure 8-12).

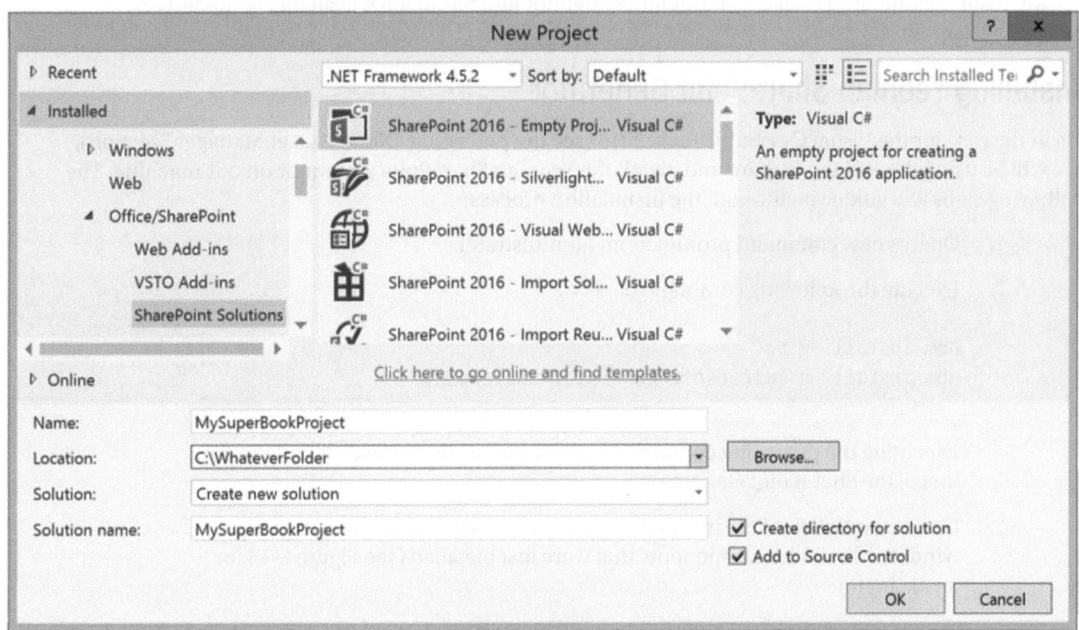

Figure 8-11. *New Project wizard in Visual Studio*

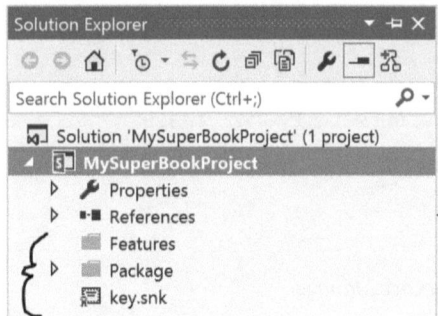

Figure 8-12. *Scaffolding of a SharePoint 2016 Empty Full Trust Code solution*

Of course, you could go in and manually create all of these files and folders yourself, but everyone needs a little bit of automation in their life, don't they? Scaffolding is there to make everyone's life easier, and just for the record, currently an empty SharePoint Framework client web part is made up of a few thousand files, so you may be my guest if you wish to create them manually, but I choose to use scaffolding. There are several other Scaffolding tools available out there in the wild: yoga, cookiecutter, Mimosa, Assemble, etc. The SharePoint team has settled on Yeoman as its default scaffolding tool.

The idea behind Yeoman is that you don't directly install a Yeoman client per say on your machine. Instead, you have to create what we refer to as a Yeoman Generator, which is then responsible for defining the scaffolding workflow to be executed. These generators are what must be installed on your development machine. They can be hosted and made discoverable on any repositories in your organization. Luckily for us, Microsoft has already created a SharePoint generator and has made it available on its servers.

Installing Yeoman SharePoint Generator

As in the case for the Visual C++ Build Tools 2015 (see the preceding "Node Packet Manager" section), we will be using the NPM to acquire and install the Yeoman SharePoint generator on our machine. The following steps will guide you through the installation process:

1.   Open a new command prompt as an administrator.

2.   Execute the following commands:

```
npm install -g yo
npm install -g @microsoft/generator-sharepoint
```

     Executing the preceding command will automatically retrieve, download, and install the SharePoint Generator.

3.   Upon completion of the installation, you should see displayed in the output window a list of the components that were just installed (see Figure 8-13 for an example).

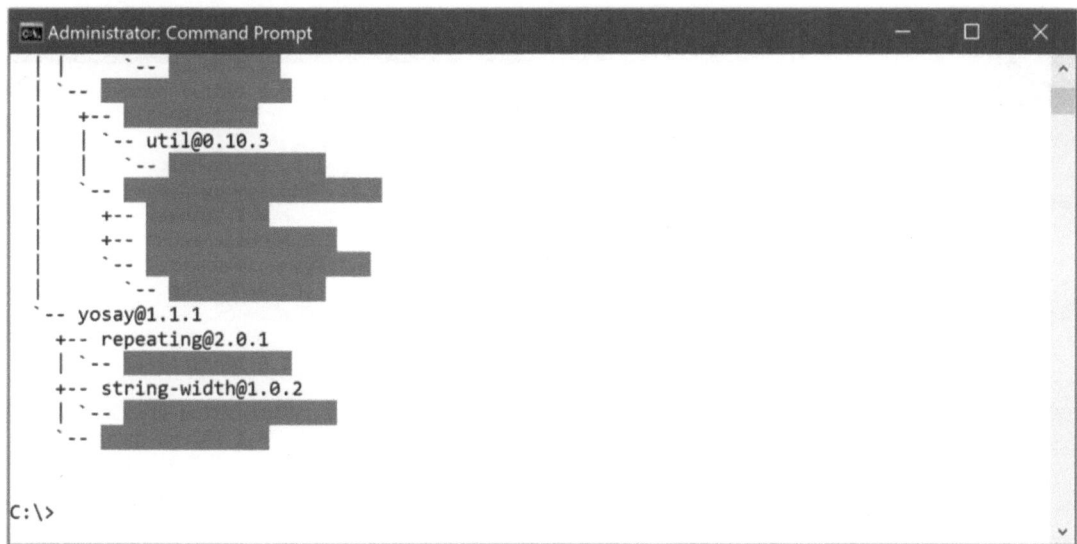

Figure 8-13. Completed installation of the Yeoman SharePoint generator

If you are like me and are always curious by nature, you may wonder what exactly has been downloaded to your machine by executing the preceding command. By default, the Node Package Manager keeps all its packages under the following path:

`C:\Users\<user name>\AppData\Roaming\npm\node_modules\`

If you navigate to this location, you will find a folder named `generator-sharepoint` that contains all the files associated with our generator. While I will not be covering the creation of a Yeoman generator in this chapter, it may be useful for you to take a look at the `index.js` file located under the `/app` folder. It contains the execution flow for the Yeoman SharePoint generator.

Scaffolding a Project

Once the Yeoman SharePoint Generator has been properly installed on your machine, we can initiate the scaffolding process for a SharePoint Framework project. Before initiating a scaffolding operation, which will generate a good number of files, I recommend that you go ahead and create a new folder somewhere on your development machine. This will ensure that we keep everything isolated. In my case, I will be creating a new folder called SPFxDemo, which will be located directly at the root of my c:\ drive (Figure 8-14).

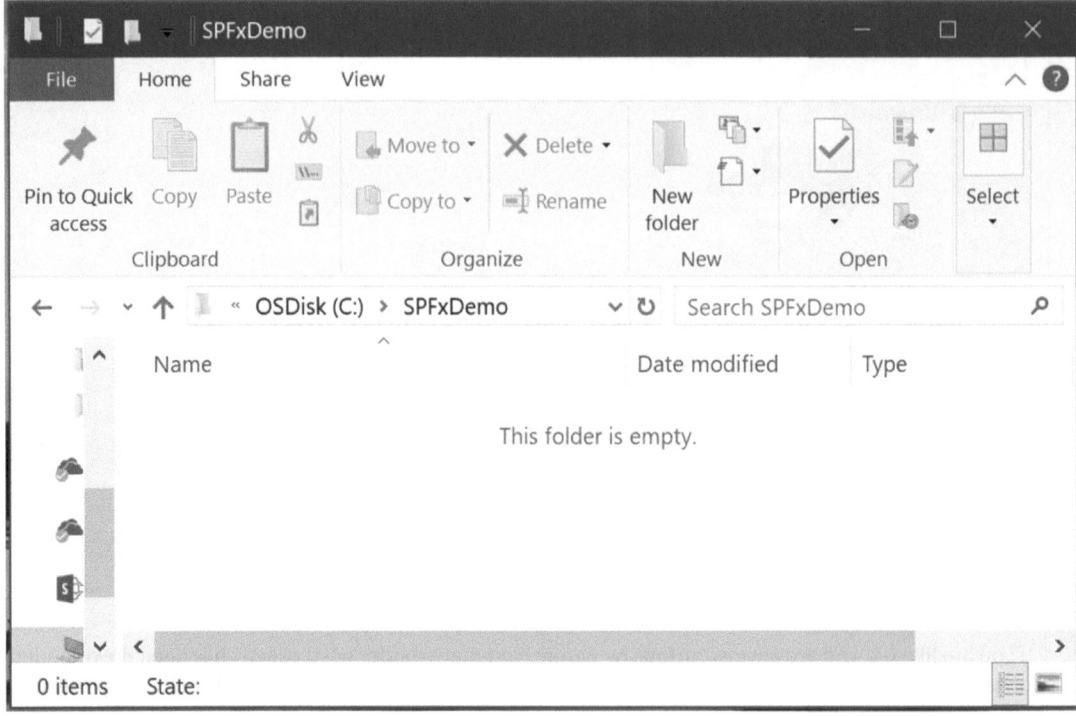

Figure 8-14. *New empty folder at the root of my C:\ drive*

Open a command line console and navigate to the newly created folder. To initiate the scaffolding operation, simply type in the following Yeoman command in your console:

```
yo @microsoft/sharepoint
```

Upon executing this line of code, Yeoman will prompt you to specify a name for the solution you are about to create. Pick a name and press Enter. In my case, the solution will be called SPFxDemo1. Upon entering a name for your solution, Yeoman will then proceed to ask you if you wish to reuse the current folder to create the solution in, or if you wish for it to create the folder structure for you. In our case, since we already created an isolated folder, we will simply choose the option to use the current folder. Yeoman is currently only allowing us to create client web part projects. It will, therefore, ask you to pick a name for that new web part you are about to create. For this example, we will be naming our web part "StockPrices." Yes, you've guessed right, our example will be about creating a client web part that allows us to display the current stock price of a given registered company. Input the name for the web part and provide a description of what it will be doing, as shown in Figure 8-15.

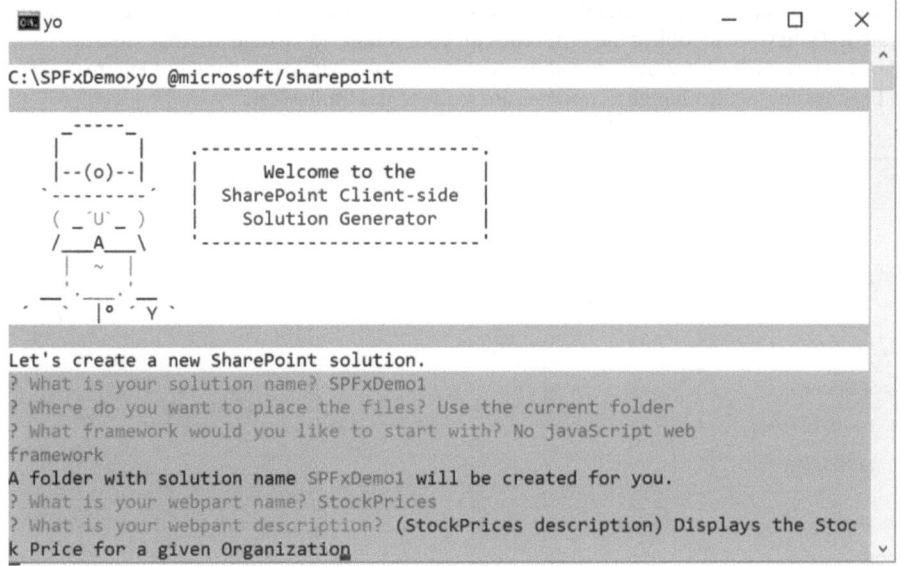

Figure 8-15. *Yeoman inputs for a new client web part*

The last prompt from Yeoman will ask you to pick what flavor of JavaScript you wish to use for your solution. Based on your choice, Yeoman will properly scaffold your solution to include any dependencies required by the library you chose. In either case, we want to keep things "low-level," in order to properly demonstrate how everything works internally. We will, therefore, be choosing the option "No JavaScript web framework," which will allow us to use pure JavaScript as our programming language. Upon choosing what flavor of JavaScript to use, Yeoman will go ahead and generate all the required files for us. If everything went as planned, you should see something similar to Figure 8-16 in your PowerShell session.

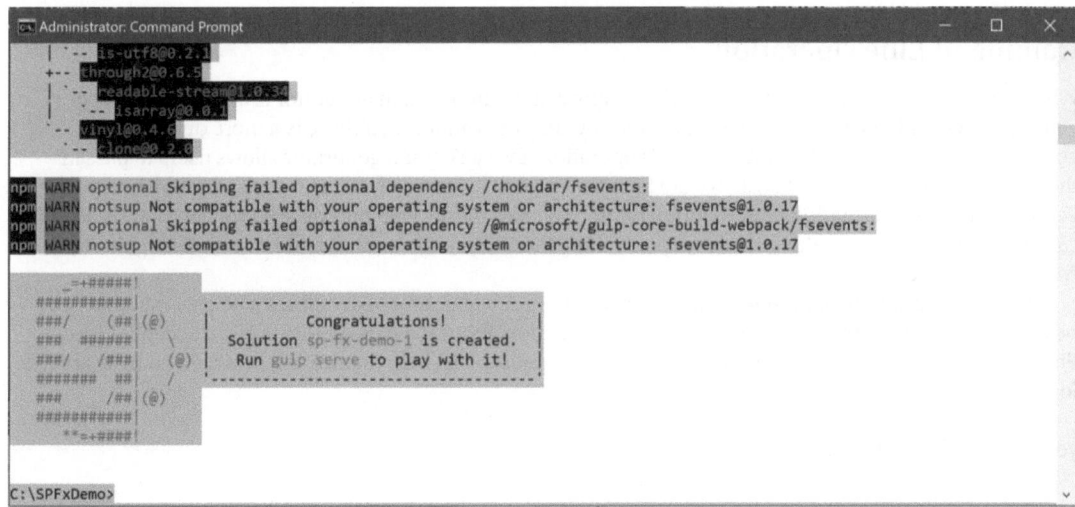

Figure 8-16. *Results from a successful Yeoman scaffolding operation*

Once the operation has completed, you can open Windows Explorer and take a look at the files that were automatically generated. If you were to look at the properties for your folder, you would see that there are more than 30,500 files that have been generated, together representing over 208MB of data (see Figure 8-17). Note that these numbers are subject to change as updates are made to the framework.

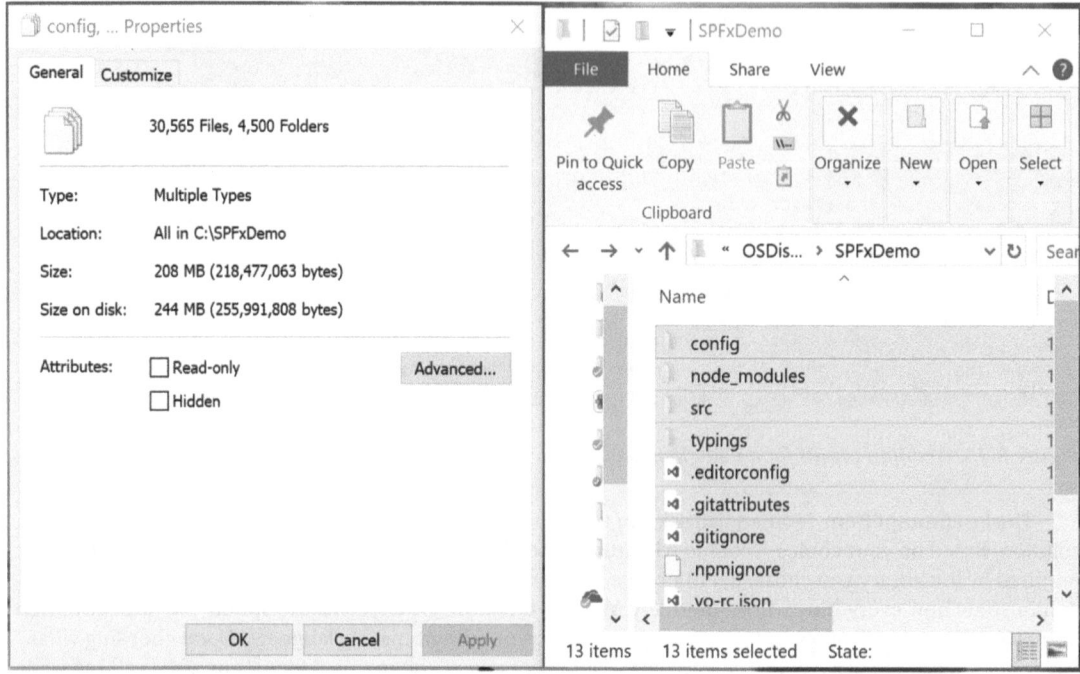

Figure 8-17. *Files generated by Yeoman and their associated file size*

Command Line Operation

While initiating the Scaffolding operation by simply calling the Yeoman generator is an effective way of getting started with the SharePoint Framework, you may be wondering if there is a more direct way to generate the files, or at least to automate this operation. Every Yeoman generator allows users to pass in the required parameters directly, so we are in luck. No need to manually answer each question every time Yeoman requires information (e.g., solution name, web part name, web part description, etc.). Instead, we can simply pass all these values at once, upon calling the Yeoman generator, and have the files generated with a simple line of code.

On top of accepting parameters directly, every Yeoman generator also defines a help switch that can be called with --help and provides additional information about the parameters that are accepted (see Figure 8-18). In the case of the SharePoint Yeoman generator, this help feature can be accessed by using the following command:

```
yo @microsoft/sharepoint --help
```

Figure 8-18. *Help output for the SharePoint Yeoman generator*

Based on Figure 8-18, we can see that the generator only requires values for four parameters: solutionName, componentType, componentName, and framework. Therefore, we are not required to pass the web part's description as a parameter. If we want to initiate the scaffolding of a new SharePoint Framework client web part with a single line of code, we can do so by calling the following:

```
yo @microsoft/sharepoint:app --solutionName="SPFxDemo1" --componentType="webpart"
--componentName="StockPrices" --framework="none" --component-description="Displays the Stock
Price for a given Organization"
```

With Yeoman, arguments must be provided in the order they are defined. In our case, if we look at the result from the help operation (Figure 8-18), the first argument is solutionName, and the last one is to be framework. Options, on the other hand, are to be provided as a key/pair entry. If you pay closer attention to the preceding code example, you can see that the web part's description is passed using the --component-description= clause. Calling the preceding command will automatically initiate the scaffolding of the SharePoint client web part project into a new folder called SPFxDemo1. Figure 8-19 shows the execution of this command to initiate the scaffolding operation.

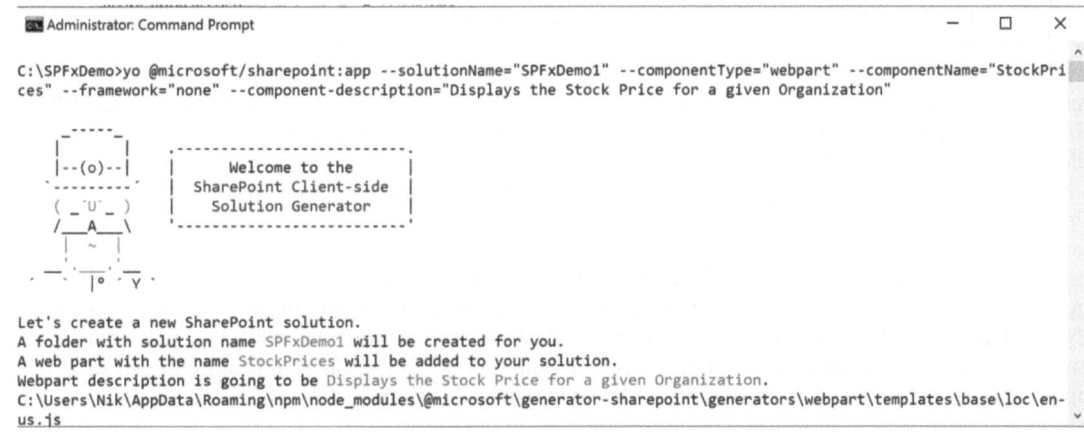

Figure 8-19. *Yeoman scaffolding of a SharePoint client web part by passing arguments*

Overview of the Ecosystem with Yeoman

To recap what we have covered so far, the new Microsoft SharePoint Framework requires Node.js to render files to the user. It acts as a web server to render content. The files to be rendered by Node.js are generated by Yeoman, using the SharePoint generator that is provided by the SharePoint Product Group. Figure 8-20 shows the evolution of the SPFx ecosystem with the pieces we've covered thus far.

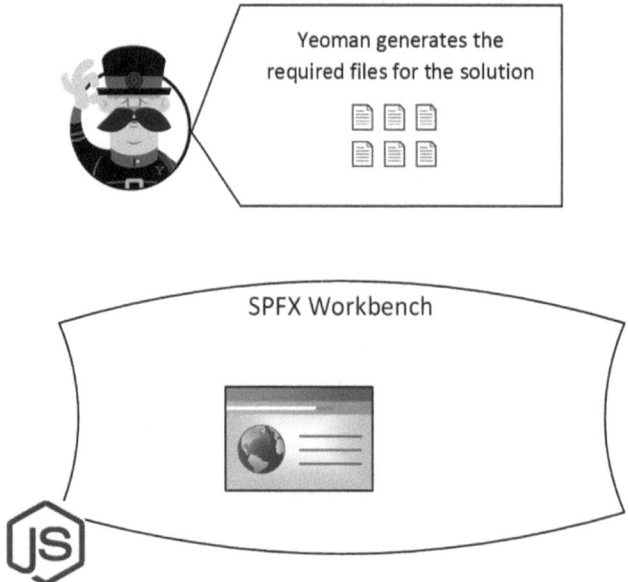

Figure 8-20. *The SharePoint Framework ecosystem with Node.js and Yeoman*

Gulp

The final piece of the puzzle is what glues together everything we have seen so far. Gulp is a way to streamline your development process. While this may seem great in writing, you are probably wondering what it is concretely used for within the context of the SharePoint Framework. In recent days, development is all about making things more performant, saving milliseconds of execution here and there. One of the best ways to improve performance of web sites is to minify resources. Minifying is the process by which we try to reduce the overall size of a given file by removing useless empty spaces and carriage returns in the file. While this often makes the file less readable to a human eye, it helps speed the process of acquiring the resource files by the network, because these are now smaller in size.

The process of minifying files is a somewhat repetitive task in our development pipeline. Automating this process would not only save us time but would allow us to make modifications to code on the fly and test the results within seconds, without having to "recompile" the resources or do any manual intervention on them. This is what Gulp is there to do: automate the repetitive tasks of the development flow to speed up development. With the help of Gulp, you can edit your files in what I would call their "maxified" shapes. By that, I mean that their content will have spacing and tabs to make it more readable. Once your changes are done, the simple fact of saving them will kick off a Gulp process that will automatically take care of optimizing your files and deploying them back to Node.js to be rendered.

Installing Gulp

As in the case for Yeoman, we will be using NPM to install Gulp onto our development machine. To initiate the installation process, make sure you navigate to the folder where your files have been generated by Yeoman and simply execute the following command (Figure 8-21 shows the execution of the command):

```
npm install gulp-cli -g
npm install gulp -D
```

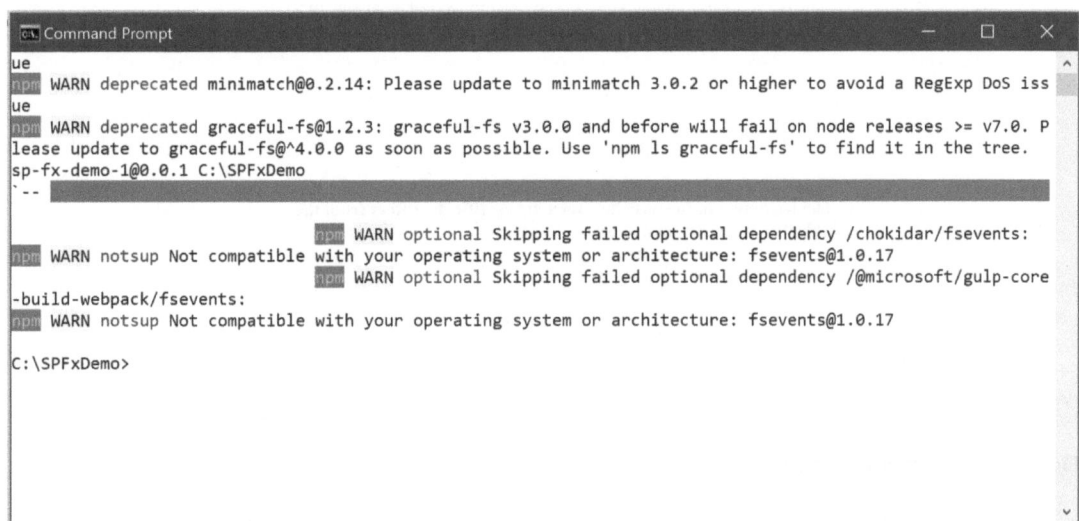

Figure 8-21. *Gulp installation using NPM*

Serving Pages with Gulp

Now that Gulp is properly installed on our development box, we can go ahead and have Gulp initiate a pipe to server our files and allow us to render the content of our solution. In order to initiate the Gulp process, you must execute the following command (make sure you navigate to the root of your solution folder first, e.g., `C:\SPFxDemo\SPFxDemo1`):

```
gulp serve
```

Because Gulp uses an SSL end point to serve the pages, it requires a developer to configure a default certificate, in order to render the pages through HTTPS. If you simply run the preceding command, you will receive the following warning in your console (Figure 8-22):

> *Warning - [serve] When serving in HTTPS mode, a PFX cert path or a cert path and a key path must be provided, or a dev certificate must be generated and trusted. If a SSL certificate isn't provided, a default, self-signed certificate will be used. Expect browser security warnings.*

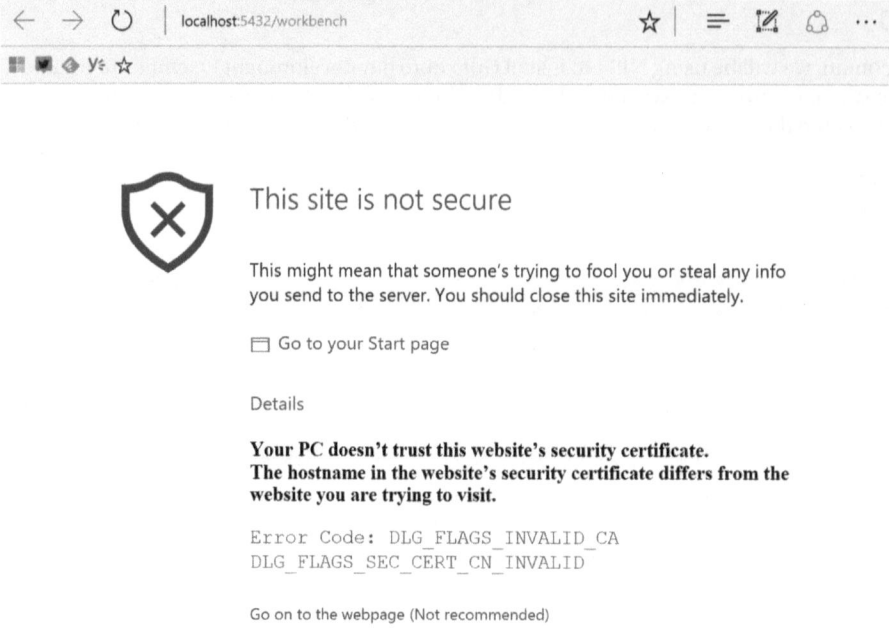

Figure 8-22. Certificate error running Gulp

Luckily for us, the framework comes with a developer certificate that we can use to get around this error. This development certificate can be easily configured by simply executing the following Gulp command:

```
gulp trust-dev-cert
```

Upon executing this command, you will be prompted to install the certificate, as seen in Figure 8-23. Simply click Yes to have the certificate installed and configured.

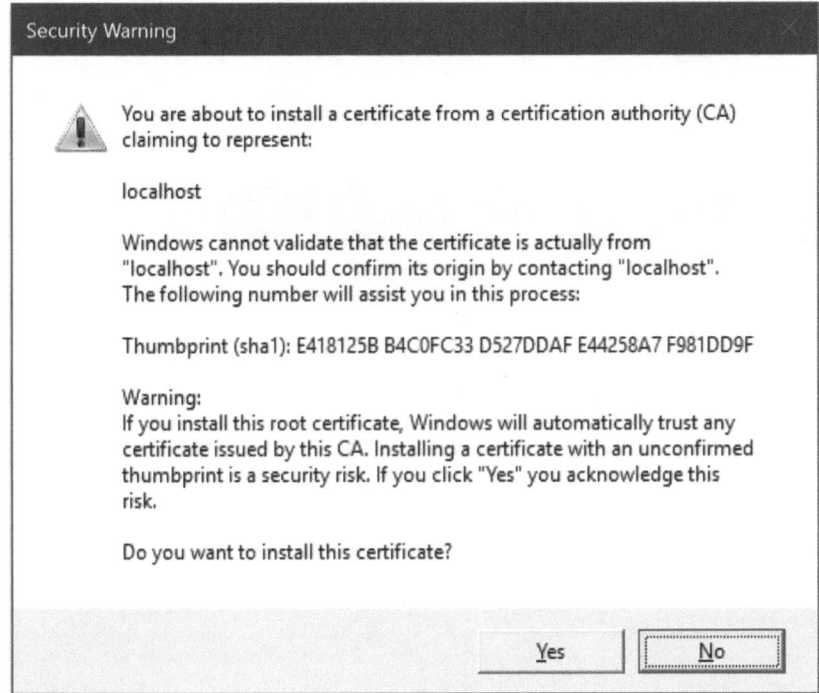

Figure 8-23. *Installation prompt for the SharePoint Framework developer's certificate*

With the certificate configured, you can now initiate a new Gulp process, by running Gulp Serve, and this time, you shouldn't receive any certificate errors and be able to view the SharePoint Framework workbench, as shown in Figure 8-24. What you are seeing here is what we refer to as the SharePoint Framework workbench. It is the component that allows you to locally test your solution without having to deploy it to Office 365.

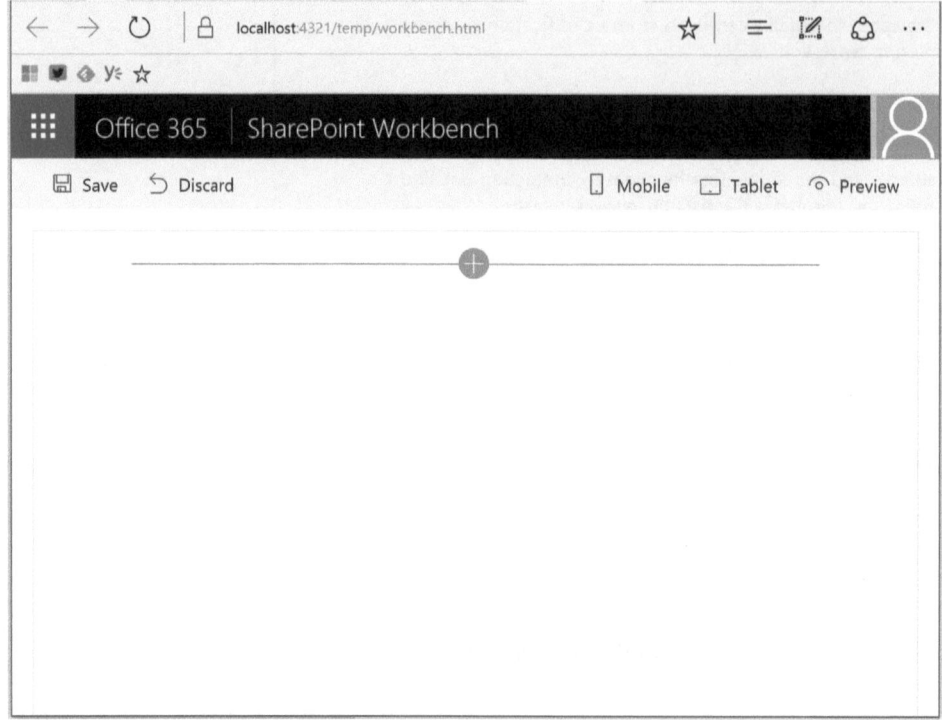

Figure 8-24. *SharePoint Framework workbench*

Overview of the Ecosystem with Gulp

We have now completed the tour of our SharePoint Framework tool chain that is used to serve our solutions locally. Figure 8-25 gives a complete picture of what the three main pillars of the SharePoint Framework are and how they each fit within the bigger picture.

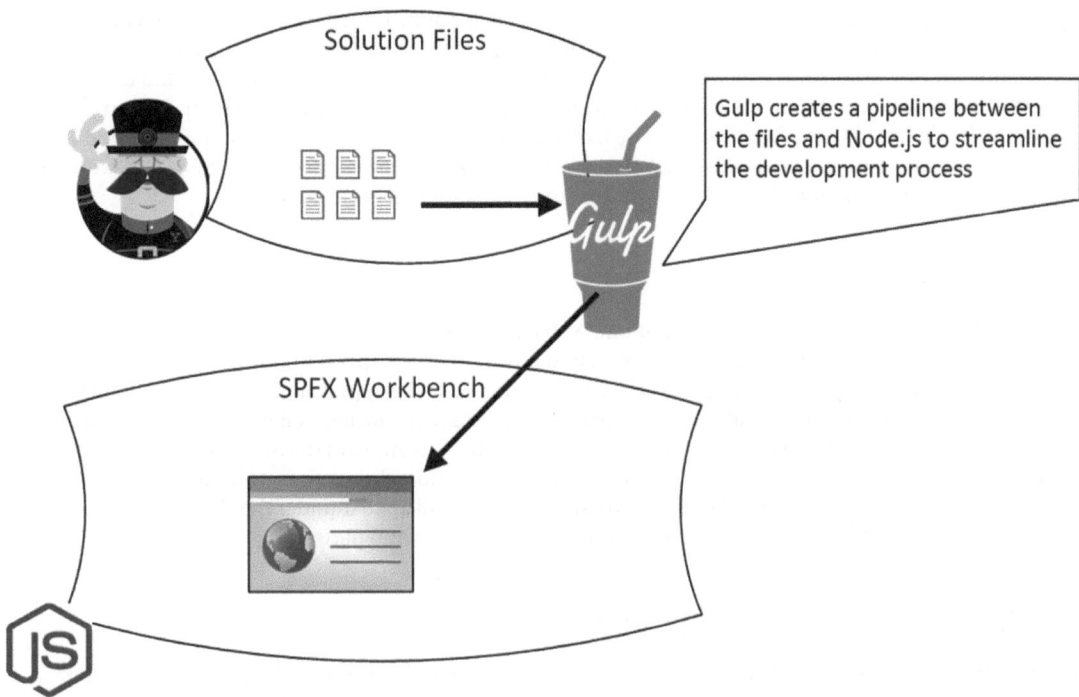

Figure 8-25. *Complete SharePoint Framework ecosystem with Gulp*

SharePoint Framework Workbench

I have already mentioned the SharePoint Framework workbench several times throughout this chapter. The workbench is what allows you to run and test your solutions locally. Concretely, the workbench is an HTML file generated by the SharePoint Yeoman Generator and is located under the temp folder in our solution folder (Figure 8-26).

> This PC > Local Disk (C:) > SPFxDemo > temp >			
Name	Date modified	Type	Size
stats	3/15/2017 11:25 AM	File folder	
manifests.js	3/15/2017 11:30 AM	JavaScript File	64 KB
manifests.json	3/15/2017 11:30 AM	JSON File	17 KB
workbench.html	3/15/2017 11:30 AM	HTML Document	1 KB

Figure 8-26. *The SharePoint Framework workbench file*

If you were to take a closer look at the file's content, you would see that it simply contains about 20 lines of HTML and JavaScript imports. I don't recommend that you modify this file directly in any way. This file is meant to provide you with an offline way of testing a solution that is targeted for a remote SharePoint 2016 instance (be it SharePoint Online or on-premises). Modifying that local file may lead to things not working as expected when the time comes to deploy it remotely.

The fact that the workbench is really nothing more than a classic HTML page in nature, which is served by Gulp, means that it is platform-agnostic. People working with Mac can easily obtain, deploy, and run the SharePoint Framework's workbench on their machine. Once you deploy your solution onto the remote SharePoint server, you will soon realize that the workbench is actually hosted as a .NET application page located at /_layouts/15/workbench.aspx. The fact that it is running as a .NET page on the other end will not affect how your solution behaves between your local and remote development environment. The workbench had to be generalized as an HTML file locally, to ensure a broader platform support.

Client-Side Web Parts

We are all familiar with the traditional SharePoint web parts that have been around since the early versions of the product. Those are contained pieces of functionality that serve a specific purpose and can be connected to other web parts on a page, to create rich dashboard type applications. With SharePoint 2013, Microsoft introduced the concept of App parts, which were iframes exposing a client-side app hosted outside the given SharePoint site (SharePoint-hosted or Provider-hosted). Now, with the SharePoint Framework, we are now talking about Client-Side Web Parts, which are nothing more than a classic SharePoint web part, but running entirely on the client side. TheseCclientSide Web Parts will appear under the web part section under the Insert tab of the ribbon, and not under the App Part button, like App parts do.

Creating Your First Client-Side Web Part

Let us now look at how we can get started and create our very first Client-Side Web Part. By default, the Microsoft Yeoman generator automatically generates all the required files for our web part. If you remember correctly from the previous examples, we have already created our Client-Side Web Part called StockPrices. In fact, if you just attempt to run gulp serve on the project folder created earlier, you will see that the workbench already allows you to add that web part to your page (see Figure 8-27).

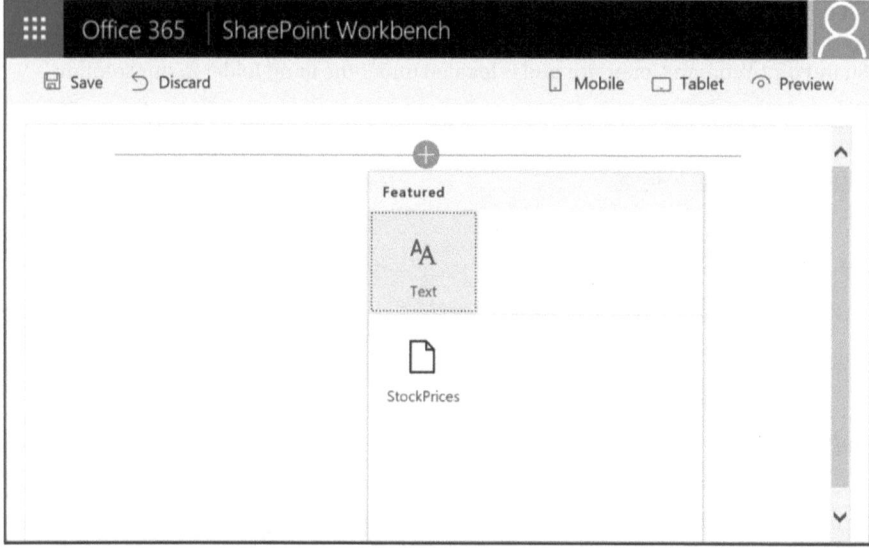

Figure 8-27. *New Client-Side Web Part showing on the workbench*

If we were to add this web part to the workbench as it stands, it would simply generate generic HTML to indicate that no logic or content has been included with that web part (see Figure 8-28).

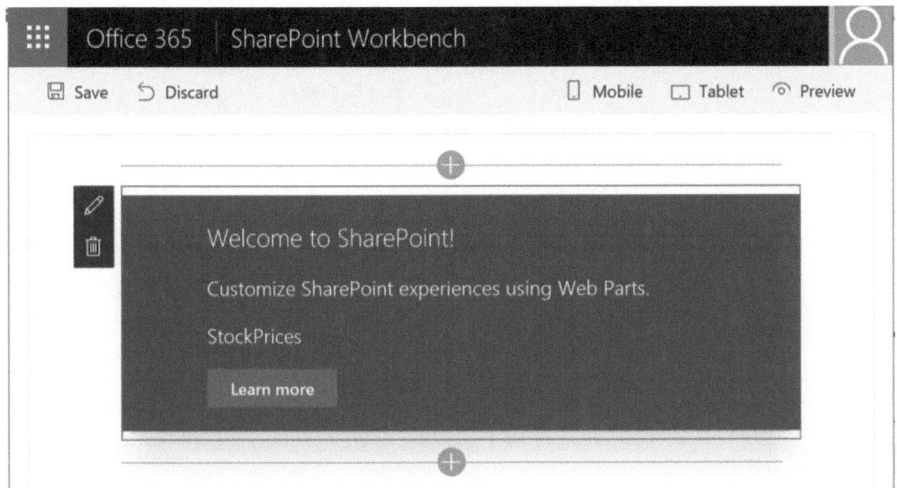

Figure 8-28. *Adding a newly created Client-Side Web Part to the local workbench*

If you take a closer look at the set of files that were automatically generated by the Microsoft Yeoman generator, you can see that under the src folder, we have a folder named webparts, which contains a subfolder having the name we gave to our solution (see Figure 8-29).

Name	Date modified	Type	Size
loc	3/15/2017 10:59 AM	File folder	
tests	3/15/2017 10:59 AM	File folder	
IStockPricesWebPartProps.ts	3/15/2017 10:59 AM	MPEG-2 TS Video	1 KB
StockPrices.module.scss	3/15/2017 10:59 AM	SCSS Style Sheet	2 KB
StockPrices.module.scss.ts	3/15/2017 11:25 AM	MPEG-2 TS Video	1 KB
StockPricesWebPart.manifest.json	3/15/2017 10:59 AM	JSON File	1 KB
StockPricesWebPart.ts	3/15/2017 10:59 AM	MPEG-2 TS Video	2 KB

Figure 8-29. *Generated content for our Client-Side Web Part*

To modify the code of our web part, I will be using Visual Studio 2017; however, feel free to use whatever your favorite editor software happens to be, because remember that in the end, all we will be editing is HTML and JavaScript. Inside of Visual Studio, I will simply choose the option to open a folder and will browse to the C:\SPFxDemo\SPFxDemo1 folder I created earlier (see Figures 8-30 and 8-31).

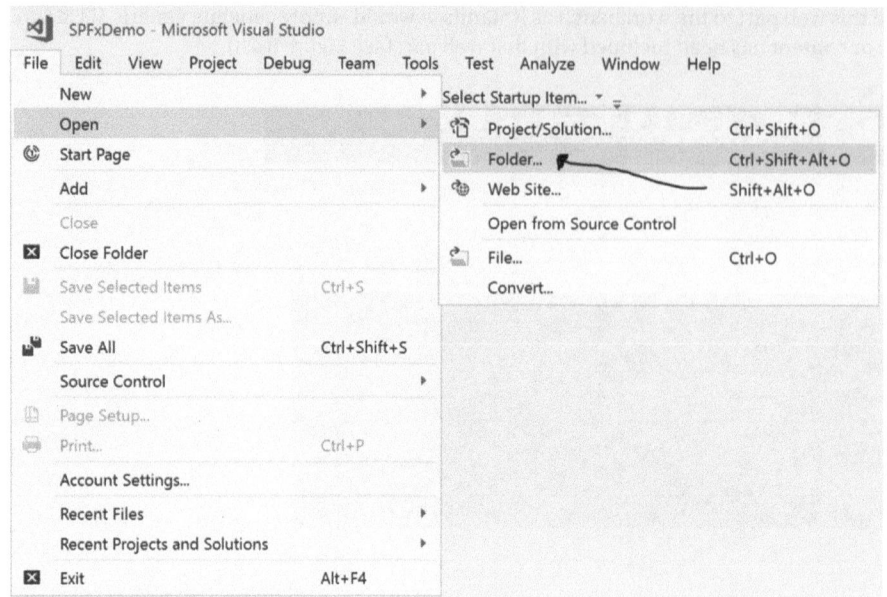

Figure 8-30. *Opening a folder in Visual Studio 2017*

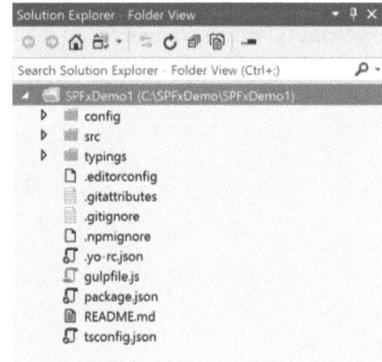

Figure 8-31. *Viewing our Client-Side Web Part folder with Visual Studio Solution Explorer*

The file we are interested in modifying first is named StockPricesWebPart.ts and is located directly under our stockPrices folder. This is a TypeScript file, and it contains the core logic for our Client-Side Web Part. If you take a closer look at the render() method in there, you will see that it is where the HTML printed out by default when we add our web part to the workbench is declared. For the purpose of our example, our web part will accept the name of an organization as part of its properties and will randomly display a fictive stock quote for that given organization. To achieve this, we will start by modifying the render() method, by replacing its entire content with the following:

```
public render(): void
{
    this.domElement.innerHTML = `<div id="StockPricePanel">
      <p>The stock price for ${escape(this.properties.Organization)} is ` +
```

```
        Math.round((Math.random()) * 100).toString()+ `$</p>
    </div>`;
}
```

This tells the web part that upon rendering its output back to the client, it has to display a sentence that will use the provided organization name in the properties panel, along with a random number between 0 and 100. This may not be the most exciting web part ever created, but the important thing here is to ensure that you have an overview of the various pieces involved in creating a new Client-Side Web Part.

Simply trying to run a Gulp process with this code in place will generate errors, because TypeScript doesn't know anything about that Organization property we just specified. For us to make TypeScript aware of the fact that this property exists, we have to define it in our web part's interface, which is named IStockPricesWebPartProps.ts. Replace the entire file's content with the following:

```
export interface IStockPricesWebPartProps
{
    Organization: string;
}
```

This tells our web part that we must expose a custom property named Organization and let the users be able to modify its value. Now, if you go back to our main web part file (StockPricesWebPart.ts), we will modify the property panel to reflect the new Organization property we wish to capture. At the bottom of the file, there is a method defined, which is called getPropertyPaneConfiguration(). This method is expected to return a structured set of properties and values that will contain information about how our web part's property panel will be displayed to the user. We are particularly interested in changing the labels that will be displayed, to show messages that are specific to the Organization property we are trying to capture. If you pay close attention to the structure returned by this method, you'll see a section named groupFields. This is the section we wish to modify, to affect the rendering of the property panel. Replace the entire content of the groupFields section by the following lines of code:

```
groupFields: [
    PropertyPaneTextField('Organization', {
        label: strings.OrganizationLabel
    })
]
```

We are almost there. We now have only to make two more minor modifications for our web part to be functional again. As part of the groupFields property that we just modified, we are now specifying that the property we will be capturing is a property named Organization, and that the field that is exposed in the web part property panel allowing the user to enter a value should have a label defined in a localized string variable named OrganizationLabel. This localized string must be defined in a TypeScript definition file named mystrings.d.ts, which is located under the /src/webparts/<project name>/loc folder. Open the file and replace the content of the IStockPriceStrings interface with the following lines of code:

```
declare interface IStockPricesStrings {
    PropertyPaneDescription: string;
    BasicGroupName: string;
    OrganizationLabel: string;
}
```

We have now defined that our property panel will expose a localized label named Organization, but we have not specified what the value for that label should be. By default, our web part is localized for English US and, therefore, under the loc folder, you will find a JavaScript file named en-us.js that will contain the localized values for our labels. Open that file, replace the default labels, and add our new one, by replacing the entire content with the following lines of code:

```
define([], function() {
  return {
    "PropertyPaneDescription": "Stock Price Properties",
    "BasicGroupName": "Settings",
    "OrganizationLabel":"Patate"
  }
});
```

Our web part is now fully functional. As mentioned previously, the purpose of this example is not to build a real-life web part that you can use immediately in your production environment. It is, rather, to give you all the information and tools you need to get started on your own projects.

Testing Your Web Part

We are ready to test our web part. Remember that for your code to be deployed and the workbench to be made available, you have to run the gulp serve command in a command prompt that is currently pointed onto our project's folder. Upon launching the workbench, you will see that you have the option of adding your StockPrice web part to your page. Once the web part has been added, you will have the option to edit its properties, by clicking the pencil icon at its top leftmost corner. This will bring up the property panel we just modified, with all the proper labels we set up for it (see Figure 8-32).

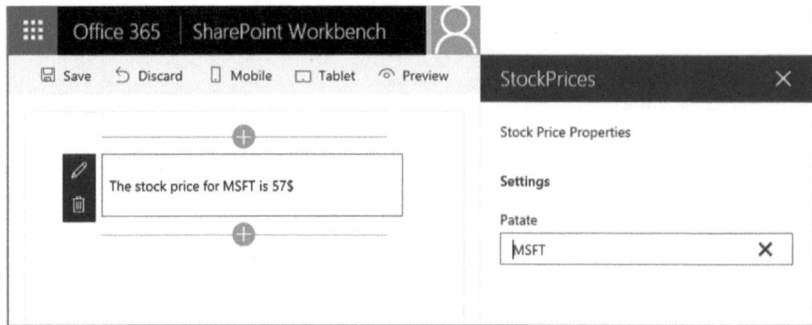

Figure 8-32. *Displaying our custom web part property panel*

Packaging Your Client-Side Web Part

Once you are done making the changes to your web part, you are ready to bundle it into a .sppkg package. We will need to use Gulp to achieve this. In a new console, browse to your project's folder and type in the following line of command:

```
gulp package-solution --ship
```

This will automatically generate your .sppkg package, under the folder <project path>/SharePoint/ solution/ (see Figure 8-33).

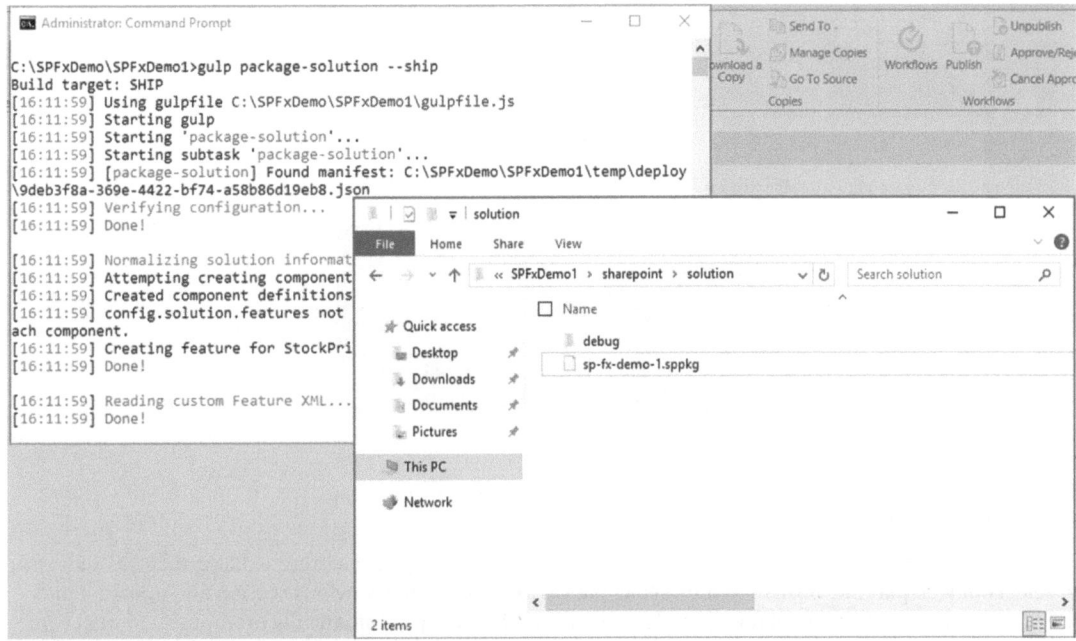

Figure 8-33. *SharePoint Client-Side Web Part Package generation*

Deploying Your Client-Side Web Part

The question you are probably asking yourself now is how to actually deploy this Client-Side Web Part onto your Office 365 tenant. This is actually done the same way you would deploy a SharePoint Add-in: via the Add-in Catalog. To deploy your web part to the rest of your organization, simply navigate to your Office 365 tenant's Add-in Catalog and browse to the Apps for SharePoint library (see Figure 8-34).

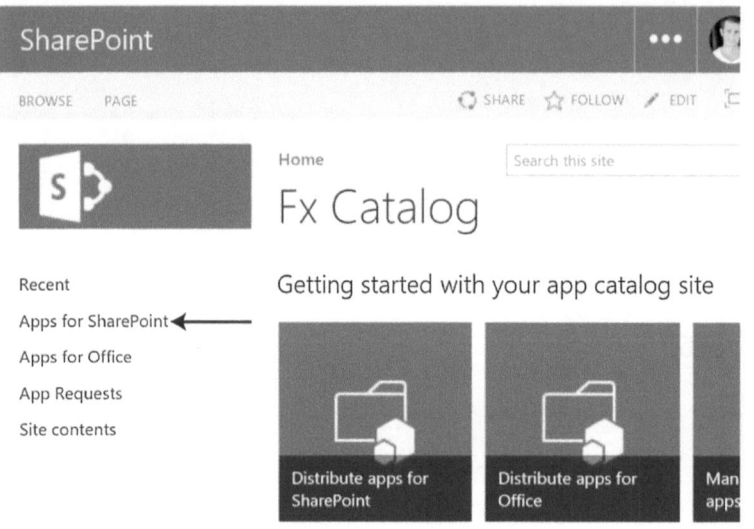

Figure 8-34. *Apps for SharePoint in a SharePoint Online Add-in Catalog site*

Once you are in the library, simply click the Upload button to open the browse dialog that will allow you to select our web part file. Browse to the .sppkg package created in the previous section and upload it into the library. Upon completion of the upload process, SharePoint will automatically prompt you to trust your new web part (see Figure 8-35). Simply click Deploy, to have that new Client-Side Web Part available to the rest of your organization.

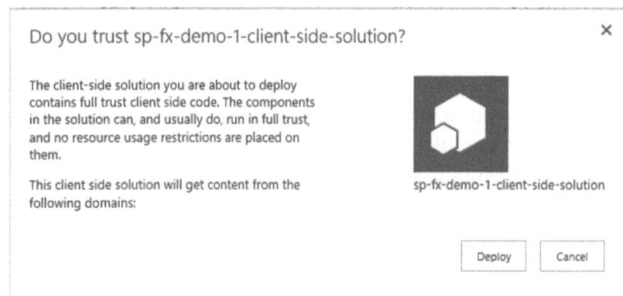

Figure 8-35. *Deploying a Client-Side Web Part via the Add-in Catalog*

Reuse Your Client Side Web Part

Now that your web part has been properly deployed in the Add-in Catalog, you can go and install it onto any SharePoint site within your organization. Because it has been deployed through the catalog, in order to use it within a site, you must proceed the same way you would if it were a SharePoint Add-in: you need to install it at the web level. The first thing you have to do is navigate to the site in which you wish to use your newly created Client-Side Web Part. Once you are there, click the Site Action icon at the top right (cog icon), then select Add and App. In the left navigation, select From your Organization. This will automatically filter the list of available add-ins and display our newly uploaded solution (see Figure 8-36).

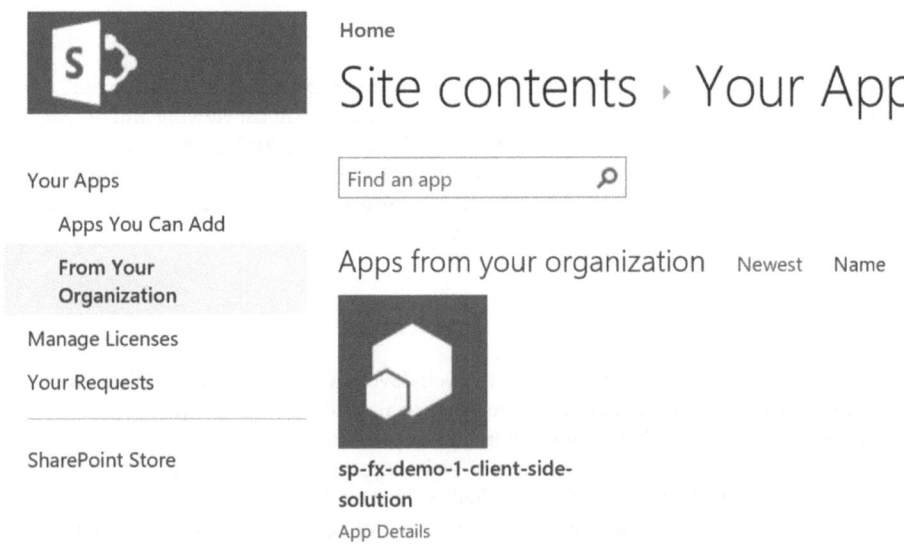

Figure 8-36. *Adding our custom Client-Side Web Part solution to a SharePoint site*

From there, simply click your solution's icon, to install it onto your SharePoint site. Once the installation completes, you will be able to access your web part, by editing a page on your site (see Figure 8-37).

Name your page

Figure 8-37. *Adding a custom Client-Side Web Part to a page*

What's Next

It was announced at build 2017 that the SharePoint Framework will soon be extended to include what we refer to as Extensions, which will also allow users to embed client-side code in list viewing and other components of SharePoint. That, combined with the announcement on May 16, 2017, at the Virtual SharePoint Summit, that Microsoft will be making the framework available to on-premises environment via Feature Pack 2 for SharePoint 2016, is a testament of Microsoft's promise to make the SharePoint Framework the most attractive development model for users to build rich and modern experiences.

Summary

The SharePoint Framework offers lots of potential for modern web developers. By providing a platform-agnostic development tool chain, it opens the door for developers of all kinds to leverage the "Rapid Application Development" component of SharePoint. Where developers used to inject JavaScript code directly in the page, by using Content Editor and Script Editor Webparts, the new framework offers a supported way of packaging and reusing contained sets of client-side logic. Any developer who is serious about getting into the SharePoint development space should start by looking at this new way of building rich and dynamic interfaces.

CHAPTER 9

■ ■ ■

Understanding and Troubleshooting Protection in Office 365

BY ANDREW STOBART

According to Talos, a digital threat research division of Cisco Systems, 86% of all e-mail traffic is unsolicited junk mail. This works out to approximately 400 billion spam messages being sent every day. In addition to stopping spam, we are also faced with a never-ending assault of phishing messages, messages containing malware, and messages containing URLs to malicious web sites. Attacks are more sophisticated than ever before, and technology is ever-evolving to keep ahead of the attacks.

In this chapter, we will explore the protection aspects of Exchange Online. Features will be explored, and troubleshooting tips and experiences will be shared. These will be presented as "notes from the field," from my own knowledge and experiences that I have gained with troubleshooting this product daily.

EOP processes Billions of messages every day. → *Include other EOP related statistics?*

Exchange Online Protection (EOP), formerly Forefront Online Protection for Exchange (FOPE), and Business Productivity Online Suite (BPOS) before that, is the protection system of Exchange Online. From a high level, this includes all aspects of the service that work to prevent spam and malicious messages from landing in users' inboxes. Whether we are talking about spam, malware, phishing, safe or block lists, the Sender Policy Framework (SPF), Domain-based Message Authentication Reporting and Conformance (DMARC), DomainKeys Identified Mail (DKIM), or data loss prevention (DLP), these topics and many others all fall under the protection umbrella.

Header Analysis

Message headers contain a wealth of information that can be used when troubleshooting messages that pass through EOP. You just need to know where to look. The following headers are the main places to look when troubleshooting false positives and false negatives.

© Nikolas Charlebois-Laprade et al. 2017
N. Charlebois-Laprade et al., *Expert Office 365*, DOI 10.1007/978-1-4842-2991-0_9

X-Forefront-Antispam-Report

Whether a message has been sent out of Exchange Online or received by Exchange Online, this header will be present on the message. This header is the first place to look when troubleshooting false positives and false negatives. This header will look something like the following:

```
X-Forefront-Antispam-Report: CIP:xx.xx.xx.xx;IPV:NLI;CTRY:;EFV:NLI;SFV:NSPM;SFS:(8156002)
(2980300002);DIR:INB;SFP:;SCL:1;SRVR:DM2PR21MB0028;H:NAM01-BY2-obe.outbound.protection.
outlook.com;FPR:;SPF:Pass;PTR:mail-by2nam01on0139.outbound.protection.outlook.
com;MX:1;A:1;LANG:en;
```

I have found that the following items are the most important from the preceding message.

- **CIP (Connecting IP Address)**: This is the IP that delivered the message to Exchange Online.

- **SFV (Spam Filter Verdict)**: Most of the time, we will either see NSPM (Not Spam) or SPM (Spam) beside this property. However, this is where we will see if a trusted sender or blocked sender caused the SCL to be altered, for example, if an end user received a spam message that should have been marked as spam. If the preceding header contains SFV:SFE, this indicates that the sender is on the recipient's trusted senders list, so spam filtering was bypassed.

- **SCL (Spam Confidence Level)**: A -1 indicates that spam filtering was skipped. This could be because of a transport rule, a white listed IP, or the sender being in the recipient's trusted senders list. A 1 indicates the message was scanned for spam but was deemed safe. A 5 indicates spam, and a 9 indicates high-confidence spam. Sometimes, we will see SCL:6. This is an indication that the sender was on the recipient's blocked senders list. In this case, we should also see SVF:BLK in this header, which would verify that the sender is on the recipient's blocked senders list.

X-Forefront-Antispam-Report-Untrusted

If the X-Forefront-Antispam-Report header exists in a message that is received by Exchange Online, the pre-existing header will be renamed "X-Forefront-Antispam-Report-Untrusted." This prevents an attacker from adding their own X-Forefront-Antispam-Report header, in hopes that it will trick Exchange Online.

We see this behavior for all messages that pass from one Office 365 tenant to another. When the message is out one Office 365 tenant, it will be stamped with X-Forefront-Antispam-Report. When the recipient Office 365 tenant receives the message, the original header will be renamed to have "-Untrusted" at the end, and a new X-Forefront-Antispam-Report header will be stamped on the message. While most of the analysis will be looking at the X-Forefront-Antispam-Report header, it can sometimes be interesting to see how a message was stamped when it left a tenant, by looking at the header with -Untrusted on the end of it.

X-Microsoft-Antispam

This is the header in which you will find the Bulk Confidence Level, or BCL, that a message has been given. A BCL of 0 indicates the message is not bulk, whereas a 9 indicates that the message is absolutely bulk mail. When talking about spam and bulk, bulk mail can be thought of as newsletters that you may have inadvertently signed up for, and spam mail is completely unsolicited mail. The X-Microsoft-Antispam header looks as follows:

```
X-Microsoft-Antispam: UriScan:;BCL:0;PCL:0;RULEID:(22001)(81800161)
(13002);SRVR:BL2PR03MB289;
```

X-Original-Forefront-Antispam-Report

When a message is sent to the Quarantine, the X-Forefront-Antispam-Report header is renamed "X-Original-Forefront-Antispam-Report." The reason for this is persistence. If the message is released from the quarantine, a new X-Forefront-Antispam-Report header will be stamped on the message with SCL:-1. The X-Original-Forefront-Antispam-Report will still be present on a message that has been released and will contain the original SCL and SFV that were stamped on the message.

If you are troubleshooting a false positive that an end user has already released, you'll still be able to pull the original stamp, by looking at the X-Original-Forefront-Antispam-Report header.

X-Original-Microsoft-Antispam

Like the X-Original-Forefront-Antispam-Report header, the X-Microsoft-Antispam header will be renamed "X-Original-Microsoft-Antispam" when it lands in the quarantine.

Authentication-Results

The Authentication-Results header will display information about the SPF, DMARC, and DKIM checks. It will also display the From and MailFrom domains that were used. Here is an example.

```
Authentication-Results: spf=pass (sender IP is xx.xx.xx.xx)
smtp.mailfrom=contoso.com; microsoft.com; dkim=pass (signature was verified)
header.d=contoso.com;microsoft.com; dmarc=pass action=none
header.from=contoso.com;microsoft.com; dkim=fail (body hash did not verify)
header.d=contoso.com;
```

In the preceding example, we see SPF pass but dkim fail. DMARC, however, passes, because SPF passed and because theMailFrom domain matches the From domain. There is much more information on SPF, DMARC, and DKIM in the section "Identifying Spoofing Attacks and Technologies That Can Protect Your Domain."

X-CustomSpam

In the Spam Filter, there is an advanced options section (see Figure 9-1).

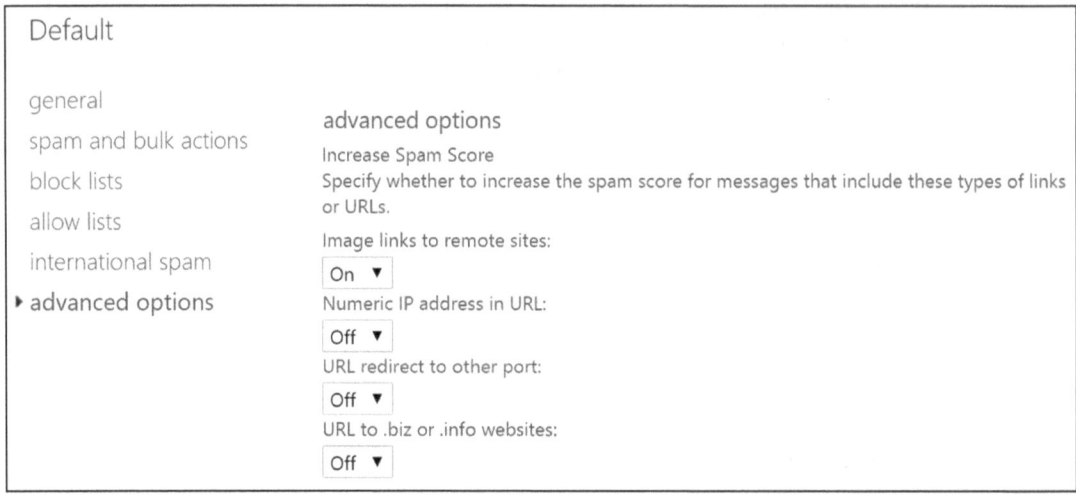

Figure 9-1. Spam Filter advanced options

The items listed here allow you to increase the aggressiveness of the Exchange Online Protection spam engine. If one of these options is enabled and causes a message to be marked as spam, you will find the X-CustomSpam header present in the header of the message. If a message that was marked as spam does not have the X-CustomSpam header present, then one of the preceding options was not the reason the message was marked as spam.

Example: I enabled the advanced option "URL redirect to other port" (see Figure 9-2).

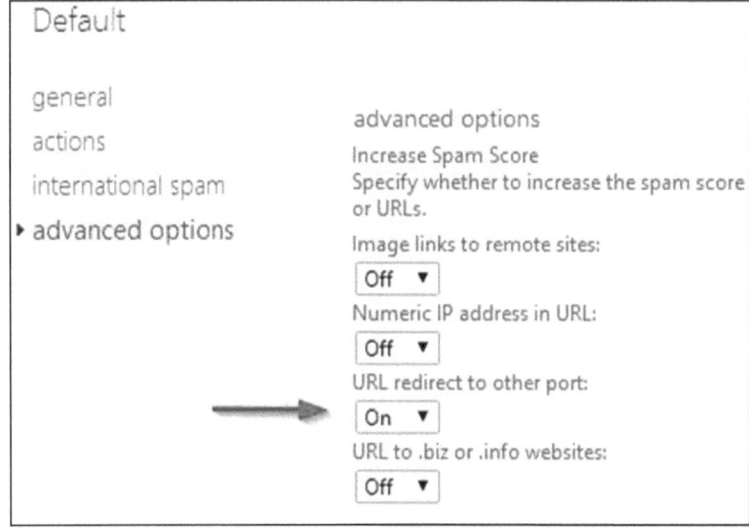

Figure 9-2. URL redirect to other port in advanced options

I then sent a message that contained the link http://www.contoso.com:123 in the body. This message triggered the preceding ASF in the Content Filter and caused the message to be marked as spam. Looking in the headers of this message, I see the following:

```
X-CustomSpam: URL redirect to other port
```

Right away I can see exactly which item in the Advanced Options of the spam filter caused this message to be marked as spam. When educating customers on these advanced options, I often recommend the following. When configuring EOP for the first time, don't initially enable all ASF options, as this can cause a large number of false positives. Instead, leave them off and, after evaluating mail flow, turn them on one at a time. I have found that the top-four ASF options are the most prone to causing false positives.

For organizations concerned about phishing, it is recommended that both SPF record: hard fail and Conditional Sender ID filtering: hard fail ASF options be enabled. Before enabling an ASF option, when possible, put it in Test Mode, to evaluate what impact it will have.

Tip for Obtaining Message Headers

In my line of work, I am constantly requesting message samples from customers, so that I can analyze the headers. Whether an end user has received a message that they believe should have been marked as spam, or they receive a message that was marked as spam that should not have been, step one of the troubleshooting starts with asking for the original message. Forwarding a sample message does not work, as the original headers are destroyed.

Less known by most people is that forwarding a sample as an attachment is also problematic (Figure 9-3).

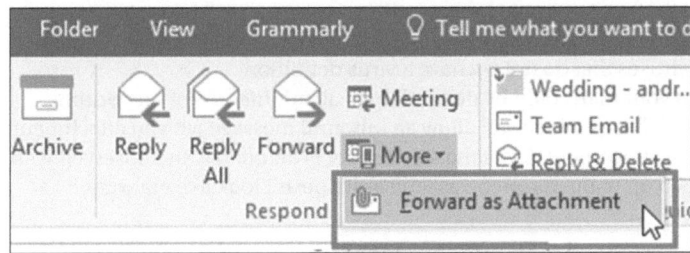

Figure 9-3. *Forwarding an attachment in Outlook*

When this message is sent, the Outlook desktop application will convert the .msg file that is attached to an .eml file. In this process, the attached message will become smaller in size before sending. The problem with this is that headers in the original message will be stripped, and oftentimes, the EOP headers that we are looking for will be gone.

To guarantee a message is forwarded intact, it first must be saved to your desktop, compressed (I recommend adding the message to a .zip archive), and then sent as an attachment. The Outlook Desktop client will not modify a message in a zip file, and this will ensure that the complete message, with all headers intact, will arrive at the destination.

Best Practices for Configuring Protection Features

This is the meat and potatoes of Exchange Online Protection. TechNet does a wonderful job of documenting how the various features work, such as the Spam Filter, the Malware Filter, Advanced Threat Protection, etc. Instead of copying TechNet, I'm going to provide best practices from my field knowledge, as well as some advanced troubleshooting tips for when problems arise.

One benefit that EOP has over on-premises spam filters is that the EOP filters are continually updated throughout the day. Spam analysts are constantly adding rules and tweaking existing ones, based on current attacks. Our customers also submit spam samples to us (both false positives and false negatives), and these are also used to update our spam filters on a continuing basis. These actions ensure that our filters are updated quickly and efficiently. Once we are aware of an attack, we can stop it very quickly.

The same applies to the EOP anti-malware engine, of which there are three. It is guaranteed that at any time, at least two of the malware engines will scan a message. Usually, all three are engaged, but this gives us the ability to pull one out of rotation for maintenance work. The three malware engines have their definitions updated continually throughout the day.

Advanced Threat Protection

Advanced Threat Protection is a feature set that can be added to Exchange Online for an additional price. The two main features of Advanced Threat Protection are Safe Attachments and Safe Links.

Safe Attachments

With Safe Attachments, all inbound mail that contains attachments will be, as we call it, "detonated." Attachments will be executed in a virtual environment, and we will look for malware characteristics. The idea here is that this can catch zero-day viruses that do not yet have a virus definition.

The catch to using this feature is that your mail could be delayed up to 30 minutes. As of this writing, Microsoft will soon be releasing dynamic delivery, which will allow an inbound message with an attachment to be delivered right away, but without the attachment. Once the attachment is detonated and observed with Safe Attachments, it will then be forwarded on to the recipient, as long as it doesn't look like malware.

Safe Links

Safe Links will rewrite any URL that is found in an e-mail. We can see the rewritten link in the following example when we hover the mouse over the embedded URL (Figure 9-4).

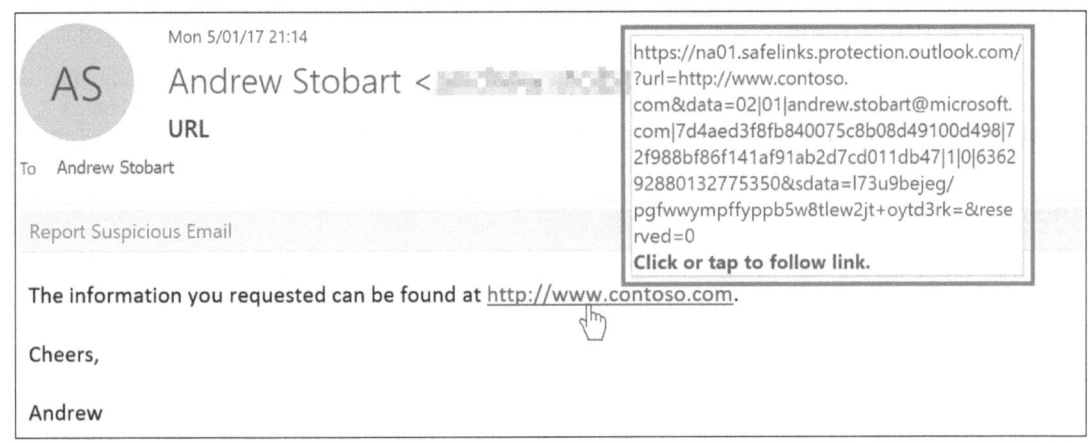

***Figure 9-4.** Safe Links rewrite*

When an end user clicks the link, they will be directed to Microsoft servers. If the link is good, they will be redirected to the actual web site. This redirection is seamless for the end user. If, at a later date, the link is determined to be malicious, users that click this link will instead be shown a page noting that the link is malicious and that they should not continue. As an administrator, you can choose to have the warning page contain a link to allow the user to continue to the actual web site.

With this proxying, we can track which users have clicked a link. If a malicious message has come into your organization with a phishing URL, you can run a report to find out exactly which users clicked the link, allowing you to start your remediation with those users that may actually be impacted.

Identifying Spoofing Attacks and Technologies That Can Protect Your Domain

SPF, DMARC, and DKIM are technologies that can be used to help protect your domain against spoofing. By using these technologies, a recipient can verify that a message they received from your domain really did, in fact, come from you, as opposed to coming from an attacker. Before discussing the three aforementioned technologies, I would first like to discuss header terminology that will be used in this section.

Header Terminology

The following excerpt from a message header will be used to identify the various headers that are important when dealing with a spoofing attack.

```
Authentication-Results: spf=none (sender IP is 167.220.24.220)
 smtp.mailfrom=contoso.com; microsoft.com; dkim=none (message not signed)
 header.d=none;microsoft.com; dmarc=none action=none
 header.from=tailspintoys.com;
From: From header FromHeader@tailspintoys.com     ← 5322.From header
To: Andrew Stobart andrew.stobart@microsoft.com
Subject: Different MailFrom and From headers
Return-Path: MailFromHeader@contoso.com     ← 5321.MailFrom
Reply-To: replyto@adventure-works.com     ← Reply-To address
```

5321.MailFrom Header

The MailFrom address represents the address that was sent in the envelope of the message. The domain used in this address is what the SPF check will be done against. In an SMTP conversation, this will be specified as MailFrom. In a message header, this will be identified as the Return-Path.

5322.From

This is the "From" address that you see in your mail client (Figure 9-5).

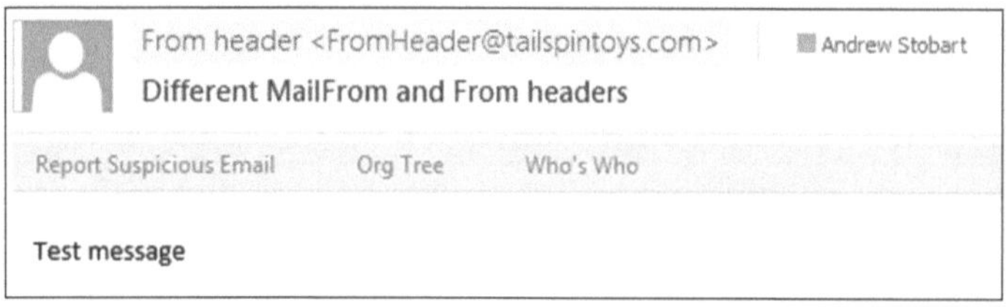

Figure 9-5. *From address in an e-mail*

In the message header, this address will be the "From" header.

```
From: From header <FromHeader@tailspintoys.com>
To: Andrew Stobart <andrew@contoso.com>
Subject: Different MailFrom and From headers
```

In most scenarios, the From and MailFrom headers will match; however, these will typically be different in messages in which spoofing is used (they also tend to be different for bulk mail). Typical spoofing attacks will only spoof the From header, because SPF will not check the domain specified in this header, therefore bypassing SPF.

Authentication-Results Header

This header will provide the results of the SPF/DKIM and DMARC checks. It also contains the following:

```
Smtp.mailfrom = Specifies the domain used in the 5321.MailFrom address.
Header.from = Specifies the domain used in the 5322.From address.
SPF = Results of the SPF check.
DKIM = Results of the DKIM check.
DMARC = Results of the DMARC check.
```

Reply-To Header

If this header is set, when a mail client replies to the message, the reply will be directed to this address, regardless of what the original From or MailFrom addresses were.

Spoofing Methods

The following are examples of the most common type of spoofing attacks.

5322.From Header Is Spoofed, but the 5321.MailFrom Is for a Domain Controlled by the Attacker

Consider the following SMTP commands for a sent message:

```
S: Helo woodgrovebank.com
S: Mail from: phish@phishing.contoso.com  <-- 5321.MailFrom
S: Rcpt to: astobes@tailspintoys.com
S: data
S: To: "Andrew Stobes" <astobes@tailspintoys.com>
S: From: "Woodgrove Bank Security" security@woodgrovebank.com  <-- 5322.From
```

The recipient would see the message being sent from security@woodgrovebank.com (Figure 9-6).

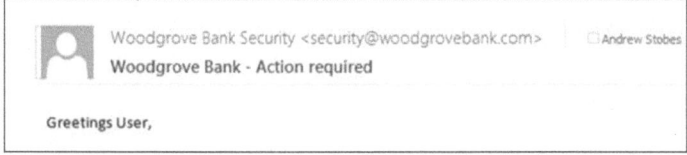

Figure 9-6. *E-mail from security@woodgrovebank.com*

The SPF check will be done against phishing.contoso.com, which will pass (or be none), because the attacker will own this domain. This is why this type of attack is so frequently used. This type of spoof can be identified when you see a Return-Path header that is different from the From header. Here's an excerpt of the message header for the preceding message:

```
From: Woodgrove Bank Security <security@woodgrovebank.com>
To: Andrew Stobart <andrew.stobart@microsoft.com>
Subject: Different MailFrom and From headers
Return-Path: phish@phishing.contoso.com   ← SPF only checks this domain
```

In these types of messages, the attacker will usually not expect the user to reply to them (as the message would go to the spoofed address, which the attacker will not control). These types of messages typically contain a URL to a phishing site that the attacker is hoping the recipient will click. SPF, combined with DMARC, would detect this type of spoof. SPF on its own would not, as SPF only checks the domain in the 5321.MailFrom address.

5322.From Header Spoofed and 5321.MailFrom = 5322.From

Like the preceding attack, but in the headers, you will see the From header and Return-Path header match. These attacks typically contain phishing links that the attacker hopes will be clicked. SPF will detect this attack; however, it is strongly recommended to implement DMARC along with SPF.

Homoglyph Attacks (Attacker Owns a Domain That Is Similar to the Customer's)

Again, these types of attacks are similar to the preceding ones, except that the domain being spoofed is owned by the attacker and is very similar to the company that they are attacking. Consider the message shown in Figure 9-7.

Reply
Reply All
Forward
IM
attacker@miicrosoft.com
Andrew Stobart
Wire transfer request

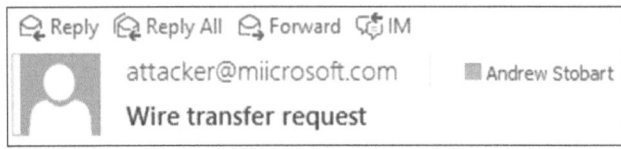

Figure 9-7. *E-mail message from* `attacker@miicrosoft.com`

In this case, the attacker hopes that when the recipient replies to the message, they will not notice that the domain they are replying to isn't actually their own. We also see a similar type of attack used, in which the attacker spoofs the customer's domain exactly but then sets a Reply-To header that is set to a domain that is similar to the customer's but owned by the attacker.

Attacks That Use the Reply-To Header

When a Reply-To header is present, when a recipient replies to a message, the reply will be directed to the address specified in the Reply-To header. For example, consider the following spoofed message (Figure 9-8). Notice how even the profile picture appears.

Reply
Reply All
Forward
IM
Joe Someone < @microsoft.com>
Andrew Stobart
Wire transfer request

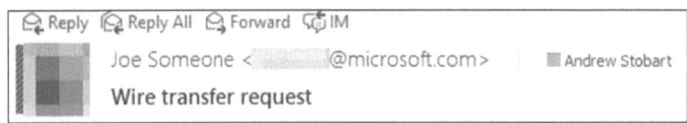

Figure 9-8. *Spoofed message with picture*

Here's what happens when I hit the Reply button (Figure 9-9).

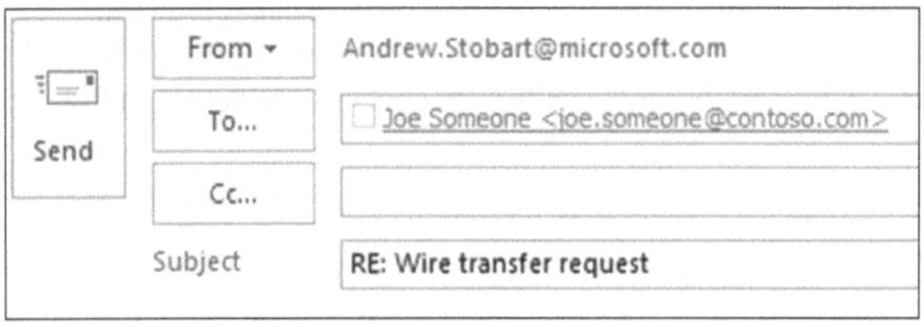

Send
From
Andrew.Stobart@microsoft.com
To...
Joe Someone <joe.someone@contoso.com>
Cc...
Subject
RE: Wire transfer request

Figure 9-9. *Replying to an e-mail*

Note that the reply is being sent to a domain that the attacker will own. The attacker hopes that the recipient won't notice that the Reply-To address is different from the sending address. Here's what the header looks like for this type of attack:

```
From: <name redacted>@microsoft.com
To: <name redacted>@microsoft.com
Reply-To: joe.someone@contoso.com
Subject: Wire transfer request
Return-Path: <name redacted>@microsoft.com
```

SPF and DMARC will detect these types of attacks. In addition, end-user education is also highly recommended.

Anti-Spoofing Technologies

You should understand the following technologies.

Sender Policy Framework (SPF)

SPF is a technology for sender authentication. SPF uses a DNS TXT record to store a list of authorized sending IP addresses for a given domain. A receiving mail server performs an SPF check by confirming that the connecting IP address is in the SPF record for the 5321.MailFrom domain. In Exchange Online, the results of the SPF check are recorded in the Authentication-Results header and the Received-SPF header.

Because SPF only checks the domain in the 5321.MailFrom address, SPF cannot detect spoofing attacks in which the 5322.From address is spoofed and the 5321.MailFrom address is set to a domain that the attack owns and, therefore, can ensure that SPF passes. This is where DMARC comes in.

Domain-Based Message Authentication, Reporting and Conformance (DMARC)

DMARC uses SPF and/or DKIM to authenticate the 5322.From address. DMARC will pass if an SPF or DKIM check passes and the domain in the 5321.MailFrom and 5322.From addresses match. This means that DMARC will always fail if the domain of the 5321.MailFrom does not match the domain of the 5322.From.

DomainKeys Identified Mail

With SPF records, you can only add up to ten DNS lookups in the record. If you have many third parties that can send on your behalf, you will quickly hit this wall. This is where DKIM comes in.

DKIM allows you to sign outbound mail with a signing certificate. The public key for the certificate is present in your Public DNS, which will allow recipients to verify that the sender is authorized.

User Education

End-user education is an extremely important part of preventing spoofing attacks. End users should be educated about the following conventions:

- Hover over URLs in your e-mail client to verify that they are going to a known location.

- Don't click URLs from people you aren't familiar with.

- When replying to a message, always verify that the expected address is present on the To line.

Advanced Troubleshooting and Tips

The following section provides some advanced guidance to help troubleshoot complex issues.

Extended Message Trace

Regular message traces are sufficient for most mail flow troubleshooting, but, occasionally, we need more data, which requires obtaining an extended message trace. These traces (provided as a CSV file) contain a plethora of information. However, parsing them can be a very overwhelming experience. Next, I will share the work flow that I use when I must extract data from an extended message trace.

Obtaining an Extended Message Trace

Obtaining an extended message trace can be tricky, if you've never requested one before. In the Message Trace tool, set a custom date range and ensure that the starting date is at least a week in the past (this is the key to enable the extended trace). Add either a sender, recipient, or Message ID, and check the "Include routing events and routing details with report" box (Figure 9-10).

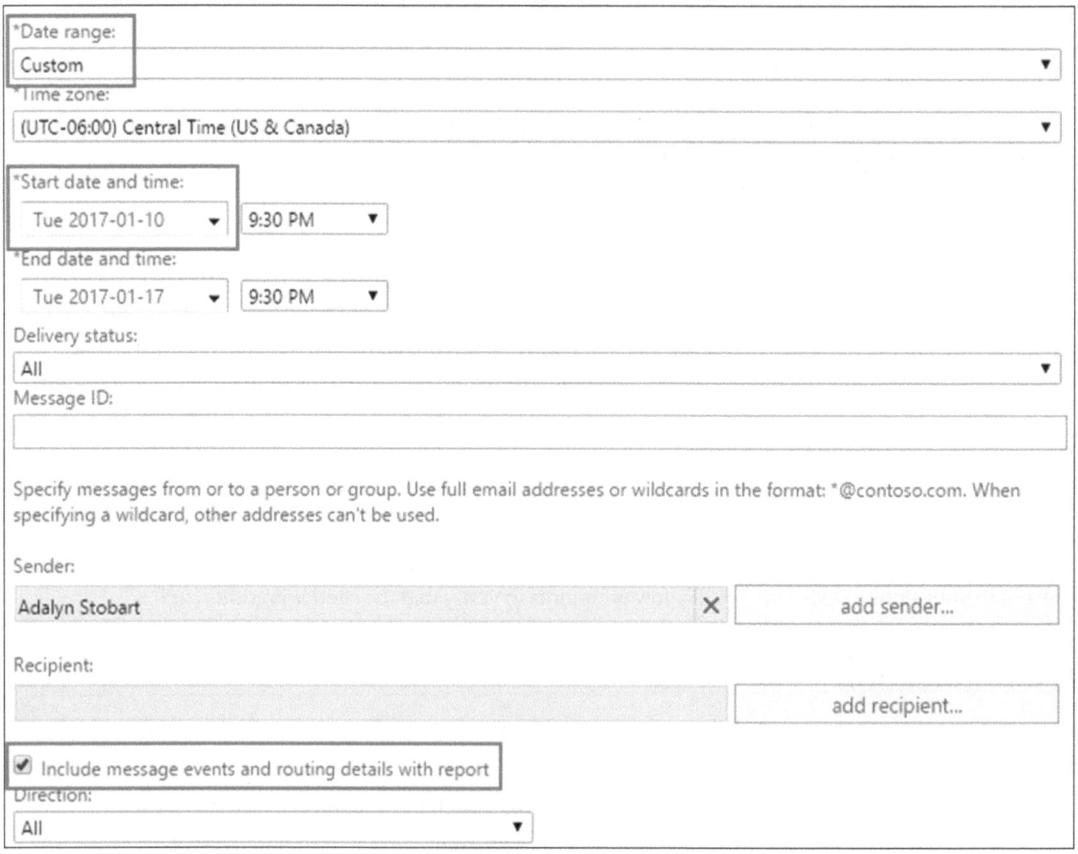

Figure 9-10. *Message trace tool*

These traces typically take about an hour to complete. Once completed, you can download the CSV file at the link View pending or the completed traces on the Message Trace page. After opening the CSV file in Excel, you should see something like what is shown in Figure 9-11.

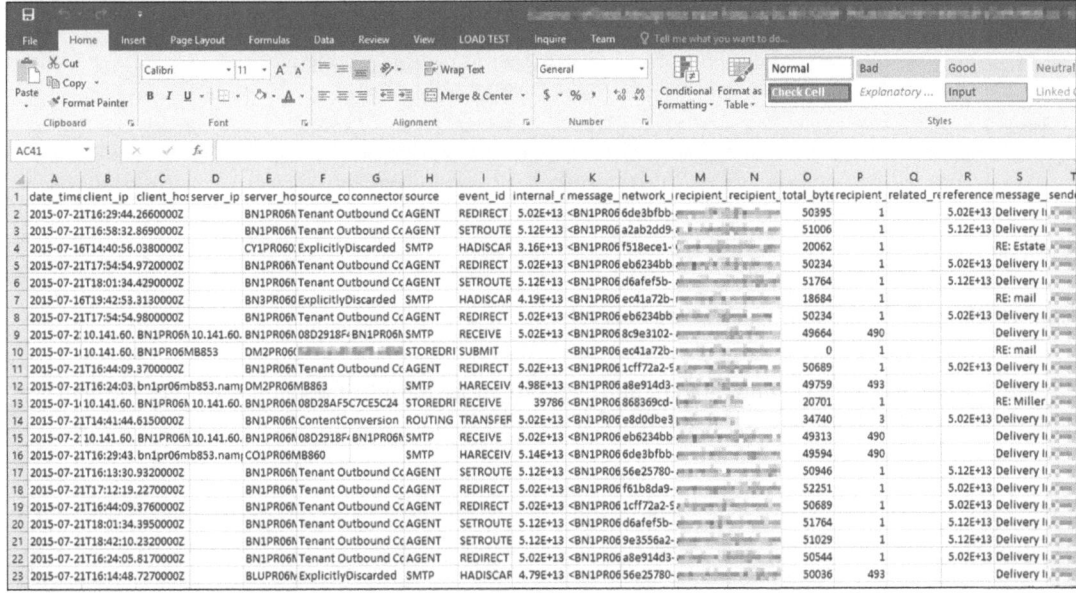

Figure 9-11. *Excel spreadsheet*

Parsing an Extended Message Trace in Excel

Message traces do not come sorted by date and time (in fact, they aren't sorted by anything), and so this is the first order of business. Next, highlight the first row, then click the Data tab, and then Filter (Figure 9-12).

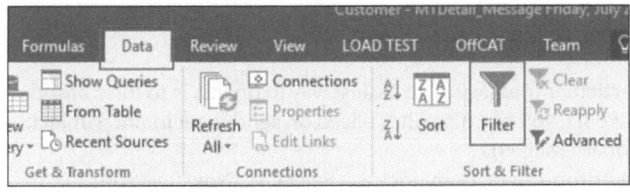

Figure 9-12. *Filter option in Excel*

To make reading our headers easier, highlight the entire first row again, and then click Format, under the Home tab, and then AutoFit Column Width (Figure 9-13).

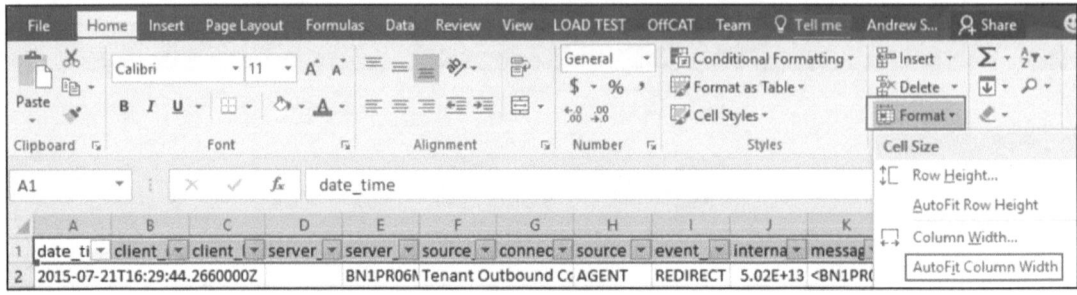

Figure 9-13. *AutoFit Column Width option in Excel*

Expand the date_time column (first column), so you can see the full timestamp, then click the filter drop-down for that column and select Sort A to Z (Figure 9-14).

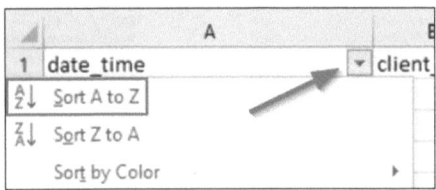

Figure 9-14. *Sort A to Z option on an Excel column*

Now that we have our trace sorted chronologically, we next have to start removing messages that aren't part of our investigation.

Only Show Rows Pertaining to a Particular Message

Typically, we only want to see details from a particular message. The easiest way to do this is to filter based on the Message ID. If you don't have the Message ID, you can also filter based on sender, recipient, subject, etc. For this example, I'm going to filter based on Message ID.

Find the message_id column, click the filter drop-down, then uncheck Select All. Now find your Message ID in the list, check it off, then hit OK (see Figure 9-15).

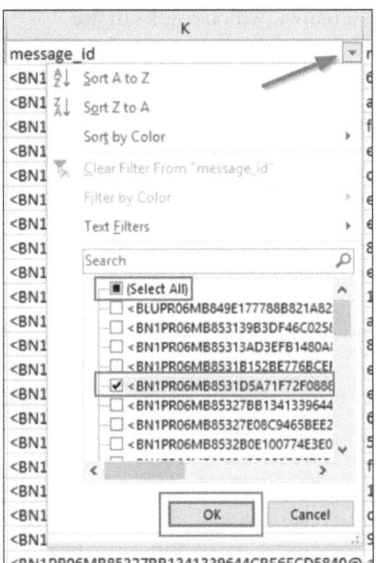

Figure 9-15. *Filtering entries in Excel*

I am now looking at 7 rows, compared to my starting point of more than 7,000 rows! Each of the now remaining rows represent a different EOP server that this message traversed through. Some rows are more interesting than others, and, typically, the most important row is that in which the EOP header (x-forefront-antispam-report) values are stamped on the message.

Extracting the EOP (X-Forefront-Antispam-Report) Header

One of the most important items we can pull from the extended message trace is the x-forefront-antispam-report header information for a message. This is especially helpful when we do not have the original .msg file for a message we are investigating.

This data can be found in the custom_data column. Look for the cell that starts with S:AMA=, as shown in Figure 9-16.

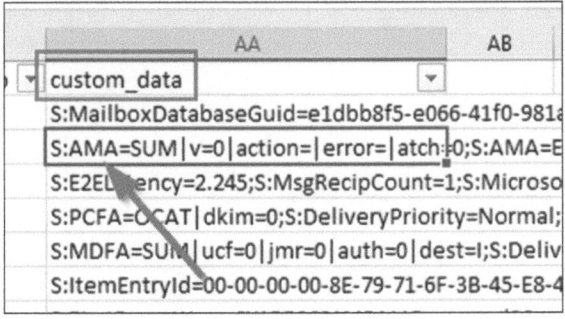

Figure 9-16. S:AMA= *entry in our Excel spreadsheet*

For my workflow, I copy the contents of this cell and paste it into Notepad++, which results in the following view (Figure 9-17).

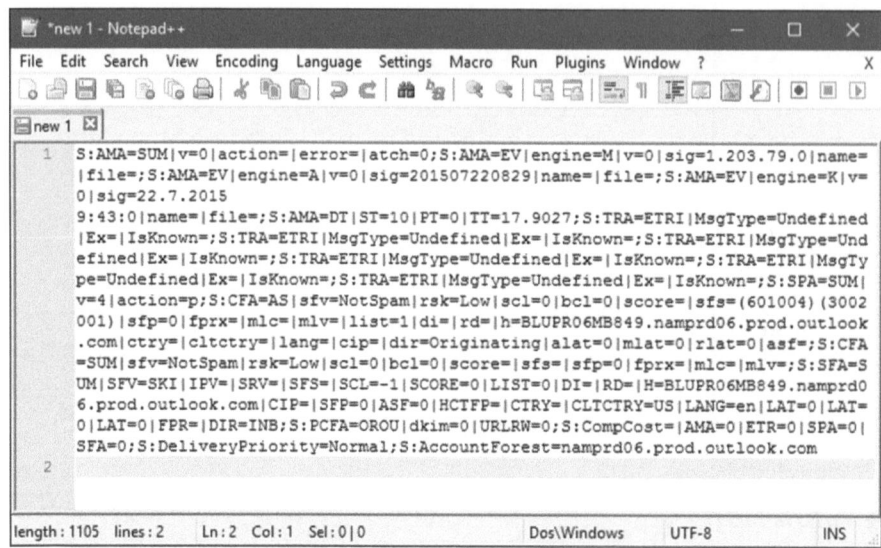

Figure 9-17. *Entry viewed in Notepad++*

To clean this up, I use the Replace action. Use the following options in the Replace window, then click Replace All (Figure 9-18).

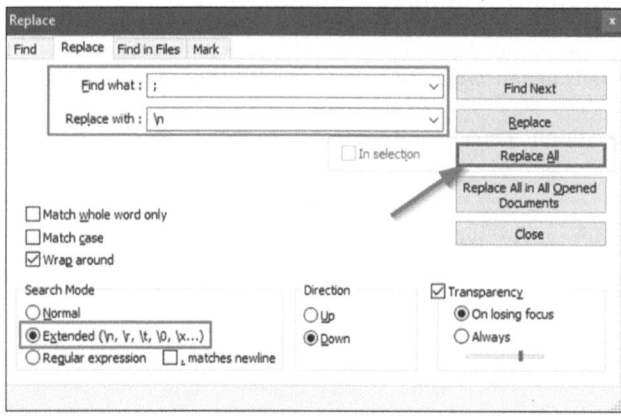

Figure 9-18. *Replace All in Notepad++*

I can now very easily pick out the various EOP results (Figure 9-19).

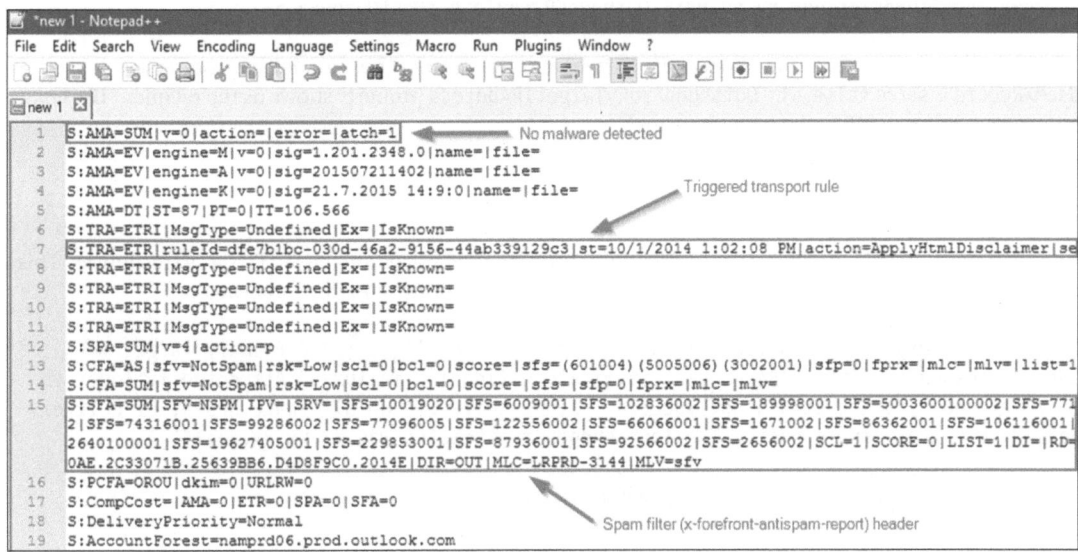

Figure 9-19. EOP Results in NotePad++

Some interesting items we can quickly pull from here are as follows:

- **S:AMA—Anti-malware Agent**: Will indicate if any viruses were detected.

- **S:TRA=ETR—Transport Rule Agent**: ETR|ruleid=[guid] will indicates the GUID of any transport rules that triggered (Note: S:TRA=ETRI and S:TRA=ETRP do not indicate rules that have been triggered)

- **S:SFA—Spam Filter Agent**: Will display contents from the X-Forefront-Antispam-Report header (Spam Filter Score, Spam Filter Verdict, message direction, etc....)

Here is the S:SFA string from an extended trace with the SCL, SFV, and direction values highlighted.

S:SFA=SUM|**SFV=SKN**|IPV=|SRV=|SFS=|**SCL=-1**| SCORE=0|LIST=0|DI=|RD=|H=BLUPR06MB849.namprd06.prod.
outlook.com|CIP=|SFP=0|ASF=0|HCTFP=|CTRY=|CLTCTRY=US|LANG=en|LAT=0|LAT=0|LAT=0|FPR=|**DIR=INB**

This was an inbound message that EOP gave an SCL of -1. The Spam Filter Verdict for this message is SKN, which indicates that the safe listing was done prior to the spam filter (ex. Transport rule).

For more information on the custom_data column, see Run a Message Trace and View Results. On this page, expand information under "View message trace results for messages that are greater than 7 days old."

EOP Outbound Connector That Was Used

For mail that is leaving your Office 365 tenant, the extended trace can tell us which EOP outbound connector was used to deliver the message. For an outbound message, look in the custom_data column for a row that begins with S:E2ELatency=. In this example, my outbound message was sent using an EOP outbound connector, called xbox.com outbound, that I created.

```
S:E2ELatency=32.140;S:ExternalSendLatency=3.155;'S:Microsoft.Exchange.Hygiene.TenantOutbound
ConnectorCustomData=Name=xbox.com outbound;ConnectorType=Partner;UseMxRecord=False';S:Outbou
ndProxyTargetIPAddress=xx.xx.xx.xx;S:OutboundProxyTargetHostName=xx.xx.xx.xx;...
```

I can also see that this connector is type Partner and uses a smart host for delivery, because
UseMXRecord is set to false. The OutboundProxyTargetIPAddress property shows us the recipient IP. (I have
obfuscated the actual IP in the preceding text).

Server SMTP Responses

Another interesting piece of data that we can pull from extended traces are the SMTP server responses. This
data can be found in the recipient_status column. As an example, consider the following:

```
'450 4.7.0 Proxy session setup failed on Frontend with  ''451 4.4.0 Primary target IP
address responded with: "454 4.7.5 Certificate validation failure." Attempted failover to
alternate host, but that did not succeed. Either there are no alternate hosts, or delivery
failed to all alternate hosts. The last endpoint attempted was xx.xx.xx.xx:25'''
```

Note that this data can also be seen in regular message traces.

Delivery Folder

For inbound messages destined to mailboxes hosted in Exchange Online, an extended message trace
will show which folder in the recipient's mailbox the message was delivered to. Note: This only works if
the recipient mailbox is located in Exchange Online, and only for server-side mailbox rules that cause a
message to be delivered to a particular folder. For example, here's an inbox rule that I have configured on my
Exchange Online mailbox (Figure 9-20).

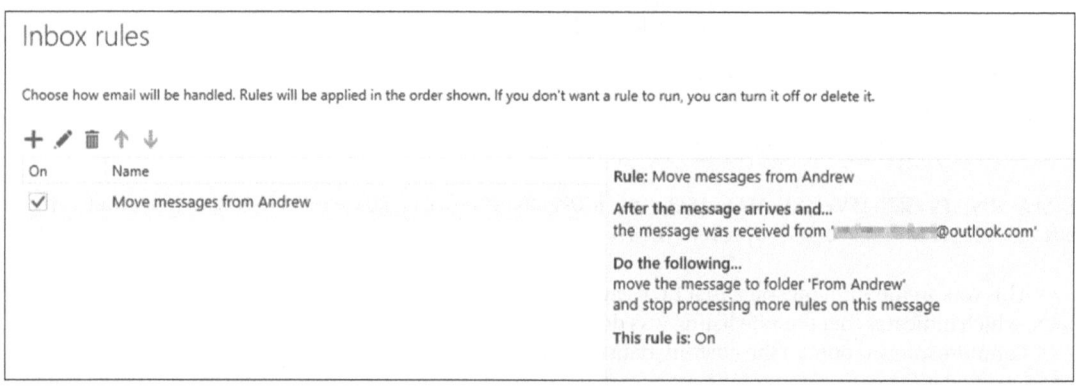

Figure 9-20. *Exchange inbox rule*

When I run an extended message trace on a message that would have triggered this mailbox rule, I can
see the folder where this message was delivered (Figure 9-21).

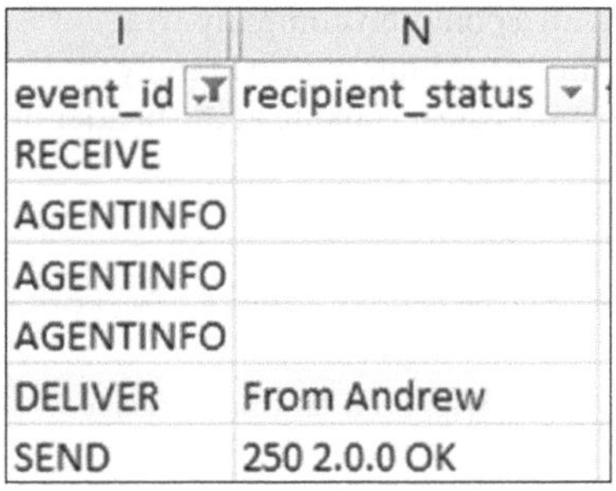

I	N
event_id	recipient_status
RECEIVE	
AGENTINFO	
AGENTINFO	
AGENTINFO	
DELIVER	From Andrew
SEND	250 2.0.0 OK

Figure 9-21. *Deliver field from the message*

Just look for the DELIVER event in the event_id column, and note the recipient_status column. A semicolon in the recipient_status column indicates that the message was delivered to the recipient's inbox.

Which Transport Rule Triggered on My Message?

While a message trace can be used to determine which rule(s) triggered on a message, it is not always fast. With the following trick, you can determine which rule(s) triggered on a message, by looking only at the headers.

In all your transport rules, add the predicate "Set the message header to this value," as shown in Figure 9-22.

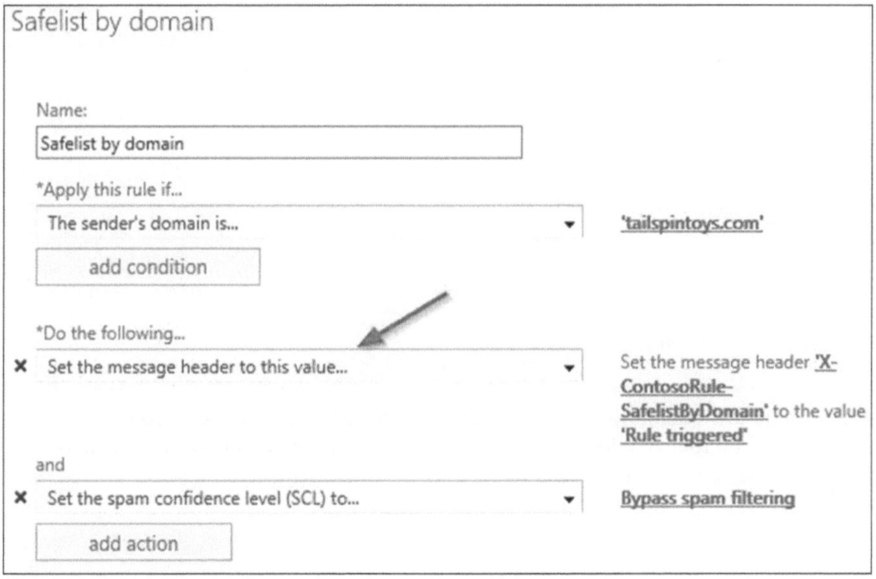

Safelist by domain

Name:

Safelist by domain

*Apply this rule if...

The sender's domain is...   ▼   'tailspintoys.com'

add condition

*Do the following...

✗ Set the message header to this value...   ▼   Set the message header 'X-ContosoRule-SafelistByDomain' to the value 'Rule triggered'

and

✗ Set the spam confidence level (SCL) to...   ▼   Bypass spam filtering

add action

Figure 9-22. *Setting a value to the message header*

When configuring this predicate on your transport rules, come up with a common company-wide header name (I used X-ContosoRule). Then, in each rule, append a unique string after this, to identify it.

As an example of this, I had a message that triggered two of my transport rules. Looking at the header of the message, I found the following:

```
X-ContosoRule-SafeDomainFound: Rule triggered
X-ContosoRule-ExecutableFound: Rule triggered
```

Without even running a message trace, I could see right away which rules triggered on this message.

Reporting

All the Exchange Online Protection reports can be found under the main Office 365 page, under Reports, and then Security & compliance (Figure 9-23).

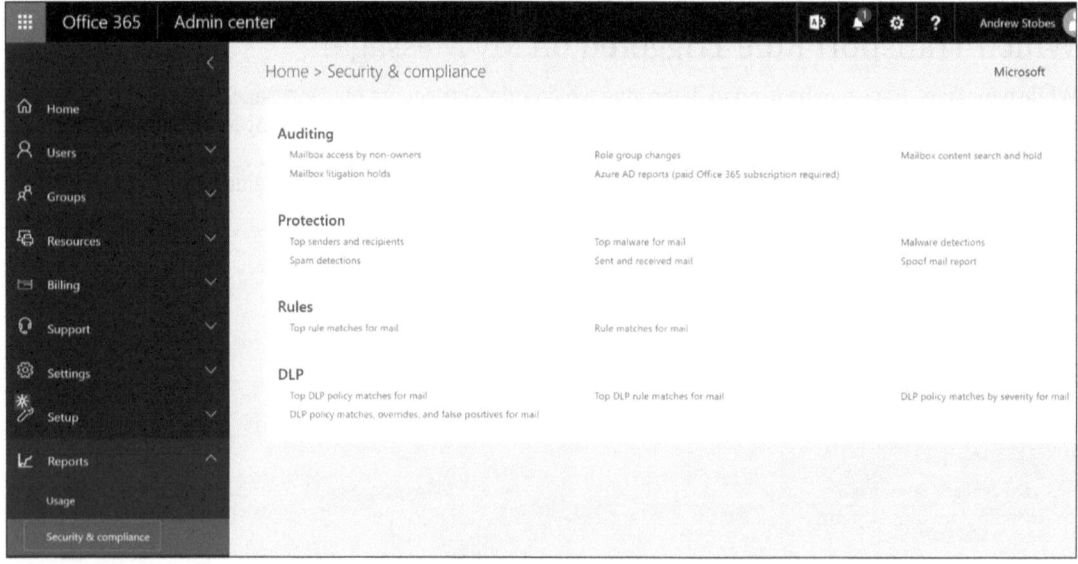

Figure 9-23. *Security & compliance portal in Office 365*

While the reports are available on demand, it can very beneficial to schedule these reports to be delivered to your inbox on a set schedule. In addition to the ease of getting information, it will also allow trending, as data is only kept for so long in Exchange Online.

Not all reports can be scheduled, but for the ones that can, you will see something similar to what is shown in Figure 9-24.

Figure 9-24. Schedule this report link

Reports can be scheduled to be sent on a weekly or monthly basis.

Additional Resources

The following links are additional resources that can help you troubleshoot common issues:

- *EHLO Blog*: https://blogs.technet.microsoft.com/exchange/

- *EOP Field Notes Blog*: https://blogs.technet.microsoft.com/eopfieldnotes/

- *250 Hello Blog*: https://blogs.technet.microsoft.com/rmilne/

- *Remote Connectivity Analyzer*: https://testconnectivity.microsoft.com/

Summary

This chapter covered protection features in Exchange Online. With knowledge of network captures, message tracing, and what various EOP headers mean, you can easily determine why a message was marked the way it was and then troubleshoot mail-flow problems. With implementation of SPF, DMARC, and DKIM, you can protect your domains against spoofing. Knowing what tools exist, and how to use them, can significantly cut down on remediation work, following a spam or phishing attack.

CHAPTER 10

■ ■ ■

Understanding and Troubleshooting Office 365 Mail Flow

BY BRUCE WILSON

Office 365 Exchange Online (ExO) with Exchange Online Protection (EOP) is the successor to Business Productivity Online Service (BPOS) and Forefront Online Protection for Exchange (FOPE) services. While BPOS and FOPE were separate services managed completely independently, Office 365 brings them together into one service and administration center, running on a common platform, Exchange. Since the service initially launched, it has received many updates, bringing new and improved functionality to users along the way.

In this chapter, we will look at the various aspects of mail flow, as they relate to Office 365, starting with what happens to an e-mail message when it is first received by the service. We will then review the steps the message takes before it is handed off to the destination e-mail system or target mailbox. We will also cover where anti-malware and antispam checks fit in, but I will not go into depth about this in this chapter. Next, we will look at the most common deployment scenarios and what properly functioning mail flow looks like in each. Then we will look at several troubleshooting techniques that can be used to isolate where an e-mail delivery failure is occurring. Other topics covered will be the different kinds of logging that are available, which one to use when, and how to use them.

Office 365 Mail-Flow Architectural Overview

Office 365 is based on the current generation of Exchange, which means that mail flow does not differ from what you would expect from an on-premises server deployment. When a message is received by Office 365, it first passes through an edge server, where connection and reputation filtering occurs, before being passed on to a mailbox server for filtering and further processing. The message is then processed by anti-malware, Transport & Data Loss Prevention (DLP) rules, antispam agents, and, if enabled, Advanced Threat Protection (ATP) safe links and safe attachments, before being delivered to its destination (Figure 10-1).

© Nikolas Charlebois-Laprade et al. 2017
N. Charlebois-Laprade et al., *Expert Office 365*, DOI 10.1007/978-1-4842-2991-0_10

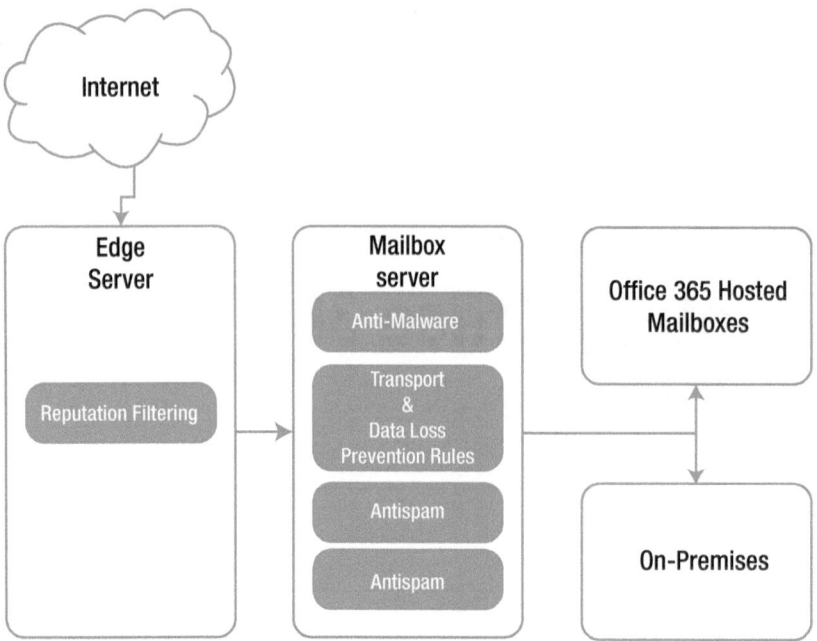

Figure 10-1. Overview of the overall Exchange Online architecture

The service uses what we call Opportunistic TLS (Transport Layer Security) to secure communication between itself and external servers, providing end-to-end TLS encryption. This means that if TLS is offered, we will always prefer it over a non-TLS connection.

For messages being sent to Office 365, the sending server is responsible for setting up the TLS connection. Connectors can be configured to force TLS communication for messages coming in to the service. Messages being sent from the service to external parties will always attempt TLS first. If the receiving MTA does not offer the STARTTLS SMTP (Simple Mail Transfer Protocol) verb or there is an issue establishing the connection, the service will fall back on unencrypted SMTP communication. Connectors can also be used to specify the security and routing of messages leaving Office 365.

There are two broad categories of customers who use Office 365: Exchange Online Protection (a.k.a. Filtering Only) and Exchange Online (a.k.a. Fully Hosted or Hybrid) customers. Aside from the physical servers that messages for these customers pass through, there is no difference between how messages are processed.

Fully hosted is by far the simplest configuration, as connectors are not required to set up mail flow to or from these customers. When a message is sent to a fully hosted customer, once it passes through filtering, it will be delivered to the destination mailbox. Messages sent from these customers will be delivered, based on the destination domain's MX record or via an outbound partner connector, if configured.

For filtering-only customers, once messages have passed through filtering, the service uses an outbound on-premises connector to route the message to the customer's on-premises environment, where it will be delivered to its destination. Messages sent from these customers enter the service through an inbound on-premises connector, then go through the same filtering as inbound messages, before being delivered, based on the destination domain's MX record or via outbound partner connectors to enforce TLS delivery.

As there are many variations of hybrid configurations, we will look at the simplest setup here. After a message passes through filtering, the service will first look for a mailbox in the cloud to deliver to. If a mailbox cannot be found, Office 365 then uses the domain type, Internal Relay or Authoritative, to determine what happens to messages when a mailbox cannot be found in the cloud. When the domain is set to Internal Relay, the service will route the message out of the service for delivery to the destination mailbox. If the domain is set to Authoritative, a mail object is required, to tell the service that a mailbox exists on-premises. In both cases, an outbound on-premises connector is required, to ensure that the message is routed to the correct end point for delivery to the destination mailbox.

How Does the Service Know If a Message Is Being Sent to or from a Customer?

When a message is sent to Office 365, the edge servers that process the message determine if it is originating, coming from a customer, or incoming, going to a customer. This process is called attribution.

- **Originating:** A message that originates from a tenant's on-premises server (matches the tenant's inbound on-premises connector) or from a cloud mailbox. If Office 365 is unable to identify the message as originating, and the recipient domain is an accepted domain in an Office 365 organization, the service will identify the message as incoming to the recipient organization instead.

- **Incoming:** Messages sent to accepted domains that are in Office 365 that do not match an incoming on-premises connector.

During the attribution process, the service uses the following information to make the determination as to whether the message is originating or incoming:

- Certificate Details and/or Connecting IP

- MailFrom domain

- RcptTo domain

Common Mail-Flow Deployment Styles

Office 365 allows for many different mail-flow configurations, from very simple filtering only or fully hosted to complex hybrid deployments. When deploying Office 365, understanding how you plan to configure your MX record in the long term is important. For example, if you plan to keep your MX record pointing to a third party, you will have to create Partner connectors to enable secured mail flow.

Filtering Only

With a filtering-only configuration, your MX record is pointed to Office 365 and then to configure inbound and outbound on-premises-type connectors, to enable mail flow for your organization (Figure 10-2).

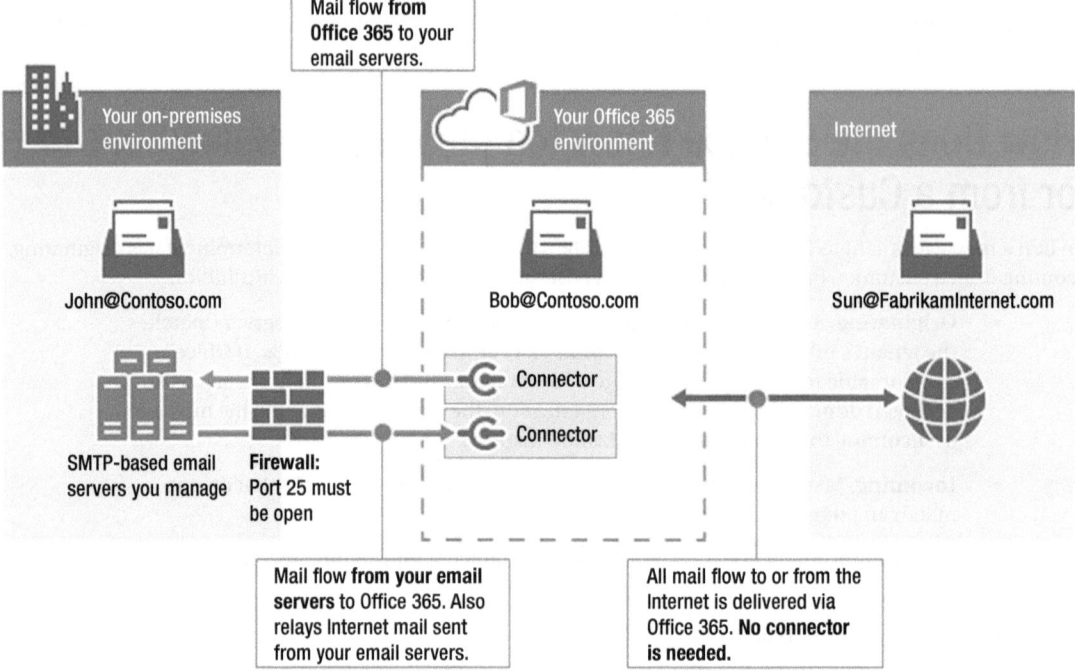

Figure 10-2. *Filtering-only configuration*

In a filtering-only configuration, there are four different failure points that you must be aware of.

- From the Internet to Exchange Online Protection

- Exchange Online Protection to on-premises

- On-premises to Exchange Online Protection

- Exchange Online Protection to the Internet

Fully Hosted

With a fully hosted configuration, your MX record is pointed to Office 365. No connectors are required with this configuration, unless you have a business necessity, such as TLS with business partners (Figure 10-3).

Hosted mail flow

MX record points to Office 365

Office 365 routes and filters all email messages for contoso.com.

Office 365

Internet

MX record
contoso-com.mail.protection.outlook.com
SPF record
v=spf1 include:spf.protection.outlook.com -all

Figure 10-3. *Fully hosted configuration*

In a fully hosted configuration, there are two different failure points that you must be aware of.

- From the Internet to Exchange Online
- From Exchange Online to the Internet

■ **Note**   If you configure connectors to enforce business requirements, these introduce additional failure points that you must be aware of.

As there are many different hybrid configurations that can be configured, I will only cover the main scenarios. Additionally, I will not go deep within on-premises but instead will reference it at a high level. With hybrid configurations, as the complexity increases, so do the number of failure points.

MX to On-Premises

With this configuration, your MX record will continue to be pointed to the on-premises server. Messages destined to mailboxes not hosted within the on-premises environment will have their e-mail address rewritten to the TargetAddress, which is the service domain in Office 365, and relayed up to the cloud for delivery (Figure 10-4).

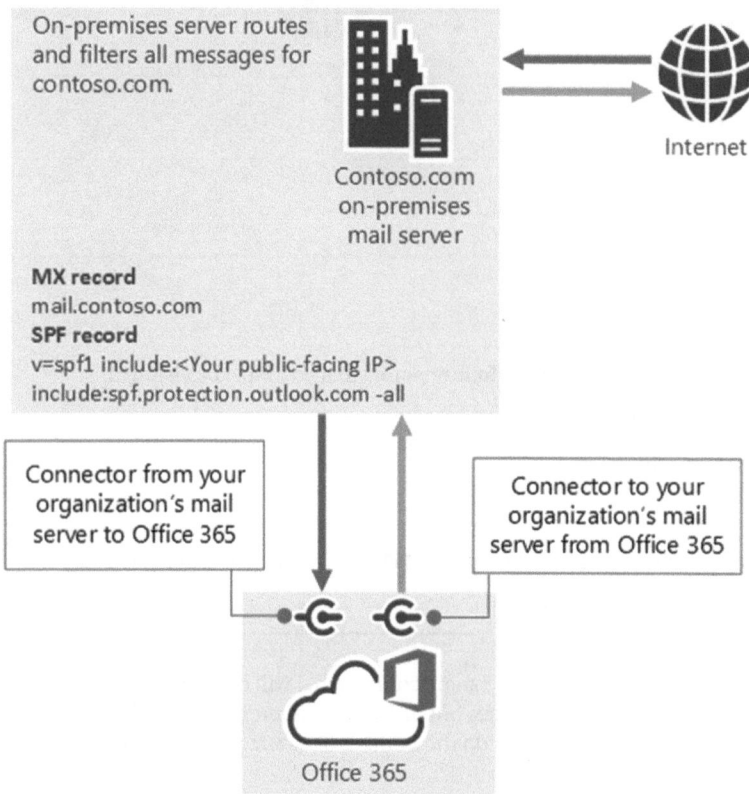

Hybrid mail flow – MX record points to on-premises server
Filtering happens on-premises

On-premises server routes and filters all messages for contoso.com.

Contoso.com on-premises mail server

Internet

MX record
mail.contoso.com
SPF record
v=spf1 include:<Your public-facing IP>
include:spf.protection.outlook.com -all

Connector from your organization's mail server to Office 365

Connector to your organization's mail server from Office 365

Office 365

Figure 10-4. *Hybrid mail flow with MX pointing to on-premises server*

In this configuration, there are five failure points that you must be aware of.

- From the Internet to on-premises
- Within the on-premises environment
- On-premises to Exchange Online
- Exchange Online to on-premises for internal recipients
- Exchange Online to Internet for external recipients

MX to Cloud

With this configuration, your MX record is updated to point to Exchange Online, and connectors are configured to route mail between the cloud and on-premises for users not hosted in Exchange Online (Figure 10-5). When a message is sent from an on-premises user to a user that is hosted in Exchange Online, the recipient's address is rewritten to the TargetAddress, which is the service domain in Office 365, and relayed to the cloud for delivery.

Hybrid mail flow – MX record points to Office 365 and Office 365 filters all messages
Filtering happens in Office 365 (Recommended for most hybrid organizations)

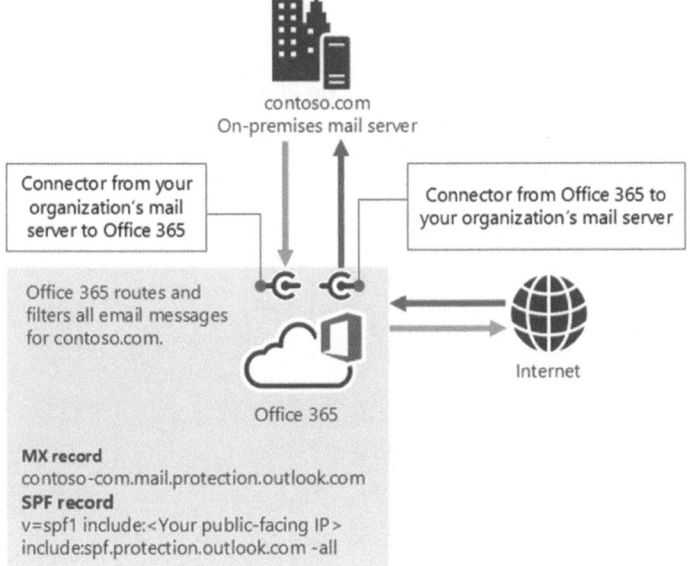

Figure 10-5. Hybrid mail flow with MX pointing to Office 365

In this configuration, there are five failure points that you must be aware of.

- From the Internet to Exchange Online

- Exchange Online to on-premises

- Within the on-premises environment

- On-premises to Exchange Online

- Exchange Online to the Internet

Centralized Mail Transport

Centralized Mail Transport, sometimes referred to as Centralized Mail Control, requires that all messages be routed through the on-premises environment first, before being delivered (Figure 10-6). This type of configuration is typically used when there are compliance requirements that must be enforced within the on-premises environment.

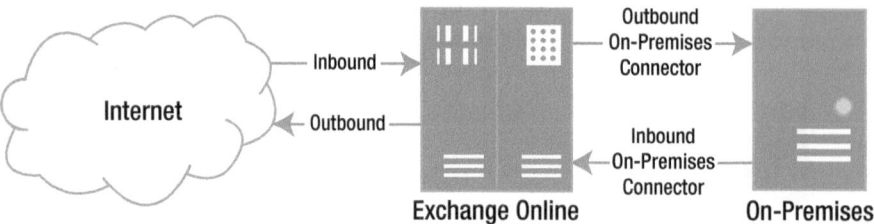

Figure 10-6. *Centralized Mail Control*

In this configuration, owing to the complexity, I will break down the failure points to inbound and then outbound.

For inbound:

- From the Internet to Exchange Online

- Exchange Online to on-premises

- Within on-premises environment

- On-premises to Exchange Online for hosted recipients

For outbound:

- Exchange Online to on-premises

- Within on-premises environment

- On-premises to Exchange Online

- Exchange Online to the Internet

Common Troubleshooting Techniques

When troubleshooting mail flow, it is critical to isolate the fault as much as possible. To do this, it is best to break the process into multiple steps: scoping, data collection, solution identification, and solution implementation.

During the scoping phase, you will want to look at the following: When did the issue begin? This is important to know, as issues that suddenly occur are often a result of a change within the environment or an unexpected service incident. If mail flow has never worked, this would indicate an initial setup issue, and the approach to resolving it will be different.

Who is affected by the issue? What you are looking for here is whether the issue is isolated to a subset of users or if it's affecting all users. If the issue is isolated to a specific set of users, you start by looking at commonalities between those users. For example, are they all in the same branch office, and are other tools also impacted. This could indicate a general connectivity issue.

Are there any error messages generated? In mail flow, we call these NDRs (non-delivery reports/receipts) or DSNs (data source names). Both will often tell you exactly what the issue affecting mail delivery is or the behavior being seen.

During the data-collection phase, you want to collect additional information that you will use with the information collected during scoping, to determine the solution. Generate test messages to identify which aspects of mail flow are not working. Often, mail-flow issues affect only some aspects of mail flow, meaning that some mail will still work. You just have to identify which ones are working. To do this you can test the following scenarios:

- External sender to hosted mailbox

- Hosted mailbox to External Recipient

- External sender to on-premises mailbox

- On-premises mailbox to External Recipient

- Hosted mailbox to on-premises mailbox

- On-premises mailbox to hosted mailbox

- Hosted mailbox to hosted mailbox (Note: This should always work. If it does not work, and you do not have a criteria-based routing rule configured in Office 365, you should engage support).

Collect any Message Tracking Logs, NDRs, and e-mail headers showing the issue. With mail-flow issues, this data will likely show you exactly where the issue is, reducing the need for further troubleshooting.

Because mail flow is linear, once you have collected the scoping data and the empirical data outlined previously, troubleshooting becomes a matter of determining where in the message flow the issue is occurring and then looking at the configuration of the step directly before the break.

Once you have identified the configuration change that is necessary to resolve the mail delivery issue, it is time to implement the fix. When you update connectors in Office 365, changes will typically replicate out in 15 minutes, but they will sometimes take longer. This is important to note, as you will not be able to test your changes immediately. Changes within your on-premises environment will replicate out faster, except for changes to DNS, if necessary, as these are dependent on the Time-To-Live (TTL) that was configured during the last DNS update.

Reading NDRs

When an NDR is generated, it will provide valuable information needed to determine where a delivery failure is occurring and the cause of the delivery failure. An NDR is always generated by the last mail server to have the message in the queue. In the case of Office 365, it will generate a friendly NDR format that is broken into multiple sections. The first section of the NDR is intended to provide end users with a quick explanation of what happened and what steps need to be taken to resolve the issue (Figure 10-7).

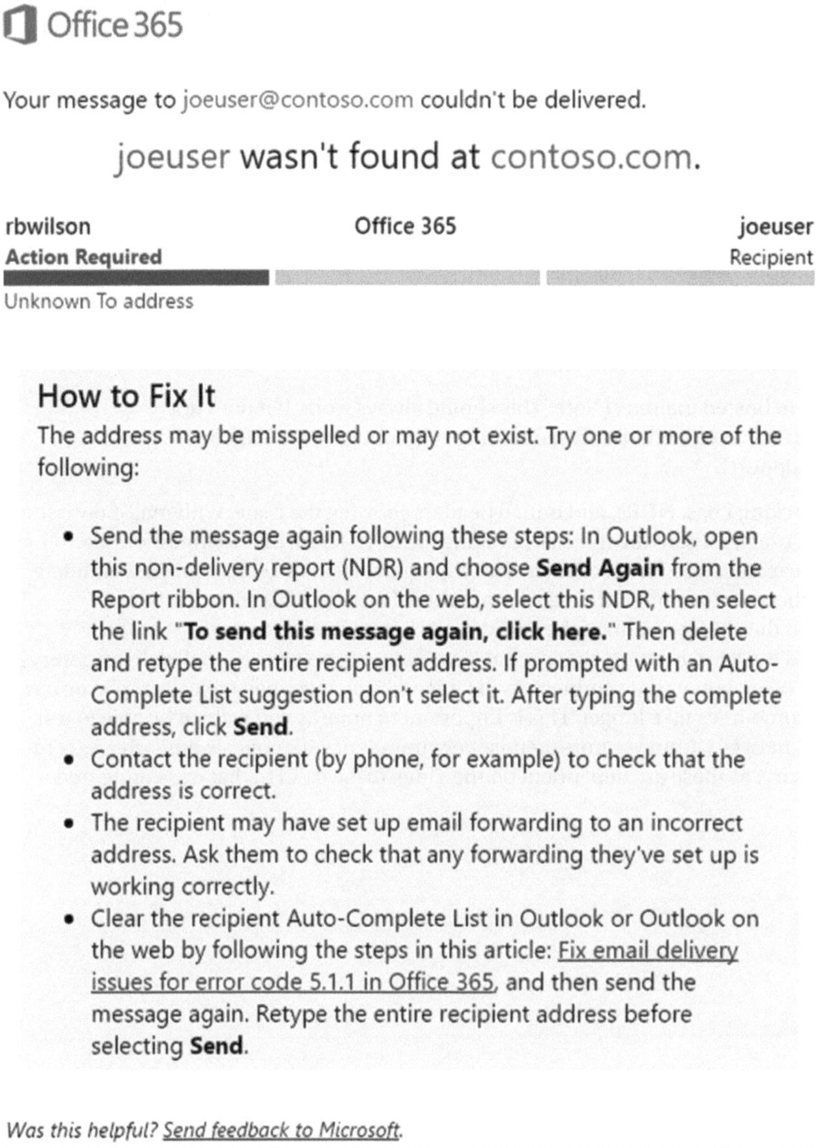

☐ Office 365

Your message to joeuser@contoso.com couldn't be delivered.

joeuser wasn't found at contoso.com.

rbwilson	Office 365	joeuser
Action Required		Recipient

Unknown To address

How to Fix It

The address may be misspelled or may not exist. Try one or more of the following:

- Send the message again following these steps: In Outlook, open this non-delivery report (NDR) and choose **Send Again** from the Report ribbon. In Outlook on the web, select this NDR, then select the link "**To send this message again, click here.**" Then delete and retype the entire recipient address. If prompted with an Auto-Complete List suggestion don't select it. After typing the complete address, click **Send**.
- Contact the recipient (by phone, for example) to check that the address is correct.
- The recipient may have set up email forwarding to an incorrect address. Ask them to check that any forwarding they've set up is working correctly.
- Clear the recipient Auto-Complete List in Outlook or Outlook on the web by following the steps in this article: Fix email delivery issues for error code 5.1.1 in Office 365, and then send the message again. Retype the entire recipient address before selecting **Send**.

Was this helpful? Send feedback to Microsoft.

Figure 10-7. *Undelivered message in Office 365*

The next section of the NDR is intended for administrators and provides more details about the most common resolutions (Figure 10-8).

More Info for Email Admins
Status code 554 5.4.14

Typically this error occurs because the recipient email address is incorrect or doesn't exist at the destination domain. This can usually be fixed by the sender. However, sometimes the issue needs to be fixed by the recipient or the recipient's email admin. If the steps in the **How to Fix It** section above don't fix the problem, and you're the email admin for the recipient, try one or more of the following:

The email address exists and is correct - Confirm that the recipient address exists, is correct, and is accepting messages.

Synchronize your directories - If you have a hybrid environment and are using directory synchronization make sure the recipient's email address is synced correctly in both Office 365 and in your on-premises directory.

Errant forwarding rule - Check for forwarding rules that aren't behaving as expected. A forwarding rule can be configured by an admin via mail flow rules or mailbox forwarding address settings, or by the recipient via the Inbox Rules feature.

Mail flow settings and MX records are not correct - Misconfigured mail flow settings or MX records can cause this error. Check your Office 365 mail flow settings to make sure your domain and any mail flow connectors are set up correctly. Also, work with your domain registrar to make sure the MX records for your domain are configured correctly.

Mail loop detected - This error also indicates that the receiving organization's email settings are misconfigured, creating a mail loop when a message is sent to an address that isn't found in their directory. This usually won't disrupt mail flow for recipients that actually exist, but the recipient's email admin should fix the misconfiguration to reduce the chance of any other mail flow issues. A common cause for this loop is that the recipient's domain is configured as "Internal Relay" when it should be "Authoritative." Another common cause for the loop is that both the sender and recipient are part of the same organization, but the sender's mailbox is hosted by Office 365, while the recipient's mailbox is hosted on-premises, and an outbound connector from Office 365 to the on-premises email servers is missing or misconfigured. To fix this, the recipient's email admin should create a correctly configured outbound connector in Office 365 to route the message to the on-premises mailbox.

For more information and tips to fix this problem, see <u>Fix email delivery issues for error code 5.4.14 in Office 365</u>.

Figure 10-8. *More information content from Office 365*

You will see the exact error details, which server generated the NDR, which server it was attempting communicate with, and a table showing the individual hops that the message took before the NDR was generated (Figure 10-9).

Original Message Details

Created Date:	2016-12-18 7:59:05 PM
Sender Address:	rbwilson@hotmail.ca
Recipient Address:	joeuser@contoso.com
Subject:	Test Message

Error Details

Reported error:	554 5.4.14 Hop count exceeded - possible mail loop ATTR34
DSN generated by:	BN6PR06MB2450.namprd06.prod.outlook.com
Remote server:	BY2FFO11FD022.mail.protection.outlook.com

Message Hops

HOP	TIME (UTC)	FROM	TO	WITH	RELAY TIME
1	2016-12-18 7:59:06 PM	CY1PR11MB1032.namprd11.prod.outlook.com	CY1PR11MB1032.namprd11.prod.outlook.com	mapi	1 sec
2	2016-12-18 7:59:06 PM	CY1PR11MB1032.namprd11.prod.outlook.com	SN1NAM01FT020.mail.protection.outlook.com	Microsoft SMTP Server (version=TLS1_2, cipher=TLS_ECDHE_RSA_WITH_AES_256_CBC_SHA384_P384)	*
3	2016-12-18 7:59:06 PM	SN1NAM01FT020.eop-nam01.prod.protection.outlook.com	SN1NAM01HT072.eop-nam01.prod.protection.outlook.com	Microsoft SMTP Server (version=TLS1_2, cipher=TLS_ECDHE_RSA_WITH_AES_256_CBC_SHA384_P384)	*
4	2016-12-18 7:59:07 PM	NAM01-SN1-obe.outbound.protection.outlook.com	BLU004-OMC1S21.hotmail.com over TLS secured channel	Microsoft SMTPSVC(7.5.7601.23008)	1 sec
5	2016-12-18 7:59:08 PM	BLU004-OMC1S21.hotmail.com	BN1BFFO11OLC004.mail.protection.outlook.com	Microsoft SMTP Server (version=TLS1_2, cipher=TLS_ECDHE_RSA_WITH_AES_256_CBC_SHA384_P384)	1 sec
6	2016-12-18 7:59:08 PM	BN1BFFO11OLC004.protection.gbl	BY2PR06CA056.outlook.office365.com	Microsoft SMTP Server (version=TLS1_2, cipher=TLS_ECDHE_RSA_WITH_AES_256_CBC_SHA384_P384)	*
7	2016-12-18 7:59:08 PM	BY2PR06CA056.namprd06.prod.outlook.com	DM2PR06MB526.namprd06.prod.outlook.com	Microsoft SMTP Server (version=TLS1_2, cipher=TLS_ECDHE_RSA_WITH_AES_256_CBC_SHA384_P384)	*
8	2016-12-18 7:59:09 PM	NAM02-CY1-obe.outbound.protection.outlook.com	BY2FFO11FD010.mail.protection.outlook.com	Microsoft SMTP Server (version=TLS1_2, cipher=TLS_ECDHE_RSA_WITH_AES_256_CBC_SHA384_P384)	1 sec
9	2016-12-18 7:59:09 PM	BY2FFO11FD010.protection.gbl	CO2PR06CA052.outlook.office365.com	Microsoft SMTP Server (version=TLS1_2, cipher=TLS_ECDHE_RSA_WITH_AES_256_CBC_SHA384_P384)	*
10	2016-12-18 7:59:10 PM	CO2PR06CA052.namprd06.prod.outlook.com	BN6PR06MB2820.namprd06.prod.outlook.com	Microsoft SMTP Server (version=TLS1_2, cipher=TLS_ECDHE_RSA_WITH_AES_256_CBC_SHA384_P384)	1 sec
11	2016-12-18 7:59:12 PM	NAM03-CO1-obe.outbound.protection.outlook.com	BY2FFO11FD026.mail.protection.outlook.com	Microsoft SMTP Server (version=TLS1_2, cipher=TLS_ECDHE_RSA_WITH_AES_256_CBC_SHA384_P384)	2 sec
12	2016-12-18 7:59:12 PM	BY2FFO11FD026.protection.gbl	BY2PR0601CA0018.outlook.office365.com	Microsoft SMTP Server (version=TLS1_2, cipher=TLS_ECDHE_RSA_WITH_AES_256_CBC_SHA384_P384)	*
13	2016-12-18 7:59:12 PM	BY2PR0601CA0018.namprd06.prod.outlook.com	BN6PR06MB2450.namprd06.prod.outlook.com	Microsoft SMTP Server (version=TLS1_2, cipher=TLS_ECDHE_RSA_WITH_AES_256_CBC_SHA384_P384)	*

Figure 10-9. *Message hops table*

The final section of an Office 365–generated NDR contains the original message headers.

If the NDR was not generated by Office 365, at a minimum, you will be presented with the SMTP response code generated by the remote server and the server that generated the NDR. The SMTP response code will be either a 4xx series, indicating a temporary delivery issue, or a 5xx series, indicating a permanent delivery issue. With a 5xx series response, the sending mail server will make no further attempts to deliver the message. For a 4xx series response, the sending server will attempt to deliver the message again, based on the configured retry interval and time frame.

Reading Headers

While troubleshooting mail flow, you will often end up looking at lots of e-mail headers, to determine the exact path that a message took. This can be done manually using Notepad or your favorite text editor, but this can become tiresome, owing to formatting and the sheer amount of information that is contained within the header. Microsoft provides a great tool that makes this process much easier called the Header Analyzer, available at `https://testconnectivity.microsoft.com/` (Figure 10-10).

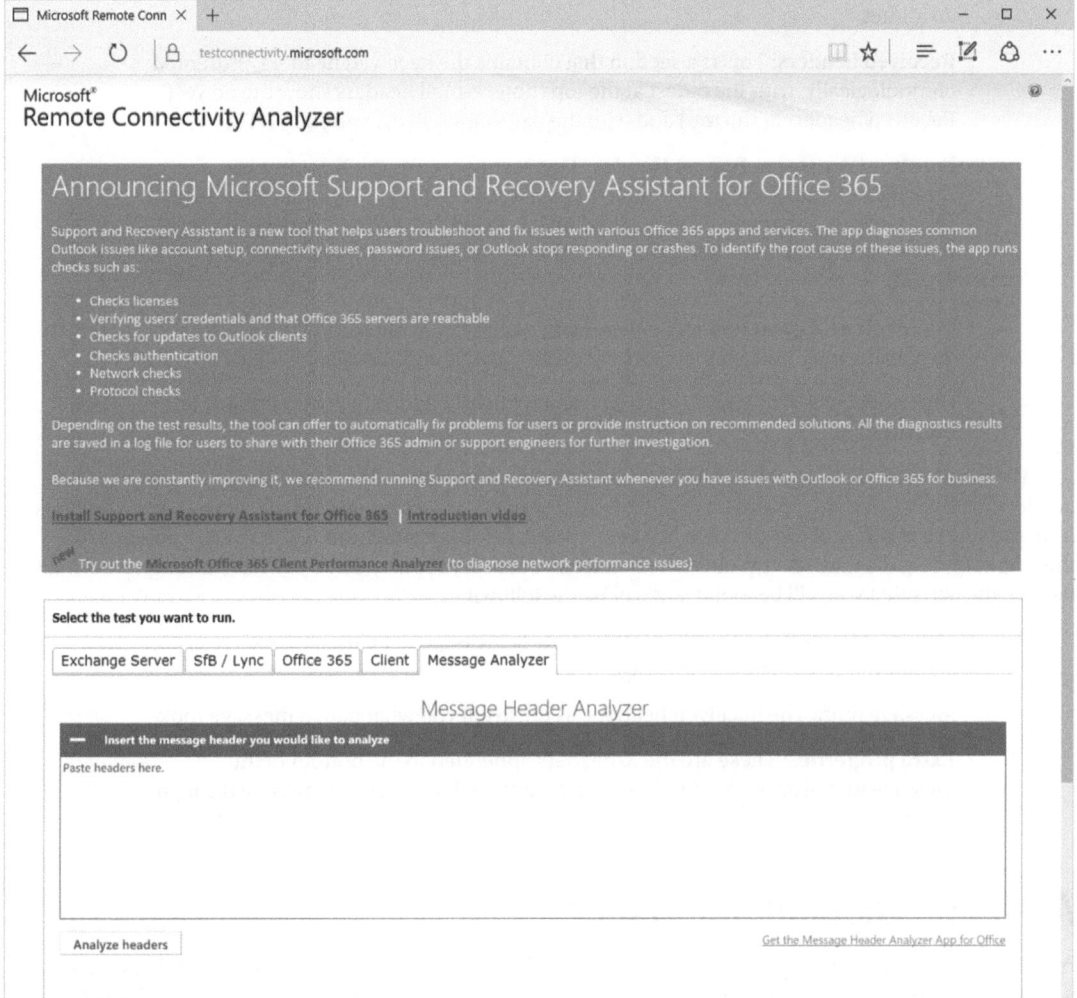

Figure 10-10. *Remote Connectivity Analyzer*

The Message Analyzer parses the header for you and then displays the contents in a table format broken down as follows:

- Summary: contains the Subject

- Message ID

- Message Creation Date/Time

- From address

- To address

    Received headers: This is a section that contains the Received headers, presented chronologically, with the oldest at the top (note: e-mail headers show the newest Received headers at the top) and with the date/times all converted to UTC.

    Forefront Antispam Report Header: This section parses the X-Forefront-Antispam-Report header, if present, to display the Country/Region the sending IP belongs to, Language, Spam Confidence Level (SCL), Spam Filtering Verdict, IP Filter Verdict, HELO/EHLO String of the sending server, as well as the PTR-Record.

    Microsoft Antispam header: This section parses the X-Microsoft-Antispam to display the Bulk Complaint and the Phishing Confidence Levels.

    Other headers: This section displays all the other headers that were present in the message.

When working with e-mail headers, it is important to ensure that you always have the complete headers. To ensure that you always have full e-mail headers, it is recommended that you copy the headers from the source mailbox. If the message has been forwarded as an attachment, there is the potential for the client sending the mail to strip out extra headers, to conserve space. Once you have a complete e-mail header, the parts that you will be looking at will be the following:

    Message details: The To, From, Date/Time & Message Id fields, as these are used, should you have to trace a message

    Message path: The Received headers, as these tell you what path a message took

    Extra properties: These are the X-headers appended to the bottom of the message that provide details about what happened to a message passing through the network.

Available Logging and Usage

As an administrator of Office 365, you will have, at some point, to be able to see exactly what happened to a message as it passes through the service. To assist administrators with these queries, the service provides multiple options.

- Message trace via the Office 365 Exchange Administration Center (EAC).

- Via PowerShell cmdlets:

    - `Get-MessageTrace` and `Get-MessageTraceDetail`

    - `Start-HistoricalSearch`

As there are multiple options, the key becomes knowing which option to use, as there are limitations that must be understood. To decide which option to use, you must first start by determining how far back you have to trace: the preceding 7 days or up to 90 days in the past.

Seven Days or Fewer

If the message is from the previous seven days, the easiest option is to perform the trace via the EAC (see Figure 10-11). For very recent messages, there is typically a delay of just a few minutes between the time the message was sent and the time it can be traced. The trace can be initiated as follows:

- Log in to Office 365 as an administrator

- Navigate to the Exchange Administration Center

- Click mail flow

- Click message trace

- Enter your search criteria

- Click Search

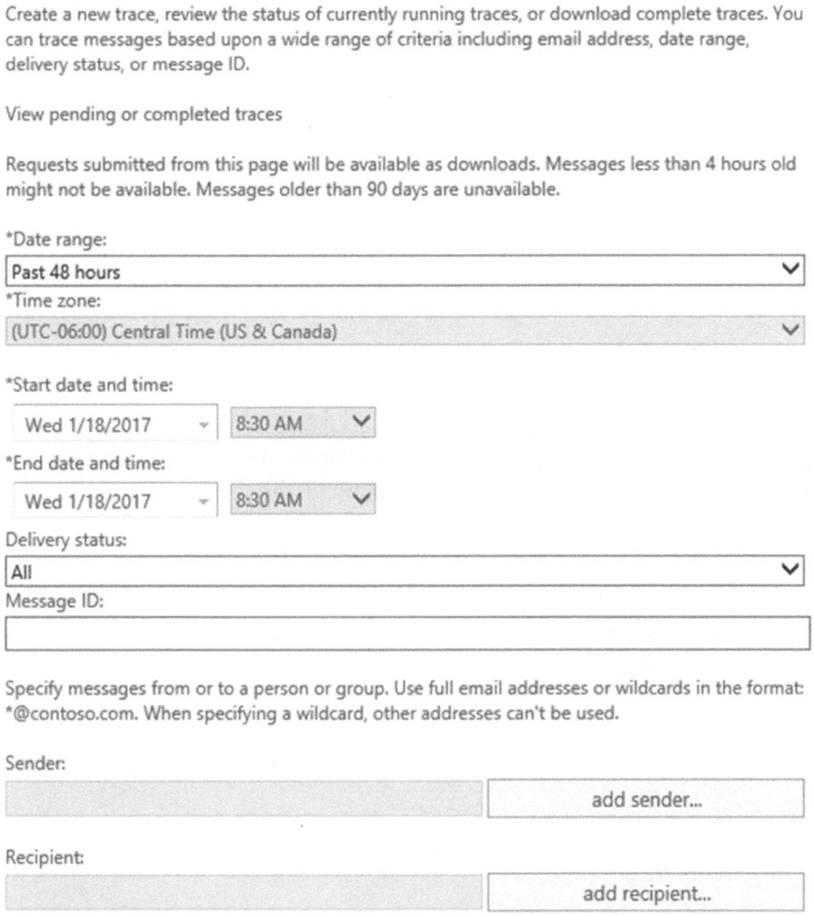

Create a new trace, review the status of currently running traces, or download complete traces. You can trace messages based upon a wide range of criteria including email address, date range, delivery status, or message ID.

View pending or completed traces

Requests submitted from this page will be available as downloads. Messages less than 4 hours old might not be available. Messages older than 90 days are unavailable.

*Date range:

| Past 48 hours | ∨ |

*Time zone:

| (UTC-06:00) Central Time (US & Canada) | ∨ |

*Start date and time:

| Wed 1/18/2017 | ▾ | 8:30 AM | ∨ |

*End date and time:

| Wed 1/18/2017 | ▾ | 8:30 AM | ∨ |

Delivery status:

| All | ∨ |

Message ID:

| |

Specify messages from or to a person or group. Use full email addresses or wildcards in the format: *@contoso.com. When specifying a wildcard, other addresses can't be used.

Sender:

| | add sender... |

Recipient:

| | add recipient... |

***Figure 10-11.** Exchange Administration Center*

Once the search has been initiated, you will be presented a results box showing the matches that were found. You can then get more details on individual messages, by double-clicking the message in question or by clicking the edit icon (Figure 10-12).

Figure 10-12. *Additional message events information*

Alternatively, the same trace can be performed via PowerShell. Often when tracing for a message, you already have the Message-ID, so start by using the Get-MessageTrace cmdlet and filter the results, to show you the Message-IDs that will return a list of matching messages (see Figure 10-13).

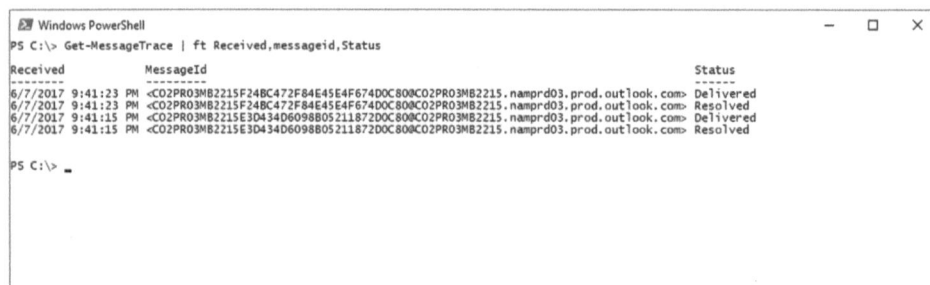

Figure 10-13. *Get-MessageTrace cmdlet results*

Next, to get additional details about the message, you can then use the `Get-MessageTraceDetail` cmdlet, which will return more information, such as what we saw through the EAC (Figure 10-14).

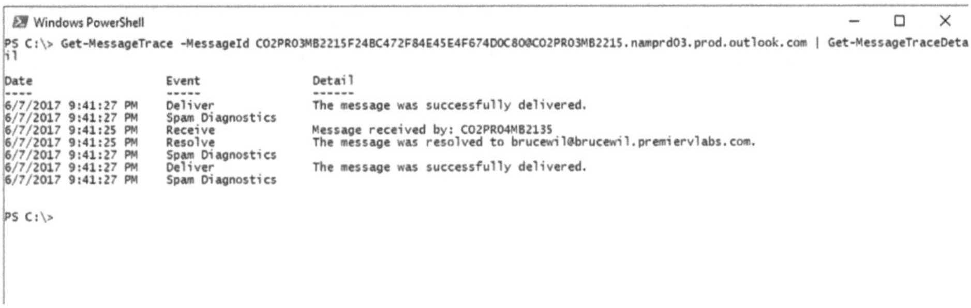

Figure 10-14. *`Get-MessageTrace` in PowerShell filtered by `MessageId`*

You will notice that this is the same detail presented through the EAC, but it is possible to get additional details. You can do the same via PowerShell, by adding | FL to the previous cmdlet (Figure 10-15).

Figure 10-15. *Full details from the `Get-MessageTrace` PowerShell cmdlet*

Greater Than Seven Days to Ninety Days

These traces can be initiated from the EAC the same way as a trace for the previous seven days. The key difference, though, is that the traces are run on the back end and then once the results can be downloaded by administrators. When setting up the trace, it is important to select the Include message events and routing details with a report option, as this will ensure that all details about what happened to the message are included in the results (Figure 10-16).

Create a new trace, review the status of currently running traces, or download complete traces. You can trace messages based upon a wide range of criteria including email address, date range, delivery status, or message ID.

View pending or completed traces

Requests submitted from this page will be available as downloads. Messages less than 4 hours old might not be available. Messages older than 90 days are unavailable.

*Date range:

| Custom | ∨ |

*Time zone:

| (UTC-06:00) Central Time (US & Canada) | ∨ |

*Start date and time:

| Tue 1/10/2017 ▼ | 8:30 AM ∨ |

*End date and time:

| Wed 1/18/2017 ▼ | 8:30 AM ∨ |

Delivery status:

| All | ∨ |

Message ID:

| |

Specify messages from or to a person or group. Use full email addresses or wildcards in the format: *@contoso.com. When specifying a wildcard, other addresses can't be used.

Sender:

| | add sender... |

Recipient:

| | add recipient... |

☑ Include message events and routing details with report

Direction:

| All | ∨ |

Original client IP address:

| |

*Report title:

| Message trace report Wednesday, January 18, 2017 9:01:05 AM |

Notification email address:

| |

> Select this check box only if you're targeting one or a few specific messages. Including event details will result in a larger report that takes longer to process.

Figure 10-16. *Creating new trace in Office 365*

The results will be presented in a comma-separated value (csv) file, which can be opened and reviewed via Excel. After opening the file in Excel, start by sorting the report, based on the Date column, and then filter to a Message-ID in question, to restrict the amount of data requiring review (see Figure 10-17).

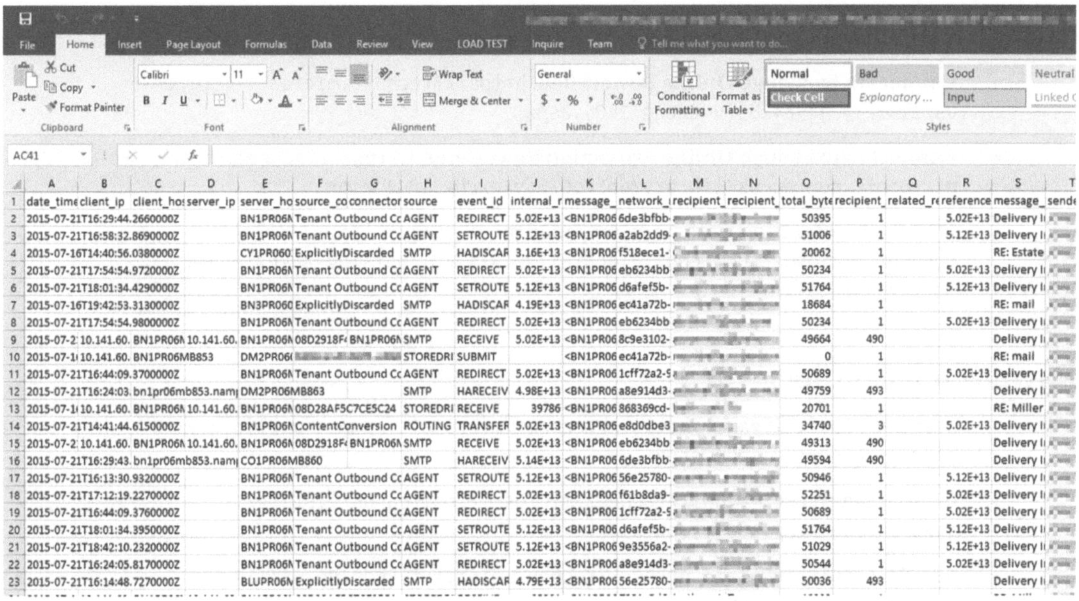

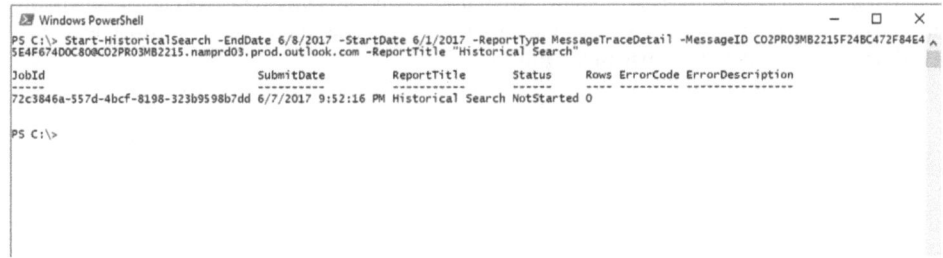

Figure 10-17. *Exported traces in Excel*

Alternatively, the same trace can be initiated via the Start-HistoricalSearch cmdlet with the -ReportType MessageTraceDetail parameter, to ensure that all the events and routing details are returned (Figure 10-18).

```
Windows PowerShell                                                    —    □    ×
PS C:\> Start-HistoricalSearch -EndDate 6/8/2017 -StartDate 6/1/2017 -ReportType MessageTraceDetail -MessageID CO2PRO3MB2215F24BC472F84E4
5E4F674D0C808C02PRO3MB2215.namprd03.prod.outlook.com -ReportTitle "Historical Search"

JobId                                SubmitDate             ReportTitle       Status     Rows ErrorCode ErrorDescription
-----                                ----------             -----------       ------     ---- --------- ----------------
72c3846a-557d-4bcf-8198-323b9598b7dd 6/7/2017 9:52:16 PM Historical Search NotStarted 0

PS C:\>
```

Figure 10-18. Start-HistoricalSearch *cmdlet in PowerShell*

Sometimes, you want to get the message tracking report for messages that are fewer than seven days old. To do this via the EAC, you can set the Start Date to eight days prior to the current date/time. The most efficient option, though, is to use the Start-HistoricalSearch cmdlet.

Additional Resources

The following resources are recommended for further information.

Miscellaneous

- **Connect to Exchange Online PowerShell**: https://technet.microsoft.com/en-us/library/jj984289(v=exchg.160).aspx

- **Connect to Exchange Online Protection PowerShell**: https://technet.microsoft.com/en-us/library/dn621036(v=exchg.160).aspx

- **EOP Field Notes Blog**: Parsing an extended message trace: https://blogs.technet.microsoft.com/eopfieldnotes/2015/12/01/parsing-an-extended-message-trace-2/

PowerShell Cmdlets

- **Start-HistoricalSearch**: https://technet.microsoft.com/en-us/library/dn621132(v=exchg.160).aspx

- **Get-MessageTrace**: https://technet.microsoft.com/en-us/library/jj200704(v=exchg.160).aspx

- **Get-MessageTraceDetail**: https://technet.microsoft.com/en-us/library/jj200681(v=exchg.160).aspx

Summary

In this chapter, we looked at how a message gets routed from the Internet through to an intended recipient in Exchange Online or an on-premises messaging environment. As mail flow is performed via SMTP, we can rely on built-in capabilities, such as NDRs and DSNs, to get alerts when something is not working correctly. Using message headers and message-tracing capabilities built into Office 365, we can dig deep into exactly what happened to a given message or set of messages. I hope this chapter leaves you with a deeper understanding and set of tools that you can use in the future.

CHAPTER 11

■ ■ ■

Final Thoughts

BY KIP NG, TECHNICAL DELIVERY MANAGER

The New World

Digital transformation seems to be the key talking point for all businesses nowadays. Everyone is discussing it. All businesses, from large financial services organizations, governments, and telecommunication companies to small retailers, coffee shops, etc., are looking at transforming digitally. The word *transformation*, according to the Oxford Dictionaries site, is a synonym for "reorganization," "overhaul," "remodeling," "metamorphosis," and "revolution." These words have one thing in common—that is, change, and, in many cases, it means introducing uncertainties.

As this book is drawing to a close, I wanted to reiterate the vision for this volume and, at the same time, share my opinions on the mentalities an information technology (IT) technical resource must embrace to be successful in this journey of digital transformation revolution.

> *Digital transformation is the change associated with the application of digital technology in all aspects of human society.*[1]

The scope is huge, because you are looking at almost everything that technology touches. For that reason, it is not always easy to understand the full impact of how such revolution affects our businesses, jobs, and interactions with people, as well as our lives. In fact, it isn't always clear what one must do or how to get ready for it.

Fortunately, for all of us, digital transformation is a process. It isn't something that happens overnight in a magical way. It means that you can't just become a digitally transformed organization overnight, especially for a well-established large organization. There are phases to follow. Now, it is not my intent to discuss how a business goes through digital transformation. However, I do want to share some of my thoughts about where and how this digital transformation will affect us all, specifically IT infrastructure technical resources in days to come.

---

[1]Erik Stolterman, Anna Croon Fors, "Information Technology and the Good Life," in: "Information Systems Research: Relevant Theory and Informed Practice," 2004, ISBN 1-4020-8094-8, p. 689.

© Nikolas Charlebois-Laprade et al. 2017
N. Charlebois-Laprade et al., *Expert Office 365*, DOI 10.1007/978-1-4842-2991-0_11

"Keeping the Lights on" vs. Productivity-Focused IT

IT is meant to empower an organization. However, that is not what we always observe in many institutions. In fact, many have viewed IT as a cash consumer, a huge expense item. As a result, most organizations just want to retain the status quo: that is, to do the minimum to keep the lights on. In fact, many will even go to the extent of cutting huge chunks of the IT budget as a starting point. There is no right or wrong here, but history has shown that, in most cases, deep cuts to IT budgets without thorough consideration usually results in a loss of competitiveness, reduced productivity, and an increase in unplanned system downtime, etc.

The good news is that many companies are beginning to realize that they can do more with IT and use IT to help accelerate their business growth, instead of viewing it as just another expense. The not-so-good news is that most of the technical IT personnel have grown accustomed to the "keeping the lights on" modus operandi. Many still do not see the need to change the way they operate, their mindset to be a more productivity-focused IT resource.

For all IT personnel, this must change. I believe the time to re-skill is now. Moving the IT infrastructure to the cloud is only step one, the beginning of the digital transformation process for many IT applications and solutions in enterprises. As companies move toward a more productivity-focused IT or, as I like to call it, a more "business-purpose-driven and intentional IT," that old mindset is just not going to cut it. Those "keeping the lights on" and a heavily technically focused skill set for many of the on-premises technologies will also start to lose their relevance. The expectation is that all IT personnel must be more business savvy, not just technically skilled.

Cloud Isn't Replacing IT People, Not If They Evolve

So, what does that really mean? Does that mean moving to the cloud will eventually result in job loss and a reduction in many current-generation IT workers? The answer is yes—and no.

Yes, because the demand for the current skill set is decreasing as IT evolves as part of this digital transformation. At the same time, no, because this digital revolution will create a lot of other opportunities, as many businesses are being disrupted by this digital transformation. It will, however, require re-skilling.

In fact, the re-skilling isn't just for the IT workers, it starts from the top and goes all the way to the bottom. I want to end this section by bringing to your attention Microsoft's company mission statement. For the last few months, I have gone through mission statements from different companies, but Microsoft's current mission statement, in my opinion, really captures the essence of how the IT personnel of the current generation should evolve their thinking.

> *Our Mission is to empower every person and every organization on the planet to achieve more.*

—Microsoft's Mission Statement

Staying Relevant

The following guidance is recommended.

Don't Fight It, Embrace It; It Is Here to Stay

Looking at the current digital transformation trend, it reminds me of the time when PC servers were growing in popularity and replacing those large mainframes. I remember speaking to a friend when I was working for Compaq, and he told me that PC servers, client servers would go away after a while. Enterprises would never adopt those PC servers as their mission-critical systems. Well, we know he was wrong.

Fast forward to just six years ago, in 2011. I was discussing with a customer the prospect of moving their enterprise messaging system to a hosting cloud solution. I was laughed at and was told a similar reason: enterprises such as large financial services will never adopt cloud for their mission-critical systems. We all know this is happening as we speak, whether we want it or not. Digital transformation is here to stay, and it is not a matter of if, but when. You can't fight it. Rather, ride the wave.

Expand Your Technology Breadth

Am I saying that all your skill sets will become obsolete and irrelevant? No, absolutely not, at least not all of it. As technology changes, and as we journey through this digital transformation, the only way for anyone to stay relevant to the market is to continuously learn and pick up new skills.

For example, those who now know only Microsoft Exchange Servers may have to start learning more, not just about Exchange Online in Office 365, but the whole Office 365 suites, which may include messaging, collaboration, unified communications, and, perhaps, even identity and networking.

The process of re-skilling in this case is more about building on top of your experience and your current skill set than a complete replacement. IT is still relevant; however, next-generation IT will demand a next-generation skill set. My advice to all IT administrators and technical resources is to continue to expand your boundaries: be more solution focused and business savvy. Embrace a growth mindset and learn, learn, and learn.

Know the Business, Expand Industry Knowledge

As discussed earlier, IT is moving away from being an expense item in the business. IT should be able about enablement, helping people to do more. This naturally means a closer integration between IT and business.

What does that mean for employees in the IT industry? We must get to know the business better and expand our industry knowledge, because only with that can we learn to think of IT as part of the business and to solutions that will ultimately help the business to grow and be more efficient. Don't limit yourself to just acquiring technology-related knowledge. You will find that equipping yourself with some business and industry knowledge will go a long way in this digital transformation era.

This Is Just the Beginning, After All...

This book was written by some of the best technical engineers and consultants I know at Microsoft. They are experts on the subject, working closely with various customers day in and day out in the areas that they are writing about.

At a glance, this book may seem unorganized and unfocused, because it touches on different parts and technologies related to the whole Microsoft Office 365 solution. It does not seem to be one of those typical, orthodox books that flows thematically from one chapter to another. This is intentional. Each chapter is quite self-sufficient and highly focused on a specific area. These are the key areas these experts have found most companies or IT administrators having the most questions, issues, and challenges with, for example, areas such as Azure Rights Management, Exchange Hybrid, Hybrid Team sites, or installing SharePoint in Azure instead of using the SharePoint Online from O365.

Each of the chapters was carefully written by someone who not only has in-depth knowledge of that specific area but who is highly experienced in real-life production deployment. Finally, we know that moving some of the services to the cloud, such as the Office 365 solution, is just the beginning, step one toward the full digital transformation. We certainly hope this book will cover some of the critical areas that will help you and increase your knowledge, as you embark on the digital transformation journey.

Index

© Nikolas Charlebois-Laprade et al. 2017
N. Charlebois-Laprade et al., *Expert Office 365*, DOI 10.1007/978-1-4842-2991-0

Get the eBook for only $5!

Why limit yourself?

With most of our titles available in both PDF and ePUB format, you can access your content wherever and however you wish—on your PC, phone, tablet, or reader.

Since you've purchased this print book, we are happy to offer you the eBook for just $5.

To learn more, go to http://www.apress.com/companion or contact support@apress.com.

Apress®